Muhammad Ali in Africa

Muhammad Ali in Africana Cultural Memory

Edited by

James L. Conyers Jr.

Christel N. Temple

ANTHEM PRESS

Anthem Press
An imprint of Wimbledon Publishing Company
www.anthempress.com

This edition first published in UK and USA 2024
by ANTHEM PRESS
75–76 Blackfriars Road, London SE1 8HA, UK
or PO Box 9779, London SW19 7ZG, UK
and
244 Madison Ave #116, New York, NY 10016, USA

First published in the UK and USA by Anthem Press in 2022

British Library Cataloguing-in-Publication Data
A catalogue record for this book is available from the British Library.

Library of Congress Control Number: 2024932333

ISBN-13: 978-1-83999-231-5 (Pbk)
ISBN-10: 1-83999-231-X (Pbk)

Cover Image: Boxing gloves hanging nailed to wall as concept of retirement,
By Khakimullin Aleksandr / Shutterstock.com

This title is also available as an e-book.

In memory of

Dr. James L. "Naazir" Conyers Jr.

June 17, 1961–January 25, 2021

Author, visionary, leader, collaborator, mentor

and

Godfather to generations of scholars

CONTENTS

ILLUSTRATIONS

FOREWORD

I still remember the shouts "Ali *boma ye*" (Ali kill him) as we all listened on October 29, 1974, in my village Ntumbaw, in the northwest region of Cameroon, to the broadcast of the most important heavyweight fight between Muhammad Ali and George Foreman, which was called (no one knows why) "Rumble in the Jungle." The fight took place in Stade Tata Raphseël in Kinshasa in the then Zaire, now the Democratic Republic of the Congo. Our sports analysts on Radio Cameroon, Abel Mbengue, and Peter Esoka,[1] all filled us in on the details and sophistication of what to some of us who did not understand the sport would have been merely a nightmarish fun that could have left someone dead. Yet, like everyone, I nursed the feeling that I wish I were at the stadium in Kinshasa, that enigmatic city and capital of African popular music and whose grandeur was enhanced by the life blood of the country, the mighty *ebale ya Kongo* (the River Congo) immortalized in a song by Le Grande Joseph Kabasele and the African Jazz.[2]

The history of the fight is shrouded in controversy, but for the many Congolese and Africans who followed this international sporting event that pitted two sons of the African world on African soil, it was a real big deal, something that has not been repeated on the African continent. Most people do not know exactly why it took place, but we must give Don King the credit. He wanted someone to sponsor this big event, and General Mobuto Seseseko Kuku Ngbendu Wa Za Banga, who had seized power in the country in 1965, stepped to the plate and offered to pay for the cost of the fight. Regardless of what one thinks of the cost for an African country at the time, one can say this for sure that this was one of the few times when watching that fight one could say the people enjoyed the benefit of the taxes they paid into the treasury.

As I listened on that day, I wondered why the 60,000 people gathered there on that day to cheer and applaud one son of Africa to kill another son of Africa and shouted "Ali *boma ye*" (Ali kill him). Did these people really want Ali to kill his fellow American and, for that matter, his Black brother in a sport that was meant to entertain? Many thought this is just the way things are and when you enter the ring, you can expect the worst thing to happen to you. But did they really want a descendant of Africa to kill another descendant of Africa on African soil? I think most people would agree that "kill him" in sports is a euphemism for "beat him" and take the crown; in this case it was the heavyweight boxing championship.[3] Defeating some on a game is a type of killing, which does not physically destroy the opponent, but establishes who is the most skillful competitor in the sport at that time of the game.

This book on Ali certainly invites us to think of the many ways we can and should celebrate the champion and the hero of the African world (Africa, North America, the

Caribbean, and Latin and South America) and all areas where Black civilization exists in some form. The African world and the rich scholarship in every area of our intellectual engagement that have been produced often stand on the shoulders of the people, who have led, in Du Boisian terms, our strivings. The story of those strivings has been led by Black women and men of all backgrounds. Ali, one of the most emblematic, articulate, inspiring, and, yes, direct, honest, and one who says it like it is, remains very endearing to many people. It is wonderful to see this work conceived and executed by Professors James Conyers and Christel Temple, two brilliant minds of Africana thought and its numerous cultural mythologies, come to fruition. Each contribution to this book is a gem in itself and gives us a portrait of the champ who lives every day in our memories.

As you read, you join others in affirming that Ali (and for that matter every Black athlete, child, or person) should win. But we know also that if the chant in Kinshasa made Ali to *boma* Foreman in the stadium on that day, people would have been shocked and frightened. They would have wondered why the gods of Africa had sent such a clear signal that something was terribly wrong. Why did the gods and ancestors not warn them? Why would they allow something like that to happen when Africans and their brothers across the Atlantic should really have been working on a giant reconciliation! I suspect if the worst had happened and someone had died, African leaders would bring in the best *ngangas* (the spiritual and ritual experts) in the Congo to determine why someone would be killed in what to the observers was "just a game or fight." I suspect those *ngangas* would have carried out the required rituals to cleanse the stadium and the land, and may be all of Africa. I still think that such a cleansing must happen to keep the souls of millions who perished in the Middle Passage, all Black people who still perish at the hands of those who should protect then in America, and the many Black bodies who are brutalized by the political system on the homeland. Such an inquiry would not be some hocus-pocus, but an inquiry into the spiritual condition of all the people, White, God-fearing Christians who traded human beings, and the Africans who lacked either the power or the will to reject this dehumanizing enterprise and its legacy that continues to haunt humanity today.

I think it may be the case that no one in the Congo on that day wanted Foreman to die. But one does not know why there was no demonstration of neutrality, leaving the crowd to call out "Ali *boma ye.*" But after reading the contributions in this book, I cannot help but ask the question, what if we reverse the chant, because we cannot easily run away from the idea of *boma*, and instead chant *boma yangó* (kill it).[4] We could and I suspect rethink the chant of the "Rumble in the Jungle" to reflect what was and continues to be the big legacy of the fight for Black liberation and restoration of Black dignity that began with resistance to White determination and their will to capture and enslave Africans (something that needs more documentation). *Boma yangó* thus invites us to see the life of Muhammad Ali, the greatest, in new light. Therefore, the human project initiated and sustained by Ali and many others is not merely a metaphor to defeat a competitor, but to engage every day in a different type of killing. It helps that Ali exemplified what it means to remain steady, focused on the task because it was late in the fight when the tide turned in his favor and Ali beat his opponent. The struggle for Black identity and dignity is not a sprint, but a series of marathons that must be coordinated using all resources, including the master's tools.

Ali therefore invites us to see *boma yangó* as the long struggle and resistance. I want to indicate only three aspects to what has been documented in this marvelous collection of essays. First, *boma yangó* is a different kind of killing because it represents a life that asserts the will to be and the resolve to kill the 1619 racial project, which marked, targeted, captured, and dehumanized Africans' to build a world, they would have to fight to be recognized as inhabitants. Ali won the rumble in the jungle, and dedicated his life to *boma yangó* racism and dehumanization. In this regard, his life was a *boma yangó* of the inhumanity that began with "slavery," an endemic inhumane indignity project that targeted Black bodies drawing on the narrative of the sacred Bible that Blacks were descendants of a cursed son who would forever serve his brothers. The internationalization of this nefarious form of servitude and inhumanity was championed by Christians, one of then penning the most meaningful hymn that remains a favorite of Black churches today, "Amazing Grace." With the rise of modernity, slavery became a veritable Christian project that would despise, debase, depopulate, yet depend on Black labor and ingenuity to build the Western rim of European civilization and its instincts of domination.

Second, Ali's *buma yangó* project puts him in a class of his own because he believed he must be heard on his own terms as a "Black man in America." For Ali, it was all about substance and style. On the question of substance, he celebrated who he was as a Black man and his ability to compete and become the world heavyweight champion. In his effective communication, he adopted a rhetorical style that would have made any of the ancient African Griots proud. The Middle Passage scholars of the Africana world, beginning with communication and historical luminaries like Professor Molefi Asante, remind us that the eloquence of Black people is not lost. It is eloquence that is grounded in the rich cultural, social, intellectual, and kemetic traditions of the Black world.

Boma yangó for Ali, who talked fast, meant that he called things the way he saw them, a reality that for some seemed uncomfortable, but that was Ali's way of resisting prejudice and injustice. He was a political activist who condemned the war in Vietnam, thus rejecting the human will to kill. This is a stance that is often not appreciated because war and violence often bring up a sense of nationalism, which in many cases means that we have to set aside the best of our human sentiments to kill to maintain national glory. Ali would also be involved in the civil rights movement in different ways, identifying with his people and thus offering the leadership on one the most compelling human projects of all times, the assertion of Black rights in a world where color (and here we mean Whiteness) had blinded many people of faith.

In a world where one must *boma ye* and dehumanize another person, in the name of religion, one could and should say Ali's *boma yangó* moved him to embrace religion and reject all forms of religious beliefs that legitimized superiority and grounded White normativity as the human standard. Ali choose Islam, eventually becoming a Sunni Muslim, the community that adheres to the practices of the Prophet Muhammad, may peace be upon him. Ali throughout his life was a prominent Muslim, who said what he thought and saw, even though some thought he talked trash. Such talk was an authenticity that demonstrated his "courage to be" and his will to confront social practices in the world that in many ways were calculated to deny Black humanity and creativity. In talking what some may have considered trash, Ali was engaged in the *boma yangó* of the false views of Blacks. More importantly, he used critical Black rhetoric to offer his own philosophy and command attention by a society that could not resist, even if some members of the society disagreed with some of his ideas.

What is fascinating about Ali's religion is that he lived his life as a Sunni Muslim; adored Black people; expressed his commitment publicly in a demonstration that as a Black man in America, he knew himself as a child of God; and had accepted himself as he was, fully a child of God who did not need any validation from the structure of Whiteness. Any study of Ali's life cannot miss the fact that he was a dignified Black man who knew and accepted himself. His philosophy and life remind me of the words of the Islamic philosopher Al-Ghazali, who began his book *On Knowing Yourself and God* by stating clearly: "Know that the key to the knowledge of God, may He be honored and glorified, is knowledge of one's own self. For this it has been said: he who knows himself knows his Lord."[5] Ali, the star, knew himself and wanted to live, fight, and speak as one who knew his life was as a follower of God and was not contingent on racist prescription and practices.

Ali carried out a public *boma yangó* of Parkinson's disease and gave a human face to the illness. The champ refused to cave in, and we all saw him live his life to the fullest, engaging in philanthropic activities and raising his voice to speak even for those who did not live with his health challenges. He remained resolute as a champ and to some the greatest person to take the gloves and enter the ring, talk, and fight his way onto victory. Ali was a graceful man.

Finally, if I can echo Christel Temple, Ali was a bold living example whose life created an enduring cultural mythology that will continue to invite us to think of what it means to train, fight, worship, be an activist, engage in philanthropy, and take the constraints of physicality with grace and dignity.[6] Christel Temple argues that Ali was more than the rich pride that celebrated Blackness; he was part of Black cultural mythology. The life of Ali was full of the kinds of mythic rhythms of life. He fought like the gods, talked as one who was sure of himself, cared for his body as only an angel would, and from my perspective will become and remain a mythic figure for many Black boys and men around the world. Is this hero worship? It may be, but why not? A man who takes care of himself, trains to be the greatest fighter, takes a stand on the most controversial yet patriotic engagements that kill, and speaks his mind and builds a philanthropic organization to meet the needs of others and *boma yangó* destitution is surely a mythic figure, who showed us how to fight, win, teach, give, and bear pain. The authors of the essays in this book invite us to reflect on their perspectives on the immortal Ali.

This is a significant text on the champion, Muhammad Ali. I am honored to invite you to join James Conyers and Christel Temple as well as a distinguished group of scholars on a fascinating journey with Muhammad Ali.

Elias Kifon Bongmba
Houston, May 8, 2021

Notes

1 Veteran Cameroonian journalist Ben Bongong told me these two journalists would have been the ones who reported on the fight and might have been at the stadium in Kinshasa.

2 Joseph Kabasele, *Grand Kallé & African Team* (Paris: Sonodisc, 1997).

3 See "Ali *boma ye*: The Chant that made Muhammad Ali an African hero." *This Week*, June 7, 2016. https://www.theweek.co.uk/muhammad-ali/73369/ali-boma-ye-the-chant-that-made-muhammad-ali-an-african-hero.

4 I am indebted to Professor Aliko Songolo of the University of Wisconsin for giving me this term.

5 Hujjat al-Islam Abu Hàmid Muhammad Ghazzali Tusi, *Al-Ghazzali on Knowing Yourself and God*, transMuhammad Nur Abdus Salam, intro. Laleh Bakhatiar (Chicago: Great Books of the Islamic World, 2011), 7.

6 Christel N. Temple, *Black Cultural Mythology* (New York: SUNY Press, 2020).

PREFACE

Michael Ezra, author of *Muhammad Ali: The Making of an Icon* (2009), titled the book's introduction "Why Another Book on Muhammad Ali?" He suggests that Ali is a world record holder, credited with being the one person who has the most books written about him.[1] Johnny Smith highlights the fact that Ali "has received little attention from historians" and his legacy in published collections and biographies has been managed mostly by sports journalists (and not by *academic* historians) who have "confined Ali to the history of sports."[2] In a shift that represents the priorities, methodologies, and critical frameworks of the academic discipline of Africana Studies, this collection articulates the wonder and scope of Muhammad Ali from a curricular perspective of Africana cultural memory studies. This approach reveals how Ali's life and legacy are teachable and quantifiable within the core subject areas of the discipline (history, politics, psychology, economics, communication, community development, pan-Africanism, etc.) and within the Black nationalist methodologies of its origins and ongoing priorities.

Sports Illustrated writer and backlash critic and biographer Mark Kram derisively asks, "Why do we need to be so intense about our heroes?" and then complains, "The intensity of hero worship out there is almost sick."[3] Yet African Americans such as Spike Lee and journalist Armstrong Williams have culturally centered answers. Lee said, "He will always be a hero for a lot of us" and "He was like our prince."[4] Williams acknowledges that Ali was the "embodiment of masculine striving."[5] He asserts further that African American heroes

> transcend the physical or cultural laws that enmesh the rest of us. Certainly, that is what Ali accomplished when he perched himself atop the sporting world then sang the sublime truth of self-worth. Along the way, he gave countless American Blacks a model of achievement. Failure suddenly seems less customary. And the possibility of playing the part of a champion seems a little more possible.[6]

Inevitably, it is okay to engage with Ali in historical, cultural, or symbolic terms, and the discipline's subfield of Africana cultural memory studies makes room for the philosophical and thoughtfully engaged *conceptual* understanding of memory, heroics, and commemoration that is a vantage point for comparatively engaging with the legacies of numerous Africana legends.

In the preface and introductions to *Black Light: The African American Hero* (1993), Paul Carter Harrison, Danny Glover, and Bill Duke describe the nature of heroics with beauty and awe. Their framing of the project is grounded with profound, philosophical orientations that stabilize *Black Light*'s photo-essay genre "celebration of 90 of the greatest black heroes of the twentieth century, men and women who through their achievement have significantly illuminated the African American experience."[7] Harrison is a cultural godfather whose work on Africana aesthetics and ritual performances would naturally imbue such a collection with a sense of sacred inheritance, and his introduction as well as text for each selected hero is grounded with deep historical sentiment. Both Duke and Glover are acclaimed actors and film directors. Glover's Black Studies background and his grounded cultural worldview of the meaning of celebrity status have given him additional compelling insight into the nature of heroics and memory. The ideas he selected to convey the gravity of the meaning of African American achievement for the collection's introduction are compatible with the conceptual framework outlined in *Black Cultural Mythology* (2020).

Itemizing Muhammad Ali's persona and legacy based on *Black Light*'s broad philosophical grounding and on its brief biographical treatment of Muhammad Ali, in particular, gives us an informal starting point and snapshot of the public's *general* approaches to historicizing and demonstrating reverence for Ali. This contextualized snapshot then sets the stage for a more in-depth survey and analysis of Ali through this volume's 17 essays, which are based on deeper conceptual and theoretical summations of how academic research, multiple lifetime and posthumous biographies, documentaries, and Ali's own autobiography and memoir stabilize Ali in Africana cultural memory, perhaps in even more ways than we have routinely realized.

In *Black Light*, the preface and introductions that reflect on heroics are worth analyzing for their depth. The lyricism with which Harrison, Glover, and Duke describe their endeavor is remarkable for how the heroic embodies a sense of cultural memory storytelling. Duke establishes the urgency of a photo-essay biography of nearly one hundred accomplished African Americans as a corrective to the practices of "a historically forgetful world."[8] He also tells an important story about heroics:

One day, in my first grade class, we were given a history lesson that I would not soon forget. On a corkboard, the teacher displayed pictures of all who had made America great: Abraham Lincoln, Benjamin Franklin, George Washington, Thomas Jefferson. The pictures were endless. I saw the pride that beamed through my white classmates. The teacher then turned to me and the other lone black child in the class with a sense of letting us know that we had not been forgotten. She then presented the class and myself with three portraits that encapsulated her understanding of "Negro" history. The first was a stoic picture of George Washington Carver, the second was a stern Booker T. Washington, and last but not least a brilliant yellow-clad dark-faced little black Sambo. Intuitively, I understood these two distinct and separate realities, the reality of the nation of America and the reality of my place in it. I also realized that being black was a bad idea because to be white was to win and to be black was to lose. To be white was to be on the side of the good guys and to be black was to be on the side of the bad guys and the insignificant. It was not until I was an adult that I fully understood the impact and implications of that history lesson on that day so long ago in my youth.

This book is dedicated to all the children of all ages who have not yet had the finger of dignity pointed to the beauty of their black existence. It is also dedicated to the endless unrecognized courage of the mothers, fathers, uncles, aunts, grandmothers, and grandfathers.

A dark-skinned or mulattoed, wide-lipped, broad-nosed courage that has put and continues to put pride and hope in the eyes of their children.[9]

Duke has a detailed grasp on what is at stake in how we articulate and model Africana hero dynamics. His range is intergenerational and futuristic, for Black progeny. He links the processes of historical awareness, storytelling, and image creation with dignity and pride, yet with the caveat and reminder that schools and non-Black teachers will not be *the* agents that sustain the personhood, motivation, and self-determination of Black children and communities.

Glover extends his understanding of his community's local heroic toward the discourse of survival. He describes "survivalists who fueled the imagination" and recalls that "there were always adults and peers whose special knack for survival made them appear invincible in my eyes. Heroic!"[10] They seemed to "magically soar above the fray [...] or move forward with such spiritual buoyancy in their rhythmical swagger that their feet seemed to never touch the ground."[11] To Glover's younger self, "these people seemed so much bigger than ordinary men and women that they were sometimes frightening. They were frightening because they reminded you of your own limitations and how far you had to go to arrive at such a posture of personal security if not invincibility."[12] Among his community, regardless of class or legal activities, he observed among certain men "a demeanor of power and self-reliance."[13] These experiences invoked an understanding that

> heroism is not an achievement everybody will be able to claim in life. The hero is like a mediator between God and ordinary folk. The hero transcends the limitations that bound the aspirations of mere mortals. Perhaps the original heroic model belongs to the ancestors who survived the Middle Passage, endured the dehumanization of slavery, then transformed the hardship of such an experience into a newly evolved people, the African American. Our ancestors had to come up with many creative strategies for survival in order to retain optimistic values that dignified their humanity in an alien social context that did everything to dehumanize them as victims of slavery. So it's not easy to be heroic.[14]

Glover historicizes African American heroics by meditating on the journey African people endured at the beginning of their American saga, and he reiterates the high standard for heroic attainment based on survival, transcendence, endurance, transformation, evolution, strategic creativity, optimistic values, and humanistic dignity. He casually mentions Muhammad Ali in this introduction, comparing boxer Mike Tyson (good skill with bad choices) to Ali: "On the other hand, the heroic gesture of Muhammad Ali's sacrifice of his career while resisting going to war on his principles shows greatness."[15] Many writers, critics, and observers describe Ali as a hero, as the greatest, and as principled, but the context of the sacred logic of Africana survival extends the meditation and demands a greater specificity in our deciphering of precisely what inheritance we gain from Ali's legacy. An even more remarkable inference is Glover's description of heroics as a type of cultural glow with psychological import. He credits heroes such as Katherine Dunham and Alex Haley with successfully initiating an "enlargement of the black psyche" through

a commitment "to the task of legitimizing our African heritage," and he writes passionately about how restoring memory works to "fortify the psychological integrity of African
Americans in future generations."[16] He has concerns for the youth "self-image" whose
worth "can be fortified by recognition" of its culture's ability "to achieve in spite of their
limited circumstances."[17]

Paul Carter Harrison's contextualization of the photo-essay on Black achievement
reinforces cultural priorities related to survival. He writes, "The hope of securing greater
stability and self-worth is the Black Light, those men and women of African descent who
serve the community as beacons in the struggle for survival."[18] Harrison defines heroes as
those whose "actions alter the status quo of black experience and foster, socially and spiritually, the necessary collective illumination for social change" and who model "a spirit
of survival through rediscovery."[19] Harrison's existential depth in describing the effect of
the heroic goes even deeper to suggest how "the heroic impulse seeks to heal the wounds
when the spirit is embattled and threatened with devastation."[20] Its priority is "collective
perseverance."[21] Finally, "the hero, as a model of ingenuity and tenacity, is a reflection of
the human spirit's aspiration toward a cosmic sense of potency bordering on godliness."[22]
Thus, Harrison's cosmological orientation of the African American hero dynamic places
even more pressure and responsibility on us to best narrate legendary personas' mortal
and immortal effect through intergenerational heroic exposure, storytelling, and symbolic reference, often through the arts and aesthetic memorialization.

While Duke's, Harrison's, and Glover's contextualization of African American heroics
is tucked in an obscure introduction to a book of heroes aimed at a generalist audience,
their collective transmission of the higher calling of cultural heroics is a treasure that is
compatible with contemporary frameworks for Africana cultural memory studies such
as Black cultural mythology. Black cultural mythology insists upon a reorientation away
from the premise of an ongoing trauma that has been active since enslavement. Similarly,
Harrison ends his foreword emphasizing that "the slaves' suffering cannot be ennobled
unless there is evidence of transcendence, a renewed desire for survival through self-
affirmation, as opposed to self-destruction, which reflects an enlightened capacity for
the human condition to be transformed."[23] As Harrison's text from *Black Light* shares, Ali
was remarkable for his verbal prowess and "colorful pre-fight signifying matches with his
opponents"; for the cultural audacity to change his name and demand that "adversaries
in and out of the ring recognize it"; for athletic credentials of being a Golden Glove,
Olympic Games, and professional heavyweight champion; as a religious icon for and
minister in the Nation of Islam; as an "undaunted" activist for conscientious objection; as
a successful litigant in a Supreme Court case that ended his suspension from boxing; and
as an "outspoken opponent to racism."[24] Ali lived for 23 more years beyond Harrison's
biographical entry on him in *Black Light*, and these years bore witness to even more honorable and heroic behavior that culminated in Ali's decision to become a highly visible
survivor of Parkinson's disease until his death. Ali did not hide the toll the disease took
on him, even as the symptoms of trembling and reduced communication were a direct
reversal of the physicality and verbal agility that defined his heroics for most of his life.

We highlight the approach to legacy, achievement, and heroics in *Black Light* in
order to map the expansion of how this academic study takes the raw material of Ali's

biography and filters it through even more tributaries. The sports biographies are invaluable and have collected data about Ali on which most of this volume's essays rely. The philosophy behind the coffee-table book, first-exposure achievement bibliography that we find in *Black Light* is also foundational because it reminds us of the pantheon of African American heroes and leaders who are household names but not always *studied* in extended biographical depth.

We have structured the essays to offer a journey of viewing Ali's value in terms of theoretical and methodological innovation, historical breadth, international legacy, and finally his applied value. In Chapter 1, Christel N. Temple approaches Ali's legacy as a case study that relies on the conceptual framework of Black cultural mythology to pinpoint a functional methodology of remembrance that fulfills the Black family's need for an ideal *mythological structure* to build confidence, self-esteem, and lifetime success for Black children and families. In Chapter 2, James L. Conyers Jr. links Ali's personhood, Black nationalist religion, and chosen sport into an expression of spiritual prowess. Molefi Kete Asante offers an important pre-Ali worldview as Chapter 3 decenters Ali, for a moment, to resituate the cultural memory of the Black boxers and athletes who came before him and who fought within and against the intricacies of the European fabric of domination to gain such sports accolades as *Black* men. Wade W. Nobles's Chapter 4 is a psycho-historical analysis of Ali as a "spirit being," defined from traditional Ifa and Vodun perspectives that counter the Western superlative and moniker of "The Greatest" that society considers to be a final word on Ali. In Chapter 5, Abdul S. Pitre, Ruby Holden-Pitre, and Natalie Williamson frame Ali's reeducation in terms of a theorization of critical Black pedagogy.

The next several chapters represent a shift from theoretical valuations of Ali's legacy and cultural memory to historical excavations. In Chapter 6, Bayyinah S. Jeffries decenters Ali's boxing superlatives to prioritize, instead, Ali's most derided identities—being a Black man and being a Black Muslim—as the contexts for his most enduring legacy. In Chapter 7, Suzuko Morikawa mines Ali's fascinating international experiences in Africa and Asia in the 1970s to highlight his lifelong friendship with a Japanese wrestler. Rounding out the lesser known legacy of Ali in an international realm of cultural memory, Anju Reejhsinghani's Chapter 8 explores Ali's cyclical visits to and experiences among Cuba's populations who valued him as a boxer, as a humanist, and as a Black man.

The second half of the collection is a more diverse look at Ali, reflecting how scholars envision his applied cultural memory status, which influences or is conversant with activism, community engagement, advocacy, policy, health and nutrition, exercise, cross-religious allyship, veteran's rights, and gender constructs in sport. In Chapter 9, Rebecca Hankins dissects the struggle between American and African American claims to Ali's iconography as either a race-less patriotic hero or a Black nationalist hero by mapping his travels and community engagement, particularly in the state of Texas. In Chapter 10, Derek Wilson provides an African-centered differentiation to counter the United States' tendency to whitewash and culturally neutralize Ali, by relying on the South African Zulu philosophy of Ubuntu, or "I am because we are," to culturally locate Ali's memory. In Chapter 11, Billy Hawkins adds an economic analysis to Ali's function in Africana cultural memory by measuring how society views Ali as either an athletic commodity or in terms of his sociopolitical capital.

In an unexpected but profound analysis of the discourse that Ali's legacy and cultural memory inspire, in Chapter 12, Akilah R. Carter-Francique takes a bold step to compare and contrast the gendered traditions of sports fame, notably discussing Ali's African American women athlete counterparts and how media and society differentiate between male and female athletic prowess. In a similarly unique study of how Ali's legendary status and iconic value to cultural memory influence the topic of African American and sport, a group of scholars—Karen E. Alexander, Ryan Moore, Jeanette Anderson, William Kouba, and Waveney LaGrone—takes a visionary step in Chapter 13 to consider the cultural memory realm of antiheroics, wherein the military status that Ali rejected in his celebrated conscientious objection to the Vietnam War draft was actually an act of self-preservation that shielded him from the mental health crises that some veterans subsequently face after military service.

The closing essays of this volume reiterate some of the more personal, localized, and contemporary memories in which Ali is central. In Chapter 14, Howard Bartee Jr. reflects on Ali's legacy based on a narrative inquiry into Ali's autobiography, revealing Ali's process of developing a *sense of self* from his humble Louisville origins and how his life can be inspiration to striving youth. In Chapter 15, Autumn Raynor shows how Ali found allies and friends among the Catholic religion's populations. In Chapter 16, Brandon Allen evaluates Ali's iconic status as memorialized figure who, like the contemporary Colin Kaepernick, stood for radical change. Finally, Angela Branch-Vital, Andrea McDonald, Park Atatah, Catherine Kisavi-Atatah, and James L. Conyers Jr. collaborate in Chapter 17 to address how Ali's diet and exercise regimen is an important health and wellness consideration that is attentive to the Africana Studies subject area of health/science/technology.

The vitality of this collection is that each researcher or research team relies on a grounded Africana methodological lens to mine the archive on Muhammad Ali to present invigorated idea formation on a cultural hero. As an Africana cultural memory study on Ali, his prowess in sport does not overshadow his prowess in living successfully as an admired, radical, strategic, often reinvented, courageous, and culture-loving African American man who was also an African in America. As an embodiment of an *African American* hero (not as the oft-framed *American* hero found in sports biography), Ali is a symbol of the trials and victories of the African American experience. Whether we focus on his identity as a grandson of enslaved Africans in Louisville, Kentucky, as a member of a thriving Black nationalist religious organization or as an iconic African American Parkinson's disease fighter carrying the Olympic torch, he is the progeny of an ingenious African people who practiced surviving a hostile and racist terrain for hundreds of years in the United States. This perspective answers Michael Ezra's question about why we need another book on Ali, and it redirects us away from Mark Kram's negative critique of the celebrated intensity of Africana heroics and cultural memory.

Notes

1 Michael Ezra, *Muhammad Ali: The Making of an Icon* (Philadelphia: Temple UP, 2009), 1. Johnny Smith describes this world record claim as unsubstantiated, in "Reflections: Remembering Muhammad Ali: Myths, Memory, and History," *Reviews in American History* 45, no. 1 (2017): 177–88 (178).

2 Smith, "Reflections," 177–88 (178, 182).

3 Qtd. in Armstrong Williams, "The Ali Myth," *Afro-American Red Star*, December 28, 2001, A27. In his review essay on Ali, Johnny Smith also categorizes journalist Mark Kram as dismissive and critical of Ali's hero dynamic in Kram's *Ghosts of Manila* (2001).

4 Williams, "The Ali Myth," A27.

5 Ibid.

6 Ibid.

7 Paul Carter Harrison, Danny Glover, and Bill Duke, *Black Light: The African American Hero* (New York: Thunder's Mouth Press, 1993), back cover.

8 Harrison, Glover, and Duke, *Black Light*, xi.

9 Ibid., xiv.

10 Ibid., xv.

11 Ibid.

12 Ibid.

13 Ibid., xvi.

14 Ibid.

15 Ibid., xxiv.

16 Ibid.

17 Ibid., xxviii.

18 Ibid., xxvix–xxx.

19 Ibid., xxx.

20 Ibid.

21 Ibid.

22 Ibid.

23 Ibid., xxx–xxxi.

24 Ibid., 24–26.

ACKNOWLEDGMENTS

Within a year of Muhammad Ali's passing in 2016, James L. Conyers Jr. contacted me to share his interest in doing a coedited volume on Muhammad Ali. Conyers had just released an edited collection on *Black Lives: Essays in African American Biography* (2015), and he had previously included me on edited projects such as *The Frederick Douglass Encyclopedia* (2009), which he coedited with Julius E. Thompson and Nancy J. Dawson; *Malcolm X: A Historical Reader* (2008), which he edited with Andrew P. Smallwood; and *Charles Hamilton Houston: An Interdisciplinary Study of Civil Rights Leadership* (2012).

One of Conyers's many strengths was his vision for the study of intellectual biography. His significant repertoire, and now *legacy*, include monographs, edited collections, book chapters, articles, and bibliographies that document a uniquely Afrocentric and Africana Studies–based corpus of ideas and approaches to intellectual biography. His publications often use the phrasings of *culture and memory* or *biography and Africology* to contextualize his work on additional figures such as Carter G. Woodson, Elijah Muhammad, Domingo Alvares, John Henrik Clarke, Martin Luther King Jr., Maulana Karenga, Molefi Kete Asante, and Charles H. Wesley. My work on the transmission of the West African funeral dirge tradition and on the conceptual framework of Black cultural mythology—an Africana Studies–based point of view on sacred remembrance that adds to the field of Africana cultural memory studies—made us an ideal pair as coeditors. Additionally, Conyers had published *Race in American Sports* (2014).

As the senior scholar who has been among the most instrumental forces promoting the legacy of pioneers in the field as well as using his edited collections to challenge newer generations of scholars to develop their most brilliant idea formation, Conyers was the administrative lead in our edited collection aimed at exploring what Muhammad Ali means from an Africana Studies point of view. Because we lost Conyers too soon, I can only guess the names of the many scholars and community activists whom he would have thanked and acknowledged. We both value the support and patience of our families—especially our children—who have grown up in sites and environments where they have seen our dedication to the discipline of Africana Studies. We extend a special thanks to the administrative staff of the University of Houston's Department of Africana Studies. Especially, we thank Jasmine Grant, who managed this project's files. We are grateful to our editor, Meghan Grieving with Anthem Press, and to the production staff who has seen our project to fruition. We extend thanks to our many contributors, each of whose visions of Muhammad Ali's depth and legacy add important layers to this volume. Finally, we thank our reviewers for their clarifying insight and helpful suggestions.

In the end, this project is attentive to the ancestral cycle. It is about the ancestor Muhammad Ali and what we learn from his trials, ethos, and victories. It is also about the ancestor, James L. Conyers Jr., and his tireless and dedicated work to create many of the texts that are a curricular foundation of our work. In a final acknowledgment, scholars in the disciplines of Africana Studies, History, and Sociology recognize and salute his contributions.

Chapter One

"SOMETHING GREATER THAN PRIDE": MUHAMMAD ALI AND BLACK CULTURAL MYTHOLOGY

Christel N. Temple

Heroics and mythology are both aligned with a focus on legacy worldviews that determine more assertive and more stylized behaviors and actions whose resistance is the compelling force that sustains achievement and prowess. Applying Black cultural mythology methodology to this case study on Muhammad Ali will reveal how the "behaviors of recollection, writing, and retelling are cyclical and self-sustained processes of the culture's intergenerational self-awareness."[1] Mythology is benignly embellished, cyclical storytelling about legendary figures and events that helps to elevate the memory, meditation, and valuation of a persona toward sacred cultural remembrance, and it differs from one of its constituent elements—*heroics*.

In articulating an Africana Studies methodological approach to the critical depth of cultural memory, the theorization of *Black cultural mythology* is a twenty-first-century itemization of a set of terminologies and a conceptual language that facilitate the exploration of the meaning and implications of legendary behavior. The theorization is attentive to "itemizing not only processes of cultural survival but also the memorialization practices that support the broad narrative of this survival."[2] Also, "a hallmark of this mythology is its heroics, recalled in collective recognition of the culture's hearty legacy of historical figures whose acts of self-preservation and prowess in surviving incredible odds are the source of rich cultural remembrance and inspiration."[3] This mining of the heroics for reproducible models of self-preservation, survival, inspiration, and prowess from the life of Muhammad Ali is incredibly rich because of Ali's multiple personas.

Black cultural mythology's concern for the *cyclical transmission* and *preservationist function* of storytelling and recollection of Africana heroics is a method for more deeply asking the simple question, What did Muhammad Ali's life teach us that is essential for increasing our life chances and life experiences in a manner of cultural wholeness? This question prompts us to be more deeply reflective and more meditative as we inquire into "the humanistic vitality of the cultural logic" that has sustained people of African descent in the diaspora since the enslavement experience required us to *begin again* and *engrave identity* on new soils.[4] Its answers will relate to Black cultural mythology's variables of hero dynamics, epic intuitive conduct, hyperheroic acts, immortalization philosophy, and resistance-based cognitive survival.

The framework alerts us to be mindful of the grit of achievement and survival in order to "jolt the reader-spectator out of [the] gaze" that causes us to be overly *casual* in the ways we remember.[5] Black cultural mythology prompts us to articulate *specificity* in remembrance similar to the translation and itemization of Muhammad Ali's hero dynamic in the entry in Harrison's *Black Light*. Similarly, Houston A. Baker's contribution to this critical framework is his assertion that consciousness and "nonmaterial counterintelligence" have been essential elements of African American survival.[6] This is particularly true for Ali's survivalist heroics, physically against sports foes, mentally against systemic racism, and mortally against Parkinson's disease. These are aspects of legacy that come to mind when we *meditate* on the specificity of the culture's inheritances from Ali and on the logic of immortalizing him. With Black cultural mythology being an "organic effort to begin to map, label, categorize, and formalize the heretofore random, yet consistently illuminated ideations of myth, memory, mythology, and heroics," Muhammad Ali's legacy is a fruitful case study that allows us to exhaust the critical possibilities.[7] From the vantage point of his feats and accomplishments, often stylized within an identifiable tradition of African American folk sensibility, the emergent *philosophy of heroism* keeps us attentive to his "achievement against the odds, and the extension of human capacity beyond the ordinary."[8] So far, there are concentrated Black cultural mythology studies on Harriet Tubman, Paul Robeson, and Malcolm X that survey superlative self-emancipation and sociopolitical activism.[9] Adding to this corpus, this study on Ali, documenting a more sustained and professional sports-related prowess layered with sociopolitical activism, breaks new ground in sports criticism and modeling a unique orientation to Africana cultural memory studies.

In terms of methodology, this exploration of the superlative analysis of Ali's legacy functions much like the case study from *Black Cultural Mythology* on Malcolm X that measured the superlative language that emerged as critics and reviewers assessed Malcolm's legacy after the release of Manning Marable's revisionist biography on him.[10] Most studies and narratives on Ali have dedicated book titles and/or chapters that address some version of what I theorize here as his mythological status, and a review of these, particularly of key historiographical (or *sports* historiography) sources on Ali culled for their use of the word *myth*, allows us to begin with a good sense of the *mythological vocabulary* that represents Ali's legacy: legend, king of the world, man of destiny, marvelous mouth, most famous man in the world, a man with amazing grace, worthy of death, resurrected, blessed, a prophet, a dreamer, exuberant, a martyr, trickster, crown prince, an icon, favorite son, a person of moral authority, people's champ, hero, an *American* hero, revolter, rebel, protest symbol, lion, rebirthed, and champion.

Beyond the titles of volumes and their chapters, within the texts, those who have studied and narrated Ali's life offer an even more intriguing list of heroic and mythological metaphors and descriptions. Ferdie Pacheco refers to him as a "many-sided meteor," "teenage giant," "on a quest," "special," "unique," "goal motivated," and "able to overcome adversity."[11] David Remnick calls him a "new species of athlete," "the most charismatic sports figure of the century," and "most adored," and described him as having "resonance" and "brilliance."[12] Gerald Early notes his "adulation" and how he is "overesteemed," and identifies him as a "trickster-like black comic."[13] However, Early's more critically balanced observations that honestly embrace contradictions and superlatives require quoting at length: "What Ali had was an irresistible combination of talent, showmanship, and a genius conceit of himself that bordered on both the heroically self-possessed and the insufferably megalomanic."[14] He adds, "Ali, far from being a victim, is perhaps one of the most remarkable examples of triumph over racism in our century."[15] He was "intuitive, glib, richly gregarious, and intensely creative, like an artist."[16] Norman Mailer names him "America's Greatest ego," "the swiftest embodiment of human intelligence we have yet," "the prince of mass man and the media," and a "Black Prince" who "behave[s] like a young god."[17] Ezra references him as "revered" and as "an iconic international figure."[18] Robert Lipsyte shares a story about how, in following Ali around as a reporter, he "learned a great deal about racial politics, celebrity, decline and fall and resurrection, hope and nostalgia, and the fakelore that fuels our dreams."[19] Barbara L. Tischler frames his legacy in terms of him being "a survivor, and a humanitarian."[20]

Biographers such as Pacheco have full chapters "in appreciation" of Ali. Pacheco registers acclaim for Ali for being "A *fanatic believer* in Islam […] with the guts to stand by his beliefs" and as "generous," "loving," "nonviolent," and "peaceful."[21] These descriptions culminate in a thwarted realization that immortalization is expected but not necessarily fulfilled. In "Great Men Die Twice," Mark Kram references Ali's 1989 health crisis and his "surface romance with immortality" and, inevitably, describes the awe of this moment's mortal distance away from Ali's former "radiated glow" of "invulnerability."[22] In describing Ali's physical appearance as an aging man whose appearance reveals the medical toll taken by the brutality of boxing, Pacheco laments that "we thought he would never grow old, would never slow down, would never stop being fun—would never stop being Ali."[23] There is a physical myth of immortality and a cosmological view of immortality, the latter of which is based on how memory and cyclical storytelling about prowess, character, and deed contribute to a *narrative* mythological status. This duality allows us to be not only pragmatic about life and mortality but also grounded in the culture's awareness of how the identities heroes engraved in our memory are sacred inheritances from which current and future generations can learn about different modes of cultural greatness as inspiration.

Thomas Hauser defines Ali, first, prior to writing the authorized biography, and he observed that the Ali society recognizes is incomplete. Specifically, "the true Ali is largely unknown. Stories about him have been embellished and retold to the point where they assume biblical proportions. People worldwide recognize his face. Yet, even as the Ali chronicles grow, new generations are born, and to them Ali is more legend than reality, part of America's distant past."[24] Hauser alerts readers that "this book is not an attempt to mythologize Ali," which means he does not fabricate and cushion the narrative in a hagiographic act to elevate and celebrate Ali toward epic or heroic status.[25] The operational definition of mythology that is at the core of the Africana conceptual framework of Black cultural mythology is the lesser known meaning of the genre, which is "storytelling and symbolism that narratively utilize the core factual variables of an event, phenomenon, or persona and assume license to enhance the story's dimensions with benign or innocuous embellishment" that reinforces the actual, lived dynamics and memorial value of the legendary figure.[26]

Pacheco's summary of why society should appreciate Ali is particularly thoughtful among an array of biographies that meander in their ability to offer an Africana cultur- ally grounded commemorative, then later, *memorial*, reflection. In a rather cosmological reflection, Pacheco writes,

> This is another part of the role he has been playing on earth. Now, he is Ali, the retired fighter. Happily married, living on a peaceful farm outside Detroit, roaming the world as a goodwill ambassador for his religion, for boxing, and for his race. He is an object of ven- eration. He is a man to be envied. He is a man with great inner peace. He has received the harvest of love from the seeds he sowed in his twenty years of world travel.[27]

This is a rare, organic statement on Ali's mythological value because it is a type of final eyewitness testimony of Ali's mythological *journey*. It invokes the restfulness that comes toward the end of an Africana life cycle that emphasizes the processes of birth, living, and transition from conception and existential destiny, through youthful vitality, and finally to the mellowing wisdom of eldership that leads to ancestral placement.

In a second chapter on "appreciation," Pacheco grounds Ali's post-Olympic develop- ment in a setting defined by his apprenticeship among a greater, methodical pantheon of boxing advisors who anoint Ali and confirm his destiny. This passage addresses the community heroics of the trainers, promoters, and managers who cultivated an folkloric persona and even transmitted to Muhammad Ali a type of inheritance that supported his process toward the legendary. These are the "boxing cognoscenti" who work in the "mecca of boxing learning."[28] Pacheco understood Ali's success in terms of "luck, for- tune, destiny, serendipity—call it what you will, but all his life, Muhammad Ali has been at the right place at the right time. He has been one of those people whom fate has chosen."[29] If we are truly itemizing what we can *learn* from Ali's mythological status, Pacheco is a grand storyteller of Ali's gifts and excellence:

> Clay genuinely loved to "shock and amaze you." Like a kid showing off in front of adults, Clay loved to find an unusual thing to do, to create strange events, to behave in the exact opposite way expected of him. To provoke. To irritate. To put himself out on a limb, then saw it off, and still prevail. This was his way to worldwide celebrity.[30]

Pacheco ends his book with a chapter on "Ali's Place in History," and he provides a summary of Ali's cultural memory value that has interesting variables. To him, Ali "transcended the sport" and "possessed all the attributes of a perfect hero: he was young, handsome, brash, witty, irreverent, chance-taking, religious, clean, and entertaining."[31] Yet, Pacheco also aligns Ali with a core subject area in Africana Studies—technology, noting that he "was clearly made for the electronic age. He emerged as new technology was developing that gave him the possibility, hitherto unthought of, of appearing on a worldwide stage."[32] The only other Black cultural mythology case study that addresses technology's role in maintaining a figure's (in the case of Paul Robeson) hero dynamic is a comparative analysis on how the documentary film structure further illuminates a heroic figure's mythological status beyond his autobiography.[33] However, there are also debates that conjecture about whether Michael Jordan's accolades within the "satellite era" that give him easy international heroic exposure is greater than the international regard that Ali garnered from exhibitions, leisurely travel, and networking.

Ali is unique because he is among the legendary figures who seized the opportunity for *self-mythologizing*. We have a trove of descriptions and phrasing from Ali's competitive self-aggrandizement that function in the best traditions of folk prowess and sportsmanly intimidation. In fact, in 1963, Columbia released a record titled *The Greatest* that was a recording of Ali performing a litany of his phrases and monologues. Thomas Hauser samples them in *Muhammad Ali: His Life and Times*: "I'm so great, I impress even myself. [...] It's hard to be modest when you're as great as I am. [...] I'm a perfect role model for children; I'm good-looking, clean-living, cultured, and modest."[34] Pacheco celebrates Ali's relationships with Harlem's clever wordsmith and motivational speaker, Drew Bundini Brown, who mentored Ali's existing verbal and performative rambunctiousness. Brown is credited with coining Ali's famous "Float like a butterfly / sting like a bee" lyric, and Ali continued the folkloric sensationalism by nicknaming all of his opponents, memorably as the Rabbit, the Bear, the Mummy, and the Gorilla.[35] Yet in the midst of our memory of Ali's performances and rhyming taunts, he lived long enough to wisely invest in his hero dynamic:

> I'll tell you how I want to be remembered: as a black man who won the heavyweight title and who was humorous and who treated everyone right. As a man who never looked down on those who looked up to him and who helped as many of his people as he could—financial and also in their fight for freedom, justice, and equality. As a man who wouldn't embarrass them. As a man who tried to unite his people through the faith of Islam. [...] And if that's too much, then I guess I'd settle for being remembered only as a great boxing champion who became a preacher and a champion of his people.[36]

Remnick published this on the last page of his book, yet he subtitled his book with the identity "An American Hero." To the contrary, Ali frames his legacy in terms of being an *Africana* hero with steady concerns for *his* people. Ali provides the final reflection in Hauser's authorized biography, which is a collection of reflections from dozens of witnesses to Ali's life. When the book was published, his attention and gaze were beyond the sport of boxing. He was intent on moving beyond the bold and playful banter of his sports career and attentive to more important things: "There's bigger work I got to do. The whole world is in trouble. Crime is on the rise; the environment is deteriorating; you've got people fighting and the threat of nuclear war; no long-term friendships; corruption in government [...] no respect for elders; people hijacking planes. [...] Everything in nature is in perfect order except man."[37]

Like another Black cultural mythology icon and exemplar—the nineteenth-century abolitionist Maria W. Stewart, who used a late-life windfall to fund the gathering and publications of her essays and writings in order to situate herself and achievements into posterity's grasp—Ali promoted the same method of self-immortalization with the creation of GOAT, Inc. (Greatest of All Time). As David Maraniss suggests, "Ali wants the world to know that he is just another goat, one living thing in this vast and miraculous universe. But also the greatest there ever was [...] arguably the best known and most beloved figure in the world. Who else? The Pope? Nelson Mandela? Michael Jordan? Ali might win in a split decision."[38]

In a Black cultural mythology reading that is attentive to a figure's hyperheroic acts, resistance-based cognitive survival, memorialization, ancestral status, immortalization, and processes of reconciliation and renewal, several texts on Ali present compelling chapters that relate to these variables. This also includes Elizabeth Alexander's poem "A Poem in Twelve Rounds" that serves as the epilogue to Elliott J. Gorn's *The People's Champ*. Along with Gerald Early's critique of "preposterous propositions" from Ali's autobiography, also in that volume, and Michael Ezra's chapter from *A Making of an Icon*, in which he assesses how Thomas Hauser's *Muhammad Ali: His Life and Times* is a "literary rehabilitation of Ali's legend," a Black cultural mythology *literary* analysis comes to fruition. Ezra accurately observes the way an authorized biography could "jump-start the moribund movement to canonize the ex-champion as a global figure and all-time moral authority."[39] Most personal narrative genres—especially autobiography and biography—have natural biases and motives bordering on the hagiographic. Early addresses this in a reading of Ali's *The Greatest: My Own Story*. He views the autobiography

> not as a true or "authentic" picture of the fighter, but as a tactical or strategic representation of his politics and his political image as America's most famous, most fanciful, most physically striking, and most "far-fetched" dissident. Particularly important here, Ali's autobiography addresses the political meaning of black masculinity, a natural obsession for a black prizefighter, the most perverse and the most telling symbol of the masculine-as-performance in American culture.[40]

Early is adept in deconstructing Americanism to include Black masculinity. As an aside, the biographies on Ali, especially the later ones that reflect on his final marriage with Lonnie Ali, pay tribute to women's gendered roles and functions that, in another study, would be of interest to a Black cultural mythology analysis. The experiences of Coretta Scott King, Myrlie Evers, Betty Shabazz, Eslanda Robeson, and even, to some, Michelle Obama bear witness to additional narratives valued for these women's leadership roles and their partnerships as spouses and companions to masculine heroes.

The public is comprised of both critical readers who comfortably navigate through episodes and draw their own conclusions, and readers whose imprint of an accomplished figure is fixed and impermeable in an elevated heroic space. The latter group reads with the goal to honor and pay tribute, and deconstruction is of no interest to their particular memory goal. There is no hierarchy among these readerships; however, there are deeper philosophical and cosmological matters at hand when Africana people engage with their ancestors. The ancestral methodologies grounded in Africana culture and its African and African-derived spiritual practices are not beholden to an emergent contemporary American biographical obsession with icon deconstruction that is occurring with books, documentaries, and film. Literature is entertainment, education, literacy-building, and reinforcement or escape from established cultural worldviews. The flexibility in remembrance and memorialization is not offensive, but an Africana Studies orientation has unique, culturally relevant, and culturally stabilizing goals in processing its heroics and mythological structures.

Black cultural mythology additionally functions as a methodology for literary criticism. Its properties have multidimensional conceptual depth for mythological analysis. They are critical tools used to decipher and itemize the methods Black creative writers utilize as the most consistent agents who recycle the content and superlatives of acclaimed legendary lives in symbolic, narrative, and lyrical form. The literary also includes the *folkloric*, which receives steady attention from Tom Wolf regarding Ali's "marvelous mouth," or lyrical oral prowess, and from Norman Mailer, who is attentive to Ali's ego, or arrogant bravado.[41] Elizabeth Alexander's poem "Narrative: Ali (A Poem in Twelve Rounds)" is the epilogue of Gorn's edited collection *Muhammad Ali: The People's Champ*, and even in its structural sparseness, it is biography, memory, history, storytelling, folk narrative, reconciliation, and Black cultural mythology from a first-person point of view that approximates Ali's autobiographical journey.

Pacheco suggests that Ali's wins and losses in sport and in court allowed him to "come back and prove himself a folk hero because he is willing to go to jail for his beliefs."[42] He also includes Ali's relationships and fatherhood in this folk hero dynamic, describing that Ali "marries four times, sires six children, yet he remains highly admired by society."[43] Early is even more detailed when he credits Ali with having "magnetism, inventiveness, a heroism that did not evade the trickster black of black folklore or the minstrel black of the nineteenth century American stage but embodied them as both the antithesis and fulfillment of himself, not as a person but as his own individualized archetype."[44] In the end, because Early gives such a ruthlessly honest critique of Ali, we almost must side with Early's comfortable litany of Ali's strengths, weaknesses, challenges, genius, and faults. Ali was "elusive, often theatrical, ever-eroding, ever-reconstructing," which means that his lifetime has cycles of meaning, cycles of change, and cycles of evolution and adaptation. This example of a lifetime of growth does not diminish his mythological status, which is stable based on a merging of historical fact, narrative embellishment, and symbol formation. Early's staunchly critical essay aside, most biographers on Ali simply tell the story and allow readers to celebrate the inspiration from the story and to file away any contradictions. Mythology allows an elevation of narrative details of any ilk as long as they are functional to teach lessons—lessons of what to *do* and lessons of what *not* to do. Mythology is a collective inheritance from the ancestors, and progeny wizens from both the victories and errors of a superlative life. Early admits his 14-year-old "boyish hero worship," which was functional for that age and should be a privilege for other 14-year-olds in the present and future who have the chance to encounter Ali's greatness.[45]

Early is a balanced, yet comically cynical, critic, whose honest appraisal of Ali and his contradictions is both refreshing and exhausting in its complexity. Nonetheless, we must hear him when he illustrates "the uses and disadvantages of having athletes [like Ali] serve as all-purpose black icons."[46] Early reminds us that Ali's legacy also ushers in a discourse, as conceptualized in Black cultural mythology, on antiheroics. Michael Ezra's discussions of Ali as "the most hated man in boxing" and of the backlash and contradictory meanings in Ali's legacy are key examples of antiheroics, for naturally, Ali is *not* everyone's hero. One frame of reference for his antiheroic is the context wherein one culture's hero can be another culture's villain, depending on points of reference and worldview. Many biographers write of America's guilt—the losses the country's laws and public opinion afflicted on Ali because of his Vietnam stance, and then a reconsideration of his stance in a better light due to the fact that the Vietnam War evolved into an American nightmare rather than into a quantifiable victory. Hauser's chapter "Underdog" captures this well. In one breath, Americans said, "He most emphatically is not to be held up as an example to the youngsters of the United States."[47] However, eight years later after Ali won against Foreman, Maury Allen called for reconciliation:

> There are certain heroes of sports who transcend the games they participate in. They become folk heroes, figures of such enormity they cross the standard barriers. […] Muhammad Ali does it best of all. It is time to recognize Ali for what he is; the greatest athlete of his time and maybe all time and one of the most important and brave men of all American time. The time has come to end the bitterness and forget the past. It seems time to appreciate and enjoy this incredible athlete, this wondrous man.[48]

In a Black cultural mythology sense, exploring the prospect of antiheroics in Ali's life is a matter of discerning what and who opposed him as an enemy or detractor, or a matter of tracing instances of anti-Black heroics, wherein Ali can be found on both the delivering and receiving end. On the delivering end, he employed the dozens to harass Liston—"You big ugly bear. […] You so ugly, when you cry, the tears run down the back of your head. You so ugly, you have to sneak up on the mirror so it won't run off the wall."[49] Norman Mailer gives Ali credit for having the "most unsettling ego of all": "He never pretends to step back and relinquish his place to other actors. […] It is intolerable to our American mentality that the figure who is probably most prominent to us after the President is simply not comprehensible, for he could be a demon or a saint."[50] On the other hand, Pacheco frames Whites as the Black cultural mythology antiheroes, when in Dr. Pacheco's clinic, Ali "was safe from the dangers of mixing with white folks, whom he viewed with guarded suspicion."[51]

As Ali created his persona, with input from some of the successful fighters who insisted on having a gimmick, Pacheco notes how Ali's persona was emerging as the opposite of the *traditional* sports hero: "In those days boxers wore black or dark trunks [Ali wore white], and definitively black shoes. The perfect role model for a champion was Joe Louis. Humility was a quality much appreciated in American heroes. A champion didn't brag outside the ring, but let his fists speak for him in the ring. A champion was a model of decorum. A champion was circumspect."[52] Religion further tested the public's opinion as he "went into the Liston fight as one of the most disliked contenders since Max Schmeling had fought Joe Louis in 1938. It [his conversion to Islam] turned him from a hero to a villain in one headline."[53] Even contender Larry Holmes offered an antiheroic critique in 2015, noting that "he got tired of people behaving as if Ali were the Dalai Lama, tired of people carrying on as if Ali were a superhero and all other heavyweight champions were mere mortals. Ali was a good man and a great fighter, Holmes said, but he'd been a fool to take so many punches. 'He wasn't no hero,' Holmes said."[54]

Remnick interviewed Ali during his struggle with Parkinson's disease, and he acknowledges the disease as an ironic twist for which Ali's haters would revel: "No, for him the special torture was speech and expression, as if the disease had intended to strike first at what had once pleased him, and pleased (or annoyed) the world, most. He hated the effort that speech now cost him."[55] In Ali's life, antiheroics merges with the way "the world tends to forget its old kings when new ones come around."[56] While no one escapes the transitions to elderly status, the world watched Ali's aging and illness with unfair expectations. Eig challenges the way society attempted to mangle Ali's racialized memory, and even this social act is one of antiheroic assault:

> Some writers said that Ali had 'transcended' race. It was an attempt to whitewash his legacy, and it was dead wrong. Race was the theme of Ali's life. He insisted that America come to grips with a black man who wasn't afraid to *overcome* race. He didn't *overcome* racism. He called it out. He faced it down. He refuted it. He insisted that racism shaped our notions of race, that it was never the other way around.[57]

Robert Lipsyte describes the racial issue concerning Ali, the United States, and the world in terms of colorblindness, noting,

> After all he went through, the affection for him is largely colorblind. Late in his career, Ali developed a quality that only a few people have—except maybe he didn't change; maybe it was the rest of the world changing. Ali reached a point where when people looked at him, they didn't see black or white. They saw Ali. And for a long time, that mystified him.[58]

In an Africana analysis, the colorblindness is a baby step toward equitable racial relations that falls short of an ideal uninhibited respect for cultural identity, specificity, historical experience, and functional worldview. The biographical reflections on Ali are valuable for documenting the norms of the racial gaze he encountered.

Ezra's thesis in *Muhammad Ali: The Making of an Icon* is *culturally* peculiar. While this study on cultural memory emerges from an immersive Africana cultural framework—Black cultural mythology—Ezra takes liberty to define *culture* in a different, perhaps American capitalist way. His thesis is that people decipher Ali's value based on a moral understanding of his "cultural image." Yet, to Ezra, his cultural image is economic and based on capitalism, namely, how his cultural image "has come from their perception of who is making money by associating with him—the commercial manifestations."[59] In essence, he is interested in cultural interpretations of "economic entanglements," but the question is, "whose culture does Ezra explore?"[60] Here, *American* culture is prioritized instead of Ali's ethnic and racial culture, which is a priority interest to an Africana audience. Michael Oriard, in his essay on the nature of the *sports* hero, takes issue with this type of thesis that David Halberstam articulated. Oriard's response is as follows: "Here is a truly radical proposition, however casual its statement. Heroes have long been said to embody personal qualities that a people most value. If heroes in America are now the products of the products they peddle on television and in magazines—if our heroes are not just used by but *created* by Madison Avenue—the implications are stunning."[61] To some, the discourse on heroics is less tied to culture and storytelling and, now, is a postmodern shift in which products and endorsements determine a figure's epic impact. A related fruitful outcome linked to economics and capitalism is the Muhammad Ali Boxing Reform Act of 2000, which was an enhancement of the original Professional Boxing Safety Act of 1996. Its goal is to "promote safety and protect the contractual rights of boxers and to regulate the industry that had no league structure or other oversight beyond the state boxing commission."[62]

Maraniss narrates Ali's appearance at the Academy Awards: "The shimmering house of movie stars seemed diminished, their egos preposterous, when Ali rose and stood before them. Yet some saw in the appearance a hint of the maudlin: poor Ali, enfeebled and paunchy, dragged out as another melodramatic Hollywood gimmick. Was he real or was he memory? What was left of him if he could not float and sting?"[63] This is a striking public observation that is antithetical to the Africana expectation of elder respect, grounded in the natural order of birth, life, and death processes that reify cultural memory and that cement cultural history, accomplishment, tales of greatness, and philosophies of well-earned wisdom.

Remnick's *King of the World* is subtitled "Muhammad Ali and the Rise of an American Hero," and thus lies one worldview challenge of mythological status that this volume seeks to address. In what orientation do we examine Ali as an *Africana* hero? This question prioritizes Afrocentric methodology wherein we narrate our own Africana histories from a cultural subject-place. We make the adjustments of lexical refinement to, for our cultural edification, define Ali as an Africana hero, and then, we define the nature of hero dynamics, mythology, and cultural memory from an Africana logic, historical context, cultural definition, and ancestral determination. In his introduction to this biography that many general American readers would easily classify as an American cultural memory source on Ali, Remnick describes Ali's corner man, Drew "Bundini" Brown, as "moon-faced and young and whispering hoodoo inspiration in Ali's ears."[64] This is not a fruitful description because of its racially derogatory imaging even though Remnick describes Ali as "one of the most compelling and electric American figures of the age."[65] This is what an *Africana* cultural memory reading counters and rearticulates in order to suggest what an Africana cultural reader-response to Ali's legacy would produce in terms of remembrance and memorialization. Remnick narrates with sentimentalism, describing that "he was a warrior who came to symbolize love" and "nearly every American now thinks of Ali with misty affection."[66] Gerald Early unforgivingly describes this type of American weeping as "a sign of some organic confusion, a mythic yet turbulently defective pietism."[67] It approaches the unforgivable because, intergenerationally, White Americans shifted between extreme racism and liberal antiracist confession and apology with a psychotic dexterity that has been an affront to Ali's agency in particular and to Black people's lives and freedoms in general.

Pacheco also has an American cultural memory reference to Ali: "He was everything an American kid could aspire to be: rich, famous, handsome, the best in his field, sought after, trendsetter, icon, idol, good, charitable, kind, gentle, sweet, father, husband, lover, raconteur, magician, entertainer, drug-free, vice-free, individualist, revolutionary, religion leader."[68] Yes, Ali was also an American Olympian, but as Remnick notes, he recants the American patriotism and "good citizenship" he showed in his Olympic gold-earning era, particularly when he shamed a Russian reporter's homeland when the reporter asked him about the paradox of boxing to represent a country that strictly and violently enforced segregation.[69] Once back in Louisville after his gold medal win, Ali had an encounter with segregation. Even though his parents had painted their front porch steps red, white, and blue to celebrate their son's American Olympic victory, when he tried to order juice at a luncheonette, the owner was not impressed with his status as an Olympian. The racist said, "I don't give a damn who he is. [...] Get him out of here!"[70] This poses another Africana cultural memory lesson—that levels of patriotism vary for African Americans depending on time, place, and context. Ali's major act of defying America came with his rejection of the draft.

White Americans abandoned their "goodwill" for Ali after he refused the draft, and as Remnick recounts Ali's story about a White woman's condemnation, "My son's in Vietnam and you no better than he is. I hope you rot in jail!" Gerald Early's reflection on Ali's resistance is a model of how an Africana hero dynamic has a positive impact on youth. Early writes:

> When he refused, I felt something greater than pride: I felt as though my honor as a black boy had been defended, my honor as a human being. He was the grand knight, after all, the dragon-slayer. And I felt myself, little inner-city boy that I was, his apprentice to the grand imagination, the grand daring. The day that Ali refused the draft, I cried in my room. I cried for him and for myself, for my future and his, for all our black possibilities.[71]

Remnick uses Early's observation to reveal how Ali's act was inspiring, but the Africana use of Early's emotional response to a cultural heroic is to exalt this observation to its proper place in the Africana worldview—the logic and organic cultural way of viewing history, the present, and the Black role in the processes of cognitively surviving based on cultural know-how and on tools passed from one generation to the next.

Gerald Early also begins his "Introduction: Tales of the Wonderboy" from the edited collection *The Muhammad Ali Reader* with an interrogation of Ali's renewed Americanism. This does not exactly parallel Black cultural mythology's conceptual prioritization of *reconciliation and renewal*, yet it is close. In Early's view, after Ali's 1996 Olympic torch experience, there was a generational fissure. Ali became "the Great American Martyr" in opposition to his earlier identity wherein "nobody embodied American popular culture, its excesses, its barbarities, its disarming densities, more than Muhammad Ali."[72] His concern is that it is difficult for Americans to respect the aging process, especially "when the figure in question is a black man, a cunning archetype who is already so burdened by a baggage of both sentimentality and taboo as to be likely a virtual walking expression of the culture's irrationality even if his old age had been a bit less marked by illness."[73] Early, indeed, identifies a reawakening due to the Oscar-winning documentary *When We Were Kings*.

Jonathan Eig's *Ali: A Life* captures well Ali's relationship with America. He chronicles the fights that Jack Johnson, Joe Louis, and Muhammad Ali all had with America, and in Ali's case, "during a period of national turmoil, he had jabbed and danced and lashed out, unworried about angering the white man, insisting America's glory had been built by the thrashing of black backs, the destruction of black families, and the mothering of black voices, and that Black Americans would never truly be free until they whipped the whole system."[74] With Parkinson's disease, the vocal, prodding, revolutionary now had "routines [that] were mostly wordless. But the less Ali spoke, the sweeter and more saintly he became—at least in the eyes of America."[75] He even apologized for calling his other Black opponents "ugly," which is a Black cultural mythology act of renewal and reconciliation that is also a lesson.[76] Thus, when Africana people visit the Muhammad Ali Center—which Leigh Montville describes as an 80 million dollar "monument to his perfect life" that "resembled a presidential library, a patriotic or religious shrine"— and when we recall his 2005 Presidential Medal of Freedom and reflect on his post-911 message that claims both Muslim and American identities, there are also Africana cultural memory lessons here.[77] The center's motto is "Be great. Do great things."[78] Also, it encourages visitors to embrace "The Six Core Principles," which are confidence, conviction, dedication, giving, respect, and spirituality.[79]

The goal is to understand, with finesse, how being Black in America is a multidimensional act, wherein Africana worldview is stable, but at times, momentary labels and priorities of culture, ethnicity, nationality, and citizenship are moveable parts, depending on context. In the end, President Barack Obama's memorial to Ali leaves the most lasting impact of what is the challenge when we label Ali an *American* hero: "'I am America,' he once declared. 'I am the part you won't recognize. But get used to me—black, confident, cocky; my name, not yours; my religion, not yours; my goals, my own. Get used to me.'"[80] As Smith describes, "We must not forget that Ali was a black hero long before he was accepted as a universal American hero. In his boasts of preeminence, Ali projected racial pride and asserted his freedom when it had been long denied to black people."[81]

To Remnick's credit, he contextualizes his study on Ali within Ali's cultural goal that existed in response to the stereotypes of his opponents. Floyd Patterson was "the Good Negro," and Sonny Liston was the "Bad Negro."[82] Remnick notes this Black masculinist struggle to control his own public image, "Each man, in his own way, represented the world that Ali would encounter then transcend."[83] Ali then stated it best: "I had to prove you could be a new kind of black man. [...] I had to show that to the world."[84] Thus, in some ways, Remnick's study is not so true to its subtitle (*An American Hero*), and is indeed part of the *Africana* cultural memory of Muhammad Ali. Remnick quotes journalist Dick Schaap, who met Ali when he was 18 years old and observed, "It was like meeting a great actor or an electrifying statesman, some sort of figure that had a glow, an energy inside him, and you knew right away that you'd be hearing about him for years."[85] This is a good memory to relay to Africana children who want to imitate the best qualities of a cultural ancestor.

The Black cultural mythology variable of ancestor acknowledgment or ancestral status is an important feature of Remnick's introduction to the volume. His recorded conversations with Ali reflect the champion's Africana worldview in terms of focusing on living an honorable life with good deeds that will ensure ancestral status. This is an important part of Ali's mythological structure that we narrate to our children and families in memorial exercises of cultural storytelling: "He thought about death all the time now, he said. 'Do good deeds. Visit hospitals. Judgment Day coming. Wake up and it's

Judgment Day.' Ali prayed five times a day, always with death in mind. 'Thinking about *after*. Thinking about paradise.'"[86] Pacheco shifts his emphasis on Ali's value to what he exhibited beyond the ring, as well:

> But it is in the area of little kindnesses, of generous gestures, of anonymous gifts, that I came to appreciate Ali most of all. His daily life was filled with the small tokens of affection. He'd stop his Rolls-Royce to shake hands with old men, play with kids on a playground, or kiss old ladies; those actions indicated a man who loved people, who loved to "shock and amaze," and who loved to entertain.[87]

In an era when children view heroics in terms of financial wealth, entertainment or sports celebrity, or even infamy, Pacheco's observation of Ali's character is an important part of the story we convey about Ali. In our narratives, we may not go as far as Pacheco's final line in the book, "He is [...] the best example of how man is made in God's image and likeness."[88] However, each of Ali's contemporaries deserves to remember him in his or her own way. Remnick's version of this near-ancestral journey is an emphasis on how "he hit people for a living, and yet by middle age he would be a symbol not merely of courage, but of love, of decency, even a kind of wisdom."[89]

So far, the narrative assessments and remembrances of Ali have been from the perspectives of mostly American witnesses and observers; however, to reinforce the diversity of viewing Ali as not only an American hero but also African American icon, this final extended analysis is an example of how *African* scholars view Muhammad Ali. From the Africana cultural memory perspective that distinguishes this project, having a more global evaluation of Ali is essential. Ali A. Mazrui, who observed that "black people must admire their heroes whatever happens, be they warrior or runners, be they jumpers or boxers," wrote an interesting article in 1977 examining Ali in the context of being an international political symbol reflecting the bioeconomics of sport.[90] In this essay, he considered the possibly *natural* selectivity of warriors (broadly defined) based on superior physicality plus this physicality's relationship to the linkages between play, sport, and warfare. This essay is a theoretical gem in the analysis of Ali's function in Africana cultural memory because of Mazrui's philosophical and anthropological deduction of how physical capability allows the strongest (usually males) to rise to social significance in terms how society most efficiently utilizes its citizens' physical abilities. He considers how "the division of labor between men and women in most societies in the world is partly a case of bioeconomic calculation. Who shall till the land? Who shall look after these children? Some of these issues were probably resolved on considerations which linked biology to economics."[91]

Merging Mazrui's best examples, he chronicles the development of prowess in a traditional African life wherein a pastoral herdsman, who routinely develops stamina from long-distance herding, develops skills of protectionism wherein he can defend his family and herds from raiders. He demonstrates how these types of experiences of traditional labor prompt the attainment of "personal valor," which, when utilized on behalf of the society or nation state, are transferable to military honors in the "*collective* combat against a collective external enemy."[92]

It is unusual to discover a comparison between Muhammad Ali and Idi Amin, but Mazrui reminds us that Amin held a nine-year title as Uganda's heavyweight boxing champion. Focusing on the men's superlatives as "two significant individuals in the recent history of black people," Mazrui gives us a different itemization of how technology (television and film) enables a figure who is already superior in physicality to emerge as a cultural symbol.[93] This is the most salient point that relates Mazrui's assessment of Ali to Africana cultural memory. While Mazrui's comparative analysis to Amin is fascinating, his treatment of Ali is the priority for this chapter. Mazrui's analysis provides additional attributes of Ali's cultural memory. He remembers him for his "physical fearlessness," "exhibitionist self-confidence," that he (like Amin) "feared no one but God," combative "colorful language" against "political or sporting foes," and "irreverence for his adversaries in the ring."[94]

As a formula that links physicality, protectionism, and social significance, Mazrui's study highlights core elements of the historical epic narrative, wherein the types of prowess that both Ali and Mazrui demonstrated in play and sport are the seeds that would hypothetically continue to bloom in the production of an epic cultural hero. The way a herder's personal valor attained through local protectionism could be transitioned to, per se, protecting or being a bodyguard for the king, to fighting in combat in the name of the king, has parallels to Olympic sports battle in the name of one's nation. This emerges as a subtle pan-African analysis, with Mazrui presumably advancing a comparison of two *African* examples, one in the United States and the other in Uganda, based on traditional African models of the development of valor. In fact, Mazrui refers to successful African American boxers as "black athletic giants [that] have come not from Africa but from among the exported Africans."[95] On the one hand, he is aware of the survivalist narrative of African Americans as those who have "experienced some of the harshest forms of slavery in the recent times [and] have also borne worse scars of humiliation and degradation than those sustained by the majority of blacks left behind on the African continent itself."[96] On the other hand, Mazrui is also aware that

black Americans by being citizens of the United States, subject to the commercial and economic culture of the United States, and modern beneficiaries of American technological affluence, have been economically the most affluent single group of blacks anywhere in the world. Their standard of living, ranging from possession of cars and televisions sets to the number of calories available in the diet, places them on a pinnacle of relative advantage compared to the great majority of black people anywhere else in the world.[97]

Mazrui speaks directly to this general Pan-African commonality in terms of

two simple attributes—they are both black and they are both male. These attributes encompass in themselves important issues concerning the roles of race, class and sex in sports and war. Why has heavyweight boxing at the global level been so overwhelmingly dominated by black men in much of this century? Why have those black men been disproportionately from the Black Diaspora in the western hemisphere rather than from the heartland of the black world in Africa? Why has war, as well as much of the sporting world, been dominated by men as against women?[98]

Mazrui acknowledges that he cannot answer all of these questions, but he returns to the topics of bioeconomics and "the general infrastructure and technological change" to address what seems to be an Africana cultural memory conversation about the disproportionate emergence of heroic *masculine* prowess. He terms this "masculine bias" and laments how women have been given "a subsidiary role" in sports and war.[99] In terms of technology, his focus relevant for this chapter is on how globalized communication (radio and satellite transmissions) internationalizes spectatorship and helps to create global icons whose iconography will linger in our cultural memory because of this international sensationalism. In this sense, witnessing international competition in an individualized sport (vs. team sport) makes the hero memorable because of the sensationalism of broadcast and the global range of spectatorship. The "planetary vision" of the Ali versus George Foreman fight in Kinshasa, Zaire, is, to Mazrui, the epitome of this.[100] Mazrui even describes Ali's and Foreman's view of Africa as "their shared ancestral continent" and partially credits "black solidarity" as part of the rationale for holding the fight in Africa.[101]

A final aspect of Mazrui's comparison introduces a more organic valuation of how Ali's hero dynamics function in cultural memory. He gives an Afrocentric definition of masculinity, which is based on fairness and playing according to the rules (which in the sport of boxing has its own inherent honor). Amin's proclivity toward brutality and cruelty is antiheroic and disqualifies him from earning any accolade in this area.[102] Otherwise, "certain rules of African concepts of masculinity would have had to be invoked as constraints on arbitrary behavior. Taking easy advantage of one's opponent was not regarded as manly in many traditional African cultures. There were rules of chivalry governing the conduct of warriors."[103] In comparison, the sport of boxing, with a referee guaranteeing opponents' adherence to rules, allows a fairer contest, more philosophically aligned with the conduct of African warriors.

In this sense, the lessons we can infer from Mazrui's survey of what features of Ali's prowess are most important to transmit intergenerationally are that there is an African masculinist foundation that explains some of his physicality, which can also be viewed in a continuum based on the African heritage of African American men. Also, we gain an Afrocentric classical reference point about the development of traditional African male valor and military honor that are the basis of a cultural sense of the function of protectionism. Finally, there is honor in fair play and in complying with rules that may be the basis for one's defeat. In much of the commemorative discourses on Ali, the processes and choices of retirement—particularly, realizing when victory and success are no longer expectations based on aging and other matters that reduce one's physical prowess—are also seen as honorable. We remember what Ali did beyond the combat and contests within the ring, and the fact that Ali was able to maintain his hero dynamic beyond the ring as a philanthropist and humanitarian is of additional memorial value. Mazrui's essay is also explicit in rejecting the racial stereotypes that Black athleticism and strength exist at the expense of Black intellect. Instead, he suggests that celebrity athletic stature is inspiring and reproducible among youth, whose early development of "strengthening competence" in non-capital-intensive sports, such as basic running and jumping, is a basis of athletic success.[104] So in terms of cultural memory, Mazrui leads us toward qualifying the nature of attainments and achievements of strength, dexterity, and overall athletic physicality that can lead to sports success and also is a basis of good health.[105]

Mazrui's unexpected comparison of Ali and Amin is a unique perspective in the sport of boxing and for the topic of African masculine physicality. As a final, minor link to the broader discussion of Africana cultural memory, of which Black cultural mythology is one orientation, Mazrui identifies a "new possessiveness concerning ancestors" among African people that is related to both religious and more broadly cultural notions of the sacred.[106] He describes how African soccer teams have engaged with some sort of divination prior to matches and how Amin always saw a "witch doctor" the day before a boxing match. The fact that Mazrui relates an essay on cultural heroes, political symbols, and sport to the spiritual and the supernatural corroborates Black cultural mythology's theorization that sacred observation and ritual remembrance are priorities in Africana cultural memory. Mazrui even introduces Ali's devout Islamic religious practice as a religious heroic feature, as he expresses awe that Ali's bragging and playful banter did not detract from his spiritual seriousness. This suggests that Ali also gives a heroic cultural memory model of balance. Inevitably, Mazrui describes this as "a strange interplay between faith and fist, science and sorcery, [and] technology and belief" amid Ali's "physical performance and spiritual existence."[107]

In an Africana cultural memory exercise, modeled for both layperson and curricular value in terms of an Africana cultural remembrance, we are called upon to reproduce Remnick's sentence to convey that nearly every *African* American now thinks of Ali with (insert any number of cultural memory variables inspired by Black cultural mythology). Black cultural mythology is a conceptual framework offering a set of critical language that allows Africana celebrants to be more culturally centered in our superlative remembrances of our legendary figures. Gorn frames this as follows: "Ali has become one of those figures who helps us to make sense of the history, to give it shape and meaning. Our stories about Ali keep our past alive, and they give us a personal connection to the larger chronicle of our days."[108] Gorn's edited collection *Muhammad Ali: The People's Champ* seeks to convey "why Ali looms so large in our collective memory," particularly the memory of the 1960s and 1970s.[109] Remnick is aware of this duality, or even multidimensionality, very much like the novelist Colson Whitehead's treatment of everybody's folk hero John Henry in the novel *John Henry Days*. Remnick reflects, "Ali is an American myth who has come to mean many things to many people; a symbol of faith, a symbol of conviction and defiance, a symbol of beauty and skill and courage, a symbol of racial pride, of wit and love."[110] Early describes the inheritance as this: "Like all great heroes he showed us the enormous possibility of the true meaning, the incendiary poetics, of self-determination."[111] This study of Muhammad Ali expands to focus on Ali as even more than merely a symbol of racial pride, and a Black cultural mythology critical methodology enables such full Africana cultural memory analysis. This becomes a fascinating model in Africana cultural memory practices because Ali had dyslexia, was not a strong reader, and prepared himself with prolific notes on cards and legal pads in order to have talking points and speeches on hand.[112] Biographers are aware of Ali's lower score on the IQ test and that he graduated 376th in a high school class of 391 students. Yet his success and accomplishments are inspiring. This is a remarkable methodology for a man who knew his literacy shortcomings. There is also an Africana cultural memory lesson in this reflection.

Additionally, as Black psychologist Amos Wilson articulates in *The Developmental Psychology of the Black Child*, we ensure that our children and families are rooted in optimum modes of confidence and self-esteem-sustaining narratives of cultural achievement. This is not mere storytelling, and in the case of Ali, it is fully developed storytelling about statistics, opponents, and the ebb and flow of sports and aging. As Bryant Gumble narrated the key variables of Ali's principled choices, one story we should tell is that Ali courageously forged ahead through the consequences of standing up for his beliefs. Gumble says,

> He was a man of principle. Whether you agreed with his principles or not was almost irrelevant. It's very difficult for anybody, even his most ardent critics, to argue that he wasn't willing to accept the consequences of his beliefs. You could argue with his beliefs till you were blue in the face, but by the time he was willing to go to jail and be stripped of his title and lose the opportunity to make millions of dollars, it was apparent that this wasn't a publicity gimmick. He symbolized optimism and the hope that anything was possible, even for the most downtrodden person. That a young black man with a limited education could rise to become the world's best-known human being; that's an extraordinary accomplishment.[113]

This is the type of story that we tell in Black cultural mythology. As this chapter seeks to explain using Black cultural mythology methodology, the narrative must be conceptually grounded in order to maximize its potential as rewarding cultural storytelling that transmits not only legacy but inheritance, modes of resistance-based cognitive survival, epic intuitive conduct, and criteria of immortalization. Achieving a high, stylized, critical analysis of these variables then allows us to properly commemorate and memorialize figures whose accolades dominate our cultural heritage and our Africana cultural memory.

Notes

This title is phrasing from Gerald Early, "Introduction: Tales of the Wonderboy," in *The Muhammad Ali Reader*, edited by Gerald Early (Hopewell, NJ: Ecco, 1998), xix. The context of the phrasing is Early's reaction to Ali's principled follow-through to reject the draft: "So when he refused, I felt something greater than pride: I felt as though my honor as a black boy had been defended, my honor as a human being" (xix).

1 Christel N. Temple, *Black Cultural Mythology* (New York: SUNY, 2020), 253.
2 Ibid., xiii.
3 Ibid.
4 Ibid., xv–xvi.
5 Ibid., 3.
6 Qtd. in Temple, *Black Cultural Mythology*, 15.
7 Temple, *Black Cultural Mythology*, 14.
8 Ibid., 18.
9 Temple, "Harriet Tubman and Aesthetic Memorialization," *Black Cultural Mythology*. The volume also includes a chapter on Malcolm X, "Mythical Malcolm in an Age of Marable." See also Temple, "Malcolm X and Black Cultural Mythology," in *International Journal of Black*

Studies 12.2 (2006): 213–21. See also her additional study on Paul Robeson, "Autobiography and Documentary Forms of *Here I Stand* as Black Cultural Mythology," in *Transcendence and the Africana Literary Enterprise* (New York: Lexington Books, 2017).

10 In the chapter on "Mythical Malcolm in an Age of Marable," *Black Cultural Mythology*, Temple uncovers an extensive "mythological vocabulary" (209) from the ways critics and reviewers framed Malcolm's legacy. See also Manning Marable, *Malcolm X: A Life of Reinvention* (New York: Penguin Books, 2011).

11 Ferdie Pacheco, *Muhammad Ali: A View from the Corner* (New York: Birch Lane, 1992), 3, 5, 44.

12 David Remnick, *The King of the World: Muhammad Ali and the Rise of an American Hero* (New York: Vintage, 2014), xv, xvi, 299.

13 Gerald Early, *The Muhammad Ali Reader* (New York: Ecco, 1998), vii, viii.

14 Ibid., xii.

15 Ibid., xii–xiii.

16 Ibid., xvi.

17 Norman Mailer, "Ego," in *The Muhammad Ali Reader*, edited by Gerald Early (New York: Ecoo, 1998), 101, 109.

18 Michael Ezra, *Muhammad Ali: The Making of an Icon* (Philadelphia: Temple UP, 2009), 1.

19 Robert Lipsyte, "When You're with Me, You Always Got Something to Write About," in *Muhammad Ali: The People's Champ*, edited by Elliott J. Gorn (Urbana: University of Illinois, 1998), 1.

20 Barbara L. Tischler, *Muhammad Ali: A Man of Many Voices* (New York: Routledge, 2015), 1.

21 Pacheco, *View from the Corner*, 45 (emphasis in original).

22 Mark Kram, "Great Men Die Twice," in *The Muhammad Ali Reader*, edited by Gerald Early (New York: Ecco, 1998), 246, 248.

23 Pacheco, *View from the Corner*, 45.

24 Thomas Hauser, *Muhammad Ali: His Life and Times* (New York: Simon & Schuster, 2012), 9.

25 Hauser, *His Life and Times*, 9.

26 Temple, *Black Cultural Mythology*, 1.

27 Pacheco, *View from the Corner*, 46.

28 Ibid., 48.

29 Ibid.

30 Ibid., 49.

31 Ibid., 206.

32 Ibid.

33 See chapter 5 in *Transcendence and the Africana Literary Enterprise* by Christel N. Temple (New York: Lexington, 2017), which addresses "Autobiography and Documentary Forms of *Here I Stand* as Black Cultural Mythology." This chapter is conversant with Kariamu Welsh's and Molefi Kete Asante's contention that Western technology "destroys the traditional myth. [...] Because technology introduces machines that reduce mystery, it also reduces the possibility of transcendence of the spirit" (See "Myth: The Communication Dimension of the African Mind," *Journal of Black Studies* 11, no. 4 (1981): 387.

34 Hauser, *His Life and Times*, 56. See also Muhammad Ali, *The Greatest* (Columbia Records, 1963).

35 Pacheco, *View from the Corner*, 52.

36 Remnick, *The King of the World*, 306

37 Hauser, *His Life and Times*, 514–15.

38 David Maraniss, "Ali's Amazing Grace," in *The Muhammad Ali Reader*, edited by Gerald Early (New Year: Ecco, 1998), 287.

39 Ezra, *The Making of an Icon*, 167.

40 Gerald Early, "Preposterous Propositions from the Heroic Life of Muhammad Ali: A Reading of *The Greatest: My Own Story*," in *The People's Champ*, edited by Elliott J. Gorn (Urbana: University of Illinois Press, 1995), 72.

41 Tom Wolfe, "Marvelous Mouth," in *The Muhammad Ali Reader*, edited by Gerald Early (New York: Ecco, 1998). Wolfe uses this phrasing in his title.

42 Pacheco, *View from the Corner*, 45.

43 Ibid.

44 Early, *The Muhammad Ali Reader*, xiv.

45 Ibid., xviii.

46 Ibid., xv.

47 Qtd. in Hauser, *His Life and Times*, 280. The original appeared in *Ring* magazine, March 1967.

48 Ibid., 281. The original is from the *New York Post*, October 31, 1974.

49 Wolfe, "Marvelous Mouth," 15.

50 Mailer, "Ego," 101.

51 Pacheco, *View from the Corner*, 50.

52 Ibid., 49–50.

53 Ibid., 52.

54 Jonathan Eig, *Muhammad Ali: A Life* (New York: Houghton Mifflin Harcourt, 2017), 533.

55 Remnick, *King of the World*, xiv.

56 David Maraniss, "Ali's Amazing Grace: Still Preaching, Teaching, Now He Contemplates His 'House in Heaven,'" in *The Muhammad Ali Reader*, edited by Gerald Early (New York: Ecco, 1998), 288.

57 Eig, *Muhammad Ali: A Life*, 535; original emphasis.

58 Hauser, *His Life and Times*, 328.

59 Ezra, *Muhammad Ali: The Making of an Icon*, 2.

60 Ibid.

61 Michael Oriard, "The Hero in the Age of Mass Media," in *The People's Champ*, edited by Elliott J. Gorn (Urbana: University of Illinois Press, 1995), 7; original emphasis.

62 Tischler, *Muhammad Ali: A Man of Many Voices*, 185.

63 Maraniss, "Ali's Amazing Grace," 288.

64 Remnick, *King of the World*, xii.

65 Ibid., xvi.

66 Ibid., xiii.

67 Early, *The Muhammad Ali Reader*, x.

68 Pacheco, *A View from the Corner*, 208.

69 Remnick, *King of the World*, 102.

70 Ibid., 106–7.

71 Qtd. in Remnick, *King of the World*, 291. The original source was Gerald Early's "Introduction: Tales of the Wonderboy" from *The Muhammad Ali Reader*, xix.

72 Early, *The Muhammad Ali Reader*, vi, vii.

73 Ibid., viii.

74 Eig, *Ali: A Life*, 526.

75 Ibid.

76 Ibid, 528.

77 Leigh Montville, *Sting Like a Bee: Muhammad Ali vs. The United States, 1966–1971* (New York: Doubleday, 2017), 4.

78 Ibid.

79 Ibid.

80 Eig, *Ali: A Life*, 535.

81 Smith, "Reflections," 184.

82 Remnick, *King of the World*, xiii.

83 Ibid.

84 Ibid.

85 Ibid., 101.

86 Ibid., xiv; original emphasis.
87 Pacheco, *A View from the Corner*, 209.
88 Ibid., 212.
89 Remnick, *King of the World*, xvi.
90 Ali Mazrui, "Boxer Muhammad Ali and Soldier Idi Amin as International Political Symbols: The Bioeconomics of Sport and War," *Comparative Studies in Society and History* 19, no. 2 (1977): 189–215 [210].
91 Ibid., 189.
92 Ibid., 191; original emphasis.
93 Ibid., 190.
94 Ibid., 196, 197, 198.
95 Ibid., 207.
96 Ibid.
97 Ibid.
98 Ibid., 198.
99 Ibid., 214.
100 Ibid., 199.
101 Ibid., 209, 210.
102 Ibid., 196.
103 Ibid., 202.
104 Ibid., 206.
105 Mazrui does exaggerate a bit in his assumption of what skills poor populations learn. His essay has loaded observations such as "fist fights in the ghettos of America, again against a background which precludes expensive toy trains, could provide the beginnings of training" (p. 206) and "early socialization into the skills of running, jumping, and fist-fighting lies within the means of the poor" (206). His casual assessment that fist-fighting is a normal sport among the poor is overstated.
106 Mazrui, "Boxer Muhammad Ali," 211.
107 Ibid., 213.
108 Gorn, *The People's Champ*, xii.
109 Ibid., xv.
110 Remnick, *King of the World*, 304.
111 Early, *The Muhammad Ali Reader*, xiv.
112 Eig, *Ali: A Life*, 259.
113 Hauser, *His Life and Times*, 506–8.

References

Early, Gerald. *The Muhammad Ali Reader*. New York: Ecco, 1998.
———. "Preposterous Propositions from the Heroic Life of Muhammad Ali: A Reading of *The Greatest*." In *My Own Story. The People's Champ*. Edited by Elliott J. Gorn, 70–87. Urbana: University of Illinois Press, 1995.
Eig, Jonathan. *Muhammad Ali: A Life*. New York: Houghton Mifflin Harcourt, 2017.
Ezra, Michael. *Muhammad Ali: The Making of an Icon*. Philadelphia: Temple UP, 2009.
Gorn, Elliott (ed.). *Muhammad Ali: The People's Champ*. Urbana: University of Illinois Press, 1998.
Harrison, Paul Carter, Danny Glover, and Bill Duke. *Black Light: The African American Hero*. New York: Thunder's Mouth Press, 1993.
Hauser, Thomas. *Muhammad Ali: His Life and Times*. New York: Simon & Schuster, 1992.
Kram, Mark. "Great Men Die Twice." In *The Muhammad Ali Reader*. Edited by Gerald Early, 244–58. New York: Ecco, 1998.

Lipsyte, Robert. "When You're with Me, You Always Got Something to Write About." In *Muhammad Ali: The People's Champ*. Edited by Elliott J. Gorn, 1–4. Urbana: University of Illinois Press, [1977] 1998.

Mailer, Norman. "Ego." In *The Muhammad Ali Reader*. Edited by Gerald Early, 101–21. New York: Ecco, 1998.

Maraniss, David. "Ali's Amazing Grace: Still Preaching, Teaching, Now He Contemplates His 'House in Heaven.'" In *The Muhammad Ali Reader*. Edited by Gerald Early, 285–96. New York: Ecco, 1998.

Mazrui, Ali. "Boxer Muhammad Ali and Soldier Idi Amin as International Political Symbols: The Bioeconomics of Sport and War." *Comparative Studies in Society and History* 19.2 (1977): 189–215.

Montville, Leigh. *Sting like a Bee: Muhammad Ali vs. The United States, 1966–1971*. New York: Doubleday, 2017.

Oriard, Michael. "The Hero in the Age of Mass Media." In *The People's Champ*. Edited by Elliott J. Gorn, 5–23. Urbana: University of Illinois Press, 1995.

Pacheco, Ferdie. *Muhammad Ali: A View from the Corner*. New York: Birch Lane, 1992.

Remnick, David. *The King of the World: Muhammad Ali and the Rise of an American Hero*. New York: Vintage, 2014.

Smith, Johnny. "Reflections: Remembering Muhammad Ali: Myths, Memory, and History," *Reviews in American History* 45.1 (2017): 177–88.

Temple, Christel N. *Black Cultural Mythology*. New York: SUNY, 2020.

Tischler, Barbara L. *Muhammad Ali: A Man of Many Voices*. New York: Routledge.

Williams, Armstrong. "The Ali Myth." *Afro-American Red Star*, December 28, 2001:A27.

Wolfe, Tom. "Marvelous Mouth." *The Muhammad Ali Reader*. Edited by Gerald Early, 15–26. New York: Ecco, 1998.

Chapter Two

MUHAMMAD ALI, THE NATION OF ISLAM, AND SPORT: THE GRIND OF SPIRITUALITY

James L. Conyers Jr.

Muhammad Ali was a former boxing champion, humanist, and civil rights activist. Collectively, these topics offer a general survey regarding the life of the subject. Described as the greatest heavyweight champion of all time, his legacy still impacts the world of professional athletics in America. Referenced in another way, Muhammad Ali was the only professional boxer to win the heavyweight championship three times. Mockingly, American society labeled Ali as: (1) unpatriotic, (2) un-American, (3) radical, and in the final years of his life (4) a humanist. With the contingency of racism applied, he was never allowed to grow and mature as a human. Instead, Ali was belittled, scorned, and ostracized as a leper. As an alternative, he turned inward toward his religion and spirituality, as a protective shield to retain humanism and peace. From an Africana cultural memory perspective, particularly from the discipline of Africana Studies, scholars are searching beyond news media to find more culturally introspective analyses of how we should value Ali's legacy.

Yet Ali exhibited leadership and an example for African American men and women around the world with his political and religious views. He made an impactful surrender in his professional, athletic, and spiritual life, which forfeited time. Conyers defines the term "sacrifice" as "an unwarranted giving of oneself, in order to advance the cause and trajectory of others."[1] Born as Cassius Clay in Louisville, Kentucky, he was reared in a Black labor-class working family. Paradoxically, the Black labor class can be explained as unskilled waged or salaried workers, who are either under- or unemployed. Joyce Carol Oates says:

> Born in 1942 in Louisville, Ky., Cassius Marcellus Clay Jr. was, as Eig notes, the great-grandson of a slave, the grandson of a convicted murderer and the son of a gregarious man who had a penchant for fighting when drunk, was known to have beaten his wife, and once, in a drunken rage, slashed his young son Cassius Jr. with a knife.[2]

From these humble beginnings, Ali's life reached a level where he had influence on an international and national level. Emerging from the Deep South, he engaged communities regarding civil and human rights. This essay will examine three points: (1) Muhammad Ali, (2) the Nation of Islam (NOI) and (3) sport. Likewise, the subtitle of

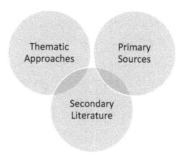

Figure 2.1 Intersectional research mode.

this essay refers to the grind of spirituality, which is the continuous pursuit of peace and intuitive thought and action of the human experience. Oates in her article titled "Muhammad Ali, Beginning to End for the First Time in a Book," writes the following regarding *Ali: A Life* by Jonathan Eig:

> As Herman Melville observed, to write a mighty book you must choose a mighty theme. In American sports culture no individual has inspired more first-rate commentary than Muhammad Ali: There are at least 50 books about this most celebrated of American heavy-weight champions, including Norman Mailer's intensely narrated "The Fight" (1975); Thomas Hauser's compendium of witness accounts, "Muhammad Ali: His Life and Times" (1991); and David Remnick's "King of the World: Muhammad Ali and the Rise of an American Hero" (1998), combining biography and social history (race in America, organized crime and sports) with the contagious enthusiasm of a fan's notes. Now comes Jonathan Eig's "Ali: A Life," the first biography of Ali's entire life, completed in the wake of his death, at 74, in June 2016.[3]

Using existing secondary literature, there has been an infusion of primary sources and tools. In this study, scholarly articles, interviews, and alternate sources have been employed, to examine the subject in place and time. Likewise, this essay extends the transcendence of Africana culture, race, and class in the Americana market culture. Figure 2.1 shows the interconnectedness of using various tools of research analysis, which outline thematic approaches, primary sources, and secondary periodical literature.

Muhammad Ali

Equally important, the issue of consciousness that Muhammad Ali embraced was under the tutelage of the NOI. Without a doubt, it is the family's foundation, which Ali established in Louisville, Kentucky. Yet the consciousness of a global pan-Africanist perspective, in the context and interpretation of African American culture, is filtered through the tutorials of the NOI. Townsend et al. cite the following regarding the subject of study:

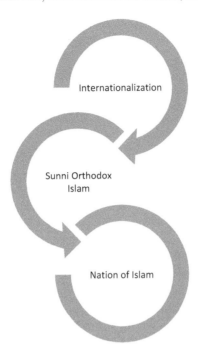

Figure 2.2 Critical influences on Ali, 1930 to 1985.

Perhaps more than any other athlete, Ali's names are inextricably linked to his cultural significance. The changing ways the press referred to Ali throughout the 1960s and 1970s reveal insights into race relations in the United States, the civil rights and Black Power movements, twentieth-century press discourses, and the cultural power of names.[4]

Figure 2.2 offers a generic framework to outline these outliers. Allegedly Ali disclosed the acceptance of the teachings of the Honorable Elijah Muhammad in 1964; however, the initial point of cultural consciousness could have occurred earlier, in the process to intake, input, and improvise the teachings of self and Black cognizance.

The Nation of Islam

The subject of Ali's alignment with the NOI and his unorthodox boxing style is intriguing. His selection of an alternative religion in Al-Islam was unconventional of most African Americans' choice of sanctuary during the period of industrialization. Secondly, most heavyweight fighters during this era were defensive brawlers, whose end game was victory by knockout. Mutually, the organizational structure of the NOI and the combatant stratagem of Muhammad Ali were unconventional relative to race relations in America during the Jim Crow era. Augmented with the idea of advocacy, agency, and autonomy, by the late 1950s, the NOI was the largest Black-owned business in America. Linking with Ali, the heavyweight champion, established a base of Black sovereignty and power for the African American community nationally. Alexandra Sims documents the interest and involvement of Ali in the NOI: "Ali reportedly attended his first NOI meeting in 1961 and continued to attend meetings with the African American Islamic religious movement aiming to improve the condition of African Americans in the US."[5] Conyers offers the following general description of the NOI:

> The organizational structure of the NOI came about between two important periods in America historiography. The organization was founded in 1930 Wallace Fard (i.e., sometimes referred to Fard Muhammad) in Detroit, Michigan. Immediately prior to its founding during the mid and latter parts of the 1920s, African Americans were engaged in the process of redefining and re-examining themselves under the auspicious of the concept of the New Negro and the sociopolitical movements of the Harlem Renaissance.[6]

Historically there has been a pattern whenever subordinated groups have redefined, reclassified, or established reclamation; this has been encountered with xenocentricism and xenophobia. Ali was a continual pattern of this reactionary behavior. Another source cites, "Clay joined the black Muslim group Nation of Islam in 1964. At first, he called himself Cassius X before settling on the name Muhammad Ali. The boxer eventually converted to orthodox Islam during the 1970s."[7] He was given the name Muhammad Ali by the Honorable Elijah Muhammad, which means "most worthy of high praise, his attribute signaled a transition of cultural maturation in his life." The foundation of Ali's consciousness is attributed to both his family and the NOI. Grant Farred writes:

> Ali's way of viewing the world, as he makes patently obvious in his autobiography *The Greatest* (what else could this work have been called?), was grounded in the teachings of Elijah Muhammad-the Nation of Islam's leader. In this religious movement, Ali says, "I saw the liberation of black people from subjugation and slavery to freedom and equality and justice" (Ali 105). Motivated by a defense of his faith and his political principles, in addition to his customary confidence in his rhetorical and his boxing skills, Ali was his usual boisterous self in the pre-fight theatrics for the Terrell encounter.[8]

Townsend et al. describe the position of nomenclature of Ali's name assigned in the NOI as follows:

> In many accounts of Ali's life, his two names serve important narrative functions. Authors have often used them as allegories for his changing persona, whereby Cassius Clay is said to have evolved into Muhammad Ali both in a personal sense and in the eyes of the American public. Although this is a common theme in the Ali literature, there are competing theories as to when this evolution happened.[9]

Ali was born on January 17, 1942. According to the Akan tradition of day names in West Africa, his name would be Kwame, which means Saturday born. The teachings of the Honorable Elijah Muhammad provided a station for African Americans to select an alternative pivot, in defining themselves outside the rubric of being involuntary migrants.

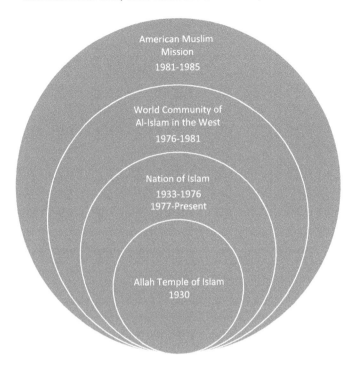

Figure 2.3 Evolution of African American Islam.

The *Black Scholar* interviewed Muhammad Ali in 1970, which was an arduous task, using the framework of a radical Black thought. Consequently, the value-added variable of a cultural imperative is detached. Yet, the *Black Scholar* asked Muhammad Ali regarding his views on consciousness. Less is more, as evident in the following transcribed commentary (Figure 2.3):

Black Scholar: What's wrong with most of the other Black celebrities, in your view? Are they failing their roles? And if so, that should they be doing differently?

Ali: We Black people could become free sooner than you think, if all the athletes and entertainers just took a stand—the famous ball players and the rock and roll artists, the big ones—took a walk through the ghetto one day and told the White man, "We're with these people and we ain't going to sell out any more."[10]

Sport

Sources report, Ali had a career record of 56 wins, five losses and 37 knockouts before his retirement from boxing in 1981 at the age of 39. Prior to 1962, his record was an undefeated score count of eight victories and zero defeats. Consequently, during this period of four years, Ali was fighting almost every two months, and, in some instances, every two weeks. This issue identifies the inequality of the boxing profession at that time, that is, the difficulty for contenders to present themselves as qualifiers for a title. Unfortunately, Ali was a part of this Black labor-class population. When provided a continuous pattern of disparate treatment, coupled with institutional racism, African Americans were provided ultimatums and not options and resources for professional occupations to retain wages and salaries. Conyers theorizes the concept of sport by noting: "For some, the idea of sport and society are interwoven parcels, which reflect each other in myriad ways. Simply put, sport is a reflection of society as we use metaphors, narratives, concepts of teamwork, and overcoming adversity as attributes to navigate transition and transcend struggle of life experiences."[11]

Figure 2.4 illustrates the intersections of race, culture, and sport. They are listed in this order because the concept of race identifies the resources for quality of life that are available for the participant. Culture then proceeds to identify one developing a level of consciousness to use occupation to attain wages, wealth, or status. Lastly, sport is the intermediary, where participants begin to develop an understanding of the business relationship, to acquire resources and to provide space in alternative spheres, for African Americans. Mentioned earlier in this essay, at birth, Ali was named Cassius Clay Jr. after his father. The *Yale News* ironically report that his father's name is connected with an alumnus of the university:

> The name Ali inherited from his father—Cassius Marcellus Clay—was in fact given to his dad in honor of Cassius M. Clay, a fervent abolitionist who graduated from Yale in 1832. Judith Schiff, chief research archivist in the Yale University Library's Manuscripts and Archives, alerted YaleNews to the connection following Ali's death on June 3 at the age of 74. Schiff noted that in "Memorials of Eminent Yale Men," Anson Phelps Stokes said of the

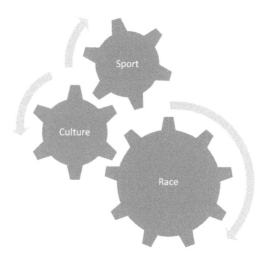

Figure 2.4 Intersections of race, culture, and sport.

Yale-educated abolitionist: "no Southern man was so active in the anti-slavery case as Clay." The Yale alumnus was born in White Hall, Kentucky, in 1810, the son of Green Clay, a land speculator who was one of the wealthiest slaveholders in that state. He attended Transylvania University (1829-1831) and Yale College (1831-1832), where he received his bachelor's degree and heard abolitionist William Lloyd Garrison speak. He returned to Transylvania to study law. Afterwards, he joined the antislavery movement and made the abolition of slavery his life's work. According to "American National Biography," Clay "developed an economic critique of slavery that some historians consider to be the most penetrating analysis of slavery produced by a Southerner."[12]

Sims discusses the transition from the English name in accepting an Islamic attribute by stating:

> Malcolm X, a key figure of the movement before his conversion to orthodox Islam, became a spiritual and political mentor for Clay, and he briefly referred to himself as Cassius X before being renamed Muhammad Ali (Praised one) in a recorded statement by Elijah Muhammad, the group's leader in 1964.[13]

Townsend et al. describe the position of nomenclature of Ali's name assigned in the NOI as follows:

> As heavyweight champion, Muhammad Ali broadcast these beliefs from a national platform, angering those who advocated more-moderate approaches to the country's racial problems. He was righteous, controversial, aggressively autonomous, and his new name symbolized this.[14]

The name Muhammad Ali, given by the Honorable Elijah Muhammad, pivoted the transition in thought, practice, and application of an Islamic attribute. It was rare for the Honorable Elijah Muhammad to bestow a name, personally, on someone. Muhammad means "worthy of praise," and Ali means "lofty."[15] Dr. Ramona Hyman notes the following in her description of this relationship:

> Resting in my historical memory is a lesson garnered concerning Muhammad Ali's transition from Cassius Clay to Muhammad Ali—a transition signaling his purpose. This eruditely noble citizen's civil and spiritual consciousness was birthed in the uniquely African American Islamic tradition as nuanced by the Honorable Elijah Muhammad. We cannot forget the tradition(s) that influence, shape, and ground us. One of the lessons in the passing of Muhammad Ali is this: An important part of his life's purpose was forged by the teachings of the Honorable Elijah Muhammad. We must know the community that provided a safe place for Ali to grow his spiritual and religious ways of being and living in the world. Therefore, we cannot forget the Honorable Elijah Muhammad; he understood the width and breath of African Americans forced to live with the twoness of being American and Negro. Like Muhammad Ali, Elijah Muhammad feared for himself and his African American brothers, sisters, children what James Cone identifies as a "lynching tree," and he provided a safe place from which men like Muhammad Ali could grow. He birthed the Nation of Islam, and he nurtured Muhammad Ali.[16]

Randy Roberts writes about the history of race and boxing in the following: "The majority of studies that examined race in boxing—and, for that matter, in other sports as well—have been biographical, which makes sense given the inherent structure of the sport."[17] From the early 1900s until the 1990s, the heavyweight champion of the world occupied status and assumed wealth of a millionaire. In a contextual framework, Farred situates the outliers of the continuous legacy of Ali in the vetting of engaging race and sport:

> The 1967 boxing match between Muhammad Ali, the world heavyweight champion, and his challenger, Ernie "The Octopus" Terrell, in the Houston Astrodome ranks as one of the most telling contests the champion ever fought inside the ring. The momentousness of this bout-for Ali-had little to do with Terrell's boxing skills. Ali was at the peak of his illustrious career. He had not yet been defeated as a professional and was going up against a badly over matched fighter. The significance of Ali's victory, by way of a point's decision, resides in the context of the fight. Ali was three years into his conversion to the Nation of Islam, a process he had inaugurated by abandoning what he dismissed as his "slave name," Cassius Marcellus Clay.[18]

Continuing the applicability of this point of information, Paul Stephen Hudson and Lora Pond Mirza describe Ali's comeback in 1970 by writing the following:

> On Monday evening October 26, 1970, Muhammad Ali, amid long enduring controversy and at the center of media frenzy, made his improbable, historic boxing comeback in Atlanta, Georgia. The fight became one of the most important watersheds in his storied career while serving as a symbolic prism for viewing the emergence of Black Power in Atlanta. Ali, who

Table 2.1 Muhammad Ali Bouts between the Years 1961 and 1965

Date	Opponent	Outcome
October 7, 1961	Alex Miteff	W-TKO
November 2, 1961	Willi Besmanoff	W-TKO
February 10, 1962	Sonny Banks	W-TKO
February 18, 1962	Don Warner	W-TKO
April 23, 1962	George Logan	W-TKO
May 19, 1962	Billy Daniels	W-TKO
July 20, 1962	Alejandro Lavorante	W-KO
November 15, 1962	*Archie Moore	W-KO
January 24, 1963	Charlie Powell	W-KO
March 13, 1963	Doug Jones	W-UD
June 18, 1963	**Henry Cooper	W-TKO
February 5, 1964	***Sonny Liston	W-RTD
May 25, 1965	Sonny Liston	W-KO
November 22, 1965	****Floyd Patterson	W-TKO

*World light-heavyweight Champion, 1952–62
**British, Commonwealth, and European heavyweight champion
***World heavyweight champion, 1964
****World heavyweight champion 1956 and 1962, US Olympic middleweight champion, 1952
W = wins; UD = undecided/draw; TKO = technical knock-out

had changed his name from Cassius Clay to Muhammad Ali when he joined the Nation of Islam in 1964, was at the lowest point in his professional life. Banned from fighting for more than three years by several of boxing's governing bodies, including the then powerful New York State Athletic Commission, he faced the specter of a prison sentence for draft evasion. In 1967, at the height of the Vietnam War, Ali had refused induction into the U.S. Army by declaring himself a conscientious objector based on his religious beliefs.[19]

Table 2.1 lists Muhammad Ali's fights between the years 1961 and 1965. During this period, he was undefeated with technical knockouts, knockouts, and one decision. Moreover, it was within this span of time that he won the world heavyweight championship and defended his title at least twice, remaining the champ. Again, holding the heavyweight championship title in the sport of boxing at that time exhibited power, presence, and political leverage in the United States.

Conclusion

The idea of working on research and writing about the late Muhammad Ali was brought up in 2015. At that time, we were still vetting the attacks on African American males' lives terminated disproportionately by local law enforcement on a national level, including the reaction and response of the 44th presidential administration of the United States.

Walking away from the topic allowed levels of maturity, reflection, and spiritual grind. Translated to this study, Ali's life is a testimony of learning about personal growth, perseverance, and the acquisition of retaining power. Indeed, these are valuable attributes of learning about life and cultural memory lessons that allow us to be most focused when enacting libation prayers to African American ancestors. The disciplinary matrix of Africana Studies allows scholars to stretch the field, in the process of describing and evaluating Africana phenomena. Lastly, James Turner outlines the following four basic tasks of a Black Studies scholar:

> We delineated four basic tasks for the Black Studies scholar: (1) Defend (legitimize) against racism and intellectual chauvinism the fundamental right and necessity of Africana Studies, at all levels of American educators for all people, but most especially for African American people; (2) to Disseminate (teach and publish) Black Studies social theory and analysis, criticism, and historiography, and to reference the work of pioneering black scholars; (3) to Generate (new) knowledge (research) and codify existing information and predicate contemporary study upon the truth's formulated by our mentors; (4) to Preserve the acknowledged value of rare and classical texts in the field (archival and library collections), and maintain the scholarly tradition and rich heritage of African people's and their descendants.[20]

Germane to this essay, I attempted to locate Muhammad Ali in the context of the Jim Crow segregation and the marketplace structure of Americana society. Overall, the relevance of this essay situates the subject threaded to ideas of Ali, in place and time. Yet we know of this figure from his quality of life, which is initiated from sport. He retains attention of the racialist ideology in America, from his alternate choice of selecting membership into the NOI during an era of industrialization.

Figure 2.5 Interdisciplinary tools of analysis.

Admittedly, the goal of this essay was to provide a survey analysis of examining the themes referred to as biographical, the NOI, and professional sport. Paradoxically, Ali lived, participated in community life, and rejected the US Army induction in the city of Houston. Being positioned in this region of the country has allowed me to reflect and focus on the resources and community, which he had access to for his growth and development.

Finally, Ali is recognized as a humanitarian and public figure internationally, after coarsening the insults, attacks, and annoyance of his livelihood and family stability. Collectively, his contribution to world history is remnant to locate him in time. Using instruments combined with a critical analysis has allowed me the flexibility of locating this subject, from an Afrocentric perspective, in the discipline of Africana Studies, using interdisciplinary tools of analysis (Figure 2.5).

Notes

1 James L. Conyers Jr., ed., *Race in American Sports: Essays* (Jefferson, NC: McFarland, 2014), 249.
2 Joyce Carol Oates, "Muhammad Ali: Beginning to End for the First Time in a Book," *New York Times*, November 8, 2017, https://www.nytimes.com/2017/11/28/books/review/jonathan-eig-muhammad-ali-biography.html.
3 Ibid. https://www.nytimes.com/2017/11/28/books/review/jonathan-eig-muhammad-ali-biography.html.
4 Stephen Townsen d, Gary Osmond, and Murray G. Phillips, "Clay vs. Ali: Distant Reading, Methodology, and Sport History," *Journal of Sport History* 46, no. 3 (Fall 2019): 380–95 [384].
5 Alexandra Sims, "Muhammad Ali: Why Did the Boxing Champion Change His Name from Cassius Clay?" June 4, 2016. Independent. https://www.independent.co.uk/news/peo ple/muhammad-ali-death-cassius-clay-why-did-he-change-his-name-nation-of-islam-a7065 256.html.
6 James L. Conyers Jr. and Abul Pitre, eds., *Africana Islamic Studies* (New York: Lexington Books, 2016), 78.
7 "Muhammad Ali." https://www.biography.com/athlete/muhammad-ali.
8 Grant Farred, "What's My Name? Muhammad Ali, Postcolonial Pugilist," *Dispositio* 20, no. 47 (1995): 37–58.
9 Townsend, Osmond, and Phillips, "Clay vs. Ali," 380–95 [381].
10 Muhammad Ali, "Black Culture," *Black Scholar* 1, no. 8 (June 1970): 32–39 [35].
11 Conyers, *Race in American Sports,* 245.
12 Susan Gonzalez, "Muhammad Ali Originally Named for Ardent Abolitionist and Yale Alumnus Cassius Clay." https://news.yale.edu/2016/06/09/muhammad-ali-originally-named-ardent-abolitionist-and-yale-alumnus-cassius-clay.

13 https://www.independent.co.uk/news/people/muhammad-ali-death-cassius-clay-why-did-he-change-his-name-nation-of-islam-a7065256.html.
14 Townsend, Osmond, and Phillips, "Clay vs. Ali," 380–95 [381].
15 Jonathan Eig, *Ali: A Life* (New York: Houghton Mifflin Harcourt, 2017), 158.
16 Ramona Hymon, "Nurtured by the Nation of Islam: Muhammad Ali's Purposeful Life." https://www.greatblackspeakers.com/nurtured-by-the-nation-of-islam-muhammad-alis-purposeful-life/.
17 Randy Roberts, "The Two-Fisted Testing Ground of Manhood: Boxing and the Academy," *Journal of American History* 101, no. 1 (June 2014): 188–91 [190].
18 Farred, "What's My Name?," 37–58 [38].
19 Paul Stephen Hudson and Lora Pond Mirza, "Controversial Comeback in Atlanta: The 1970 Return of Muhammad Ali in 'The City Too Busy to Hate,'" *Georgia Historical Quarterly* 95, no. 1 (Spring 2011): 42–55 [42].
20 James L. Conyers Jr., ed,, *Africana Studies* (Jefferson, NC: McFarland, 1997), 92.

Chapter Three

MUHAMMAD ALI AND THE EUROPEAN FABRIC OF DOMINATION

Molefi Kete Asante

From the inception of the United States under the constitution, a monotonous fabric of social, economic, and political life has been built upon the false idea of White racial superiority. One of the tenets of that false doctrine was the physical invincibility of the White man. Despite the fact that Whites have pushed this myth in one way or another from the beginning of the encounter with Black people, it is also a fact that Africans have never believed this lie. As James Baldwin understood, African Americans are some of the people in the world most likely to have seen the reality of this lie. As workers on the plantations, on the docks, and in the fields, Blacks came to recognize that the skin color myth was a delusion and that physicality did not reside in the whiteness of the skin. In fact, the idea of physicality and athleticism would be cited as reasons for Black male dominance in certain sports (Anderson, 2012; Azzarito, 2008).

Nevertheless, in the nineteenth and twentieth centuries, boxing became for Whites the ultimate test of strength, endurance, and masculinity during the rise of the American industrial age. Thus, in American history, physical prowess was always the test of White supremacy over other people, and surely in the mind of racists, since Whites were the chosen race, no Black man could ever defeat White men in boxing. This belief was a poly-textured fabric that had been richly woven by Whites into the same frame as White racial domination in every sector of society. Whites considered themselves the smartest, the most innovative, the most athletic, and also the best boxers (Birrell, 1989). This fabric had been ripped away from the raw flesh of racism many times, even before Muhammad Ali, but ultimately it was Ali who would tear to shreds any sense of White domination in boxing with a blistering set of fists and feet to match, plus he had a confidence and swagger that demonstrated a fierce determination to degrade the blanketing racism that existed in America.

Theorizing about black cultural mythology has long been an objective of numerous scholars. However, with the publication of her magnum opus, *Black Cultural Mythology*, Christel N. Temple (2020) has given us a clear path forward in ascertaining the importance and significance of heroic and antiheroic figures in our imagination. It is Temple's understanding of the links between memory and mythology operating in the African American context that advances our approach to iconic mythology. She writes: "Mythology indicates a timeless, honored and revered narrative of Africana culture's legendary impulses worthy of remembrance, celebration and memorialization because it includes an account of a *repertoire of survival* based on agency, resistance and hyper-heroic conduct" (p. 111; original emphasis). Muhammad Ali is a central part of the panoply of heroic individuals within the African American community because he embodies the repertoire of survival in the context of agency and resistance.

Prologue to Fame

Muhammad Ali was born in Louisville, Kentucky, on January 17, 1942, and given the name Cassius Marcellus Clay Jr. He died on June 3, 2016, in Scottsdale, Arizona, with the name Muhammed Ali. He rose from poverty and anonymity to become one of the most recognized sports figures of the twentieth century. He was often called the "greatest heavyweight champion" and at one time was considered the most famous person in the entire world. Herein lay the sharp knife of Ali's persona for America. In many ways he was an original, but in some important ways he had a trail to follow that had been laid down by his predecessors, especially Jack Johnson and Joe Louis, two of the most dominant fighters of their times. Each one in his own way contributed to the shredding of the monotony of White masculine superiority, which was at the foundation of slave patriarchy that ruled the imagination of White people.

Race and Sport

Jack Johnson's phenomenal entry into the world of professional boxing marked a splitting assault on the patterns of racial myth governing the American society during the first quarter of the twentieth century. Johnson was born in Galveston, Texas, in 1878 and died in 1946. His life covered one of the grimmest periods in American history when lynching of Black men was at its height, the rise of African American resistance to segregation was boiling over in periodic riots and rebellions, and the Second European War led by the racist German Third Reich was clawing at the submission of the world to the Aryan race. Thus, Jack Johnson lived during a turbulent time in racial relations as local state laws were enforced to segregate Blacks and Whites always with the idea that Black places of water fountains, schools, and even cemeteries were inferior to those for Whites. It would be about twenty years after Jack Johnson died in 1946 that those laws would be eradicated.

Race and sport were attached to the centerpiece of the White Americans' understanding of dominance (Hartmann, 2000). One can see why White Americans found Jack Johnson a threat to White manhood. He took control of the heavyweight boxing championship in 1908 and held it until 1915. His dominance in the ring made him an instant hero among Blacks and ultimately a legendary figure among the reporters of news. The fight between Johnson and James J. Jeffries was called the "Fight of the Century." This was the first fight so designated by the sporting world. Because by this time Johnson had shown that he was both a master of the ring and a master of making White men angry, the majority of Whites wanted to see him defeated by what would become one of the first "Great White Hopes." Not only was Johnson the most hated

African American by Whites, but he was also the most admired by many Blacks who were happy to see a Black champion, although they were often apprehensive about his commitment to Black solidarity. Johnson bought a nightclub, a restaurant, and other businesses and had his White wives run them. After 1912 Johnson was a target of authorities in various positions in government mainly because of his brazen public relationships with White women. Ultimately, he was arrested for violation of the Mann Act, which forbade the transporting of a woman across state lines for immoral purposes. It was clearly a racially motivated charge, but it had the effect of taking Johnson out of circulation as a boxer in the United States. With ongoing legal and public struggles with women for allegations of domestic violence, Johnson left the United States and boxed in foreign countries for seven years until 1920. Johnson later served his one-year sentence at the federal penitentiary at Leavenworth. He died in 1946 in an automobile accident. When Johnson died, the reigning professional heavyweight champion was Joe Louis, who had been born Joseph Louis Barrow in 1914 during the time that Johnson was the heavyweight champion. Louis held the title king of the ring as world heavyweight champion from 1937 to 1949, and it must be included as one the greatest heavyweight boxers of all times. He fought 26 championship fights and won so predictably that he was called the Brown Bomber, a name that stuck because of the military era of World War II. Like Jack Johnson before him, Joe Louis became an integral part of the cultural language and social discourse in the American society. Louis was a nationwide hero because of his skills, anti-Nazi positions, beliefs in equality of the human race, and the need to break down racial barriers in all sports. Furthermore, Louis was considered less outspoken and more acceptable in manner than Jack Johnson had been. Louis was married to a Black woman, Martha Jefferson, until his death in 1981.

The Dance of African Manhood

When Muhammad Ali was born in 1942, Joe Louis was the reigning heavyweight champion of the world, and although there had been other boxing champions between Louis and Ali, it seemed quite logical to Cassius Clay that he would be the greatest coming after Johnson and Louis. In 1960 Clay won the light heavyweight Olympic gold medal and was on his way to becoming a household name like the boxers he had come to admire. He would climb the ladder of African American boxing prowess until he stood at the head of the group. This was to be his fate from the first moment that he came to self-realization after his bicycle had been stolen when he was a young boy growing up in Louisville, a city that would later honor him with a magnificent museum in memory of his road to glory.

The weaving of America's racist fabric was always about the attempt to dehumanize Africans, to conceal the weakness of the White racist ethic, to create the ideal America where Blacks would always be second- or third-class people in a nation of White citizens. To be a citizen, the racial patriarchy created a Whites-only code that made its way into the very nature of White domination over Black people. Here comes Muhammad Ali with the support of several White people in Louisville behind him, having seen the possibility that they could ride the wave of this victorious Olympic star's remarkable victory to their own financial gain, only to discover years later that no one could prevent the full-fledged independence of the most audacious boxer of his generation. It is where he began to see the light and soon did what was considered his first great heresy against the shaped and patterned quilt of racial inequality that had been made for him. He joined the Nation of Islam, considered the most anti-American religious group that Black Americans could commit to. It was neither Christian nor Western and had the character of being historically in contention and competition with the European world. In 1961 as a Muslim he abandoned his "slave name" and took the Islamic name Muhammad Ali, which some of his critics claimed was another slave name. Nevertheless, in the context of the American society, it was seen as an anti-White name, and of course, it was perceived that way by African Americans.

The Rise of the Heroic Ali

In the life of subjected people, almost any time is a good time for a heroic figure to appear. There is no wonder that African Americans have been able to discover so many individuals who challenged the superstructure of White domination. Muhammad Ali's actions became the scissors that were used in an orderly cutting up of the White myths of masculinity, beauty, grace, power, and domination, by addressing in his life and speech every major aspect of the racist cover woven to blanket American society. There had been characters, heroes, and myths in the verbal repertory of African Americans that made a difference in how African Americans responded to the social, political, and economic vicissitudes of life. There was in Ali's prowess, sassy style, and poetic communication combinations of the most authentic myths of African American manhood. He was the embodiment of every male African American hero who had preceded him with strength, vigor, and physical energy: Nat Turner, John Henry, Shine, Jack Johnson, Joe Louis, and Stagolee (Leonard, 2009). Black people saw in Muhammad Ali the intersections of resistance, confidence, grace, soul, and courage in all of the possible manifestations of brilliance. He was the new icon of manliness on the American performance stage. He possessed the fearlessness of Nat Turner, determined to be a link to the liberation of African people from a consciousness of oppression without victorious thoughts, in order to demonstrate that independence can be performed. John Henry's legendary physicality was of a steel-driving man tasked with pounding a steel drill into rock to make blast holes for explosives in constructing a railroad tunnel. John Henry competed against a steam-powered drill and won the contest, only to die of heart failure. In Muhammad Ali's case, his physical strength and boxing ability showed his willingness to extend himself to prove his manhood. Of course, competing against human beings and not machines gave Muhammad Ali an advantage over John Henry, considered by all who knew of his exploits the greatest steel-driving man in the world. The legendary Shine is said to have been on the *Titanic* when it went down in 1912. While this legend started to circulate in Harlem, New York, and other metropolitan areas soon after the sinking of the British liner, it made Shine an icon of incredible Black physical strength and profound wisdom. Shine swam his way to New York and refused to give in to the blandishments offered to him by people on the ship. One can see how Shine's untutored wisdom and great belief in his invincibility became a part of the Muhammad Ali mythic image. As I have pointed out earlier, both Jack Johnson and Joe Louis had already become magical iconic figures by the time of Ali's ring mastery.

One character from African American culture that cannot be totally equated with Muhammad Ali but who also had a corona that spread toward Ali's reputation was that of Stagolee, the mythical bad Negro. Interestingly, Saeed Amir (2011), a Pakistani, wrote about Ali in iconic terms as a Muslim: "Quite simply Ali belonged to us and we would watch with a mixture of awe and envy, especially because of the way that white people respected Ali the Muslim." Amir's adoration of Ali was in the words of Christel Temple "time-transcending" and also race, culture, and class transcending (2020, p. 161). To use Temple's language about Malcolm X, it is plain to see that Muhammad Ali's "legacy is well aligned to the topic of myth" (2020, p. 200). It should be clear that Ali's mythical character was not the same as Malcolm's; indeed, Malcolm might be more effectively related to Stagolee, for instance, but in every case the legendary figure of immense charisma carried the flame of agency, capability, and resistance. In this regard, pre-Malcolm, the Black community in the United States came to see the Stagolee figure as unique in his freedom, reputation for toughness, and resistance to White domination. The ballads that were written and sung about Stagolee did not have to be precise and sometimes were purely fictional. This was not the case with Ali; his record spoke for itself, and it was large, expansive, and engaging in an international manner. Yet while satisfying a national and international audience of admirers, Ali tapped into the richly articulated layers of African American oratory, poetics, and slang to make Stagolee live again in our Black imaginations.

The African American Epic Memory

Stagolee, a principal figure in the heroic cultural imagination of most Black people in the United States, occupied a space in Black culture that Muhammad Ali stretched into, and it allowed him to act out the full symbolic and interpretative performance of the "bad" Black man who existed in every community in the United States, where there was a large population of Blacks. The bad Negro could confront Whites in every sector of society, the ring, music, school, wit, humor, sexuality, and religion. In Valdosta, Georgia, where I grew up, it was said, "None of them white people mess with Mr. Moses." He was a Stagolee figure who knew how to resist racism with dignity and in defiance of White madness that brought death to so many unsuspecting Blacks in the South of the 1960s. Muhammad Ali was the Stagolee figure writ large. He won the heavyweight championship at the age of 22 in 1964 when he beat Sonny Liston in an upset victory. Most people thought that Sonny Liston was the likely victor because of his tough guy persona. However, it was the cool, dancing, graceful, fluid, rapping Ali who would win the bout and become the darling of the sports commentators and the heroic beautiful African American icon of resistance. With victories in his hand, waving them in the face of a White reactionary society, Muhammad espoused his beliefs about imperialism, religion, and war in Vietnam. Soon the full weight of a racist political structure showed its colors and patterns by arresting him, charging him with draft evasion, and taking away his boxing titles in an effort to teach him a lesson about the power of the White system (Quintana, 2007). It was as if they wanted him to know that the system gave, and the system could take away. Yet the attacks on him by the system further embellished his shining image as a symbol of Black pride and masculine prowess (Ferber, 2007). African Americans had seen so many leaders with strong anti-racist beliefs assassinated, brutalized, stripped of rights, and exiled that they knew that the system was corrupt and someone with the stance and posture of victory of Muhammad Ali was truly reflective of what hundreds of thousands of Black people believed and thought about the society. The persecution of Ali was the persecution of the freedom-loving Black person anywhere and everywhere. Later the society would be roiled by the broadcast and publishing of images of Black men beaten by police or shot down because they were perceived by Whites to be threats. Although many incidents happened after the height of Ali's fame, nevertheless his life and actions anticipated issues such as the attack on Rodney King (Alexander, 1994, pp. 77–94).

Muhammad Ali appealed his case, and the Supreme Court overturned his conviction in 1971. He had lost four years of boxing during the prime of his career as an athlete, yet he remained famous, iconic, and free to speak about his beliefs, while supporting Elijah Muhammad, being a friend to Malcolm X, his religious mentor, and supporting racial integration (Conyers and Smallwood, 2008).

There are numerous characteristics that identify the Stagolee spirit in African American culture. Recognized as a variant of the Yoruba deity Shango, the god of thunder, Stagolee is the disrupter of the normal order, the one who through turbulence clears the world of all impurities. The first mention of the ballad of Stagolee is usually given as 1895 when Lee Shelton shot William Lyons in St. Louis. Of course, there had been other ballads of tough, rough, or dangerous Black men who had created fear among Whites and Blacks. One such person was St. Malo, a rebellious African who was sung about in the early part of the eighteenth, nineteenth, and early twentieth centuries, alongside Stagolee. Known in French as Jean Saint Malo or in Spanish as Juan San Maló, he was the leader of a maroon colony of formerly enslaved Africans in Spanish-controlled Louisiana. In one of the many cooperative ventures between African people, the free African community of Louisiana supplied Saint Malo and his community with weapons as they escaped to the swamps near Lake Borgne. The people began to sing the ballad of Saint Malo after he was captured and killed by the Whites in 1784. Malo, unlike Stagolee, was responsible for freeing Africans, not killing them. Yet these figures, and scores of others in African history in the United States, accumulated the iconic medals of being defiant personalities who would stand up to Whites. In this sense, the monumental place of Stagolee in our imagination marks him as powerful not because he fought against Shelton but because Whites appeared to admire his strength, tenacity, and confidence. Muhammad Ali combined all of these heroic ideas into one new and generative personality.

It is easy to see how one could understand Stagolee as a sustained African American male resistance and protest figure against White racial domination because over the years the ballads about him morphed. While folk heroes have existed throughout the Black sojourn in the United States, the idea of a tough guy icon cut from the Stagolee myth might appear in the presence of Adam Clayton Powell, a politician who could not be controlled by White politicians; Malcolm X, who was his own man grown up on a doctrine that emerged from the mind of a Black man (Marcus Garvey); and, of course, Muhammad Ali.

Michael Ezra (2009) spoke about the nature of Muhammad's status as an icon. I use the term "icon" in this chapter because it resonates with the history of heroic Black men and women such as Harriet Tubman, Malcolm X, and Marcus Garvey. There are, however, characters that have become iconic by virtue of tapping into the desires and wishes of the people as legendary stories. Stagolee is such an icon of resistance, protest, opposition, and often counterculture. William Wiggins, one of the most important African American anthropologists, in talking about how Jack Johnson was related to the Stagolee myth said: "He was his own man; he refused to allow anyone, white or black, to determine his place in society or the manner in which he should live (1971, pp. 35–46). Obviously, he did not shrink from confrontations with White society. In a similar vein, as we shall see, Muhammad Ali fulfilled all of the requirements for what the culture would call a "bad nigger."

Muhammad Ali's image reflected the major positive characteristics of Stagolee. He demonstrated no fear of the White man and exhibited the greatest of skill with absolute cool, the epitome of African performativity (Voulgaris, 2016). He was willing to establish the grounds of his own actions. He recognized no one, White or Black, who could show more excellence than he could. He defied the authority that they thought they had over him. He was seen and saw himself through the prism of sexual virility and physical appearance and prowess. He recognized that the world he was born into was not of his own making and that he had a right to change as much of it as he could. These were some of the main tenets of the sustained Stagolee spirit that Muhammad Ali naturally related to without having a definitive analysis of the society's woes, although he knew the dangers of patriarchy and racism.

Muhammad Ali took the code of masculinity as defined by the White society and bent it toward a collective liberation of Black people. Escaping the fate of many Black men because of his fame, he knew that the objective of Whites who hated him was to reduce him to the same fate as other Blacks (Alexander, 2012). While Black and White men have found masculinity distorted in the American culture because of patriarchy, both groups are inflicted with competition and strength. Out of the condition of enslavement, segregation, and inequality, Black men have been recreating themselves. Ali is the perfect example of how a Black man recreated the masculinity code. If Whites thought of masculinity as conquests, then who could be a better conqueror? He was the only boxer who was a three-time lineal champion of the heavyweight division, and he had a record of beating 21 boxers for the world heavyweight division. The *Ring Magazine* named him "Fighter of the Year" for an unprecedented six times. Called both the "greatest heavyweight boxer of all times" and the "greatest athlete of the 20th century," Muhammad Ali ripped to shreds the racist fabric of masculinity and race as constructed by the doctrine of White racial superiority (Hunter, 1996). On June 3, 2016, Ali died and has remained in the imagination of African Americans as the most dominant athlete of his generation.

Muhammad Ali lived an incredibly open life, dancing and confronting, poeting and fronting, jiving and moving, stinging and floating, representing the grace, beauty, and confidence of the Black man. Imperfect as he was, he never represented himself as an ethical icon, only the greatest fighter. Yet in a racist society even his physical dominance could be turned to the use of White supremacist rhetoric. Hence, the idea of White racial superiority remained stamped in the mind of some Whites even though Muhammad Ali had shown that all human beings were capable of championships in boxing or other sports. In 2020 a White Britisher, Tyson Luke Fury, became the heavyweight champion after defeating African American Deontay Wilder, proving once again that ring domination has little to do with race. Thus, the meaning of Muhammad Ali's ring domination was not that he was a Black champion, but that he was able to tear to shreds the idea of White racial invincibility in the ring. It was a path that had been opened informally many times and then formally by Jack Johnson, Joe Louis, Floyd Patterson, and others, but it was Ali who took the fabric of racial arrogance and put it into the trash heap of racist history. In so doing, he was manifesting in his authentic self the fulfillment of Temple's assessment about the meaning of myth for a people when she wrote, "When a culture elevates the narrative of its survival—not merely the memory of its heritage—to a conceptual mythological status, the philosophical refinement permanently revives the intellectual cycles of wonder and analysis" (2020, p. 253).

References

Alexander, E. (1994) "'Can you be Black and look at this?': Reading the Rodney King video(s)". *Public Culture* 7(1): 77–94.

Alexander, M. (2012) *The New Jim Crow: Mass Incarceration in the Age of Colorblindness*. New York: New Press.

Amir, Saeed (2011) "'Worthy of all praises': Muhammad Ali and the politics of identity." *Questia Soundings*, 47 (Spring): 123–29.

Anderson, E. Kian (2012) "Examining media contestation of masculinity and head trauma in the National Football League." *Men and Masculinities* 15(2): 152–73.

Azzarito, H. L. (2008) "'White men can't jump': Race, gender, and natural athleticism." *International Review for the Sociology of Sport* 43(4): 347–64

Birrell, S. (1989) "Racial relations theories and sport: Suggestions for a more critical analysis." *Sociology of Sport Journal* 6(3): 212–27.

Conyers, J., and A. Smallwood, eds. (2008) *Malcolm X: A Historical Reader*. Durham, NC: Carolina Academic Press.

Ezra, Michael (2009) *Muhammad Ali: The Making of an Icon*. Philadelphia: Temple University.

Ferber, A. (2007) "The construction of black masculinity: White supremacy now and then." *Journal of Sport and Social Issues* 31(1): 11–24.

Hartmann, D. (2000) "Rethinking the relationships between sport and race in American culture: Golden ghettos and contested terrain." *Sociology of Sport Journal* 17(3): 229.

Hunter, D. W. (1996) "Race and athletic performance: A physiological review." *Journal of African American Men* 2(2–3): 23–38.

Leonard, D. J. (2009) "It's gotta be the body: Race, commodity, and surveillance of contemporary black athletes." In Denzin, N. K. (ed.), *Studies in Symbolic Interaction*. Bingley, UK: Emerald Group, pp. 165–90.

Quintana, A. F. (2007) "Muhammad Ali: The greatest in court." *Marquette Sports Law Review* 18(1, Fall): 171.

Temple, C. N. (2020) *Black Cultural Mythology*. Albany: SUNY.

Voulgaris, Panos (2016) "Muhammad Ali: An Unusual Leader in the Advancement of Black America," master's thesis, Harvard Extension School.

Wiggins, W. H. (1971) "Jack Johnson as bad nigger: The folklore of his life." *Black Scholar* 2 (5, January): 34–46.

Chapter Four

MUHAMMAD ALI AS *SKH*

Wade W. Nobles
Ifágbemì Sàngódáre, Nana Kwaku Berko I,
Bejana, Onebunne

I would like to begin this chapter with a personal remembrance. In 1972, when I was a graduate student at Stanford University, Muhammad Ali came to speak at the university. He spoke passionately about White intellectuals' failure to acknowledge Elijah Muhammad's significance and influence. I remember him saying, "Why you don't talk about Elijah; he taught them all; that's where all the ideas come from." Elijah made him. After berating the audience of White intellectuals, faculty, and students, he picked up and held my 3-year-old son, Omar Jahmal, in his arms. He whispered something in Omar's ear and kissed him on his check. Omar was too young to remember what Muhammad said. Since I know us to be "spirit beings" and that our spirits talk to each other in ways that our minds may not comprehend or remember, the message in the whisper between Muhammad and Omar may forever be known only to their spirits. It is, however, because of the gentle way in which Muhammad held my son and my understanding of spirit now that I honor him as one of "the greatest of all times."

This discussion of Muhammad Ali as *Skh* is both an honoring and an application of Sakhu-historical analyses.[1] At the onset, it is herein stated that this discussion will be grounded in the advanced level of the discipline of Black Psychology known as *Skh Djr* that requires the need to rescue African language and logic associated with the illumination of the "spirit being" where, in my opinion, *Skh* is undeniable. In this writing as well as others, the science of Black Psychology will be held to the charge of continuing its break from the constraints of Euro-American psychology and to explore more deeply an African paradigm, episteme, and terminology as useful tools for the structuring of the science of the spirit for understanding African human functioning (Nobles, 2020). The term Sakhu (*Skh*) has been offered as the proper nomenclature for the science of African human functioning. Sakhu (*Skh*) was introduced as a deeper extension and further representation of the science of African human functioning's African essence (Nobles, 2013). As a system of thought and action, *Skh Djr* examines and utilizes the processes that allow for the illumination and liberation of the spirit. Technically, *Skh Djr* is an unfiltered (free of Western contamination) process of understanding, examining, and explicating the meaning, nature, and functioning of being human for African people by conducting a deep, profound, and penetrating search, study, and mastery of the process of "illuminating" the human spirit or essence and totality of all human experiences and phenomena. The *Skh* process requires that we interrogate the language and logic of traditional African peoples and by so doing gain greater insight into the functioning of contemporary African peoples. Understanding Muhammad Ali as *Skh* requires us to engage, however briefly, in different epistemic reflections; explore realms of reality (visible and invisible); shift the paradigm; and ultimately, accept an African science of the spirit.

African Spirit Science

In our traditional spirit science(s) that are often mistakenly called traditional religions, that is, Vodun, Ifa, there is a common recognition that force, energy, or spirit is the essence of every living expression of being. In ancient Dahomey (Benin), our ancestors believed in the idea of "Bo," which protected and directed human affairs. Bo represented the idea of the "power to activate" and was conceived symbolically as being gods in the earth, that is, little forest spirits (Aziza, Mmotia, etc.), fetishes, and Orisas. The term "Bo" in Aja, Evhe, and Fon conceptualizations is in actuality associated with what it means to be human.

Psychologically or more correctly via *Skh*, the Bo is a sign that encourages humans to understand and utilize that which is invisible in the visible. The Bo represents the potentiality of all human action to uncover the hidden potentiality of all things. In the vocabulary of the Fon, "Boko" means knowledgeable in Bo. The word "Bokomon" means master of Bo knowledge. The word for Vodou priestess, "Mambo," is derived from the Fon word "Nanbo," which means mother (na) of Bo. "Lo" means mystery and "lon" means heaven. Parenthetically, it should be noted that, on a deeper intellectual and philosophical level, the master and mother of the Bo, "Bo komon" and "Bo mena," brought together the science of the African spirit to spark the Haitian revolution (see Nobles, 2015) via the energy (spirit) vibrations embedded in the "irritated genie" as Lwa (see Carruthers, 1985) Consistent with this African idea of "if it exists, it most assuredly is spirit" is the recognition that "we are not human beings but 'spirit beings' housed in a physical container having a human experience" (Nobles, 2013). As "spirit beings," what I call "spiritness,"[2] we as African people have a metaphysical connection and ethereal extension into and between the supra world of the deities, the interworld of other beings, and the inner world of oneself. It should be noted here that the very use of African language and logic forces the use (and for some a difficult/different level of comprehension) of a new paradigmatic lens.

Accordingly, to understand and "illuminate" Muhammad Ali's personhood as *Skh*, we must frame his story as the workings of a "knowing and knowable spirit" whose human experience is both African and not African at the same time. However, before discussing Muhammad Ali as a *Skh*, it may be helpful to briefly discuss the Bântu-Kôngo[3] understanding of what is actually reality. The Bântu-Kôngo believe that diverse forces and waves of energy govern life around humans. It is believed that the heated force of Kalunga blew up and down as a huge storm of projectiles, *Kimbwandende*, producing a huge mass in fusion. The fire force called *Kalunga* is complete in and of itself, emerges within the emptiness or nothingness, and becomes the source of life on Earth. In the process of cooling the mass in fusion, solidification occurs giving birth to Earth. In effect, the Bântu believe that all of reality (*Kalunga*) is fundamentally a process of perpetual and mutual sending and receiving of spirit (energy) in the form of waves and radiations. *Kalunga* or reality is the totality, the completeness of all life. It is an ocean of energy, a force in motion. *Kalunga* is everything, sharing life and becoming life continually after life itself. As the totality or the complete living, *Kalunga* is comprised of both a visible realm (*Ku Nseke*) and an invisible realm (*Ku Mpemba*). The visible physical world has spirit (energy) as its most important essence/element. Referred to as *Nkisi* (medicine), the spirit element of the physical (visible) world has the power to care, cure, heal, and guide. The invisible (spiritual) world (*Ku Mpemba*) is comprised of human experience, ancestor experience, and the soul–mind experience. The *Ku Mpemba* has spirit (energy) as its most important essence/element. In effect, as noted above, if reality is (visible and invisible), it is spirit.

Different Episteme and Paradigm

Unfortunately, almost all formal knowing has been filtered through a Western grand narrative that gives priority to epistemic considerations of separateness, different/distinct, and oppositional categories that privileges an epistemic orientation to only the material/physical world. This discussion will intentionally break ranks with Western orthodoxy. Embracing a different episteme requires the simultaneous adoption of culturally congruent African-centered language and logic as central to the paradigm shifting and new narrative for exploring the life story and events found in African American reality. In this regard, it has been noted (Nobles et al., 2016) that African people (both continental and diasporan), though often disrespected and/or unrecognized, have always possessed a full language and systems of beliefs (logic) about what it means to be human, to whom, whose they were, and why they existed. The importance of language is fundamental (Nobles, 1996). In fact, in discussing the African origins of civilization, Diop (1974) noted that the cultural unity of Africa can be understood and obtained only by examining the domains of language, history, and psyche. As is true with language, so too is it equally true with episteme. African deep thought rightly suggests that each realm (supranatural, natural, and paranormal) of reality should be subject to its own epistemology. Knowing in the spirit (supranatural and/or paranormal) realm is, according to N'Sengha (2005), assisted by four basic ways of knowing: divination, revelation, intuition, and reason.

In traditional African thought, being human is to be spirit, energy, or power. Being spirit is to be one who lives and moves within and is inseparable from the ocean of waves and radiations of energy or power (spirit). A human being is "spirit" whose unfolding is a constant and continual inquiry into its own being, experience, knowledge, and truth (Ramose, 2002). To be human is to be a spirit in motion (unfolding). Being human is being a phenomenon of perpetual, constant, and continual unfolding (vibration sharing and exchanging) of life spirit. Humans are containers and instruments of divine spirit and relationships. A human being is likened to a living sun (unlimited power), possessing a "knowing and knowable" spirit (energy or power) through which one has an enduring relationship with the total perceptible and ponderable universe. A human being is thought to be a "spirit" who affirms one's humanity by recognizing the humanity of others and on that basis establishes humane relations with them.

The Invisible Force (Spirit)

The African science of the spirit requires that we briefly explicate Africa's understanding of the invisible forces that guide and direct our lives and living. As mentioned, in ancient Dahomey (Benin), for example, our ancestors believed that an invisible, living energy/spirit called Bo protected and directed human affairs. This living energy, though anthropomorphized (seen as having human characteristics) as Orisa or Lwa, should be thought of as expressions of concentrated energy in distinct forms with particular intelligence, attributes, qualities, and characteristics.[4]

In the Ifa sacred text it is said that when Orunmila was coming down to the world, Olodumare gave him Odu, an attribute or quality of supreme authority to speak and act and be implicitly obeyed. Olodumare had given each of the Orisa his or her own particular $\grave{A}$sẹ, a sacred divine invisible power that connects all things and beings to the Supreme Being (Olòdùmarè-Oloòrun) and the Orisas (Cuoco, 2014: 590). The entire universe is thought to have $\grave{A}$sẹ as the creative continuous energy that connects everything and all beings to the realm of creation. It is the dynamic relation between humans, the Orisas and $\grave{A}$sẹ that maintains the balance between the visible realm (material/physical) and the invisible realm (immaterial/spirit).

$\grave{A}$sẹ is the generative force presence in all things—rocks, hills, streams, mountains, plants, animals, ancestors, deities—and in utterances—prayers, songs, curses, and even everyday speech (Drewal 1992). $\grave{A}$sẹ is the power to bring things into existence, to make things happen. It is the authority, power, and life force within all creatures. $\grave{A}$sẹ is the divine (sacred) energy (force) that affects all things and is affected by all things. Each Orisa has its own power or life force, that is, $\grave{A}$sẹ.[5] For example, Sango as a knowing and knowable "force" represents the Orisa of Opposites (double axe). He is the god of thunder and lightning. As universal manifestation of spirit, energy, or force, Sango takes the concentrated form and attributes of courage, resourcefulness, preparedness, intelligence, wit, power, majesty, fertility, and procreation/sensuality. He rules the testicles. Those humans who are "Omo Sango" (child of Sango) are, in fact, spirits (forces) in human form that represent or reflect the attributes or qualities of courage, fertility, majesty, and so on.

Obatala as a knowing and knowable force represents the Orisa of "Rightness." He is the god of wisdom, happiness, and peace. As universal manifestation of spirit, energy, or force, Obatala takes the concentrated form and attributes of purity, wisdom, morality, humility, and judgment. He rules the Head. Those humans who are "Omo Obatala" (child of Obatala) are, in fact, spirits (forces) in human form that represent or reflect the attributes or qualities of rightness, purity, peace, wisdom, and so on.

The Episteme of the Invisible (and Realms of Reality)

While challenging the so-called continental Africans' monopoly on African identity or Africanity, Nobel Laureate Wole Soyinka (1990: 13) states that the idea of Africa is more than a mere material/physical spatial reality that stops wherever saltwater licks the shores of the continent. He asserts that the thought traditions, belief systems, life worlds, and language world are drawn from and contributed to by persons of African descent wherever they exist. However, in accepting the idea that the invention and retention of African thought (including episteme) can be found wherever African people exist, Sonyinka, like many of us, limits the discussion of African thought to the material/physical realm. In this remaining discussion, I want to take this opportunity to explore and engage in what I call the "episteme of the invisible." The admitted difficulty for this analysis (discussion) is that as "spirit beings" we are not accustomed to understanding or analyzing "spirit talk." Our "spirit talk" communicates in ways that our Western trained mind may not comprehend. Given that what we know and the methods we use to know have been filtered through the imposition of Western thought systems and grand narratives, the African-centered directive that will guide the interrogation of Ali as *Skh* will be how do we know what our "knowing and knowable" spirit knows and how does that translate to our being, becoming, and belonging as agents of doing.

The episteme of the invisible requires a break with knowing only via the material or physical realm. It is a totally distinct way of knowing/thinking. Though seldom respected in the Western academy, knowing/thinking in the invisible realm is common among Bântu peoples. For example, among the Bântu-Kôngo, the *ngánga* is considered a person initiated in the African way of knowing/thinking (Fu-Kiau, 2001a: 70). In this way of knowing/thinking, the idea of "Vee" is informative. The Vee is a symbolism for the representation of life across stages manifesting from the invisible to the visible. It represents the living energy[6] and is the symbolic form of attraction, repulsion, celebration, pain, individual, and community. It is the basis and/or signature of all realities whether biological, material, ideological, or immaterial. Keep in mind that these realities (material or immaterial) are not separate realities. The material (visible) is simply an expression (in physical form) of the immaterial (invisible) essence.

When placed on the *dikenga* or cosmogram, the Vee is a "living pyramid in constant motion which follows the path of life and passes across the four main points or phases of demarcation" (Fu-Kiau, 2001b: 132). And the more centered a person is in this Vee, the more powerful is the person. There are four main Vees (symbolic points of living energy) on the *dikenga*: *Vangama*, *Vaika*, *Vânga*, and *Vûnda*, analogous to the *dinga* or "events of time." The *Vangama* equates with conception and when genetic codes are set. The *Vaika* symbolizes the transition from the internal (invisible essence) to the external environment or birth (visible expression). The *Vânga* is the time of creativity and maturation of the essence as expression. It is generally thought that this is the time wherein one enters the status of mastery. The last symbolic demarcation *Vûnda* is where "one goes naturally or unnaturally into the process of dying to rest, to extinguish, leave the physical world, to re-enter the world of living energy" (Fu-Kiau, 2001c: 141) When a person reenters the world of living energy, they have a new set of experiences. According to Fu-Kiau, "it is the period of birth-growth in the invisible world and a penetration through the accumulated cultural role of the past time in order to regenerate one's own life potentialities for a possible return of that *ngolo* energy [...] in the physical world" (Fu-Kiau, 2001d: 34). After accumulation of all spiritual, moral intellectual, or genetic potentialities at *ku mpèmba* "the Kongo cosmology tells us, the dual soul mind, *mpève ngîndu* is ready to reincarnate" (Fu-Kiau, 2001d: 34). The multidimensional aspects of the person as a "spirit being" are combined with the dazzling array of forces that populate creation; the possibilities of what could be causing disharmony are equally spectacular because African concepts of healing address all factors as it involves all materials and modalities.

The episteme of the invisible and the role of a "knowing and knowable spirit" is found most clearly in the use of spirit vibrations/radiations in healing. A major characteristic of African traditional healing is that it acknowledges subtle energy and vibrations as playing the causal role in illness. For instance, a Yoruba diagnosis of illness (àrùn) would include divination to be sure that any potential spiritual causes are identified so they can be addressed in the treatment. Among the Dagara, healing must take into account the energetic or spiritual condition that is in turmoil that is affecting the physical condition (Fu-Kiau, 2001d: 30). Focusing just on the physical denies the needs of spirit and the adjustment of it in order to make the cure last. If energy vibrations (radiating spirit) play a role in healing then, given our reframing of human beings as "spirit beings," would it be too far-fetched to also recognize that spirit vibrations are the bases of all "spirit being" activity from illness to well-being?

It may also be helpful to briefly explain the idea of Egbe Orun relative to the episteme of the invisible. The Egbe Orun are spirit companions. They are our associates in heaven (the invisible realm) who guide our living in the visible realm. Hence, it is believed that every person has spirit companions in the invisible realm (an Egbe Orun) and a guiding Orisa. More accurately, one's personhood is an expression of the essence of a particular Orisa.

The Paradigm of Personhood

Generally speaking, the African (Bântu-Kôngo) word for person, *MuNtu*, represents a "set of concrete social relationships [...] a system of systems; the pattern of patterns in being" (Fu-Kiau, 2001e: 42). *MuNtu* is "*n'kingu a n'kingu*," a principle of principles (Fu-Kiau, 2001f: 70). *MuNtu* is distinguished from other beings by intelligence (Diop, 1974) and a unique human quality (Ani, 1994). According to Fu-Kiau (2001), *MuNtu* is not comparable to an animal because *MuNtu* has a dual soul–mind, *mwèla-ngindu*, which can remain in and interact with the visible (material) world and the invisible (world of invisible).

Accessing both realms of reality is codified throughout African cultures. It is the interaction with the invisible realm that is lost in Western episteme. There are, however, in fact, not two realities. To fully understand this, one must understand that African wisdom traditions posit that all that is, is spirit, and the physical is nothing more than the manifestation of the spirit that is the essence of all life. In effect, the essence (spirit) is expressed in physical form. For instance, in ancient Kmt (Egypt), the physical body is called the *zed* or *khet*, which is an expression of the *Ka* (the immortal soul) (Akbar, 1985).[7] For the Zulu, the person is an expression of Uqobo (essence). With the Nupe, the person (*Nkak*) is an expression of *Rayi* (soul). It is generally believed that the Yoruba conceive of the person as having multiple components: the physical body, *ara*; the soul, *emi*; and the inner head, *ori*. I believe it is more accurate that the *ara* (physical body) is an expression of the *emi*.

The African idea of personhood requires a shift from the simplistic notion of individuality and the role of energy or spirit in the full understanding of reality.

Muhammad Ali as *Skh*

Others may chronical Muhammad's physical achievements/experiences as a boxer directed toward boxing by the white Louisville police officer (1954); to being winner of six Kentucky Golden Gloves titles and two National Golden Gloves titles by 1960; to being a gold medal winner at the 1960s Olympics; to his two fights, 1964 and 1965, with Sonny Liston for boxing's World Heavyweight Championship; to "The Rumble in the Jungle" in 1974 against George Foreman, in Kinshasa, Zaire; to his third and final boxing match, the "Thrilla in Manila," with Joe Frazier in 1975; to his 1978 loss against Leon Spinks and his TKO defeat by Larry Holmes in 1980. Some may also find fascinating his love for women and marriages to 18-year-old Sonji Roi (1965), 17-year-old Belinda Boyd/Khalilah Ali (1967), 16-year-old Wanda Bolton/Aaisha Ali in an Islamic ceremony (while still married to Belinda), 18-year-old Veronica Porché Ali (1977), and 29-year-old Lonnie Ali (1986).

However, for this discussion my analyses will be guided by the intellectual charge of seeking answers to what Ali's "knowing and knowable" spirit knew and how that translates to his being, becoming, and belonging as an agent of doing. It is important to note here that the *Skh* is the illumination of one's spirit (essence) that is revealed (expressed) by the character, conduct, and consciousness of one's Orisa. One's personal Orisa is key to understanding the particular way in which one illuminates the character, conduct, and consciousness of one's vibrational energy (spiritness) force that is a "knowing and knowable spirit."

The following discussion will explore Muhammad Ali's life and living, not as the "Greatest Heavy Weight Champion of all Times," nor as a courageous political activist, nor as a lightning rod member of the Nation of Islam, nor as an undefeatable enemy of White supremacy, but as a "spirit being" who represented and reflected an undying African consciousness and Black identity that, like an Ifa Orisa or Vodun Lwa, represents the illumination of African spiritness.

Now I want to frame Ali as *Skh*. This is consistent with Ifa tradition where it is noted that human beings became Orisas through their great knowledge and luminous powers. The Odu Ifa in the Odu Owonrinwese explains that

> human beings become Orisa.
>   I said, human beings become Orisa. Orunmila said, don't you see Obatala? He was a human being,
>   But when he became wise and powerful He became Orisa

Orunmila said, human beings become Orisa. I said, human beings become Orisa.
Orunmila said, don't you see Sango? He was a human being,
But he became wise and powerful, He became Orisa.[8]

In discussing Orisas as archetypes, Alex Cuoco (2014: 817) notes that the Orisa Vodun (invisible living energy/forces) is the conscious and/or unconscious constant presence in the everyday lives of people. He asserts that all actions and reactions, all behaviors, characteristics, likes and dislikes, our personalities and peculiarities are an indirect effect of the deity within us. Everything we do or say and every thought that crosses our minds has a direct connection with an Orisa and each person's individual Orí. It is, to the contrary, my contention that we are not just connected to these spirit forces but also the expression of a particular spirit force or essence. We are not simply spiritual. We are totally spirit.

In conversation with the Araba of Osogbo, Nigeria, Baba Ifayemi Elebuibon (February 2020), it was determined that the forces in the invisible realm (Egbe Orun) or spirit companions of heaven along with an Orisa for Muhammad Ali was (is) Sango. As universal manifestation of spirit, energy, or force, Sango is a "knowing and knowable spirit" that possesses the attributes, qualities, and characteristics of "Thunder and Lightning" in the concentrated form of courage, resourcefulness, obsessiveness, energetic, explosive, ambivalent, exuberance, preparedness, intelligence, wit, power, majestic, courageous, humorous, fertile, and procreative/sexuality (Cuoco, 2014: 682). With the Egbe Orun in heaven and Sango as his Orisa, Ali's "knowing and knowable spirit" represents the Orisa of Opposites (double axe), the spirit force of thunder and lightning.

Many suggest that Malcolm X was the singular influence that guided Ali's entry into the Nation of Islam and deeper Black consciousness. The length of this chapter will, however, not allow for a full and exhaustive discussion about their brotherhood (Roberts and Smith, 2016). What should be noted is that the spirit companions of heaven along with the Orisa for Malcom X was (is) Obatala. Obatala is a "knowing and knowable spirit" that possesses the attributes, qualities, and characteristics of the Orisa of "Rightness and Wisdom" in the concentrated forms of purity, benevolence, trusting, responsible, stubborn, obstinate, good willed, moral, humble, judgmental, and peace (Cuoco, 2014: 836).

What then is really known of Muhammad Ali and Malcolm X's spiritness? Ali and Malcolm X met in 1962, and Malcolm quickly became Ali's friend and Jegna.[9] Malcom X was assassinated in 1965. Their three-year friendship was no less than a whirlwind of African American history. They met at a historic Saviours' Day celebration (Malcolm was the opening speaker) in 1962 in Chicago, where George Lincoln Rockwell, founder of the American Nazi Party, was invited to address the Nation of Islam members and was booed and heckled. A year later, Malcolm X was asked for a comment about the assassination of President John F. Kennedy. Malcolm X said that it was a case of "chickens coming home to roost." He added that "chickens coming home to roost never did make me sad; they've always made me glad." The *New York Times* (1963) wrote, in further discussing President Kennedy's assassination around the "chickens coming home to roost" statement, Malcolm cited the murders of Patrice Lumumba, Congo leader

(1961), and of Medgar Evers, a civil rights leader, on June 12, 1963, and, three months later, the bombing of four little Black girls (1963) in a Birmingham church. These, he said, were instances of other "chickens coming home to roost." On February 25, 1964, the underdog Cassius Clay, age 22, defeated the champion Sonny Liston in a technical knockout to win the world heavyweight boxing crown. Upon his unexpected win, he declared, "I'm the greatest! I shook up the world!" Malcolm X was at ringside. The next morning, at the traditional day, after press conference, Cassius Clay told reporters that henceforth he would be known as Cassius X, and a month later, he was given the name Muhammad Ali, which would become world famous. A year later, Malcolm was assassinated.

Embedding this time line in the "tone of the times" reveals a whirlwind of activities. What was the ideational atmosphere, as vibrating/radiating energy, that shaped this time? What was the particular vibrating/radiating energy (tone) of the spirit talk found in the vibrating knowing and knowable energy of this particular ideational atmosphere as knowing and knowable spirit? In 1959, Malcolm X took his first trip to Africa. Traveling as an ambassador for the Nation of Islam and with a passport issued in his new name, Malik el-Shabazz, he visited Sudan, Nigeria, and Egypt—and a few months later Ghana, Syria, and Saudi Arabia. Malik el-Shabazz (Malcolm) was well versed in Sudanese history, with a particular interest in Nubian civilization and Muhammad al-Mahdi, as a Black anti-colonial figure. Malcolm X's sojourn in Sudan seems to have been formative, leaving an imprint as part of Malcolm's tone and may have influenced Muhammad Ali. On January 17, 1961, Patrice Lumumba was assassinated. Approximately 13 months after Lumumba's assassination (February 25, 1962), Ali met Malcolm. A year and a half later, on September 15, 1963, four little Black girls were bombed in a church in Alabama. Two months later, on November 22, 1963, John Fitzgerald Kennedy, the 35th president of the United States was assassinated. Malcolm declared (December 1, 1963) that this represented that the "chickens are coming home to roost" and was prohibited from speaking publicly by Elijah Muhammad for 90 days. Just 14 months later, on February 25, 1964, Cassius Clay became the heavyweight champion of the world. The next day he announced he was Muhammad Ali.[10] On March 8, 1964, Malcolm X publicly announced his break from the Nation of Islam. Less than a year later (February 19, 1965), Malcolm X was assassinated.

As is well known, when notified of his draft status, Muhammad Ali declared that he would refuse to serve in the U.S. army and publicly considered himself a conscientious objector. He stated that "war is against the teachings of the Holy Qur'an" and that he was not trying to dodge the draft. On April 28, 1967, with the United States at war in Vietnam, Ali refused to be inducted into the armed forces, saying, "I ain't got no quarrel with those Vietcong They never called me nigger." Two months later, on June 20, 1967, Ali was convicted of draft evasion, sentenced to five years in prison, fined $10,000, and banned from boxing for three years.

During the above-mentioned lightning-speed "tone time," what was the spirit talk between Muhammad Ali as Sango and Malcolm X as Obatala? Ali as *Skh* expressed the essentiality-of-being as a knowing and knowable vibrational energy (spirit). Muhammad Ali's action (conduct) in placing his reputation, wealth, and freedom at stake can be understood as an expression (thunder, lightning in the concentrated form of courage, preparedness, intelligence, power, and majesty) of the essence of his Orisa, Sango.

Putting Ali's life and living, as embedded in a particular ideational atmosphere, allows us to see how the vibrational energy (spirit) surrounding his living can be seen as the "tone of that time"[11] or ideational atmosphere. What was the ideational atmosphere, as vibrating/radiating, knowing and knowable energy, that shaped Muhammad Ali? More accurately what was the "tone" (particular vibrating/radiating energy) of the spirit talk found in the vibrating knowing and knowable energy of the "tone time" (ideational atmosphere) that was in conversation with Ali's knowing and knowable spirit? The intellectuals and artists like Langston Hughes, James Weldon Johnson, Richard Wright, Claude McKay, W. E. B. Du Bois, Marcus Garvey, Cheikh Anta Diop, Léopold Sédar Senghor, Aimé Césaire, Léon-Gontran Damas, Frantz Fanon, Marvin Gaye, James Brown, Miriam Makeba, B. B. King, and the Spinners can or should be thought of as the "tone makers" of this time that made up the resonant (historical) energy ideational atmosphere that influenced Malcolm and through him Muhammad Ali. What then are the essential ideas of these intellectuals, artists, and thinkers and how do they resonate with and activate the knowing and knowable spirit? Rabaka (2009: 154) notes that the so-called Negritude poets along with the radicals of the Harlem Renaissance advocated, in common, for the idea that persons of African descent "return to or rather rediscover the teachings and texts, logic(s), and lessons of their ancestors in order to provide interpretations, clarifications, and solutions to the conceptual puzzles that confront Africans, as well as, others in the present." Malcolm's arsenal of intellectual insight had to be nurtured by the tone of his time, and his many conversations with Muhammad Ali must have been seasoned with the banquet (Du Bois, Garvey, Senghor, Césaire, Fanon, Elijah, Malcolm, Betty Shabazz) of Black thought. Identifying the above-mentioned "tone makers" and the presence of the Egbe Orun and Orisas clearly support the recognition that Muhammad Ali (and all of us) could be thought of as a "spirit being" living in a reality of spirit.

In recognizing that there were many contributors to the tone of the time or even moment(s), we should recognize that the subject of this chapter and the entire book, Muhammad Ali, as a "spirit being," was not alone. His spirit was in constant conversation with an orchestra of spirit-driven inputs. His entire professional support team, the cadre of entertainers, friends, family, and advisors, was all the unknown sources of spirit talk with Muhammad Ali. And this is not unique to Muhammad Ali. Each and every one of us is a "spirit being," and according to Ifa tradition, each of us comes from heaven (the invisible realm) having an Egbe Orun, an Orisa, and an agreement with the Divine All to be on a particular path and purpose. We just don't know it. Think about this. Have there been times when you had a thought but did not know where it came from? You may have made or designed or fixed something and could not say how you did it or what was the source of your creativity? Can you remember the instance where you were looking for some lost thing and found some other thing that was just what you needed? All of these instances, and untold others, can be better understood as the fact that you were being guided by your "knowing and knowable spirit."

As two "spirit beings" with "knowing and knowable spirits," the relationship between these two men deserves further analyses. What was the concentrated energy in distinct forms with particular intelligence, attributes, qualities, and characteristics that represented the metabolic transformation of Muhammad Ali's very being? How did the spirit companions of heaven (Egbe Orun in the invisible realm) along with their personal Orisas guide and influence Muhammad Ali as Sango and Malcom X as Obatala?

Through the "episteme of the invisible," Ali's own words and deeds reveal that he was *Skh* (illumination) and driven (like all of us) by the invisible ones. A few of the significant events in Ali's life are informative. There were a lot of factors associated with why Malcolm left the Nation and Ali didn't. Placed between what some would call the "blood feud" between Malcolm and Elijah (Roberts and Smith, 2016) where Elijah declared Malcolm to be a hypocrite, which he taught was the most hated by God, Ali was at the vortex of a major historical split. The day after he took the infamous army entrance exam, on his way to meet with Elijah Muhammad, Ali was assaulted with questions about his relationship with Malcolm X. Ali answered by saying, "Muhammad taught Malcolm X everything he knows so I couldn't go with the child, I go with the daddy."

The most talked-about issue was Malcolm's revelation about the Honorable Elijah Muhammad's extramarital affairs with his young secretaries. The attractants and performance of sexual intimacies and intrigues should not be judged by Judeo-Christian-Islamic ethics, even though all three, Elijah, Malcolm, and Muhammad, presented themselves as devout Muslims. A clearer understanding may be found through the lens of the science of the spirit. Malcolm is a child of Obatala and Ali a child of Sango. Each of these Orisas, as knowing and knowable spirits, would guide the interpretation and actions relative to the same event differently. As a child of Obatala, whose attributes, qualities, and characteristics are rightness, purity, trustworthy, moral, and so on, Malcolm as an Obatala spirit force would find Elijah's actions intolerable and unforgiving. Ali, however, as an Omo (child of) Sango spirit force would have seen the event differently. Ali's governing spirit/energy with women (three young wives) was aligned with Sango (three wives), whose attributes, qualities, and characteristics are majestic, courageous, procreative/sexual, and ambivalent. At best, Ali may have mentally struggled with knowing about these sexual liaisons, but would not have seen Elijah's infidelity (with multiple young secretaries) as problematic.

As revealed (expressed) by the character, conduct, and consciousness of his Orisa, Sango, Muhammad Ali's unseen spirit force would guide the choices made and chances taken that are hallmark and vintage Ali speech. Ali, for instance, said, "If you even dream of beating me, you'd better wake up and apologize" or "I've wrestled with alligators. I've tussled with a whale. I done handcuffed lightning and thrown thunder in jail." He once said, "I'm so fast that last night I turned off the light switch in my hotel room and was in bed before the room was dark." These should not be seen as colorful poetic quips that are meant to "play to the camera." Interpreted from the "episteme of the invisible," wherein the accumulation of all spirit energy, moral intellectual, or genetic potentialities demonstrates one being in touch with making the impossible possible. Muhammad Ali's daughter, Hana Yasmeen Ali, also noted that her father recognized that "spirituality is recognizing the divine light that is within us all. It doesn't belong to any particular religion; it belongs to everyone." What Ali was calling "divine light" are the forces in Egbe Orun (the companions in the invisible realm). Ali also said, "Service to others is the rent you pay for your room here on earth." A recognition that what one does in one realm of reality is connected to what happens in the other realm of reality.

Around the time of his death, Muhammad Ali's, friend and one-time rival in their historic fight in 1974, George Foreman, in an NPR (2016) interview, said, "A giant tree just fell and Muhammad Ali—there'll never be another." Foreman went on to say,

> What I learned from Muhammad Ali is that he [...] had a cause. He really had a cause. He left a legacy that for all athletes—I heard him say that he wanted to be more than just a boxer. The man was a great man beyond anything as far as color. [...] I've traveled the world and people have whispered in my ear from every corner of the earth Ali, Ali. He was the greatest. He was the greatest, and they knew who he was. When you say the word Ali, it would do something to your heart and make you feel a certain thing.

George Foreman's testimony actually tapped into the science of the spirit where an inner force (Bo) represents the potentiality of all human action to uncover the hidden potentiality of all things, that is, to do good because it is good to do good. One of Ali's fiercest rivals, Foreman recognized that Ali "would do something to your heart and make you feel a certain way." Could that "something to your heart" be a knowing and knowable spirit recognizing a knowing and knowable spirit?

In discussing the animosity between his father, Joe Frazer, and Ali, whom he always referred to as Mr. Ali, Marvis Frazer discussed how his father was deeply hurt by Ali's name calling (Uncle Tom, Gorilla, ugly, can't talk, etc.) even though for Ali it was part of the "show." Marvis noted that in the end, before his father passed, the two giants did come together with love and respect and the "oneness of spirit." Amid all the chatter and diatribes of the time, Ali and Joe Frazer's special friendship can be fully understood only through spirit. Our spirit knows how to speak the truth even when our minds, mouths, and chatter (hype) of the times can't articulate what we really mean. Marvis understood, though he wouldn't state it this way, that as two "spirit beings," Joe Frazer and Muhammad Ali loved and respected each other and were one in spirit.

Malcolm X's daughter, Ambassador Attallah Shabazz, can shed additional light on this particular split. At Muhammad Ali's funeral, Attallah spoke about her long, deeply paternal, and loving relationship with Muhammad Ali. She ended her remarks by pointing out that her dad would often state when concluding parting: "'May we meet again in the light of understanding' and I say to you with the light of that compass, 'by any means necessary.'" In her significant, profound, and moving remarks, she connected Malcolm and Muhammad by simply pointing to the light (illumination) that couldn't be broken by any religion or organization. A light that was them.

In discussing the special significance of her father, Laila Ali recalled that once when her father visited their home, three years after his divorce from Veronica, her mother greeted him; she started to cry and left the room. Ali asked what was wrong with her, and when she went into the room and asked her mother about it, her mother said, "Well, I looked in his eyes and I saw God." At the most, deepest esoteric level, the eyes are not just the mirror of the soul. The eyes are a window to physical insight of the sight (vision) of a divine "spirit being." We are expressions of the Divine All. Veronica's crying should be thought of as a response to see Ali's *Skh*.

While on the Arsenio Hall talk show (I Am Ali, *StarzEncore*, 2014) with Muhammad Ali, Mike Tyson, and Sugar Ray Leonard as guests, Arsenio asked if at his prime, could Muhammad Ali win the fight between Ali and Tyson. Tyson responded by saying he has an ego and knows that he is a great fighter, but "every head must bow and every tongue must confess," and pointing to Muhammad, he said, "This is the greatest of all times." I think Mike Tyson was not just referring to Ali's fighting skill. He, like others, could speak only in the language of our limited material education, but Mike's "knowing and knowable spirit" knew more.

As a "spirit being," Muhammad Ali, as a case example, expressed the essentiality-of-being a knowing and knowable vibrational energy (spirit). Muhammad Ali served to bring, shape, and share light (illuminate) to the spirit of his time.

Muhammad Ali was (and still is) *Skh*. In summary, however, I wish to caution the reader that the limitations of our training and education, grounded in the Western grand narrative that privileges separateness, opposition, and individuality, make our likelihood to default to Western historiography and read this discussion as if it is only about Muhammad Ali. It is not. Muhammad Ali, as a *Skh*, is a case study that, hopefully, reveals a deeper African-centered understanding of ourselves. As *Skh*, our illumination is the light (energy/spirit/force) that shapes and shares (sometimes subliminally and subtly, sometimes loud and startling) what we bring to the world (reality).

We are all *Skh* (illumination).

Notes

1 The Sakhu-historical analysis is grounded in African-centered historiography and was created and used in the first Black psychological (unfiltered by Western thought) analyses of the architects of the Haitian revolution, *The Island of Memes: Haiti's Unfinished Revolution*.

2 Spiritness pertains to the condition of actually being spirit and not the quality of having a spirit. Spiritness is the energy, force, or power that is both the inner essence and the outer envelope of being. As energy, spirit becomes "spiritness" and therein serves to ignite and enliven the human state of being.

3 Bântu people inhabit most of the continent of Africa and historically were the founders of highly developed sociocultural and political entities ranging from the rain forests of West and Central Africa to the plains and Kalahari Desert of Southern Africa.

4 The closest way to understand this in Western thought is found in physics, where we know that every material thing/object is really energy vibrating at different levels or speed and thereby takes on the qualities of a stone or tree or ice or elephant.

5 The *Àṣẹ* of a particular Orisa or Lwa is within each and every one. It is generally activated by initiation. The Orisas or Lwas, as knowing and knowable living energy, can and do self-activate. While it may be difficult to prove with Western empirical research methods, it is highly likely that Muhammad Ali's poetic verse, boasting, and fight predictions were empowered with the unknown (by him and others) power of *Àṣẹ*.

6 To determine if African understandings of vibration and energies operate on an Einsteinian, quantum, or sub-quantum level would involve a synthesis of knowledge from esoteric African

traditions and cutting-edge physics and medicine, interesting work for the scholars up to the challenge.

7 In ancient Kmt the definition of the human being emphasized the primacy of the person that has a soul comprised of seven dimensions. The dimensions of the soul are Ka, Ba, Khaba, Akhu, Seb, Putah, and Atmu.

8 The Araba of Osogbo recorded that "Eni to gbon nni won mbo o" (the wise ones become an Orisa to be propitiated).

9 We choose to use the African term "Jegna" instead of the Greek "mentor." Jegna (Jegnoch— plural form) are those special people who have been tested in struggle or battle; demonstrated extraordinary and unusual fearlessness; shown determination and courage in protecting their people, land, and culture; shown diligence and dedication to our people; produced exceptionally high-quality work; and dedicated themselves to the protection, defense, nurturance, and development of our young by advancing our people, place, and culture. Malcolm fits the meaning of Jegna more so than that of mentor.

10 There were of course the confused and the naysayers. When Ali called himself Cassius X, Martin Luther King Jr. charged that "Ali has become the champion of racial segregation and that is what we are fighting." Floyd Patterson condemned Ali as being unfit to be the champion.

11 Tone is most often understood to mean a particular pitch pattern on a syllable used to make semantic distinctions on a word and/or the degree of difference in the intensity of something.

References

Abímbolá, Kolá. 2006. *Yorùbá Culture: A Philosophical Account*. Birmingham, UK: I{rókò Academic.

Akbar, N. 1985. "Nile Valley Origins of the Science of the Mind," *Journal of African Civilizations*, Video.

Ali, M., and Hana Yasmeen. 2002. *Ali. The Soul of a Butterfly: Reflections on Life's Journey*. New York: Simon & Schuster.

Ani, Marimba. 1994. *Yurugu: An African-Centered Critique of European Cultural Thought and Behavior*. Trenton, NJ: Africa World.

Carruthers, J. H. 1985. *The Irritated Genie: An Essay on the Haitian Revolution and Intellectual Warfare*. Chicago: Kemetic Institute.

Cuoco, A. 2014. African *Narratives of Orishas, Spirits and Other Deities: Stories from West Africa and the African Diaspora: A Journey into the Realm of Deities, Spirits, Mysticism, Spiritual Roots and Ancestral Wisdom*. Denver, CO: Outskirts Press.

Delaney, M. 2008. "Pan African Metaphysical Epistemology: A Pentagonal Introduction," *Journal of Pan African Studies*, vol. 2, no. 3 (March): 221

Diop, Cheikh Anta. 1974. *The African Origin of Civilization: Myth or Reality*. Chicago: Lawrence Hill.

Drewal, M. T. 1992. *Yoruba Ritual Performers, Play, Agency*. Bloomington: Indiana University Press, 21.

Elebuibon, Femi. 1999. *Ìyèrè Ifa: An Exposition of Yorùbá Divinational Chants*. Bernardino, CA: Ilé Orunmila Communications.

Elebuibon, Ifeyemi, Araba of Òsobo. 2020. Personal Communication, March 7.

Foreman G. 2016. "There Will Never Be Another: George Foreman Remembers Muhammad Ali," Obituaries, Copyright © NPR.

Fu-Kiau, Kimbwandende Kia Bunseki. 2001. *African Cosmology of the Bantu-Kongo Tying the Spiritual Knot Principles of Life and Living*, 14, 34, 70, 132. Brooklyn, NY: Athelia Henrietta.

New York Times. 1963. "Malcolm X Scores U.S. and Kennedy; Likens Slaying to 'Chickens Coming Home to Roost' Newspapers Chided." December 2. https://www.nytimes.com/1963/12/02/archives/malcolm-x-scores-us-and-kennedy-likens-slaying-to-chickens-coming.html.

Nobles, Vera L. 1996. "Ebonics: The Retention of African Tongues." In M. J. Shujaa and K. J. Shujaa (eds.), *Encyclopedia of African Cultural Heritage in North America*. Thousand Oaks, CA: Sage.

Nobles, Wade W. 2002. "From Na Ezaleli to the Jegnoch: The Force of the African Family for Black Men in Higher Education," *Making It on Broken Promises African American Male Scholars Confront the Culture of Higher Education.* Sterling, VA: Stylus.

Nobles, Wade W. 2013. "Shattered Consciousness, Fractured Identity: Black Psychology and the Restoration of the African Psyche," *Journal of Black Psychology*, vol. 39, no. 3: 232, 239.

Nobles, Wade W. 2015. *The Island of Memes: Haiti's Unfinished Revolution.* Baltimore, MD: Black Classic..

Nobles, Wade W., Lesiba Baloyi, and Tholene Sodi. 2016. "Pan African Humanness and Sakhu Djaer as Praxis for Indigenous Knowledge System," *Alternation: Interdisciplinary Journal for the Study of Arts and Humanities in South Africa*, Special Edition, vol. 18: 36–59.

Nobles, Wade W., and Nhlanhla Mkhize. 2020. "The Charge and the Challenge of Illuminating the Spirit (*Skh Djr*): The Question of Paradigm, Episteme and Terminology for Therapy and Treatment." In Nhlanlha Mkize (ed.), *Alternation: Interdisciplinary Journal for the Study of Arts and Humanities in South Africa*, University of KwaZulu-Natal, 239.

Nkulu-N'Sengha, M. 2005. "African Epistemology." In Molefi Asante and Ama Mazama (eds.), *Encyclopedia of Black Studies.* Thousand Oaks, CA: Sage, 39–44.

Rabaka, R. 2009. *African Critical Theory: Reconstructing the Black Radical Tradition, from W.E.B. DuBois and C. L. R. James to Frantz Fanon and Amicar Cabral.* New York: Lexington Books, Rowman & Littlefield.

Ramose, M. B. 2002. "The Philosophy of Ubuntu as a Philosophy." In P. H. Coetzee and A. P. J. Roux (eds.), *Philosophy from Africa: A Text with Readings.* New York: Oxford University Press.

Roberts, R., and Johnny Smith. 2016. *Blood Brothers: The Fatal Friendship between Muhammad Ali and Malcolm X.* Philadelphia, PA: Basic Books, Perseus Book Group.

Somé, Malidoma Patrice. 1997. *Ritual Power, Healing and Community.* New York: Penguin Compass, 30.

Sonyinka, W. 1990. "The African World and the Ethnocultural Debate." In Molefi K. Asante and Kariamu Welsh Asante (eds.), *African Culture: The Rhythms of Unity.* Westport, CT: Greenwood, 13–38.

Chapter Five

LET US MAKE A MAN: MUHAMMAD ALI'S REEDUCATION THROUGH CRITICAL BLACK PEDAGOGY

Abul A. Pitre, Ruby Holden-Pitre, and Natalie Williamson

Muhammad Ali is widely known as the people's champ and considered the greatest boxer of all time. As the heavyweight boxing champion of the world, Ali's athletic prowess put him in the world spotlight, but it was his advocacy for equal justice for Blacks in America that distinguished him. This chapter offers a brief historical discussion of the Nation of Islam as well as Muhammad Ali's development into a fighter for equal justice. It uses the concept of critical Black pedagogy—encompassing Afrocentricity, multicultural education, critical pedagogy, and African American spirituality—to understand Muhammad Ali's reeducation through the teachings of Elijah Muhammad. Throughout the chapter, Elijah Muhammad takes center stage to demonstrate the power of proper education in transforming one's life.

Introduction

Muhammad Ali's journey to greatness is well known. He was the world's greatest boxer and a fervent defender of equal rights. What is less known is the role that Elijah Muhammad, the leader of the Nation of Islam, played in that journey. If writers on Ali's life mention Elijah Muhammad at all, it is to downplay his influence or portray him as a negative force in the development of Muhammad Ali. This chapter offers a counternarrative to the mainstream narratives. It attempts to dislodge the majoritarian narrative that hides the impact of Elijah Muhammad's teachings on the evolution of Muhammad Ali's becoming a warrior for equal justice. To those attempting to write Elijah Muhammad out of history, Ali said:

> I see everybody's picture on the wall but Elijah Muhammad's. I see Rap Brown. I see Huey Newton, Eldridge Cleaver, Martin Luther King, Abernathy. I see Muhammad Ali, H. Stokely Carmichael. You don't see Elijah Muhammad's picture up there as someone who has done something for black people. He's done more in every city for feeding and clothing and changing pimp-players and wineheads. They don't put his picture on the wall. […] Anybody around will admit that the Muslims are the most unified and the cleanest people in the country. But he's one leader that you're never told about. (*Black Scholar*, 1970, p. 20)

This chapter attempts to rectify that neglect. It first introduces the Nation of Islam and Elijah Muhammad, then moves on to address Muhammad Ali and the influence that Elijah Muhammad had on his life and his journey to become an advocate for equal justice, and finally discusses critical Black pedagogy and how education was the cornerstone of Ali's evolution from Clay to Muhammad Ali.

Elijah Muhammad and the Nation of Islam

Elijah Poole was the son of a Baptist minister, born in 1897 in the Sandersville, Georgia, area. Appalled by the horrendous living conditions of the Deep South, he moved his family to Hamtramck, Michigan, in hopes of finding better living conditions (Clegg, 2014). With only a fourth-grade education, he was unable to find employment and as a result resorted to drinking. On several occasions he would be too drunk to find his way home, causing his wife, Clara, to go in search of him. Frustrated and defeated by the oppressive conditions that prevailed for Blacks in America, he was often found in an alley too drunk to return home.

The hopes of a better life were not materializing as Elijah had planned, and Clara urged him to attend one of the lectures by Mr. Fard, hoping it might give him a glimmer of hope. Wallace D. Fard (also known as Master Fard Muhammad) had founded the Nation of Islam in the 1930s in Detroit, Michigan. As the son of a Baptist minister, and a devout Christian, Elijah Poole had no interest in hearing about Islam. But in 1931 he went to hear Mr. Fard speak (Muhammad, 1996). While listening to Mr. Fard, he reflected on his understanding of biblical scripture and saw Mr. Fard as the second coming of Jesus. Speaking about this initial experience, he said, "Finally I met him. When I looked at him, it just came to me that this is the Son of Man which the Bible prophesied would come in the last days" (Hakim, 1997, p. 36).

When the lecture concluded, he went over to shake hands with Mr. Fard, and while doing so whispered into his ear, "You are the one that the Bible prophesied will come at the end of the world." Mr. Fard whispered back, "Yes, I am the one, but who knows that except yourself? Be quiet" (Hakim, 1997, p. 36). Thus began a close relationship between the two men. Over the next three years and six months, he taught Elijah from sunrise to sunrise something about everything in the universe (Hakim, 1997; Muhammad, 1996). Before Fard's departure, he conferred on Elijah the last name Muhammad. Thus, Elijah Muhammad began his journey as the Messenger of Allah, and for the next 41 years, he would lead the Nation of Islam, transforming the lives of countless people. Herbert Berg (2009), in his book *Elijah Muhammad and Islam*, wrote that he had done more to spread Islam in America than any person to date, despite the fact that most people know more about his students Muhammad Ali, Malcolm X, Imam Warith D. Mohammed, and Minister Louis Farrakhan.

Elijah Muhammad's impact has not yet been completely realized because it extends beyond the formal members of the Nation of Islam to other people who do not attend a mosque. For example, Clarence 13X, the founder of the Five Percenters, left the building where the Nation of Islam held its meetings but kept its teachings embedded in his heart, causing him to take those teachings to the youth in the street. Today the Five Percenters have come to play a major role in raising the consciousness of youth through rap music (Allah, 2007).

A careful study of Elijah Muhammad's books, articles, and speeches will reveal his contributions to many areas of knowledge (including astrobiology and neuro-science; Hakim, 1997; Muhammad, 2012). But his greatest work was the building of human potential through reeducation. This reeducation was affected by the applica-tion of critical pedagogy to the education of Black people. Critical pedagogy has many characteristics, but the primary tenet is to use education as a tool to empower those who suffer from oppression. Peter McLaren (2015) says of it, "Critical pedagogy is a reading and an acting upon social reality by abstract things into a material force for liberation by helping abstract thought lead to praxis, to revolutionary praxis to the bringing about of a social universe that is not based on the value form of labor and financial gain but based on human need" (p. 29). Paulo Freire's (1970) classic book *Pedagogy of the Oppressed* became the foundational text for educational scholars who study critical pedagogy. The book addressed the role of schooling in domesticating those from historically under-served groups. It discussed how education could be used to keep people in a social space for benefiting those ruling the society. This coincided with the way schooling in America works to domesticate the masses of students. Chomsky (2000) noted that the primary role of schooling was to indoctrinate the youth for the benefit of the ruling group. Molefi Asante (2005) similarly stated, "I cannot honestly say that I have ever found a school in the United States run by whites that adequately prepares black children to enter the world as sane human beings" (p. 65).

Today prominent theoretical constructs like critical race theory and critical whiteness studies have similarities to Elijah Muhammad's teachings (Ignatiev, 1996; Leonardo, 2009; Delgado and Stefancic, 2017).

The now well-known tenets of critical race theory—including the permanence of racism, interest convergence, and the ideology of citizenship—were all part of the teachings of Elijah Muhammad (D. Muhammad, 2016). In his classic book *Message to the Blackman in America*, Elijah Muhammad (1965) deconstructs the term *citizenship* pointing out that it is defined as anyone not belonging to aboriginal people. Through the dictionary's definition during that era, he argues that Blacks in America could not be citizens, contending that integration was a trick. His study of history convinced him that there has never been a case in history where the slave was made the equal of his master. Unfortunately, most writers have not studied the teachings of Elijah Muhammad, and even many Black writers are the epitome of what Carter G. Woodson described as miseducated because they have been taught to view the world from a Eurocentric lens (Muhammad, 1996). The education of oppressed groups involved a deculturalization process that was designed to make non-Whites tools for those who owned the country (Watkins, 2001; Spring, 2016).

The Making of a Fighter

The ideas that Elijah Muhammad cultivated in *Message to the Blackman in America* and other writings proved to be pivotal in the development of Muhammad Ali's thinking and career. Born on January 17, 1942, in Louisville, Kentucky, under the name Cassius Clay, he was drawn to boxing after his bicycle was stolen. After telling Joe Martin, a police officer, that he wished to whip the person responsible, Mr. Martin suggested to the young Cassius that he might consider boxing. Mr. Martin trained him, and he excelled in the sport (Ali, 2018). By the age of 12 he was fully engaged in boxing but lagged behind in school. He went to Central High School in Louisville, Kentucky, and graduated 376 out of a class of 391 students (Milord, 2014)—not a promising start for someone who became known for the depth of his thinking. When asked in an interview about his education, he pointed out that he did not know the value of education (Demirel, 2016).

Clay took the world by storm at age 22 by defeating the boxing star Sonny Liston and becoming the world heavyweight champion. His shout "I am the greatest!" became the trademark of Cassius Clay, but unbeknownst to the world, Clay had begun studying Islam (whose call "Allah is the greatest" was echoed in Clay's motto). He had begun studying Islam under the tutelage of Captain Sam X, later known as Abdul Rahman, who had been privately tutoring Clay about the teachings of Elijah Muhammad (R. Muhammad, 2016; Zirin, 2017). While most writers refer to Malcolm X as being the person that most influenced Clay, it was actually the teachings of Elijah Muhammad that transformed Clay, and he soon took on the new name Muhammad Ali (D. Muhammad, 2016; R. Muhammad, 2016). Farrakhan summarizes it best when he stated, "We can't talk about Cassius Clay or Muhammad Ali or Malcolm X without talking about Elijah Muhammad because there wasn't nobody in America giving out X's and giving people names but Elijah, Elijah Muhammad" (R. Muhammad, 2016).

Ali stated that studying the teachings of Elijah Muhammad made him appreciate knowledge. He said he never imagined that he would be on the world stage with a knowledge that was like that of the prophets and great thinkers of history. Speaking about the value of knowledge, he poetically stated, "Where is a man's wealth, his wealth is in his knowledge, for if his wealth is in the bank and not in his knowledge, then he don't possess it because it is in the bank" (Demirel, 2016).

Richard Muhammad reflected, "There is an intentional effort to whitewash Mr. Ali's history by not mentioning the Nation of Islam patriarch who taught and bestowed an Islamic name on a young Black Muslim sports hero" (R. Muhammad, 2016). While attending Muhammad Ali's funeral, Louis Farrakhan and his entourage was surrounded by police officers, framing them as hostile forces. But Elijah Muhammad's influence cannot be denied. It was through his concept of reeducation that Elijah Muhammad made giants out of men like Muhammad Ali, Malcolm X, Warith D. Mohammed, and Louis Farrakhan.

For the most part, Muhammad Ali has been commercialized and sanitized to make him more palatable to the interests of the White ruling class. But as a member of the Nation of Islam, Ali shook up the White world with a body of knowledge that did not originate from them. His reeducation through the teachings of Elijah Muhammad transformed him into the heavyweight champion for the liberation of oppressed people. It was his cry for equal justice for Blacks in America that made him more than just a boxer. This transformation began when he officially became a member of the Nation of Islam in 1964 and then received the name Muhammad Ali from Elijah Muhammad shortly thereafter. The Nation of Islam is not an organization that you can just sign up to join, but its members are required to take up study. Through studying they are then required to complete exams that demonstrate a basic knowledge of the Nation's teachings. This knowledge includes the origin of the universe, the knowledge of God, and the knowledge of self. It is a rigorous curriculum, and Ali had the dedication to see it through.

Giving up his slave name of Cassius Clay and accepting the name Muhammad Ali represented what Paulo Freire described as dislodging the oppressor consciousness that resides in the oppressed. Freire (1970) wrote that the oppressed have often internalized the oppressor consciousness to such a degree that they are afraid to seek freedom. Grounded in a universal knowledge, Ali was confident, and this made him not only a boxer but a "Man" who frustrated White interviewees because they could not defeat his arguments. While the masses were listening to persons like Muhammad Ali and Malcolm X, behind the scenes Elijah Muhammad had been teaching and influencing them. The federal government kept Elijah Muhammad under surveillance for many years, even arresting him in 1942, obviously aware of his influence among his followers. Ali's reeducation with the Nation of Islam was the foundation for his refusal to be drafted by the US armed forces in the Vietnam War. Ali famously stated that he did not have any quarrels with the Vietnamese. Ali was not talking jive but was well versed in history.

Ali's decision to join the Nation of Islam sent shock waves through the country. The Nation of Islam had been framed as a destructive force, and many news stories were fabricated that became the foundation from which scholars still write today. Two examples of this were the pieces by Alfred Balk (1963), "The Black Merchants of Hate," and by Alex Haley (1965), *The Autobiography of Malcolm X*, both of which were influenced by the FBI with the intent of portraying the Nation of Islam in a negative light (Marable cited in Pitre, 2010). Perhaps what was most disturbing about the Nation of Islam and Elijah Muhammad's teachings was their declaration that "the white man is the devil." This caused C. Eric Lincoln (1994), the author of one of the first scholarly books on the Nation of Islam, to declare that these teachings were repugnant. Lincoln's summation should not be shocking because it represents how many people feel when they hear something that shakes their beliefs. Schooled in a White world in which education is a form of domestication, scholars would certainly be shocked to hear the White man is the devil. But when Elijah Muhammad used the term "devil," he was using it as a kind of technical term for any object that is grafted from an original (Muhammad, 1993). Scientists who study genetics clearly know that through grafting you can get different-colored species; it is in this sense that Elijah Muhammad used the word "devil," to indicate grafting.

Muhammad Ali's transformation into an intellectual giant was part of the resurrection process. When Elijah Muhammad was asked about his mission, he said it was the resurrection of the dead. Resurrection meant raising the Blacks in America to a new level of consciousness, one that would give birth to their creative genius. Through this creative genius they would be able to overthrow the oppressor consciousness that had made them beings for a White power structure, but they would also become acquainted with the divine force within.

Orthodox Muslims and Islamic scholars point out that Elijah Muhammad was not teaching Islam. They contend that he was teaching shirk because God could not come in the form of a person and that Islam does not see race (Fardan, 2001). But this viewpoint ignores that it was Islam at the core of Elijah Muhammad's teachings that made the Nation of Islam a problem for the ruling group. Elijah Muhammad taught that Islam means peace and that a Muslim is one who submits entirely to the will of God. To submit to the will of God required studying and putting into practice the five pillars of Islam. Praying five times a day would keep evil tendencies away—a form of washing. Fasting became an exercise to exert self-control over the lower appetites, allowing adherents to throw off the savage culture that depicted women as sex objects, to throw down their liquor bottles, and to feed themselves on the intoxicating words that came through the prophets and messengers. A new diet cleansed the body, put to death the reptilian brain, and allowed practitioners to utilize more fully power of the human mind. They would then become more Christ-like because they would have cleaned their vessel and could now hear the voice of God resonating within. The adherents of these teaching would have grown into what Imam Warith D. Mohammed (1975) describes as the "divine mind" through their study of the scriptures.

After the death of Elijah Muhammad in 1975, Muhammad Ali initially followed the leadership of Imam Warith D. Mohammed, the son of Elijah Muhammad. Imam Warith D. Mohammed, a brilliant theologian and scholar, led the Nation of Islam to what is sometimes called *Chrislam*, a theological point of view that connects Christianity, the Nation of Islam's teachings, and Orthodox Islam. His article "The Coming of the Son of Man, Part 1" (Mohammed, 1975) speaks to this transition. Ali eventually transitioned to the path of Sunni Islam, but his advocacy for Black people and against oppression that had been nurtured by the Nation's teachings never waned. His practice of Islam continued to be feared and disruptive because he was critically conscious of the forces of oppression and worked to use his platform to eradicate those inequities.

Critical Black Pedagogy

The reeducation of Muhammad Ali represents the epitome of what Pitre (2019) calls a critical Black pedagogy. Critical Black pedagogy represents the critiques of education and society offered by Black thought leaders. It is grounded in the teachings of Carter G. Woodson and Elijah Muhammad. The four cornerstones of critical Black pedagogy are Afrocentricity, multicultural education, critical pedagogy, and African American spirituality.

Afrocentricity (a term coined by Molefi Asante (1991)) means viewing the world from an African or African American perspective. For Blacks in America, schooling was designed to domesticate consciousness, causing them to view the world through a Eurocentric lens. In other words, Black people would articulate and defend positions in the best interest of their oppressors. Ali's reeducation caused him to see the world not through the lens of a highly acclaimed boxer but as a fighter for his people. The boxing platform gave him the opportunity to advocate against inequality and oppression. This made him not just a boxer or sports figure but the peoples' champion.

Multicultural education involves seeing the multiple perspectives that diverse individuals might have of the world. It more deeply explores education in the context of equality and justice (Banks, 2019). Its leading scholar and founder, James Banks, began his scholarship around many of the tenets found in the teachings of the Nation of Islam. For example, Banks's (1972) book *Black Self-Concept: Implications for Education and Social Science* discusses the knowledge of self, a key tenet in Elijah Muhammad's teaching.

Muhammad Ali in the context of multicultural education was fighting for freedom, justice, and equality for Blacks and other oppressed groups in America. His Islamic journey caused him to grow into seeing the oneness of humanity. Undergirding this oneness is the principle of Islam of the *doing of good*. It was this doing of good that made Ali loved by a sea of people from different racial, ethnic, religious, and social classes. This was the objective of Elijah Muhammad's teachings to manifest in human beings the power of doing good.

Critical pedagogy involves becoming critically conscious of self and the world in which one lives and working to dismantle oppression and human suffering (Kincheloe, 2008). It is described as educating to empower those from oppressed groups (Pitre, 2019). Muhammad Ali in several pictures can be seen holding the book *Message to the Blackman in America*, a book which contains knowledge that can liberate human beings from the oppressive conditions under which they live. Muhammad Ali—equipped with the knowledge of self, the knowledge of God, and the knowledge of the time—was catapulted into stardom and considered a major influence of social thought, not just an athlete.

African American spirituality is the connection of education to spirituality. For Blacks in America, education would no longer be centered on human capitalist ideology, the belief that education should be geared toward getting a job. Education was much more than training for job—it was about touching of the soul of people. Cornel West describes it as *soul crafting:*

> It's the cultivation of thinking critically for yourself so you're willing to speak in such a way that you exercise what Socrates called *parrhesia*, which is clear speech, frank speech, fearless speech, unintimidated speech, speech that flows from your soul not to show that you're clever and smart, but to show that you're courageous and wise. (Cunningham, 2018)

Muhammad Ali embodied soul crafting, being fearless in the face of White audiences and the US government. When speaking in an interview with *Black Scholar* (1970) about going to jail because of his refusal to go to Vietnam, he poetically stated,

Hell no,
I ain't going to go
Clean out my cell
And take my tail to jail
Without bail
Because it's better there eating
Watching television fed
Than in Vietnam with your white folks dead.

It was his courageousness that caused him to place his boxing career aside to advocate for those who were living under oppressive conditions. It was this soul crafting that Ali experienced that allowed him to find a bigger purpose in life. Farrakhan similarly writes the goal of education is to help one discover their aim and purpose in life, essentially helping them to become one with their creator (Farrakhan, 1991; Pitre, 2018).

These components of critical Black pedagogy have been joined today in academia by a field called critical White studies. Scholars in critical White studies are echoing Elijah Muhammad's teachings without even knowing them. One excellent example of this is Gary Howard's (2016) book *We Can't Teach What We Don't Know: White Teachers in Multiracial Schools*. Howard credits the book's title as coming from a saying of Malcolm X. But it was not Malcolm X who originated this phrase, but Elijah Muhammad in his 1965 classic *Message to the Blackman in America*. In it, he asks the question, who is God? He noted that those who were teaching that God is a mystery were clearly unable to teach about God. For if a mystery is something unknown, how can they teach what they don't know? Elijah Muhammad made it clear that Black students could never receive a full and healthy education within the confines of White ideology.

Conclusion

Ali's reeducation was a rendezvous with destiny. The unlettered Cassius Clay met the fourth-grade-educated Elijah Muhammad, who shared with him divine knowledge, sparking in Clay—the future Muhammad Ali—the desire for more knowledge. This reeducation gave Ali the tools to articulate the needs of oppressed peoples. These teachings touched Ali's soul to the degree he became a shining light to the whole of humanity. Muhammad Ali's practice of doing good shows the potential for human beings to grow beyond physical attributes but to the stirring of the *soul*.

Muhammad Ali became "the people's champ" through his praxis of Elijah Muhammad's mission to resurrect the dead. The only way the dead could be raised was through the acquisition of knowledge because it was the lack of knowledge that rendered them dead (Muhammad, 1965). Ali's love for Blacks in America caused him to undertake study, a study that would bring him beyond the Black experience in America to one that caused him to see the unity and beauty in diversity. It is through the theoretical lens of critical black pedagogy that his life can be more deeply explored.

Throwing off his slave name of Cassius Clay, Ali was destined to eradicate the *boy* label often prescribed to Black men to become the epitome of a *man*. Farrakhan, reflecting on Elijah Muhammad's role in making men, stated:

It's about time you meet a real man. And by the way, that's why they don't want you to know Elijah because when Elijah gets ahold to you, you might have been a boy yesterday, but from the moment you come into contact with Elijah Muhammad like Malcolm X did, like Muhammad Ali did, you become a world leader. (R. Muhammad, 2016)

Ali's adoption of his new name angered many people, and for years journalists and others refused to acknowledge him as Muhammad Ali (Townsend et al., 2018). They were angered because the name Muhammad Ali represented the birthing of a human being who was critically conscious of the forces that sought to dehumanize Blacks in America. He was now striving to become more God-like by throwing off "the slave master's name." Ironically, like the *clay* described in the Holy Quran, this Clay grew into a living spirit. The Holy Quran in chapter 15, verses 28–29, refers to *clay*: "And when thy Lord said to the angels: I am going to create a mortal of sounding clay, of black mud fashioned into shape. So when I have made him complete and breathed into him of My spirit, fall down making obeisance to him." Clay transfigured the earthly chains (materialism, racism, classism, etc.) that caused human suffering and was made complete through his acquisition of knowledge that led him to the doing of good for the whole of humanity.

And while nearly every person writing about Muhammad Ali tries to discredit or distance him from the "The Most Honorable Elijah Muhammad," it was this master teacher who did the *soul crafting* or brought out the good in him, starting by giving him the name Muhammad Ali on March 6, 1964 (Townsend et al., 2018). The name Muhammad means one worthy of praise and praised much, and Ali means high, elevated, or champion. Muhammad Ali lived up to this name because he was deeply in love with his teacher. Ali credited him directly, saying that while all these accolades were going to himself and others, they were all students of a great master teacher. He admonished those who were not giving credit to the architect of their greatness. Responding to criticism of Elijah Muhammad, he made his feelings clear: "Don't find fault in the man. Because he's for you. He loves black people" (*Black Scholar*, 1970, p. 20). It was these sentiments that Ali held in the secret chamber of his heart that will forever make him one worthy of praise and one praised much and the champion of the people.

References

Ali, M. (2018, September 12). History.com. https://www.history.com/topics/black-history/muhammad-ali.

Allah, W. (2007). *In the Name of Allah: A History of Clarence 13X and the Five Percenters*. A-Team Productions.

Asante, M. (1991). "The Afrocentric idea in education." *Journal of Negro Education*, 60(2), 170–80.

———. (2005). *Race, Rhetoric, and Identity: The Architecton of Soul*. Humanity Books.

Balk, A. H. (1963, January 26). "The Black merchants of hate," *Saturday Evening Post*.

Banks, J. (1972). *Black Self-Concept: Implications for Education and Social Science*. McGraw Hill.

———. (2019). *An Introduction to Multicultural Education*, 3rd ed. Pearson.

Berg, H. (2009). *Elijah Muhammad and Islam*. New York: New York University Press.

Black Scholar (1970, June). "Muhammad Ali," 14–21.

Chomsky, N. (2000). *Chomsky on Miseducation*. Rowman & Littlefield.

Clegg, C. (2014). *The Life and Times of Elijah Muhammad*. University of North Carolina Press.

Cunningham, P. (2018, February 5). "In keynote address, Cornel West urges integrity and soul crafting." Yale News. https://news.yale.edu/2018/02/05/keynote-address-cornel-west-urges-integrity-action-and-soulcraft.

Delgado, R., and Stefancic, R. D. (2017). *Critical Race Theory: An Introduction*, 3rd ed.. New York: New York University Press.

Demirel, F. (2016, December 1). "Muhammad Ali motivational speech: The value of education." YouTube video. https://youtu.be/qR4JwjI3ldU.

Essein-Udom, E. U. (1995). *Black Nationalism: The Search for Identity*. University of Press.

Fardan, D. (2001). *Yakub and the Origins of White Supremacy: Message to the White Man and Women of America*. Lushena Books.

Farrakhan, L. (1991). *A Torchlight for America*. Final Call.

Freire, P. (1970). *Pedagogy of the Oppressed*. Continuum.

Gardell, M. (1996). *In the Name of Elijah Muhammad: Louis Farrakhan and the Nation of Islam*. Duke University Press.

Hakim, N. (ed.). (1997). *The True History of Elijah Muhammad—Messenger of Allah*. MEMPS.

Haley, A. (1965). *The Autobiography of Malcolm X*. Random House.

Howard, G. (2016). *We Can't Teach What We Don't Know: White Teachers in Multiracial Schools*, 3rd ed. Teachers College Press.

Ignatiev, N. (1996). *Race Traitor*. Routledge.

Kincheloe, J. (2008). *Critical Pedagogy*. Peter Lang.

Leonardo, Z. (2009). *Race, Whiteness, and Education*. Routledge.

Lincoln, C. E. (1994). *The Black Muslims in America*. Africa World Press.

McLaren, P. (2015). *Pedagogy of Resurrection: From Resurrection to Revolution*. Peter Lang.

Milord, J. (2014, January 17). "Float like a butterfly, sting like a bee: Lessons of success from Muhammad Ali. Elite Daily." https://www.elitedaily.com/money/float-like-butterfly-sting-like-bee-lessons-success-muhammad-ali.

Muhammad, D. (2016, June 7). "Muhammad Ali's beloved teacher, the Most Honorable Elijah Muhammad." Finalcall.com. http://www.finalcall.com/artman/publish/National_News_2/article_103144.shtml.

Muhammad, E. (1965). *Message to the Blackman in America*. UBUS Communications.

——— (1993). *History of the Nation of Islam*. Secretarius MEMPS.

——— (2012). *Ministry Class Taught by Elijah Muhammad in the 1930s*. Medina Mohammad.

Muhammad, J. (1996). *This Is the One: The Most Honored Elijah Muhammad—We Need Not Look for Another*. Book Company.

Muhammad, R. (2016, June 19). "Made by Elijah: Farrakhan speaks on the life and times of Muhammad Ali." Final Call. https://www.finalcall.com/artman/publish/National_News_2/article_103160.shtml.

Mohammed, W. (1975, December 12). "The coming of the Son of Man part I. Cleansed by the oil of divine wisdom." Bilalian News. http://www.newafricaradio.com/articles/12-12-75.html.

Pitre, A. (2010). *An Introduction to Elijah Muhammad Studies: The New Educational Paradigm*. University Press of America.

———. (2018). *Farrakhan and education* (2nd ed.). Cognella Academic Publishers.

———. (ed.) (2019). *A Critical Black Pedagogy: The Brothers Speak*. Rowman & Littlefield.

Spring, J. (2016). *Deculturalization and the Struggle for Equality: A Brief History of the Education of Dominated Cultures in the United States*. Routledge.

Townsend, S., Phillips, M., and Osmand, G. (2018). "Remembering the rejection of Muhammad Ali: Identity, civil rights and social memory." *Sport in History*, vol. 38, no. 3: 267–88, doi.10.1080/17460263.2018.1474129.

Watkins, W. (2001). *The White Architects of Black Education: Ideology and Power in America, 1865–1954*. Teachers College Press.

Zirin, D. (2017, April 24). "'Sports Illustrated' gets everything about Muhammad Ali and Malcolm X wrong." TheNation.com. https://www.thenation.com/article/archive/sports-illustrated-gets-everything-about-muhammad-ali-and-malcolm-x-wrong/.

Chapter Six

THE CHALLENGE OF RACE AND RELIGION IN THE UNITED STATES: FROM CASSIUS CLAY TO MUHAMMAD ALI

Bayyinah S. Jeffries

Muhammad Ali emerged as one of the leading Black American Muslim voices during the 1960s and 1970s. Though his affiliation with the Nation of Islam is often overlooked, his journey as a Black Muslim athlete and the challenges he faced because of his race and religion during the civil rights–Black Power era is one of the most courageous and important historical narratives of the twentieth century. Raised in the Black church, Ali aligned himself with one of the most radical Black nationalist Muslim organizations in American history, the Nation of Islam. This chapter seeks to recapture Ali's significance as both a Muslim and as a Black man.

What did it mean to be Black and Muslim in American during the late 1960s and early 1970s? How did people navigate two marginalized positions in a society where both identities could threaten one's socioeconomic opportunities and even one's life? In the wake of his passing on June 3, 2016, millions of fans gathered across the United States as a testament to one of the world's greatest athletes, Muhammad Ali, a Black man and a Muslim. Worldwide, magazine editors, newspaper columnists, and social media fans recapped his success not only as an athlete but also as a man who defied the odds and emerged victorious in his efforts in 1971 to have the US Supreme Court support his stand as the first Black Muslim conscientious objector. While the *New York Times* referred to Ali as the "Titan of Boxing," the *Washington Post* featured his most popular soundbites concerning the Vietnam War. Yet, few emphasized Ali's significances in terms of his journey for respect as a Muslim or the ways in which the intersections of race and religion situated him as an important voice for freedom of speech and religious freedom, in the late 1960s and 1970s.

Though many important works have been published on Ali, few scholars have sufficiently acknowledged the source of his work and accomplishments, his conversion to Islam, as well as the challenges he faced as one of the most visible and celebrated Black American Muslims of the twentieth century. Given the political, economic, and social dimensions of American boxing, Ali's decision to convert to Islam stood in direct opposition to what the popular sport stood for—great American Christian nationalism.

Historically, American boxing aligned well with the "bootstrap" narrative of the poor boy who makes it big with hard work and determination, and who, not surprisingly, through his physical abilities achieved the "American Dream." Ali's story, as a great American athlete, has been void of his racial and religious identity. As the first Muslim heavyweight champion of the world, Muhammad Ali emerged as one of the foremost Black American Muslims to be widely celebrated on national and international stage in the twentieth century. Ali stood at the intersection of race and religion at one of the most tumultuous and important times in American history.

Born Cassius Marcellus Clay Jr. on January 17, 1942, in Louisville, Kentucky, Ali, like a large percentage of African Americans during the time, lived with a strict working-class Christian family. His mother, Odessa Grady Clay, was a Baptist, and his father, Cassius Marcellus Clay Sr., was a Methodist. Both of his parents were extremely proud of the Judeo-Christian values they instilled in Ali and his brother, Rudy (Rahman Ali). His parents, particularly his mother, remained determined to have the entire family attend their neighborhood church every Sunday. Ali often quipped during his public lectures that his mother in fact raised him as a "good Baptist," before he converted to Islam. He described his mother as a very spiritual person. According to Ali, his mother first introduced him to God. She modeled for him what it meant to be a principled person, and she insisted that he treat people with respect and kindness. Most importantly, Ali's mother inspired his confidence and insisted that he stand up for justice. Both of his parents, extremely proud of the Judeo-Christian values they instilled in Ali and his brother, Rahman, touted their son's Christian upbringing as a symbol of their love and loyalty to the United States when Ali later came under attack.[1] After he converted to Islam, Ali vowed and consistently voiced, "Her God is still God," in deference to his mother.[2]

While growing up, Ali's father worked as a sign painter, and like many of her Black women contemporaries, Ali's mother worked as a domestic in various neighboring White homes.[3] Even given their limited occupations, his parents worked hard to provide a stable life for their sons steeped in a politic of respectability informed by Judeo-Christian values. "I dressed them up as good as I could afford, kept them in pretty good clothes," his mother recalled. "And they didn't come out of no ghetto. I raised them on the best street I could. […] I made sure they were around good people; not people who would bring them into trouble," she proudly added.[4]

Like his religious views, Ali's racial understandings were also shaped in his youth. The family resided in a four-room house in a predominantly Black neighborhood. The boys attended segregated schools like Central High School and DuValle Junior High, and Ali and his brother interacted with Whites only in very brief instances. Ali described his parents teaching him to be proud of his Blackness, but not allowing the hate of others to induce him toward hatred. As an example, he recalled a story about his mother turned away from a restaurant when she asked for a cup of water on a hot summer day in their hometown. Despite the number of racial insults she likely endured, his mother never learned to hate Whites, Ali insisted.[5] His father, he described as someone who had very strong racial ideas, he conveyed less tolerable views. Once, according to Ali, his father expressed that "Whites should not be trusted" and that they kept Black men economically impoverished.[6] Ali's ideas about race developed not only based on the remarks or warnings of his parents but also as a result of his own observations about race relations in America. Ali often relayed the story of Emmett Till as a benchmark for understanding the racial climate. Like so many young Black people, the murder of Till touched him very deeply. "(A) picture of [Till] was in the newspaper. [...] It made me sick, and it scared me," Ali shared. "I was full of sadness and confusion. I didn't realize how hateful people could be until that day. I didn't know Emmett Till personally [but] from that day on I could see him in every black boy and girl."[7]

Other factors also shaped his early ideas about race. Although he had made his country proud by winning an Olympic gold medal for boxing in 1960, Ali still had to conform to the strict racial customs of segregated Louisville.[8] Initially overjoyed about his Olympic win, Ali felt confident that the United States would make the necessary changes to treat Black people fairly. He also believed that winning the Olympic gold medal would open doors for him, previously closed, particularly in his hometown. Consequently, "when asked by a Russian reporter about the Jim Crow laws that prevented a Black Olympic Gold medal winner from accessing something as simple as an eatery in the United States, Clay [said] [...] the USA is the best country in the world, including yours."[9] But he later modified these ideas when he realized that, no matter what he did on behalf of his country, it seemed nothing would change for Black men who sought equal treatment and access in America. Another observation concerning his second-class status came about when a local restaurant refused him service, even after he was honored by the city and the mayor.[10] Similar experiences would also shape his views regarding links between American race relations and Christianity. On several occasions, Ali spoke with his mother about biblical interpretations and images peppered with notions of racial distortions. "Momma, how come everything is white?" he pried. "Why is Jesus white with blond hair and blue eyes?"[11] Like many Black people, Ali recognized the contradictions embedded in the Christianity he was taught and how it further relegated Black people to an inferior position. Despite growing up under Louisville's racial segregation, the limitations Ali experienced as a young Black man, his evolving misgivings about White supremacist narratives of Christianity, and other factors, Ali still remained hopeful that American race relations would improve, though his worldview was circumscribed by relative isolation—that is, until the age of 12, when he entered the world of amateur boxing.

According to Huston Horn, a journalist for *Sports Illustrated*, "From the start of his boxing career in Louisville, [Ali] had been regarded as a 'good colored boy.'" In this arena, Ali had a number of White coaches, supporters, and opponents, and his prior racial experiences did not initially prevent him from taking advantage of any support offered to him by Whites. In fact, he developed close friendships with some. Throughout his teen years, White patrons presented Ali with countless opportunities that would enable him to travel internationally and take part in the Rome Olympics in 1960. As an amateur boxer, he was described in newspapers from Oklahoma to Texas as a "deceiving nonchalant high school light heavy" from Louisville, Kentucky. Many considered him to be "non-threatening" and a "well behaved" Black boy.[12] Men like Angelo Dundee (Ali's trainer), Ferdie Pacheco (his physician), Joe Martin, and the Louisville Sponsoring Group had considerable control over Ali, at least initially. The sponsoring group in particular consisted of 11 local White millionaires from Louisville, Kentucky, all of whom controlled the local industries, such as "tobacco, horse racing, and newspaper publishing."[13] Collectively, these White men tried to keep Ali within the "good colored boy" paradigm, where he would accept his second-class social and political position. Especially paternalistic, the Louisville Sponsoring Group endeavored to keep Ali away from civil rights issues and racial politics, counseling him that his success greatly depended on the acceptance of White Americans who perceived him as nonthreatening and accommodating to the existing racial order. In a 1963 *Sports Illustrated* interview, one of Ali's sponsors shared: "We are behind Cassius Clay to improve the breed of boxing, to do something nice for a deserving, well-behaved Louisville boy."[14]

Because of these racial perceptions of Ali's social place, his life as a Black athlete initially developed as expected by those shaping his career. He fought against noteworthy opponents, gained steady popularity, made his sponsors a lot of money, and did all he could to perfect his boxing skills and promote his career. Later, his evolving racial views would lead him to substitute Joe Martin, the White man who first got him started in boxing, with a Black trainer, Fred Stoner. He also replaced the 11 businessmen, who handled his early career, with Herbert Muhammad, son of Elijah Muhammad, the leader of the Nation of Islam.

Unlike his early career as a boxer, Ali's journey as an American Muslim was neither smooth nor predictable. When Ali started to associate with Black Muslims in the early 1960s, Whites closes to him, especially those in the sponsoring group, cautioned Ali against associating with perceived Black agitators. Dundee, Ali's trainer, said to reporters, amid rumors of his affiliation with the group, "The Black Muslim stuff is hokum [...] Cassius Clay likes people. The only group Cassius Clay belongs to is the Cassius Clay group."[15] Ali first heard about the Nation of Islam when he was in high school, while visiting Chicago in 1959. In early 1960, Ali frequented various Muslim temples. In 1961, Nation member Captain Sam Saxon (Abdul Rahman) formally introduced Ali to the movement. Captain Sam sold *Muhammad Speaks* newspapers on the street corners of Miami, Florida, where Ali trained. He subsequently invited Ali to the Muslim Temple in Miami to hear about the Nation and its program for Black people. During those meetings, the Nation's overall message of Black Nationalism and its emphasis on the history of the Black man in America changed Ali's life and instilled him with a strong sense of pride. "The day I met Islam I found a power within myself that no man could destroy or take away," he stated unequivocally. "When I first walked into the mosque I didn't find Islam, it found me," he beamed.[16] The Nation spoke to the unique predicament of Black people living under a strident racial tyranny. Still, given the negative perceptions of Islam in general and of the Nation of Islam in particular, and because of their strident ideas about White people, politics of respectability, and stand on racial separation, when Ali became a member in the early 1960s, he initially chose not to disclose his affiliation.[17] Understandably, Ali had to play to the racial and religious politics of his time. Any affiliation with Islam, and especially the Nation, would likely derail his career plans in becoming the heavyweight champion of the world. So, in response to rumors, Ali initially denied any links to Islam or other Black movements when reporters asked about his relationship to Black civil rights groups. In the *Western Kansas* newspaper and other publications, he shared with reporters that he had not "joined any such organization because he [had not] […] found one that offer[ed] 'an eternal solution and not just a temporary one' under the leadership of one man." He continued to distance himself from being marked as a leader of the black struggle, stipulating that "entertainers were not fit to be leaders."[18] Ali continued to play it safe, downplaying any connections to the larger Black liberation struggle. Any hope to advance the cause of Black people or any message he desired to impart would never be heard or taken seriously as a Black Muslim without first securing national recognition and respect that came with the heavyweight championship title. And, more than anything, he wanted to be a champion for his people.

By August 1963, it seemed that most rumors had quieted down about any potential links between Ali and the Muslims. His career remained on track, and his plans for his upcoming fight against Sonny Liston planned for February 1964 continued to move forward. Meanwhile, Ali signed a recording contract for a record titled "Naturally, I AM The Greatest," and though he continued to reject the title of leader as mentioned above, Ali was invited as a "Negro Leader" alongside Malcolm X, James Baldwin, Reverend Adam Clayton Powell, and others to the Afro-American Association conference titled "The Mind of the Ghetto" in August 1963 in Oakland, California.[19] Thus, Ali seemed already to be recognized as an important voice in the Black community. Then, in October 1963, Ali was seen openly attending Muslim events, such as the Black Muslim Rally in Philadelphia. His appearance seemed to suggest that he no longer felt inclined to hide his political or religious interests, but outside of a few mentions in the media, few paid attention. In January 1964, the *New York Herald Tribune* covered a story about Ali attending yet another Muslim affair in New York. The reporter wrote:

> The brash young boxer, who celebrated his 22nd birthday last week, may not be a card carrying Muslim. But, unquestionably, he sympathizes with Muslim aims and by his presence at their meetings lends them prestige. He is the first nationally famous Negro to take an active part in the Muslim movement. Yet, he still has not formally announced support for the Muslims. He will not discuss the subject publicly.[20]

Behind the scenes, and with the exception of his brother Rahman, those closest to Ali continued to try to persuade him to publicly renounce Elijah Muhammad, along with the Nation's rhetoric concerning Whites so that his supporters would be clear that he was not interested in civil rights matters and remained solely focused on his career as a boxer. Some of the sponsoring group members did as much as they could to distance him from the influence of the Muslims, such as threatening to cancel his fights and end his boxing career.[21] Between January and February 1964, Ali made no further pronouncements either for or against the Nation of Islam. However, two days after he secured the heavyweight title from Sonny Liston on February 25, 1964, Ali announced to the world that he was indeed a Muslim, and he had aligned himself with "750 million Muslims" all over the world.[22] He also shared that, as the most preeminent, albeit controversial Black Nationalist organization at the time, the Nation of Islam not only was doing good works but "were righteous people."[23]

Ali's decision to openly associate himself with the Muslims, specifically the Nation, appeared to be a rebuke of America and Christianity, thus drawing sharp reactions to his conversion. Within a few weeks after announcing his new religious affiliation, Ali demanded to be referred to as "Cassius X." However, at about the same time, during a Chicago broadcast on WWRL, Elijah Muhammad suggested that Ali take the name "Muhammad Ali."[24] Consequently, within days of the WWRL broadcast, Muhammad Ali had embraced his new name.[25] In response, Ali quickly became a target of even more resentment.

As a representation of American power, that is, the heavyweight champion of the world, Ali, like Black athletes before him, notably Jesse Owens, Joe Louis, and Jackie Robinson, was to take his place as a paragon of good American race relations. Jesse Owens had done his part never publicly remarking negatively about American Jim Crow politics during the 1936 Olympics. Joe Louis proudly enlisted in the US armed forces during World War II against Germany's fascism. Jackie Robinson also did not upset the racial applecart, but instead focused his attention on maintaining good relations in baseball. In stark contrast to Owens, Louis, and Robinson, however, Ali attacked the duplicity of White Americans and the ideological and institutional oppression faced by Black people. In place of silence or ignoring existing injustices, he openly celebrated his Blackness and commitment to Black people like Malcolm X before him; Ali loudly touted the doctrine of Elijah Muhammad and spoke openly about Muhammad's views concerning the impact of White hegemony. He shared concerning Black people:

> They've been taught to love white and hate black, we've been robbed of our names in slavery. We were robbed of our culture, we were robbed of our true history. So it left us a walking dead man. So you got black people in an all-white country and they don't know nothing about themselves. They don't speak their language, they're just mentally dead. And this is happening all over the world.[26]

According to some journalists, like Huron, Ali's apparent involvement with civil rights, especially his affiliation with the Nation, contributed to his declining support, thereby throwing him within the American good and bad guy dichotomy, where Ali would be cast as "the bad guy" because of his link to Islam.[27] Sports, like baseball and boxing, remained an important space for celebrating American identity and displaying the best America had to offer, including Black athleticism. Athletics reinforced the image of American pride and power, and Ali's refusal to play ball, so to speak, in order to maintain this image stood as an offense to American sensibilities. Consequently, in the mid-1960s, a Black Muslim heavyweight champion of the world seemed quite un-American.

Ali's journey toward self-awakening resulted in his rejection of not only the standard for American religiosity but also his birth name, Cassius Clay, which he viewed as an affront to his new identity as a Black man and a Muslim. As a result, Islam became a vital part of Ali's identity and also primed him as an emerging voice for Black liberation in the twentieth century. When Ali converted to Islam, the group provided Ali with apt male role models including Miami minister Ishmael Sabakhan, Jeremiah Shabazz, Sam Saxon, Malcolm X, Herbert Muhammad, and later Warith D. Mohammed, all of whom were guided and taught by the leader of the group, Elijah Muhammad.[28] "The Nation's programs, advanced a kind of hyper-masculinity, and affirmed Ali as a Black man. While the Nation sought to rebuild the image of Black people, many Americans, Black and White, viewed the group as Black supremacists who endangered what some saw as improved race relations."[29]

For some, becoming a Muslim during the 1960s likely seemed akin to embracing communism in the 1950s. Those who challenged capitalism, racism, and Christianity were seen as a threat to American ideas and values, even a national security threat. But some Black people turned to Islam because they felt Christianity was "not in the best interest of Black people," given the persistence of racism. They believed that American Christianity historically intermingled with White supremacy stifled their growth and development and reduced any hope for equality, justice, and freedom. Instead, American Christianity taught Black people "that salvation [would] be in the after-life […] [which helped] to keep [Black people] inferior and accept [nearly all] injustices."[30] In comparison, Islam addressed the unique condition of Black people in America and provided a blueprint for success, given their circumstances. Edward E. Curtis, professor of religious studies, explains that Black people were attracted to Elijah Muhammad's religiosity because "Islam was a religion that spoke to [their] need for a faith that addressed the practical problems of Black life. […] Islam is a religion of life while Christianity is a religion of death. […] [Christianity] was used to keep [Black] men enslaved [mentally and physically]."[31] Therefore, Islam created a new spiritual space for Black people in America, one that made them feel empowered. Unlike Christianity, Islam was not linked to "dependency, misfortune, slavery, and death."[32] Muslims believed that "Christianity was the slave masters' religion [that] […] teaches [Black people] to pray to [a] God who isn't God, and make [Black people] want to love [their] enemy but hate [their] own."[33] In a 1971 interview with BBC reporter Parkinson, Ali exclaimed, "I'm proud, and Islam did it. […] As soon as I heard the truth that Elijah Muhammad teaches us in America, it made me accept it." The Black Muslim's critique of Christianity, juxtaposed with Black people's struggles against White supremacy, appealed to Ali and provided him with a better understanding of American race relations, a view he would share many times later as a college lecturer.

In response to his affiliation with Islam and his unwillingness to conform to racial respectability politics expected of athletes, the media constructed Ali as both anti-American and anti-Christian. Those who had once supported Ali felt threatened by his new religion.[34] Even Ali's parents openly shared their dismay about his new religion, believing somehow that the Nation had taken their good Christian son and poisoned him with Islamic and racist rhetoric. In a February 1964 interview, Ali's father voiced that the Muslim "sect ha[d] brainwashed [Ali and his brother]" and taught them to "hate White people."[35] The Louisville Sponsoring Group also shared concerns that their once "good Negro boy" had been corrupted. For many people, Ali's conversion to Islam seemed a slight against everything it meant to be the heavyweight champion of the world. The Black boxer Floyd Patterson, who later lost to Ali, went on a diatribe about winning back, on behalf of all America, the heavyweight title from Ali and the Muslims and, by proxy, Christianity. Patterson spoke as "a proud Catholic":

I disagree with the precepts of the Black Muslims just as I disagree with the Ku Klux Klan— in fact so much so [that I] desire to fight Cassius X to take the title [back] from the Black Muslim leadership and will do so for no purse at all. […] I am proud to be an American, and proud of my people, and no one group of people could make me change my views. Therefore I challenge you not only for myself, but for all people who think and feel as I do.[36]

According to Ali's biographer, Thomas Hauser, "Before February 25, 1964, it seemed as though almost everything Cassius Clay did fit within the context of establishment white values."[37] But once Ali officially aligned himself with Islam, the anti-Muslim backlash in America became significant. The media "had an attitude of contempt toward Clay." According to Robert Lipsyte, a sports journalist for the *New York Times*, some reporters believed that a Muslim heavyweight champion of the world "was the worst thing that ever happened to boxing" and "might be the worst thing that ever happened to the youth of America, which needs a proper role model." Lipsyte also commented on the Patterson–Ali fight, which had been constructed as a battle between Christianity and Islam.[38] Ali was framed as the Muslim brute attacking the innocence of Christianity, which Patterson embodied. Ali was not attacked simply because he was Black, as Patterson also occupies this space, but because he was also a Muslim, specifically one linked to the Nation of Islam. According to reporter Huston Horn, when Ali acknowledged his association with the Muslims, he had personally "felt resentful and betrayed."[39] Reporter Jimmy Cannon agreed, insisting, "I pity Clay and abhor what he represents."[40] After Ali won the bout against Patterson, some went so far as to call Ali "sadist," especially since it appeared to many that Ali beat Patterson mercilessly for negative remarks about Islam.[41] "*Life*" magazine, which had been kind to Ali in the past, headlined its story on the [Patterson] fight, 'Sickening Spectacle in a Ring.'" Other snubs to Ali's religion and his desire to define himself on his own terms included the media's refusal to refer to him by his Muslim name. As such, reporters sparred with Ali over the rights to his identity, begrudgingly calling him Ali only when he refused to answer to Clay. Newspaper reporters continued to refer to Ali as Clay in their stories to demonstrate their power to define him as they saw fit. White reporters (e.g., Horn), promoters (e.g., McDonald), and their Black allies (e.g., Patterson) all were comfortable with Ali, as long as he played the racial politics expected of Black athletes during the 1960s. But Ali's move toward a group like the Nation of Islam seemed too intolerable for them. In response, Ali exclaimed, "I don't have to be who you want me to be."[42] Amid continued attacks, Muhammad Ali stood firmly in defense of Islam.[43]

Internationally, Ali emerged as a hero, and by proxy, the notoriety of the Nation of Islam also expanded. For instance, shortly after winning the fight against Liston in 1964, Ali traveled to Asia and Africa for three months. Every country he visited celebrated him as a Muslim and a Black American. Like Elijah Muhammad and later Malcolm X, Ali met with dignitaries, kings, and prominent leaders of non-European countries throughout the world. He traveled to Ghana, where he met with President Kwame Nkrumah and faced cheering Ghanaian crowds. He also traveled to Liberia, Nigeria, and Egypt, where he met with President Gamal Abdel Nasser, a longtime supporter of the Nation of Islam. While there, Ali also visited the pyramids and University of Al Ahzar.

In 1974, Ali traveled to Jamaica and met with Prime Minister Manley. The Nation of Islam delegation reported:

> More than 200,000 Jamaicans lined the streets of Kingston as a 20 car motorcade twisted through the capital city to an official welcoming ceremony at the government's National Arena. During the ceremony Prime Minister Manley lavishly praised the works of Mr. Muhammad, [stating] "The Honorable Elijah Muhammad leads one of the most remarkable movements in the world. [...]" We are proud of his work. And you let him know that this prime minister of this proud country would be very [much] honored to welcome him as our guest at any time."[44]

Ali's international reputation helped increased admiration for Black American Muslims and for the work of Elijah Muhammad. In his 1975 Saviour's Day address, Professor Ali Baghdadi, a Palestinian journalist, said of Ali and the Nation, "We love you because you love Islam. You have become the Freedom Fighters of Islam—Soldiers of Allah. Muhammad Ali stood in that ring and put Islam on the map internationally."[45]

Even with international recognition, Ali's journey as a Muslim became ever more challenging as the US government targeted him for induction into the armed forces. Previously, at the age of 18, Ali had registered for the draft as required. Prior to becoming the world champion, in 1964, US military officials conceded that Ali was not fit for service because of his low IQ scores. Even the Secretary of the Army, Stephen Ailes, submitted a letter to the House of Representatives endorsing the US armed forces' decision to reject Ali.[46] Nevertheless, at the height of his boxing career, the issue regarding his ability to serve resurfaced after the military altered the mental aptitude standard, thereby making Ali eligible for service. In 1967, people speculated that Ali would be inducted into the US armed forces. His family, close friends, and other Black athletes urged him to save his career and accept the induction. Of course, Ali was not the first Muslim to face this problem. During World War II, the US government attempted to undermine the Nation of Islam by accusing members of sedition for their refusal to be drafted. Along with other Muslim men, Elijah Muhammad served prison time for refusing to fight abroad in a war against fascism while Blacks still faced racial oppression at home. Elijah Muhammad's son, Warith D. Mohammed, also elected to go to prison rather than be inducted into the US military. Ali now faced the same dilemma being inducted or going to prison. Unlike other Black sports figures, Ali again refused to play the role of the "good Negro athlete" within the confines of American racial politics. When asked his thoughts about the Vietnam War, with his most honest assertion yet, Ali stated, "I don't know nothing about Vietnam. [...] I ain't got no quarrel with those Vietcong." Though this assertion became popular with many in the Black community, this sentiment angered many Whites and escalated attacks against Ali, who was already perceived as an anti-American Muslim and a communist. Meanwhile, Ali also received scorn from the uppermost levels of government. Some referred to Ali as an "unpatriotic draft-dodger." Representative Frank Clark and other congressmen also condemned Ali for his stance. "The heavy-weight champion of the world turns my stomach," Clark complained, "I feel that each man, if he really is a man, owes his country a willingness to protect it and serve it in time of need. From this standpoint, the heavy-weight champion of the world has been a complete and total disgrace. I urge the citizens of the nation as a whole to boycott any of his performances."[47] Many reporters, perhaps the most virulent, said "Cassius makes himself as sorry a spectacle as those unwashed punks who picket and demonstrate against the war." Moreover, "boxing should throw Clay on his inflated head. The adult brat, who has boasted ad nauseam of his fighting skills, but who squealed like a cornered rat when tapped for the Army should be shorn of his title."[48] Arthur Daley of the *New York Times* wrote, "Clay could have been the most popular of all champions. But he attached himself to a hate organization, and antagonized everyone with his boasting and his disdain for the decency of even a low-grade patriotism. [...] Not a nickel should be contributed to the coffers of Clay, the Black Muslim," Daley insisted.[49] Several people, including reporters, sports sponsors, congressmen, and the like, insisted the Terrell fight be canceled. As a result, the Illinois Athletic Commission revoked the Ali–Terrell license. Kentucky and other states followed suit, by passing resolutions to condemn Ali and pledging not to allow the fight in their states.[50] This national call to boycott Ali, mostly by Whites, was strong and successful, albeit temporary, since Ali ended up fighting the Canadian heavyweight champion George Chuvalo in Toronto, Canada. Also, a year later, the Ali–Terrell fight materialized back in the United States amid all of the controversies and calls for boycotts. As a Black Muslim man in America with few rights, Ali was expected to fight in an unjust war for a country that treated him worse than a second-class citizen. "Boys are dying in Vietnam for something they don't believe," he observed.

"Why should they ask me [...] to put on a uniform and go ten thousand miles from home and drop bombs and bullets on brown people in Vietnam while so-called Negro people in Louisville are treated like dogs? [I] [...] have nothing to lose by standing up and following my beliefs [...] I've got no jails, no power, no government, but six million Muslims are giving me strength," Ali said.[51]

In spite of the continued media bashing, hate mail, and bomb threats, on April 28, 1967, Ali appeared, as ordered, to Houston, Texas, military training center. However, he "refused to step forward" when called to be inducted in to the US armed forces.[52] Meanwhile, behind the scenes, some government officials worked with influential Whites who supported Ali to offer him a number of ways to avoid actually taking part in combat. Military officials claimed, if Ali were to be initiated into the army, he would simply be used to entertain the troops by taking part in exhibition matches as Joe Louis had done during World War II. Ali declined these compromises, citing his religious principles. Indeed, many Christians had successfully avoided induction by offering their religious objections. However, Ali's decision not to be inducted, combined with his affiliation with Islam and his criticisms of US involvement in the war, continued to ignite a firestorm of criticism from the US Congress, the Boxing Commission, the media, and later college presidents and administrators who offered condemnation as well. Gene Ward, sports columnist with the *Daily New*, said: "I do not want my three boys to grow into their teens holding the belief that Cassius Clay is any kind of hero. I'll do anything I can to prevent it." Milton Gross, of the *New York Post*, added: "Clay seems to have gone past the borders of faith. He has reached fanaticism."[53] Though other Black athletes supported Ali, none possessed the courage or the religious conviction to do what he did. According to Bill Russell, a Boston Celtics basketball player at the time, Ali "has an absolute and sincere faith. [...] He is better equipped than anyone I know to withstand the trials in store for him."[54] Yet Ali soon found himself barred from boxing; the Boxing Commission revoked his license, and the federal district court in Houston sentenced him to five years in prison, at which time they also slapped him with $10,000 fine. Since the courts denied the Nation of Islam as an authentic religious institution, Ali's position as a contentious objector held little sway. The court's decision to ignore Ali's claims that the Nation of Islam was an authentic religious community resulted in the loss of his title and his ability to earn a living, which nearly pushed Ali and his family into poverty. Thus, Ali found himself enduring rising court costs, and because his skills were quite limited to boxing, it became even difficult for him to support his family. As a last ditch effort to intimidate Ali, the federal government confiscated his passport, thereby preventing him from seeking any other economic recourse.

For nearly four years, Ali was denied any opportunity to advance his career as a boxer or pursue other avenues toward financial stability outside the United States. Moreover, during this time, there was a clear gap between how Blacks and Whites perceived Ali, which also complicated his ability to earn a living. While many White people considered Ali an anti-American draft dodger, most Black people saw him as a hero, "the people's champion," who proudly stood against a racially oppressive system.[55] Ali's association with a successful and expanding Muslim community in the mid-1960s, along with the mounting resentment young Whites demonstrated during their anti-war protests, proved helpful. While suspended, Ali looked for ways to support his family. He opened a restaurant called "Champ Burgers." He also served as a regular minister for the Nation of Islam and participated in a Broadway play titled "Big Time Buck White," which provided him with some monies. But he derived his most successful means for earning a living from a most unlikely place for a Black athlete who only completed high school and whom the US Army initially denied induction because of his low IQ. Ali, possessing only what he referred to as a lack of book knowledge, but a lot of common sense, became the most sought-after lecturer for colleges and universities across the country during the modern civil right–Black Power era.[56]

The late 1960s were fraught with college campus unrest, including student strikes, and organized protests against the ROTC . In 1968 in the wake of the assassination of Martin Luther King Jr., college campuses in Wisconsin, North Carolina, Michigan, Pennsylvania, and California exploded with scrimmages between students, college administrators, and the police. At Michigan State, students disrupted a Board of Trustees meeting in order to present a list of demands, which included the hiring of Black faculty. Rutgers University protesters gained control of a classroom building, and at Alabama's Stillman College, students boycotted classes for nearly a week. At Kent State and other schools, student protests mounted against the Vietnam War. Meanwhile, the Black student population on predominantly White campuses (PWI) continued to proliferate, along with the establishment of Black Studies programs at PWIs and Historically Black Colleges and Universities (HBCUs), all of which offered Ali a ready audience. This backdrop of student uprisings and protests created fertile ground for Ali and significantly contributed to his newfound popularity and importance in the Black liberation struggle of the 1960s and 1970s.

As Ali's case moved through the courts, Jeremiah Shabazz, the Philadelphia Temple No. 12 Nation's minister, and Ali's wife, Belinda, worked closely with Ali to keep him in the public eye. By the late 1960s, the Nation of Islam had a significant presence in the city of Philadelphia. Early on, Malcolm X, Warith D. Mohammed, and ultimately, Jeremiah Shabazz served as ministers in the city. Shabazz used his local influence to arrange speaking engagements for Ali at several colleges in the Philadelphia area, for a small fee. Prior to his suspension from boxing, Ali had conducted some college lectures at places like Tuskegee University, a historically Black college in Alabama. In November 1966, Tuskegee students invited the boxer to the school. While there, Ali spoke to students about pursuing a meaningful education that would provide them with an opportunity to give something back to their communities. He also shared why he joined the Nation of Islam and how it had changed his life. He insisted that without the "rehabilitative powers" of Islam, he would have been lost. Under the leadership of Elijah Muhammad, the Nation of Islam transformed Black people who had become hopeless, Ali argued.[57] After his suspension, Ali first spoke to students at Temple University and then Cheney University. Later he signed with the Richard Fulton, Inc. agency, which resulted in speaking engagements at more than one hundred colleges over the next few years.[58] For instance, in October 1968, students of the Student Political Forum invited Ali to Union College in Schenectady, New York. Ali spoke at length in favor of racial separation and the need for reparations for Black people in the form of land. "No one can be free and independent without some land," he stated unequivocally.[59] Ali's message to college students was honest, controversial, and impassioned. Though he did not support the movement for racial integration, his message of separation and self-determination resonated with his mostly White audiences, many of whom shared his feelings that the civil rights movement had been in many ways a failure by 1968. Reverend Martin Luther King Jr.'s assassination, urban rebellions, and campus protests across the country made the call for solutions to America's race problem ever more urgent. But the Nation of Islam had the cure, Ali reasoned. In September 1969, Ali gave a lecture on "The Black Muslim Opinion on Racial Conflict" at Appalachian State University. Ali's message to students detailed how White supremacy worked to foster a sense of black inferiority. White and Black people in America perceived that everything of value was perceived to be associated with White people. Indoctrinated at birth and through the media, biblical texts, history books, and even nursery rhymes, it seemed that close proximity to Whiteness was the most desirable position, he explained. Those who gained a modicum of success appeared especially vulnerable under this mentality. "We black people could become free sooner than you think, if all the athletes and entertainers just took a stand," he stated. "[But] as soon as they get great they go where you can't see them anymore," ostensibly away from other Back people when possible. To Ali, it seemed that although they all depended on Whites for their livelihood, they had to stand up for Black people, principles mattered. Behind closed doors, many may have shared his convictions, but to say so publicly would cost them too much. "The person known as the Negro was robbed of name, God, culture, and nationality. Now we have a nation of Negroes suffering mentally," Ali averred. He openly discussed the impact of self-hate and the loss of Black history with his college audiences.[60]

Ali's college visits offered him the opportunity to dialogue with some of the brightest minds in America at places like Howard, Harvard, and Berkeley.[61] As he traveled around the country, he gained more respect for his honest reflections on race relations, his stance against the Vietnam War, his role as a Muslim leader, and his poetic skills. Oxford University offered him a teaching position as a professor of poetry and social ethics.[62] During his college lectures, he often remarked upon topics like segregation, Black pride, Black women and modesty, the Vietnam War, and standing up for one's principles. Lecture titles included "The Intoxication of Life," "The Purpose of Life," "The Real Cause of Man's Distress," "In the Eye of the Beholder," "The Journey to the Goal in Life," and "The Heart of Man."[63] Between 1968 and 1975, Ali spoke at more than two hundred colleges and universities, and his message changed very little. However, during several lectures in 1967, Ali shared his feelings about the pending Supreme Court decision relating to his appeal; he said:

> Don't care about the verdict as long as I know I am going to jail for standing up for my people. Don't matter if you die when you dying for your people. […] I am one thousand percent Black. Let it be on the record that I fight for my people. Let it be on the record that I went down for my people. If I ain't free let it be on record for me and my kind.

As Ali's popularity increased, local and national pressures combined to prohibit Ali from speaking on college campuses. Colleges threatened to revoke funding from student organizations; some people, both on and off campuses, encouraged community protests and boycotts and strategized through various other schemes to dissuade students and faculty from inviting Ali to campus. As disagreements mounted, Ali's planned visits incited heated discussions about the issue of free speech and academic freedom. University officials who did not support Ali's stance against the Vietnam War found it necessary to push back against local and national detractors in favor of free speech. They also sought to appease students and faculty in ways that nevertheless upheld their constitutional rights and the university policies that protected all speech. In 1969, the University of Arkansas Student Government Association invited Ali to participate in a symposium lecture series. In response, a local business group, the Pulaski Businessmen's Association, wrote a letter to Dr. David Mullins, president of the university, to dissuade him not to allow "un-American" speakers like Ali to have access to college students.[64] Local organizations closed rank to block the lecture, as well. Arkansas senators also chose sides in the debate. A resolution brought before the state Senate objected to Ali's upcoming appearance. The measure, SR 19, was introduced by Senator Milt Earnhart of Fort Smith, Arkansas. Earnhart claimed that the bases for issuing the resolution included not only Ali's refusal to be inducted into the US army but also Earnhart's personal beliefs that Ali had nothing to offer Arkansas University students.[65] Other senators voiced their anxiety over Ali's planned visits, stipulating that "students should not be exposed to alien thoughts until they had had ample doses of patriotism."[66] The adopted resolutions and other threats from the top did not prevent Ali's appearances, however. The Young Republicans, which was a mostly White student group, and other student groups supported Ali's right to speak in support of free speech.

On March 19, 1969, Ali did address the University of Arkansas community with more than a thousand people in attendance. His lecture focused on his religious beliefs as a Muslim.[67] He discussed the dress of Muslim women versus non-Muslim women, the move of so-called Black radicals toward Islam, the virtues of George Wallace and racial separation, and his religious conviction concerning the war in Vietnam. He also expressed finding more satisfaction in "fighting for freedom" than being a boxing champion.[68] On the topic of women, Ali encouraged all Black women to follow the lead of Muslim women as it relates to issues of modesty. He spoke about their inner beauty and the need to protect them from unwanted advances that may be encouraged by what he saw as unfavorable clothing.

At a 1970 Michigan State University address, Ali criticized integration. "We have tried integration. It is 1970 and integration has failed to solve the race problem." Black leaders of integration are dead or powerless because "two people [Black and White] in opposition to one another by nature can never get along in peace," said Ali. "Politics is also not the answer," he shared. According to Ali,

Even if a Black man became President of the U.S. he would still be powerless to make any real change. No matter how many black people you get into political office [...] Black people will never control no white man's politics [...] he'll never write the laws. The white man got books we'll never see on law. He will change them when he's ready. [...] Politics won't solve black people's problems. We have a dope problem politics don't have no program for. We have a lack of unity problem that politics will not solve, and a disrespect for our women that politics don't preach so politics ain't gonna solve Black people's problems.

Much of the condemnation concerning Ali's visits to colleges and his message to students, seemed to be simultaneously religious, racial, and political, though many denied that racial or religious intolerance played any role at all in Ali's overall treatment. Still, comments and actions by White officials seemed most revealing. For instance, the day after Ali's appearance at the University of Arkansas, four Arkansas legislators visited the campus to discuss issues concerning free speech. In their public remarks, several confessed to reporters, "We are frank to state that we are happy that there are no more Muslims in Arkansas." Senator Guy H. Jones of Conway spoke more to the increasing fears around Islam and communism than the debates over free speech, as did other political figures. "If there is a last citadel of Christianity, it is in this country. There is no power on earth that can stop the spread of communism but the United States government," Jones boasted.[69] Religious and political ideological pollution is what senators like Jones and Earnhart feared. Meanwhile, cities that refused to allow Ali to fight also voiced concerns over Ali's possible spread of moral "corruption," namely , Islam.[70]

By the mid-1970s, Ali was no longer the most hated and despised Black athlete in American history. He had regained his popularity because of the embrace and advocacy of college students and faculty. Because the Vietnam War grew even more unpopular with the American people and explicit racial bigotry became less acceptable, Ali emerged as nearly everyone's champion. All of the anxiety and fury over his conversion to Islam, his refusal to be inducted into the US military just four years earlier, and his stance on racial separation seemed to dissipate as his popularity as a lecturer grew. Even the controversy over his link with the Nation of Islam looked to be forgiven, so much so that in 1974, President Gerald Ford invited Ali to the White House.

As a Black Muslim, Ali had popularized Black religious freedom and free speech, and became a leading voice against the Vietnam War. Throughout his suspension from boxing, financial difficulties, and the threat of prison time, there was no question about where Ali stood as he took every chance he could to confirm that he stood firmly and courageously on the side of Black and Muslim people. Ali's status as a heavyweight champion, his confidence, poetic skills, international popularity, and US Supreme Court victory further endeared him to Black people and a growing number of sympathetic Whites. Moreover, his conversion to Islam and his refusal to become yet another Black casualty for US militarism and capitalism during the 1960s also won many over to his side. The later establishment of the Muhammad Ali Center in Louisville, Kentucky, in 2005; the 1996 lighting of the Olympic torch; and his visit to Iraq to meet with Saddam Hussein in 1990 to help with the release of Americans, are all a testament to the remarkable Black Muslim man Ali became and the diverse legacy he left behind. Ali shared, "If I were not a Muslim, I might not have taken all the stands that I did," Ali averred. "If I were not Muslim I would not have changed my name or sought to spread peace, […] If I were not a Muslim […] the world would have never known Muhammad Ali."[71] No life in recent history has left such a tremendous impact on American culture and religiosity than Muhammad Ali.[72]

Notes

1 Thomas Hauser, *Muhammad Ali: His Life and Times* (New York: Simon & Schuster, 1991), 14.
2 Ibid.
3 Ibid., 17.
4 Ibid., 15.
5 Ibid., 10–11.
6 John Stravinsky, *Biography of Muhammad Ali* (New York: Park Lane, 1997), 10–11.
7 Muhammad Ali and Hana Yasmeen Ali, *The Soul of a Butterfly: Reflections on Life's Journey* (New York: Simon & Schuster, 2004), 11.
8 Michael Parkinson, "Interview with Muhammad Ali," British Broadcasting Company, October 17, 1971, https://www.youtube.com/watch?v=lRHoh8bH3BQ.
9 Hauser, *Muhammad Ali: His Life & Times*, 28.
10 Ali and Ali, *The Soul of a Butterfly*, 41.
11 Ibid.
12 As quoted in Huston Horn, "The Eleven Men behind Cassius Clay," *Sports Illustrated*, March 11, 1963, 62–70.
13 Michael Ezra, *Muhammad Ali: The Making of an Icon*. (Philadelphia: Temple University Press, 2009), 20.
14 As quoted in Horn, "The Eleven Men behind Cassius Clay," 62–70.
15 Ezra, *Muhammad Ali: The Making of an Icon*, 64–65.
16 Ibid., 65.

17 Ibid.
18 "Cassius Denies Rights Actions," *Western Kansas Press*, July 6, 1963; "Athletes Poor Leaders-Clay," *Winnipeg Free Press*, July 6, 1963.
19 "Negro Leaders Asked to Meet," *Nevada State Journal*, August 10, 1963.
20 Hauser, *Muhammad Ali: His Life and Times*, 64.
21 Ali and Ali, *The Soul of a Butterfly*, 77.
22 Bud Collins, "Clay Admits Belief in Black Muslim Credo," *Boston Globe*, February 27, 1964, 39.
23 Ibid.
24 "Clay Puts Black X in His Name," *New York Times*, March 7, 1964.
25 "'Muhammad Ali' Clay," *Chicago Tribune*, March 8, 1964, B2.
26 Parkinson, "Interview with Muhammad Ali."
27 As quoted in Michael Ezra, *Muhammad Ali: The Making of an Icon*, 65.
28 Ezra, *Muhammad Ali: The Making of an Icon*, 87–88.
29 Ibid., 88.
30 Hatim A. Sahib, "The Nation of Islam," MA thesis, the University of Chicago, 1951, 135.
31 Ibid., 39.
32 Abdul Basit Naeem, "Moslem Convention," *Moslem World & the U.S.A.*, 12–13. On the instruction Black board of every Nation of Islam Temple was the American flag, Cross, and the words "Christianity, slavery and death." On the other side were an Islamic flag, Islam, and the words "freedom, justice and equality." Edward E. Curtis, IV. *Black Muslim Religion in the Nation of Islam, 1960–1975* (Chapel Hill: University of North Carolina Press, 2006), 39. For Black Muslims, America became synonymous with Christianity and White supremacy; Elijah Muhammad, *The Supreme Wisdom*, vol 1. (Phoenix, AZ: Secretarius MEMPS, 1957), 37; Elijah Muhammad, *Message to the Black Man in America* (Newport News, VA: United Brothers, Communications Systems, 1965), 70–71.
33 Naeem, "Moslem Convention," 12.
34 Hauser, *Muhammad Ali: His Life and Times*, 66.
35 "Muslims Told Him to Hate His Mom, Says Cassius Dad," *Pittsburgh Courier*, March 7, 1964, 19; "Cassius Joined Black Muslims at 18, Father Says," *Los Angeles Times*, February 7, 1964.
36 "Patterson Challenges Muslim Clay to Fight," *Boston Globe*, March 8, 1964, 69.
37 Hauser, *Muhammad Ali: His Life and Times*, 81.
38 Ibid., 83, 141.
39 Ibid., 95.
40 David Remnick, *King of the World* (New York: Random House, 1998), 210.
41 John Micklos Jr., *Muhammad Ali: I Am the Greatest* (Berkeley Heights, NJ: Enslow, 2011), 62.
42 "The Trials of Muhammad Ali," directed by Bill Seiger (New York, NY: Kino Lorber, 2014), DVD.
43 Hauser, *Muhammad Ali: His Life and Times*, 135.
44 Charles 67X and Alonzo 4X, "Jamaica Government Host Muslim Delegation," *Accomplishment of the Muslims* (1975): 24.
45 Ali Bagdadi Savior's Day address, the Nation of Islam, "Saviour's Day" (Chicago, IL: Nation of Islam, February 26,1975), DVD.
46 Micklos, *Muhammad Ali: I Am the Greatest*, 66.
47 Hauser, *Muhammad Ali: His Life and Times*, 147.
48 Ibid., 145.
49 Ibid., 147.
50 Ibid., 146.
51 Ibid., 167; Muhammad Ali, *"The Black Scholar* Interview," in *The Muhammad Ali Reader*, ed. Gerald Early (Hopewell, NJ: Ecco, [1970] 1998), 83.
52 Ali and Ali, *The Soul of a Butterfly*, 88; Hauser, *Muhammad Ali: His Life and Times*, 169.
53 Hauser, *Muhammad Ali: His Life and Times*, 177.

54 Ibid., 170.
55 David K. Wiggins, "Victory for Allah: Muhammad Ali, the Nation of Islam, and American Society," in *Muhammad Ali: The People's Champ*, ed. Elliott J. Gorn (Chicago, IL: University of Chicago Press, 1995), 88–89.
56 Ali and Ali, *The Soul of a Butterfly: Reflections on Life's Journey*, 97.
57 "Muhammad Ali Thrills Audience with Lecture"; and Wesley Godfrey, "The Ali Shuffle Sweeps Campus," *The Campus Digest*, December 3, 1966, vol. 35, no. 9.
58 Hauser, *Muhammad Ali: His Life and Times*, 185.
59 Paul Andres, "Applause Flatters Ali; but He Wants Races Apart," *Concordiensis*, October 25, 1968, vol. 98, no. 9.
60 Mary Ann Cox, "Muhammad Ali Addresses Appalachian Crowd," *Appalachian*, September 19, 1969, vol 19, no. 2, 1.
61 Muhammad Ali, lecture remarks, Michigan State University, East Lansing, MI, March 2, 1970.
62 Ibid.
63 Ali and Ali, *The Soul of a Butterfly*, 98.
64 "Bravo Dr. Mullins," *Arkansas Gazette*, February 22, 1969.
65 "Senators Condemn Plans for Speech by Ali at U of A," *Arkansas Gazette*, March 1, 1969.
66 Ibid.
67 George Boosey, "Ali Drives into Town, Reviews Show on TV, Finds a Message in It," *Arkansas Gazette*, March 1, 1969.
68 Ibid.
69 Dick Allen, "Rule, Caldwell Are Heroes of Legislators' Debate over Appearance by Ali," *Arkansas Gazette*, March 20, 1969, 18A.
70 "*The Black Scholar* Interview," 88.
71 Ali and Ali, *The Soul of a Butterfly*, 57.
72 Davis Miller, *The Tao of Muhammad Ali* (New York: Three Rivers Press, 1996), 308.

Chapter Seven

GLOBAL INFLUENCE OF MUHAMMAD ALI'S PAN-ETHNIC VISION AND CONVICTION: AFRICA AND ASIA IN THE 1970s

Suzuko Morikawa

The multifaceted and fertile legacy of Muhammad Ali during and after his boxing period has been well-represented in the various scholarly convergences of sports, political and social activism, religion, and health and medicine. He was one of the most documented sports legends and compelling public figures, especially in the last half of the twentieth century,[1] yet his pan-ethnic vision to underscore the solidarity among people of color across the world, especially outside of the United States, has not been extensively discussed. In particular, Ali's embodiment of zeal for Afrocentric views and for recognition of cultural, social, and political determinants of sports, particularly on the African and Asian continents, has not yet been systematically analyzed. Ali's legacy of pan-ethnic consciousness for people of African and Asian descent was exemplified by his strong opposition to and condemnation of the Vietnam War and of Apartheid in South Africa, but how he has implemented such political activism through sports has not been widely publicized.

Muhammad Ali's engagement with a variety of sports and political figures from non-European continents, particularly Africa and Asia, through sports toward the end of his professional boxing career and after his retirement has been relatively overshadowed by his Afrocentric stance during his sensational earlier career. That initial engagement is represented by such visits as his first setting foot on the African continent in 1964, involving a month-long tour to Egypt, Nigeria, and Ghana, with the photographer Howard Bingham and two friends from the Nation of Islam.[2] In the midst of the Black Power Movement and Vietnam War, and during ongoing Apartheid in South Africa, Ali met with such heads of the state as Marcos Ferdinand, Sukarno, and Mobutu Sese Seko, as well as with famous sports figures and, most importantly, with ordinary citizens. As a result of these interactions, Ali consequently influenced and empowered Africans and Asians on the continents through numerous sporting events with his pan-ethnic consciousness against European supremacy and imperialism around the world.

Having regained his boxing license in 1970 after more than three years of suspension at the height of his physical fitness in his mid- and late 20s, due to his refusal to be inducted into the US army, Muhammad Ali's second phase of boxing career flourished while he resumed the demanding pace of bouts, rivalling the first half of his boxing career. Ali relaunched his career with the 1971 "Fight of the Century" and two subsequent bouts with Joe Frazier. As seen through the Ali–Frazier rivalry in boxing, the 1970s signified the importance of Black empowerment as embodied by Ali's fight against Whites' post–Civil Rights resurgence and demands for law and order against desegregation, increased crime, and urban disorders as well as conservative integrationist African American sports, cultural, and political figures.[3] This second phase of Ali's boxing career in the 1970s exemplified not only his combination of irrefutable intelligence, resilience, and raw toughness with a newly mature athleticism but also his theatric and charismatic political activism through boxing in African and Asian arenas.

Through a critical investigation of intersectionality between ethnicity, sports, culture, and politics in the international arena, this chapter demonstrates the exigency for analysis of Muhammad Ali's idea of ethnic and cultural centeredness against racism and post- and neocolonialism in the 1970s post–Civil Rights Movement and Cold War era. Ali played a key role in the advancement for contemporary African and Asian societies at a time when citizens were groping for fruitful collective knowledge, wisdom, and actions both as a source of their resilience and vitality against oppression and as a response to the instability of many postindependent African and Asian societies. By merging the mindset he demonstrated throughout his boxing career with on-the-ground experience on the African and Asian continents, Ali developed a critical and ever-evolving worldview that penetrated to the core of ethnic and cultural centeredness, inspiring generations of Africans and Asians to follow his lead. I ultimately argue that, using sports as a cultural and political tool, Ali made an indelible contribution in support of the humanity of African and Asian peoples and established a continuing legacy of pan-ethnic consciousness.

Contexualization of African and Asian Pan-Ethnic Consciousness through Sports

Muhammad Ali's iconic quote regarding his draft evasion during the Vietnam War in 1967, "I [would not] help the shooting of dark Asiatic people, who haven't lynched me, deprived me of my freedom, justice and equality, or assassinated my leaders,"[4] can be analyzed within a framework of African–Asian interaction as often described in "Black Pacific" or "AfroAsian unity" discourse since the late twentieth century. The solidarity between Asian and African countries in the modern era was politically introduced by the 1955 Bandung Conference, which aimed to discuss the role of the "Third World" in the Cold War, economic development, and decolonization.[5] The conference foreshadowed Ali's perspective on draft evasion, as participants decried incongruities in the United States' positions, particularly (a) US support of decolonization of South East Asia and Africa in post–World War II world in alliance with Britain, France, and the Netherlands and (b) the inherent contradiction of the United States' "support" for African and Asian nations' rhetoric of equality, anticolonialism, and self-determination during the ongoing

Jim Crow system in the Civil Rights Movement era. These incongruities became a vital catalyst for Afro-Asian solidarity.[6]

In *The Color Curtain: A Report on the Bandung Conference*,[7] Richard Wright assessed the 1955 Bandung Conference after prior communications with such notable luminaries of *negritude* and pan-Africanism as Aimé Césaire, Léopold Senghor, George Padmore, and Kwame Nkrumah. Wright demonstrates his support not only for the ideologies of anti-racialism, anticolonialism, national sovereignty, peace, and development but also for his perception of the core reality of racial consciousness and religion as a basis for African and Asian solidarity.[8] African American officials who attended the Bandung were empowered by linking African and Asian unity tied with anticolonialism liberation movements with African American Civil Rights Movement, but US observers, aware of the keen interest taken by European nations, especially the Soviet Union, were wary of a possible denunciation of the United States in light of discrepancies in racial inequality and the American principle of democracy. In order to strategically propagate the sign of American freedom and democracy, the US State Department sent, in addition to ongoing tours by the Harlem Globetrotters, several African American sports figures such as Jackie Robinson, Althea Gibson, Jesse Owens, and Mal Whitfield on goodwill missions to Asia during this mid-1950s Cold War period. The underlying objective was to promote capitalist democracy in the world with the idea "that if social mobility was possible for black Americans, other people of color worldwide could improve their social, political, and economic well-being by aligning with the United States."[9]

Muhammad Ali, then known as Cassius Clay, did not exhibit any challenges against existing social order during that period, not only because of the involvement of the State Department and the US Olympic Committee but also because those African American Olympians who performed as goodwill ambassadors influenced young Ali's attitudes about race, sports, and American exceptionalism.[10] When Harry Edwards, the lead organizer of the Olympic Project for Human Rights (OPHR), the organization for the boycott of the 1968 Mexico City Olympics, first met Ali during his training for the 1960 Rome Olympics, Ali's nationalist and pan-ethnic stance was not yet born, and Edwards could have never "anticipated that their paths would intersect as they ultimately did over the years."[11] Nevertheless, Ali was "an athlete of unparalleled brilliance, beauty, and bravado at a time when Black athletes (other than the Globetrotters) were expected to be seen, not heard."[12] Recognizing Ali as the "champion and the warrior saint in the revolt of the black athlete in America"[13] in the late 1960s, Edwards's establishment of the OPHR with Tommie Smith and John Carlos in 1967 ignited Black Power rhetoric. By querying African American racial identity within the context of "the hegemonic concepts of American national subjectivity,"[14] African American athletes started to criticize the morals and ethics of athletics by mainstream sports reporters and to seek an alternate approach to sports reporting from the Black perspective.[15]

The OPHR articulated five focal demands: (1) restoration of Ali's boxing title, which had been rescinded due to his draft refusal; (2) removal of Avery Brundage, the White supremacist, as head of the US Olympic Committee; (3) disinvitation of two Apartheid states, South Africa and Rhodesia; (4) boycott of the New York Athletic Club for its racist and discriminatory membership policy; and (5) more employment of Black coaches.[16]

Edwards's action brought about "an expansive international forum of transnational racialized politics in the late 1960s, particularly issues surrounding independent African nations, South African apartheid, and student social movements in the Olympic host city itself."[17] Muhammad Ali's representation of Black dignity and struggle for Black liberation changed the mindset of many African American athletes in the late 1960s, including Kareem Abdul-Jabbar, whose name change reflected both increased self-determination with regard to political and religious beliefs and decreased cooperation with the State Department's goodwill ambassadorship.[18] Since the late 1960s, Ali's ideological and instrumental nationalism as expressed through sports has caused a ripple effect through other athletes in the United States, Africa, and Asia, prompting increasingly global, pro-non-European, and culturally rooted perspectives. African and Asian solidarity emerged from the Bandung Conference to denounce Western neo- and postcolonialism, Christianity, and racism. Despite disavowals by the United States and Europe, solidarity continued to deepen through the spread of pan-ethnic ideologies in the United States through educational and political movements. Ali fomented this solidarity on the African and Asian continents further as the ambassador of cultural and ethnic pride in the 1970s.

Confluence of Boxing with Ethnic and Cultural Consciousness

Muhammad Ali's famous quote before his trip to the first international trip to the 1960 Rome Olympics, "I worry more about airplanes than I do boxing. I mean I never worry about the fight. I worry about the flight,"[19] was inverted with his numerous international trips including multiple long air flights to Asia and Africa continents in the 1970s. Ali's return to his boxing career after the three-year suspension kindled interest in the global boxing sensation. Coupled with emerging international satellite communications,[20] this renewed interest turned top-ranking heavyweight boxing fights into extravagant sporting exhibition events that journalists and media organizations followed across the world. Ali, with his flamboyant and outspoken personality, attracted many international journalists and millions of media viewers from the United States and other countries. Many of the regions Ali visited benefited from the economic boost caused by this promotion. The kickoff bout of the second half of Ali's career, the 1970 Muhammad Ali versus Jerry Quarry fight, spurred the recognition of Atlanta as a racially progressive sports capital of the South, following Atlanta's acquisition of the Braves with Hank Aaron in 1966.[21] Many countries and cities competed to host Ali's bouts, spending lavish millions as a form of cultural diplomacy in the midst of the Cold War.

Muhammad Ali brought the first professional heavyweight fight to Asia through the Ali versus Mac Forster bout in Tokyo, Japan, in 1972,[22] along with the first heavyweight world championship to Africa through the Ali versus George Foreman bout in Kinshasa, the capital city of what was then Zaire, in 1974.[23] As the 1970s transformed boxing matches into global spectacles, Ali linked his visits to Asia and Africa to his fights against anticolonial and anti-racist ideologies via his participation in political and cultural movements, thereby conveying Black Power, pan-Africanism, and Black internationalism rhetoric to different continents. The major world heavyweight championships, two of five Ali's greatest fights of all time,[24] took place in Africa and Asia in that decade.

African American promoter Don King labeled these bouts the "Rumble in the Jungle" and the "Thrilla in Manila," using his mangled rhyme schemes to manipulate enduring stereotypes against Africans and Asians. King rendered these fights successfully and profitably. His business enterprise dexterously negotiated complex deals with two major heads of state, which demonstrated brilliance in Black entrepreneurship within the White power structure on the heels of the civil rights movement.

Ali's world title matches succeeded in propelling two countries, today's Democratic Republic of the Congo and the Philippines, as well as the continents of Africa and Asia in a larger sense, into the international limelight, as Marcos Ferdinand and Sese Seko Mobutu gambled millions of dollars to bolster their own—and their respective country's—popularity. Mobutu and Marcos both used the spectacle as a distraction from their despotism. Mobutu's pro-Euro-American stance led him to order the elimination of Patrice Lumumba, who led the independence of Congo, while Marcos ordered mass killing of Muslim-majority residents of Moros under his Marshal Law. Both held up Muhammad Ali to their citizens as a symbol of Black nationalism and anticolonialism. Mobutu made an effort to advertise Zaire's modernity and unite Africans and African Americans against White supremacy with large billboards: "Black Power is sought every-where in the world," "but it is realized here in Zaire."[25] Marcos noted, "Ali symbolizes success in that part of the world which sees white men as colonial and the like. The old voices against colonialism are all over Asia again because of the Vietnam debacle, and Ali symbolizes a continuing protest against this racism and dominance because of color and birth. And while this may not be fascinating to the Western world, it is to Asians a highly charged matter."[26] Ali magnetized huge athletic event audiences in these two countries and left many Asians and Africans with a significant impression, including a vision for future generations beyond the Congo and the Philippines.

When Don King orchestrated matches between Ali versus Rudy Lubbers (of the Netherlands) in Jakarta, Indonesia, in 1973 and Ali versus Joe Bugner (of England) in Kuala Lumpur, Malaysia, in 1975,[27] Muhammad Ali made further unique and memorable impacts on Asian countries through his boxing matches against European opponents, from which political implications were obviously discerned. For both Indonesia, having experienced a long colonial rule since the Dutch East India company in the seventeenth century, and Malaysia, a former British colony, Ali's victory sent a visual and cultural anticolonial message to Indonesians and Malaysians. The 1973 bout was a nontitle fight, yet Jakarta was chosen as the site by popular demand of fervent Asian boxing fans among the 90 percent Muslim population[28] and became the first of three visits of Ali's life to Indonesia, all under the Sukarno regime.[29] Ali's win in Kuala Lumpur over a British challenger at the Stadium Merdeka (meaning "freedom and independence" in Malay), constructed at the end of British colonial rule, was also significant and with media hype's help continued Malaysians' hero worship of Ali as Malaysian legend.[30]

Athletic Humanism and Politics beyond Boxing

At the height of his worldwide popularity, with a nearly unbeatable boxing record until the late 1970s, Muhammad Ali employed expanded and versatile approaches to his career and political life, both in and outside the ring. Ali drew the interests of Muslim and newly independent nations in the 1970s, due to his employment of the rhetoric of "Asiatics" and his status as an international symbol of anti-racist, anticolonialist, and pro-Muslim support.[31] He traveled to Qatar for an open-air exhibition fight in Doha in 1971,[32] and two years after he made the Hajj to Mecca in 1972,[33] Ali met with Prime Minister Taqi al-Din al-Sulh in Beirut and then traveled to southern Lebanon to tour the refugee camps to meet the Palestinians, whom he hailed with the words "great fighting spirit."[34] The *Jewish Telegraphic Agency* reported that "[he] is losing no time throwing right hooks at Zionism"; Ali told reporters, "The United States is the stronghold of Zionism and imperialism. [...] In my name and the name of all Muslims in America, I declare support for the Palestinian struggle to liberate their homeland and oust the Zionist invaders."[35] After this trip, he played a number of matches with Libyan boxers in Libya[36] and received a guided tour of a new hydroponics project for vegetation and several local schools in Abu Dhabi by Sheikh Zayed bin Sultan Al Nahyan, His Highness and president of the United Arab Emirates.[37] Ali increasingly started to amass fame and popularity, especially among Africans and Asians who were not traditionally boxing enthusiasts.

Muhammad Ali exerted a pivotal influence on people in east and southeast Asia— as well as on himself—in the mid-1970s through his encounter with two extraordinary Asian athletes, Jhoon Rhee, the renowned South Korean Tae Kwon Do master, and Kanji "Antonio" Inoki, one of the most celebrated wrestlers in Japanese history. Ali's open-minded and critical insights into combat sports in general were evident since the early 1970s; in 1972, for instance, Ali told George Dillman, an American karate master, that "he can study the Asian arts full time" when he retired.[38] He also interacted with Joe Hess, a karate master and the kickboxing champion in 1975.[39] Rhee introduced Ali to "accupunch," a high-speed punching technique using the calculation of human reaction, that is, brain-to-wrist communication. Ali's acquisition of this skill through Rhee's instruction advanced Ali's performance; he successfully executed the technique in later critical bouts against Joe Frazier and Richard Dunn, as well as a fight against Inoki.[40] Rhee and Ali were reunited in Seoul in 1976 after the Ali versus Inoki match in Tokyo. Ali, welcomed by "hundreds of thousands of" Korean fans, left Seoul with such impression as "to tell people of the world how nice Korea is."[41]

The 1976 Muhammad Ali versus Antonio Inoki match, in Tokyo, achieved a reputation as a most rare and exclusive boxing-professional wrestling match between the current world championship holder and the most popular and unique wrestler of various martial arts. The match is infamous as the fight where a Japanese pro-wrestler— Inoki—"almost got Muhammad Ali's leg amputated"[42] and a "10 million fiasco [...] made in Japan."[43] Even today, the match generates overwhelmingly negative reactions from mainstream media and conventional Ali's fans and trainers, who consider it terrible and embarrassing.[44] Nonetheless, this match unequivocally represents Ali's quintessential traits and his magnitude both as an athlete and as a human. Firstly, this opportunity exemplifies his dexterity to turn his own inquisitiveness, inspiration, and principles into his strength. He followed his curiosity to martial arts and was open to learning totally different techniques from a palpably different cultural tradition, Asian, amid his critical winning streak of world title fights. Just as African ancestral traits led him to transform any experience into positive, effective, and productive forces against slavery, colonialism, and racism, his openness to new approaches allowed him to bring new methods into his fights. Secondly, Ali's mission of humanizing the world based on the idea of peace-loving cultural groups beyond profession, language, religion, and politics was established through collegiality and friendship between Muhammad Ali and Kanji "Antonio" Inoki. No one could have imagined a long-lasting, unparalleled, and unique relationship would be born out of this "mismatched" combat exhibition event. At his 1977 wedding, Ali gave Inoki his word that the 1976 Ali versus Inoki was the best match of his life,[45] contrary to public criticism that "Ali, Inoki fight to draw in dull bout."[46] Their relationship continued on the world stage, with Inoki following in Ali's footsteps to engage in high-profile, high-stakes diplomacy. About a month after Ali successfully negotiated the released of 15 American hostages from Iraq in Baghdad in November, 1990,[47] Inoki, who entered the House of Councillors of Japan in 1989, met with Saddam Hussein and succeeded in negotiating the release of 41 Japanese.[48] Inoki invited Ali to subsequent major events that reassured onlookers of their joint commitment to humanism and common political interests based on sports and peace, including the 1995 Sports and Culture Festival for Peace in Pyongyang, North Korea, and Inoki's 1998 Retirement Match in Tokyo.

Toward the end of his boxing career, Ali took other two atypical journeys as a sports icon to newly independent Asian countries, including Bangladesh in 1978 and China in 1979. Bangladesh, an overwhelmingly majority Muslim nation, faced economic challenges of a 70 percent poverty rate with several years of famine in the 1970s.[49] The Rahman administration honored Ali with Bangladeshi citizenship and promoted the beauty of Bangladesh through Ali's one-week visit to Dhaka and outside scenic nature preserves, including a UNESCO World Heritage Site.[50] Ali returned the gesture of cherishing the country with his words, "If I get kicked out of America, I have another home" and "If you want to go to heaven, come to Bangladesh."[51]

In December 1979, after his visit to refugee camps and other engagements in Hong Kong, Ali visited China for the first time as the first foreign athlete to be jointly invited by the Chinese Olympic Committee and China Sports Federation. As part of this visit, he met with Deng Xiaoping, three years into the aftermath of the Cultural Revolution.[52] In Hong Kong, he expressed his excitement for China and the Chinese people, saying, "I've wanted to go there since I was 10 years old. Those people are so self-sufficient; they have pulled themselves right up without asking for help from the Western world. I just admire them so much."[53] Boxing had been banned in China since 1959. Deng was receptive to Ali's advocacy of reviving boxing in China, which led to the lifting of the boxing ban in 1986, followed by China's first national boxing championship, Chinese boxers' participation in the 1992 Olympics, and the first international boxing match held in Beijing in 1993. Ali's ongoing efforts to support these developments led to his second and third trips in 1985 and 1992.[54] During his second visit, Ali wrote in the *China Youth News*: "Now that you are open to the world, never lose your culture, because others will try to give you their culture. It will be a great fight."[55]

Legacy of Muhammad Ali's Global Vision and Cultural Conviction

A significant amount of criticism emerged as a result of Muhammad Ali's travel to five countries on the African continent in 1980. Ali visited Tanzania, Kenya, Liberia, Nigeria, and Senegal, as part of a trip organized by the Carter administration to earn support in "black Africa" for a boycott against the Moscow Summer Olympics.[56] After Ali's meeting with Julius Nyerere of Tanzania and Alhaji Shehu Shagari of Nigeria, Nigerian government-run radio criticized the 1980 Olympics boycott as hypocritical and inconsistent with United States' positions over the African boycott of the 1976 Montreal Olympics, when 28 African countries boycotted to protest New Zealand's presence after that country's participation in sports with Apartheid South Africa.[57] Ali had an ongoing interest in South Africa, as he attempted to schedule a fight in South Africa in 1972 and again in 1978, though both failed. When reporters challenged him on these points at an interview, Ali appeared to have no knowledge of the Soviet Union's support for southern African liberation movements or of the United States' dismissal of the 1976 Montreal Olympics boycott.[58] When confronted with the incongruity of his role as the "Carter Administration's diplomat," he straightforwardly acknowledged, "They didn't tell me in America that Russia supports these countries. Maybe I'm being used to do something that ain't right. You have given me some questions which are good and which are making me look at this thing different."[59] He further stated, "I'm not representing America," then elaborated: "Nobody made me come here and I'm nobody's Uncle Tom."[60] Michael Ezra, the author of *Muhammad Ali: The Making of an Icon*, argues,

> If Ali could be contradictory, it was in part because he remained open to opposing ideas, and that made him precisely the wrong choice to deliver a clear American message on the Olympic boycott. Even as someone who had renounced the most strident of his black nationalist views, Ali still had a strong anti-colonial leaning toward black self-determination. Carter's position that African nations should follow the U.S. lead was one that Ali simply could not bring himself to deliver from the heart.[61]

Muhammad Ali could never be a diplomat for any state or administration because of his refusal to juggle double consciousness in himself. Rather he was a diplomat for human or cultural relationships with his constant pursuit of mutual ground and voice.

Ali's extensive travel record throughout his life has been widely publicized,[62] yet little attention has been given to *how* he traveled. Even at the height of his boxing career in the 1970s, Ali made time to pay visits to many corners of different countries, particularly in Europe, such as Germany, Spain, England, Ireland, and Switzerland, but also in Asia, Africa, and the Americas. These visits undoubtedly further advanced his popularity and accumulated wealth for the entire business enterprise surrounding Ali. His global fame and reputation accelerated via extensive coverage in *Sports Illustrated*, one of the most internationally popular sports magazines both in the 1970s and today, as well as the first pay-per-view TV broadcasting boxing match between Ali and Frazier in 1975.[63] These financial considerations cannot be dismissed, but neither should they eclipse his commitment to witness, affect, and become involved with ordinary people and to raise funds for charitable organizations. In particular, he made a conspicuous and conscious effort to build itineraries around travel to Muslim and non-European nations, regardless of distance, location, or convenience, even when incorporating those visits required additional travel shortly before or after important physically and mentally strenuous world-class bouts.

Ali's core principles of empathy and respect informed his interactions with ordinary citizens, especially countless Africans and Asians during and after post- and neocolonialism. Ali's ease in his body and apparent comfort with his always-evolving self served as an undreamed-of mirror, a conduit to appreciate and respect the beauty and strength inside themselves. Ali held babies in the Philippines, danced with children in Congo, spent an extra hour to sign autographs for Palestinian refugees, and got knocked down by a 12-year-old Bangladeshi boy in the exhibition ring. Some may argue that, in comparison to Joe Frazier, Ali's upbringing was much more secure and affluent and that, therefore, Ali's enduring consideration for needy populations reflects a fixation with charity or philanthropy, or emerges from mercenary celebrity self-interest. This contention devalues the impact of his conscious efforts to grow, learn, and question as an activist and advocate. Rather, he found goodness through brutal honesty with himself as he evolved as an African and African American, Muslim, and most importantly human, and modeled a process of growth for others. Ali touched the mind and souls of people, especially many boxers and wrestlers in Asia and Africa. In *Erasing Racism* (2003), Molefi K. Asante explicates the Afrocentrists, noting that they "are like the young visionaries, committed to finding their own centers: to inquiring about their own identities, their own culture, and their own history as a way of contributing to the grand flow of humanity without being mere imitators who follow others without first essaying their own experiences."[64] Muhammad Ali, armed with originality, unpretentiousness, and idiosyncrasy as he expanded his visions of the world, truly was an Afrocentrist full of courage and humility. As he himself affirmed, "My purpose is to be right in front of the world—as big as you can get, but at the same time humble, work with my people."[65]

Notes

1 Heather McKintosh, " 'The Trials of Muhammad Ali' Uncovers Missing Chapter behind the Legend," Documentary News, PBS, October 29, 2013, http://archive.pov.org/blog/news/2013/10/trials-of-muhammad-ali-uncovers-missing-chapter-behind-the-legend; Dick Heller, "Floating like a Butterfly, Having Stung Like a Bee," *Washington Times*, November 29, 1998, B8.

2 Mike Marqusee, "Bringing It All Back Home." In *Redemption Song: Muhammad Ali and the Spirit of the Sixties* (New York: Verso, 1999), 102–61.

3 Johnny Smith, "Reflections: Remembering Muhammad Ali: Myths, Memory, and History," *Reviews in American History* 45, 1 (2017): 182.

4 Gregory Sean. "Why Muhammad Ali Matters to Everyone," *Time*, June 4, 2016. http://time.com/3646214/muhammad-ali-deadobituary.

5 US Department of State, Milestones: 1953–1960 – Office of the Historian, "Bandung Conference (Asian-African Conference)," 1955, https://history.state.gov/milestones/1953-1960/bandung-conf.

6 Ibid.; Vijay Prashad, "Bandung Is Done: Passages in AfroAsian Epistemology," In *AfroAsian Encounters*, edited by Shannon Steen and Heike Raphael-Hernandez (New York: NYU Press, 2006), xi–xxi.

7 Richard Wright, *The Color Curtain: A Report on the Bandung Conference* (Cleveland: World Publishing, 1956).

8 Babacar M'Baye, "Richard Wright and the 1955 Bandung Conference: A Re-Evaluation of the Color Curtain," *Journeys* 10, 2 (2009): 31–44; Prashad, "Bandung Is Done," xi—xxi.

9 Damion Thomas, *Globetrotting: African American Athletes and Cold War Politics* (Champaign: University of Illinois Press, 2012).

10 Johnny Smith, "Reflections: Remembering Muhammad Ali: Myths, Memory, and History," *Reviews in American History* 45, 1 (2017): 181.

11 Harry Edwards, *The Revolt of the Black Athlete*, 50th anniversary ed. (Champaign: University of Illinois Press, 2017), vii.

12 Ibid.

13 Ibid., 75.

14 Amy Bass, "The Race between Politics and Sport," *Not the Triumph but the Struggle: The 1968 Olympics and the Making of the Black Athlete* (Minneapolis: University of Minnesota Press, 2002), 4–5.

15 Edwards, *Revolt of the Black Athlete*, 30.

16 Dave Zirin, "The Explosive 1968 Olympics," *International Socialist Review* 61, September–October (2008), http://www.isreview.org/issues/61/feat-zirin.shtml.

17 Bass, "The Race between Politics and Sport," 4–5.

18 Kevin B. Witherspoon, "Going 'to the fountainhead': Black American athletes as cultural ambassadors in Africa, 1970–1971," *International Journal of the History of Sport* 30, 13 (2013): 1508–22.

19 *What's My Name: Muhammad Ali*, episode 1, Chapter One, directed by Antoine Fuqua (2019; HBO Sports), https://www.kanopy.com/product/chapter-one, 83 min.

20 John Matthew Smith, "The Resurrection," *Southern Cultures* 21, 2 (Summer 2015): 6–8.

21 Ibid., 15–17.

22 John M. Lee, "The Ali Bout: Just a Japanese Sandman," *New York Times*, April 2, 1972, sec. S, 2, https://www.nytimes.com/1972/04/02/archives/the-ali-bout-just-a-japanese-sandman.html.

23 Lewis A. Erenberg, "'Rumble in the Jungle': Muhammad Ali vs. George Foreman in the age of global apectacle," *Journal of Sport History* 39, 1 (2012): 82.

24 Steve Bunce, "Muhammad Ali's five greatest fights: From the Thrilla in Manila to the Rumble in the Jungle," *Independent*, June 4, 2016, https://www.independent.co.uk/news/people/muhammad-ali-dead-greatest-fights-rumble-in-the-jungle-thrilla-in-manila-rumble-jungle-cassius-clay-a7065211.html.

25 Erenberg, "'Rumble in the Jungle'," 90.

26 Mark Kram, "Manila for Blood and for Money," *Sports Illustrated* 43, 13 (September 29, 1975): 29.

27 Dave Anderson, "The King of the Boxing Promoters," *New York Times*, April 28, 1975, 52, https://www.nytimes.com/1975/04/28/archives/the-king-of-the-boxing-promoters.html.

28 "Ali-Lubbers Bout Fiscally in Dutch," *Washington Post, Times Herald (1959–1973)*, October 20, 1973, D2.

29 Heri Gagarin, "Commentary: Remembering Muhammad Ali's Visit to Indonesia," *Jakarta Globe*, June 23, 2016, https://jakartaglobe.id/opinion/commentary-remembering-muhammad-alis-visit-indonesia.

30 Syed Nadzi, "When we were struck by 'Ali fever,'" *New Straits Times*, June 5, 2016, 4.

31 Amir Saeed, "'Worthy of all praises': Muhammad Ali and the politics of identity," *Soundings* 47 (Spring 2011): 128.

32 Anand Holla, "The champ, once more!" *Gulf Times*, July 4, 2016, https://www.gulf-times.com/story/500408/The-Champ-once-more; Victor Bolorunduro, "When Muhammad Ali graced Doha and fought a bout," *Qatar Tribune*, June 5, 2016, https://www.qatar-tribune.com/news-details/id/5613.

33 Ali Khaled, "How Muhammad Ali became a sporting hero to the Arab world," *Al Arabiya*, June 3, 2016, https://english.alarabiya.net/en/sports/2016/06/04/How-Muhammad-Ali-became-a-sporting-hero-to-the-Arab-world.

34 Michael R. Fischbach, *Black Power and Palestine: Transnational Countries of Color* (Redwood City :Stanford University Press, 2018), 140–41.

35 Jewish Telegraphic Agency, "Ali Bets Zionism," *Daily News Bulletin* 12, no. 47, March 8, 1974, 4.

36 Ali Al-Qataani, "Fight for your right," *Correspondents.org*, July 23, 2012, https://correspondents.org/en/2012/07/23/fight-for-your-right.

37 James Langon, "Time Frame: Muhammad Ali tours Abu Dhabi," *Lifestyle*, November 4, 2011, https://www.thenational.ae/lifestyle/time-frame-muhammad-ali-tours-abu-dhabi-1.424855; Ali Khaled, "How Muhammad Ali became a sporting hero."

38 Robert W. Young, "The 1970s: Highlights from the martial arts world during black Bbelt's first half-century," *Black Belt*, 49, 2 (February 2011): 49.

39 Dave Anderson, "The karate king wants Ali for kicks," *New York Times*, May 10, 1975, sec. Archives, https://www.nytimes.com/1975/05/10/archives/the-karate-king-wants-ali-for-kicks.html.

40 Young, "The 1970s," 51.

41 "Ali gets real 'soul' welcome in Seoul," *Pacific Stars & Stripes*, June 29, 1976, 17.

42 "The Japanese pro wrestler who almost got Muhammad Ali's leg amputated," *Los Angeles Times*, June 9, 2016, https://www.latimes.com/sports/sportsnow/la-sp-japanese-muhammad-ali-20160606-snap-htmlstory.html.

43 "Ali, Inoki rope the dopes: So fans are disappointed?" *Los Angeles Times*, June 26, 1976, C3, 2.

44 Andy Bull, "The forgotten story of … Muhammad Ali v Antonio Inoki," *Guardian*, US Edition, November 11, 2009, https://www.theguardian.com/sport/blog/2009/nov/11/the-forgot ten-story-of-ali-inoki.

45 *Shukan Puroresu (Weekly Professional Wrestling)*, the 40-year anniversary of the Antonio Inoki vs. Muhammad Ali edition, *Baseball Magazine*, Tokyo, June 21, 2016, 28.

46 Andrew H. Malcolm, "Ali, Inoki fight to draw in dull bout," *New York Times*, June 26, 1976, sec. Archives, https://www.nytimes.com/1976/06/26/archives/ali-inoki-fight-to-draw-in-dull-bout-ali-and-inoki-fight-to-draw-in.html.

47 "Boxing's Muhammad Ali meets with Saddam, hostage release promised," *Associated Press News*, November 27, 1990, https://apnews.com/ae7d3a67b1cb4abd5e100821ce810805.

48 "Profile of Antonio Inoki," Coralz, https://www.coralz.co.jp/profile.html.

49 S. R. Osmani, "Notes on some recent estimates of rural poverty in Bangladesh," *Bangladesh Development Studies* 18, 3 (1990): 75–87.

50 "Rare video when Muhammad Ali visited Bangladesh 1978" ("Muhammad Ali goes east: Bangladesh, I love you"), *Dailymotion*, 2020, https://www.dailymotion.com/video/x4ek 60g, 42 min.

51 Palash Ghosh, "Muhammad Ali in Bangladesh: 35 years ago the champ visited a new nation in turmoil," *International Business Times*, August 12, 2013, sec. World, https://www.ibtimes.com/muhammad-ali-bangladesh-35-years-ago-champ-visited-new-nation-turmoil-1382005.

52 Bo Bai, "Tencent: Ali helped restore boxing to glory in China," *ESPN.com*, June 4, 2016, https://www.espn.com/boxing/ali/story/_/id/15948776/boxing-muhammad-ali-vis its-china-meets-deng-xiao-ping.

53 Dave Hadfield, "China trip ends dream for superstar Ali," *South China Morning Post*, December 18, 1979.

54 Mike Ives, "How Muhammad Ali helped revive boxing in China," *Aljazeera*, June 9, 2016, sec. Feature/Sports, https://www.aljazeera.com/indepth/features/2016/06/muhammad-ali-hel ped-revive-boxing-china-160608063601546.html.

55 Jun Mai, "How Muhammad Ali helped land knockout blow to end China's 20-year ban on boxing," *South China Morning Post*, June 4, 2016.

56 Victoria Brittain, "Ali retreats on boycott of Moscow," *Washington Post*, February 5, 1980, https://www.washingtonpost.com/archive/politics/1980/02/05/ali-retreats-on-boycott-of-moscow/5c18c0a8-8b44-434d-b1f0-6c958b4bf1de/.

57 Ibid.

58 Stephen R. Wenn and Jeffrey P. Wenn, "Muhammad Ali and the convergence of Olympic sport and U.S. diplomacy in 1980: A reassessment from behind the scenes at the U.S. State Department," *Olympika: The International Journal of Olympic Studies* II (1993): 51.

59 Ibid.

60 Ibid.

61 Michael Ezra, "Muhammad Ali's strange, failed diplomatic career," *POLITICO Magazine*, June 5, 2016, https://www.politico.com/magazine/story/2016/06/muhammad-ali-diplomat-213941.

62 "Muhammad Ali's passports for sale," *Brampton Guardian*, June 8, 2016, 1.

63 Neven Šerić and Jasenko Ljubica, *Market Research Methods in the Sports Industry* (Bingley: Emerald, 2018), 4.

64 Molefi Asante, *Erasing Racism: The Survival of the American Nation* (Amherst, NY: Prometheus Books, 2003), 242.

65 Jim Colonna, "Ali decks press to open promotional tour," *Stars and Stripes*, October 11, 1975, https://www.stripes.com/news/ali-decks-press-to-open-promotional-tour-1.7753.

Chapter Eight

MUHAMMAD ALI'S CUBA CONNECTIONS

Anju Reejhsinghani

I was in Havana the day Muhammad Ali died. The news reached me the following day through the Cuban news media, though I quickly confirmed it flipping through the multiplicity of foreign cable channels in my simple hotel room, which, like most others in Cuba, lacked WiFi. Without phone alerts and messages barraging me, without my close-knit boxing circle to process the news with, it did not feel quite real. As retired *Miami Herald* sports columnist Edwin Pope, who covered young Cassius Clay through his phenomenal rise and transformation into Muhammad Ali, wrote, "I was actually a little surprised to hear he had died. You see, I had felt he died a long time ago."[1] Pope was referring to the glorious young Clay/Ali who twice defeated the once-invincible Sonny Liston. Other obituaries referenced the Ali–Frazier trifecta, the Rumble in the Jungle against George Foreman, and, of course, the battles Ali waged out of the ring to avoid going to Vietnam before he was redeemed in full by the courts and by history, leading to his triumphal lighting of the Olympic flame in 1996. For many who came of age after Ali had left the ring, however, he could not die because he had already been beatified. The students on my study abroad program were saddened, of course, as they would be by the loss of any beloved sports figure. But they had no memory of Ali the upstart, Ali the braggart, Ali the champion, Ali the rebel, Ali the visionary, Ali the peacemaker. He was just Ali to them.

Cuban president Raúl Castro, attending the Havana summit of the Organization of American States (OAS), issued a public statement in response to Ali's passing. To robust applause from delegates (slightly jarring to ears used to moments of silence on such occasions), Castro expressed condolences and a message of solidarity to the Ali family, to the people of the United States, and especially to the African American community, "whose rights he [Ali] always defended." Speaking on behalf of the Cuban people, he said, "We will never forget his chivalry and ethics, his rejection of war, and his defense of peace." He praised Ali for "his respect and friendship with Comrade Fidel," his then ailing older brother, who would pass away that November, shortly after the election that swept Donald Trump into the US presidency.[2]

Raúl Castro did not use the occasion to delve into Ali's connections with Cuba. For Cubans and Americans of a certain age, the primary one was the fight that never was—a long rumored 1970s professional heavyweight championship matchup between Ali and eventual three-time Cuban Olympic gold medalist, Teófilo Stevenson. More than any actual Cold War bout, it epitomized the seemingly impassable distance between these two nations, one that could be bridged only in a heavyweight championship ring. The failed event may have simply become a relic of a bygone era had not Ali, retired and suffering from Parkinson's syndrome, met Stevenson in the 1990s while on humanitarian missions to the island, the first trip immortalized by Ed Bradley on the US news program *60 Minutes* and by Gay Talese in a feature for *Esquire*. Awed observers saw glimpses of the two old fighters' magnificence as they mock sparred in an Old Havana gym, determined young boxers waiting their turn for a go at Ali.[3] It remained in question who would have bested the other back in 1976 or 1977, and what that might have meant for US–Cuba relations at the time, not to mention for boxing history.[4]

Yet as this essay briefly explores, Ali's pugilistic connections with Cuba began much earlier, shortly after the 1960 Summer Olympics at which he won his light-heavyweight gold medal. Cuba, at the time less than two years into its revolution, fielded a team of just 12 athletes, among them a single boxer, lightweight Estebán Aguilera.[5] Far from the Olympic machine it would become, Cuba in 1960 was still trying to maintain its once-robust prizefighting industry while building greater ties to the international amateur arena, long neglected in the prerevolutionary days when fighters were incentivized to go pro and go north. After returning home to Louisville and making his way to Miami, Ali joined the multiracial 5th Street Gym, home to a growing list of early 1960s-era Cuban exiles and US promoters and trainers who had witnessed the collapse of Cuban prizefighting.[6] Trainer Angelo Dundee and his promoter brother Chris worked with fighters from Argentina, Mexico, Puerto Rico, the Dominican Republic, and elsewhere but seemed to specialize in Cubans, "fighters like Florentino Fernández, Luis Rodríguez, Doug Vaillant, Ultiminio 'Sugar' Ramos, and José Legra among dozens more."[7]

Like many old-school boxing gyms, the 5th Street Gym, a second-floor walk-up in Miami Beach, could best be described as "funky."[8] Located at the corner of 5th Street and Washington Avenue in a neighborhood that would undergo a complete transformation in the ensuing decades, its early 1960s infusion of multiracial Latin American and Caribbean migrants was a microcosm of wider changes occurring in South Florida. The Dundees played their own small role in hastening that social change, Chris with his Cuban "import business" and Angelo by ferrying cash and jewels from wealthy Cubans at his Havana bouts who made clear their goal to flee to South Florida. At Chris's request, Angelo Dundee even learned "gym Spanglish" to communicate with the new fighters as well as the multitalented Luis Sarría, a former top Cuban trainer who would go on to become Ali's masseur.[9]

Ali, then Clay, fresh off his Olympic win and dazzling ring observers with hand and foot speed, quickly rose to the top of the gym's ranks and into position as a top heavyweight contender. Though they rarely make it into popular biographies and films about Ali, which tend to focus more on what he borrowed from wrestler-showman Gorgeous George, Ali's Afro-Cuban stablemates played a critical role in his pugilistic education. He relied on Sarría for far more than physical conditioning. Sarría, who had trained the Cuban amateur team as well as 1940s Afro-Cuban middleweight world contender Kid Tunero (Evelio Mustelier), had a wealth of knowledge that quickly led to his becoming one of the most trusted members of the gym staff and a frequent cornerman for exile fighters' title bouts.[10] Stylistically, Ali was indebted to Luis Manuel

Rodríguez, the welterweight nicknamed "El Feo" (Ugly), whose rapid-fire flurries dazzled opponents. Years later, Angelo Dundee recalled Rodríguez's velocity as exceeding even that of Ali and his later superstar, Sugar Ray Leonard: "Ray had the fastest combinations of all my fighters. Muhammad had a fast one-two. But the quickest hands belonged to Luis. He could hit you over and over again with a jab that you didn't expect to get hit with. He was fast but also nimble and graceful. And it was effortless." Ali did not, however, take to Rodríguez's defensive posture. The latter "kept his hands up," blocked hits well with his gloves, and "had this constant bouncy head movement that made guys miss just by an inch or two," while young Ali/Clay leaned away from punches, "usually with his hands down by his waist."[11] That strategy, of course, stopped working quite as well as Ali aged.

Outside the 5th Street Gym, Miami was a deeply segregated city, one that viewed the young Ali/Clay through strict racial lines.[12] The area, in particular Miami Beach, had seen a rise in its Jewish population after World War II from 5,500 in 1940 to 55,000 in 1950. As Jews and other European ethnics assimilated into Whiteness, the racial line remained heavily fortified against African Americans and Afro-Latin Americans.[13] "Running while black" remained a threat to athletes traversing neighborhood or city limits without prior notice. Police stopped to question young Clay when they saw him running across the Miami causeway; one writer noted that Black people were not welcome in Miami Beach at the time "unless you had a reason" to be there.[14] Like almost all Black athletes in the early 1960s South, Ali was forced to stay in segregated motels like the Booker Terrace in Brownsville and to eat at restaurants that catered to Black visitors unable to eat at or stay near the beach.[15] For several years, he lived in the predominantly Black neighborhood of Overtown, an area northwest of downtown that had been deemed "blighted" shortly before his arrival. As a result, sociologist Jan Lin notes, power brokers displaced "tens of thousands of residents and businesses, to make way for the elevated expressway and associated cloverleaf exchanges" of Interstate 95 that "destroyed the commercial and residential heart of Overtown." The neighborhood and other northern urban areas like Liberty City and Brownsville that were carved out for the Black community thus became both spatially and racially segregated from Anglo and increasingly Hispanic Miami.[16]

Ali's Afro-Cuban stablemates could traverse Spanish-speaking spaces but, like Ali, still faced racial profiling and segregation from Southern Whites. An additional burden was the expectation from Anglo and Cuban exile Whites that they adhere to staunch anticommunism regardless of their views on the dismantling of the most overt forms of White supremacy in Cuba during the early revolution.[17] Adding to the pressure, defectors like Rodríguez, who had been lionized during the early days of the Castro regime, also feared repercussions from the Cuban state itself.[18] In July 1961, Rodríguez, his Cuban-born manager Ernesto Corrales, and Sarría were swept up in a hijacking that took them to Havana instead of Dallas for a welterweight title fight.[19] While negotiations for the plane's return went smoothly and all passengers returned safely, the experience was apparently traumatic for Rodríguez, who lost by split decision to Curtis Cokes several days later.[20] Thus, while not himself directly connected to the political upheaval surrounding these vulnerable new exiles, young Ali/Clay would likely have been aware of them.

Differences on Castro, especially after the formal breaking of ties between the United States and Cuba, quickly became an area in which radical African Americans could differentiate themselves politically from Whites as well as more moderate Black peers. Within months of publicly embracing Cuba's rejection of racial segregation and other measures to benefit its Afro-Cuban population, African Americans seeking to operate within the mainstream, like former heavyweight champion Joe Louis—whose public relations firm briefly advertised revolutionary Cuba as a tourist site for middle-class African Americans ("first-class treatment as first-class citizens")—were forced to renounce any transformational potential in the revolution out of fear of being labeled a communist. In August 1961, the US Senate Internal Security subcommittee accused "Fidel Castro and his Communist henchmen" of trying to "subvert the American Negro against his own Government," an effort which, the subcommittee was relieved to report, had failed.[21]

The distance that these and other US-led efforts created between revolutionary Cubans and middle-class African Americans highlighted generational and ideological schisms in the US Black community. The Cuban government's eager acceptance of African American visitors and exiles helped to solidify its image as an upstart multiracial country advancing much farther and faster on race relations than the United States, but it also used propaganda effectively to contrast its seemingly peaceful progress with the tumult of the US civil rights movement. As Cynthia A. Young reminds us, "In the early 1960s, it seemed as if Cuba had succeeded where the United States had failed."[22]

The rise of Black Power interest in revolutionary Cuba preceded Ali's dramatic emergence as a Black Muslim and his rejection of the assimilationist vision of the mainstream civil rights movement. Despite the overwrought reaction of most Whites in the boxing world, Ali's conversion was less controversial than the open embrace of communist nations by Black intellectuals and artists. Though it took several years, Michael O. West argues, "Black Power recentered black internationalism. Gone was the fear of Red-baiting, the communist bogey, which had dogged the civil rights movement."[23] As activists like Robert F. Williams and Amiri Baraka gravitated to Cuba and later China, they signaled to older civil rights figures that fear of communism did not merit continued injustice against African Americans. Through a cultivation of alliances—with Black celebrities, business leaders, and tourists and, later, activist expatriates, —Castro's government ably exploited fissures in the African American and diasporic community, causing alarm in Washington and giving cover to liberal Whites calling for a more limited civil rights agenda in the United States.

It was in this context that Muhammad Ali's religious conversion and pronouncements about racial separation could be reinterpreted in ways that strengthened Cuba's invective about US anti-Black racism. In *Soul on Ice*, Eldridge Cleaver pointed an accusatory finger not only against "'white' white America" but also "'white' black America" for working against "autonomous Negroes." In boxing, the first autonomous Black man, Cleaver claimed, was Sonny Liston (no mention was made of Jack Johnson). But Liston was "nonideological"; as Cleaver wrote, "The mystique he exuded was that of a lone wolf who did not belong to his people or speak to them." In this way, explained Cleaver, Liston represented "the competitive ethic undergirding American culture. If every man is for himself, it was rational for Liston to be for *himself*." Muhammad Ali, on the contrary, was "a genuine revolutionary, the Black Fidel Castro of boxing."[24] Cleaver spared no vitriol for former heavyweight champion Floyd Patterson—a "boot-licking" "Uncle Tom" whom Ali had soundly defeated at their recent 1965 heavyweight title fight in Las Vegas—drawing an extended metaphor between Patterson's defeat and that of US-backed exile forces in April 1961:

> Muhammad Ali, in crushing the Rabbit [Floyd Patterson] in twelve [...] inflicted a psychological chastisement on "white" white America similar in shock value to Fidel Castro's at the Bay of Pigs. If the Bay of Pigs can be seen as a straight right hand to the psychological jaw of white America, then Las Vegas was a perfect left hook to the gut.[25]

Leaving aside claims about Patterson's willingness to serve "white" white America—a picture that Ali himself later cast doubt on and one that has been much complicated by recent work on this understudied champion[26]—Cleaver's narrative likens White Americans' shock at Cuba's resounding defeat of American exceptionalism to their inability to process Ali's athletic supremacy. In this way, Fidel Castro and Muhammad Ali were defeating the same enemy: hypocritical White Americans (and their Cuban counterparts) who rejected autonomy for others beside themselves. Like Castro, Ali reflected and refracted his people's "furious psychic stance." As an unapologetic militant inside the ring and out, he was thus a far more dangerous Black champion than any who had come before.[27]

Some years later, Ali himself made a similar argument about how African Americans could learn to be more autonomous from the example of revolutionary Cuba. In a November 1975 *Playboy* interview, he drew parallels to the unfinished struggle for African American freedom, which could end only with the creation of a new homeland:

> Muslims will never be satisfied with integration and all the little jobs and promises black people get. We want our own nation. We're twenty-five million black people—there's a lot of Negroes in America, you know? Man, there's only about ten million people in Cuba, and when they tell America to stay out, America *stays* out. They're just a few million, but they got their own nation and can get away with it. Nigerians and Ghanians [*sic*] have *their* own country. When I rode through Zaire and looked at their little flag and watched them doing their little dances, hey, it was *their* own country. But we're a whole nation of slaves still in bondage to white people. We worked three hundred years to make this country rich and fought for it in the Japanese war, the German war, the Korean war—in all the wars—and we *still* don't have nothing![28]

Ali may have been revolutionary owing to his adherence to the Nation of Islam, but he was not ideologically consistent. Gerald Early provocatively argues that, "Ali, despite all the talk of his brilliance, was not a thoughtful man. He was not conversant with ideas. Indeed, he hadn't a single idea in his head, really. What he had was the faith of the true believer."[29] Ali's uses of Cuba could therefore shift according to his audience, the context, and the point he was trying to get across. To promote Black separatism, Ali spotlighted Cuba as having thrown over the yoke of imperialism as had been done in newly independent African nations. In a 1989 interview, he recalled that what first drew him to the Nation of Islam was hearing Malcolm X's message of why African Americans needed to cast off "slave names." In Ali's recollection, Malcolm said, "Chinese are named after China. Cubans are named after Cuba, Russians after Russia, Germans after Germany. All people are named after the country. What country is called Negro?"[30] Far from being a country that had enslaved and colonized its own people, Cuba in this telling became a racially homogenous nation, one that cast off US enslavement to achieve true freedom.

Nonetheless, Ali could speak the language of capitalism when it suited him, as he did when trying to drum up public interest in a potential prizefight between himself and Teófilo Stevenson. The idea was floated following Stevenson's second Olympic gold medal win, in Montreal. Don King, the African American promoter who had made his name by pulling off the Rumble in the Jungle in Zaire, attempted to promote the fight and had talked about arranging a preliminary bout for Ali in Havana, with Stevenson on the undercard fighting as an amateur. To this and other offers, Stevenson flatly refused. As early as 1974, he said, "What is a million dollars against eight million Cubans who love me?"[31] Stevenson's height (6-foot-5), range (7 feet from fingertip to fingertip with arms outstretched), muscular physique (215 to 220 pounds at his peak), and youth (a decade younger than Ali) were all distinct advantages, even if as an amateur Stevenson had never fought bouts of 12 or 15 rounds. By 1976, with Ali's best fights behind him and money low, he indulged in talk of the Stevenson fight or even an exhibit.[32] The boxing world was champing at the bit for an exciting new face, and as Ali aged, the window for such a matchup was smaller by the day. In the end, Castro praised Stevenson's not giving in to "traffickers of bodies and souls." Much later, after both men had retired from the sport, they each claimed to believe the bout would have been a draw.[33] Without the fight, just as with other aborted efforts to engage in sport diplomacy in the late Nixon era, the sporting impasse between both countries remained well into the post–Cold War period.

Similarly, Ali's spirited defense of Black Muslims didn't always extend to other religious minorities. When former Cuban welterweight champion Kid Gavilán (Gerardo González)—who retired in 1958 and subsequently endured expropriation of his beloved farm as well as jail stints for proselytizing as a Jehovah's Witness—was finally able to depart for Florida in 1968, Ali had little to say publicly about Gavilán's ordeals or the importance of upholding religious freedom in Cuba. What offended him, it seemed, was the news that Gavilán was working in a Miami park:

See, once you become a Muslim, you want for your brother what you want for yourself. For instance, Kid Gavilan was a black boxing champion who had trouble in Cuba after he retired and he wound up in Miami working in a park. Newspaper reporters used to write stories about it that would embarrass Kid Gavilan and when I heard what he was doing, I thought, 'Kid Gavilan ain't gonna work in no *park.*' So I found Kid Gavilan and now he works for me, and I pay him a lot better than what he made in the park. Why should I allow one of the world's greatest black fighters in history to end up workin' in a park? He's representing all of us.[34]

The aged Kid, nearly blind from cataracts, was thus valuable to Ali for the religious merit this redemption would bring. Unfortunately for Gavilán, the relationship with Ali quickly went south. Ali grandly presented him with a $1,000 check, offering significantly more for his help training Ali in Zaire.[35] Gavilán went on to sue Ali, claiming he had been promised $200 a week and $5,000 per fight for 10 fights. He ultimately won a judgment of about $40,000 and went on to work for Trevor Berbick, Ali's final opponent. Sadly, when Gavilán died in 2003, he was buried in a pauper's grave—but later reburied with funds from former boxing stars and Mike Tyson, then still active in the game.[36]

In keeping with Ali's positive statements about respecting Cuban autonomy over the years, race was a "problem" the Castro government claimed to have solved when it eradicated the most odious remnants of the Fulgencio Batista dictatorship. In reality, structural racism continued to contribute to inequities in housing, employment, and political service, realities that many Afro-Cubans (at least those within the country) didn't feel safe articulating publicly until the 1990s. By the time Ali actually had a chance to visit Cuba, in 1996 and 1998, Cuba was undergoing a flowering of Afro-Cuban musical, art, and spiritual expression that had begun to attract diasporic interest from the United States and elsewhere. His visits also coincided with the hardening of the Cold War against Cuba, as the United States sought to destabilize one of the sole remaining communist governments in the world. Like Pope John Paul II's 1998 visit, Ali's 1996 and 1998 Havana sojourns were brief healing moments for US–Cuba ties at a moment when Cuba remained mired in crisis and the hard-right exile movement centered in South Florida approached its post–Cold War political zenith.

The collapse of the Soviet Union fueled a 40 percent contraction in the Cuban economy between 1989 and 1993 and buoyed US policymaking expectations that Fidel Castro, and perhaps communism itself, was finally on the way out. George H. W. Bush's administration oversaw passage of the 1992 Toricelli Act (Cuban Democracy Act) restricting US subsidiary trade with Cuba and hampering third-party vessels that sailed to Cuba from continuing on to the United States. Predictably, the tightening of the embargo hastened the departure of desperate Cubans, who began fleeing by the thousands across the Florida Strait in makeshift rafts. The *balsero* crisis of 1994, which led to adjustments in US policy to discourage Cuban migration by sea, was soon followed by the Republican takeover of the US House and Senate. Despite signs that the United States and Cuba were taking tentative steps toward rapprochement, the proposed Helms–Burton Act—known in full as the Cuban Liberty and Democratic Solidarity (Libertad) Act—attempted to encircle the world in the trade embargo and to bring revolutionary Cuba to its knees. In February 1996, the Cuban government shot down two jets from Brothers to the Rescue, a right-wing exile organization, after warnings about their violations of its airspace. In response, President Clinton signed the Helms–Burton into law in March 1996, thus enshrining the embargo (previously a set of executive orders) into US law.[37]

It was in this context that Ed Bradley and *60 Minutes* covered Ali's first humanitarian visit to Cuba. Ali was accompanied by his wife, Lonnie; close friend and photographer Howard Bingham; screenwriter Greg Howard; and *Esquire* writer Gay Talese, along with members of the nonprofits that he was representing. Ali was tasked to be the head of a delegation sending $500,000 in medical supplies to Cuba. His travel expenses were covered by Direct Relief International, which was hoping to drum up additional publicity about the plight of Cuba during the embargo.[38]

This was not Ali's first trip to a country with fractured relationships with the United States. In 1990, he traveled to Iraq to meet Saddam Hussein, where he negotiated the exchange of 15 US prisoners that Hussein had ordered detained after the invasion of Kuwait. Six weeks after Ali and the prisoners returned, Operation Desert Storm began.[39] This trip helped to establish his credibility as a representative for peace, especially in the Muslim world, even when it meant meeting with leaders who were reviled in the United States. Moreover, according to Lonnie Ali, the visit to Havana was nonpolitical. Despite the tightening of the embargo after Torricelli and Helms–Burton, US law permitted exemptions for humanitarian relief. Toward the end of its stay, the group—along with Teófilo Stevenson, who accompanied Ali throughout his trip, and Stevenson's young wife, Fraymaris—was granted a meeting with Fidel Castro, which was filmed for *60 Minutes* and covered by Talese for *Esquire*. The Cuban biweekly journal *Bohemia* wrote an article about the visit, focusing mostly on "the fight that never was" but also discussing Ali's humanitarian mission in some detail. According to *Bohemia*, Ali told Stevenson, "Castro is a good man," and left the journal an affectionate note in English, which it translated. Ali also signed a Bingham photograph for Castro.[40]

Following the Pope's January 1998 visit, during which he called for Cuba to open itself to the world and for the world to open itself to Cuba, Ali's second and last trip to Cuba—accompanied by Lonnie Ali, actor and activist Ed Asner, and Asner's wife—was another effort to push against the US embargo. The trip was a follow-up to the distribution of $1.2 million in aid through Direct Relief of Santa Barbara and the Disarm Education Fund of New York, which was distributed to Cuban polyclinics. The Alis visited sick children at the Juan Manuel Marquez Children's Hospital and, through Lonnie, called again for an end to the US embargo. "I think human suffering transcends barriers," she said. "I don't think politics should ever be involved in that. You cannot deny someone health and assistance based on politics. It's ridiculous. If Americans would come over here and watch these people here or go to Iraq and watch those babies die in front of their eyes, I don't think any of them would stand for that." The Alis also met again with Fidel Castro, who used the visit to declare that the US people were against the embargo. Yet the trip was notable on both ends, US and Cuban, for being apolitical, as both Alis wished.[41]

The trips did not seem to draw the ire of the hard-right exile community in the same way as did Hollywood liberals speaking out against the embargo. By the time of his Cuban visits, the 1996 Olympic torch-lighting moment had occurred, and Ali, who rarely spoke in public, was no longer seen as a threat to the political establishment. The downsides of his commodification and universalization were often remarked upon while Ali was alive.[42] More than any single human being with the possibility of the Pope, Muhammad Ali was able to bridge the US-Cuban divide at a time when every aspect of that relationship was being politicized. His visits brought to life what a new relationship between the countries might look like, even if that proved evanescent.

Ali's visits, moreover, coincided with the rise of an Afro-Cuban youth movement. By the mid-1990s, young Cubans were both covertly and openly expressing the limits of racial equality in revolutionary Cuba through hip-hop, visual arts, and other media. It remains unclear what impact, if any, these fleeting trips had upon those who were too young to remember his greatness in the ring. But at least according to Fidel, the Cuban people had never lost their veneration for Ali: "He was very much admired as a sportsman, as a boxer, as a person. There was always a high opinion of him."[43]

Ali lived to see the beginning of normalization between the United States and Cuba, though that, too, has proven fleeting. (Stevenson died in 2012.) In March 2016, President Barack Obama called out the equality of Ali and Stevenson in his speech in Old Havana. He reminded his audience:

> We share a national past time, la pelotero [baseball], and later today our players will compete on the same Havana field that Jackie Robinson played on before he made his major league debut. And it is said that our greatest boxer, Muhammad Ali, once paid tribute to a Cuban that he could never fight, saying that he would only be able to reach a draw with the great Cuban, Teofilo Stevenson.[44]

Acknowledging the athletic equality of Ali and Stevenson—something no sitting US president had done before—was a significant indication that the Obama Administration had come to accept Cuba as a sovereign, independent nation, at least in its domestic sphere. A few months later, upon hearing of Ali's passing, Raúl Castro returned the favor with his graceful words for Ali at the OAS Summit. The Cuban state-run media was uniformly adulatory in memorializing Ali, reflecting the respect and admiration personally shown by Fidel during his 1990s visits. In this telling, far beyond his athletic pursuits and even his civil rights activism, Ali is remembered as an advocate for peace; his contribution to ending the embargo will not be forgotten.

In the United States, Ali remains, in death, both ever present and startlingly absent from a narrative that owes so much to his example. . One wonders how he would have responded to the ascendance of Black Lives Matter in the wake of George Floyd's murder; to the growth of sports activism across racial lines; to the legacies of intervention in Afghanistan and elsewhere; and to the unequal impacts of the COVID-19 pandemic on communities of color. In so many ways, he was on the right side of history, but his message has perhaps been diluted in its universalization. (The commodification of the Ali legacy may have assisted with this process; following the severing of his business ties with Herbert Muhammad, Ali and Lonnie sold 80 percent of the marketing rights to his name and image to entertainment company CKX for $50 million.[45]) Ali's unsparing stances have been shaped into a mantra of sorts that further loosens him from the confines of history. The Ali Center in Louisville holds as its motto "Be Great: Do Great Things." As its six core principles, it states:

Confidence Belief in oneself, one's abilities, and one's future.
Conviction A firm belief that gives one the courage to stand behind that belief, despite pressure to do otherwise.

Dedication	The act of devoting all of one's energy, effort, and abilities to a certain task.
Giving	To present voluntarily without expecting something in return.
Respect	Esteem for, or a sense of the worth or excellence of, oneself and others.
Spirituality	A sense of awe, reverence, and inner peace inspired by a connection to all of creation and/or that which is greater than oneself.[46]

This essay intended to offer an initial glimpse into the meanings of Ali for Cuba and Cuba for Ali. Both are worthy of further study in context of the wider African American civil rights movement, Black internationalism, and Third World nationalism during the Cold War. For many in Cuba and among the Cuban diaspora in the United States, however, the roots of Ali's greatness were sometimes contradictory but nevertheless authentic, the response to what he saw as injustice at home and abroad. From his relationships with Afro-Cuban boxers in their South Beach gym to the "fight that never was" and his humanitarian visits to Cuba, Ali did more than embody the six core values discussed above. He found ways to connect with ordinary Cubans at home and in diaspora that, if not exactly healing the divide between the United States and Cuba, at least offered a much needed respite from it.

Notes

1 Edwin Pope, "Memories of Ali on His Way to Fight Liston," *Miami Herald,* January 19, 2017. The article was originally published on June 5, 2016, and rerun after Pope's passing at the age of 88.

2 Reuters, "Cuba's President Remembers Muhammad Ali," June 4, 2016, https://in.reuters.com/video/watch/cubas-president-remembers-muhammad-ali-id368785519 (video since disabled).

3 60 Minutes Overtime, "1996: 60 Minutes Profiles Muhammad Ali," https://www.cbsnews.com/news/60-minutes-muhammad-ali-ed-bradley/, June 4, 2014; Gay Talese, "Boxing Fidel," *Esquire,* September 1996, 138–47.

4 One contemporary writer has composed an answer to this question. See Tony McDougall, *The Fight We Never Saw* (London, Ontario: Lucha Comics, 2020), https://aliversus.com/.

5 Organizing Committee of the Games of the XVII Olympiad, *The Games of the XVII Olympiad: The Official Report of the Organizing Committee,* Vol. I, Rome, 1960, 721–22.

6 Ferdie Pacheco, *Tales from the 5th Street Gym: Ali, the Dundees, and Miami's Golden Age of Boxing* (Gainesville: University Press of Florida, 2010). In 1962, professional boxing was prohibited in Cuba.

7 Angelo Dundee and Bert Randolph Sugar, *My View from the Corner: A Life in Boxing* (New York: McGraw-Hill, 2009), 48.

8 Quote from Jack Newfield, "The Meaning of Muhammad," *Nation,* January 17, 2002.

9 Dundee and Sugar, *My View from the Corner,* 48, 50.

10 Enrique Encinosa, "Luis Sarria," in Pacheco, *Tales from the 5th Street Gym,* 207.

11 "Angelo Dundee: The Best I've Trained," RingTV.com, September 23, 2010, https://www.ringtv.com/124373-angelo-dundee-the-best-ive-trained/.

12 For a description of how the postwar Latinization of Miami affected the civil rights movement, see Chanelle N. Rose, *The Struggle for Black Freedom in Miami: Civil Rights and America's Tourist Paradise, 1896–1968* (Baton Rouge: Louisiana State University Press, 2015), chapters 7–9.

13 Jan Lin, *The Power of Urban Ethnic Exchanges: Cultural Heritage and Community Life* (New York: Taylor & Francis Group, 2010), 111–12.

14 Quote from Carlos Suarez, "A Look Back at Muhammad Ali's Roots in South Florida," Local10.com, June 6, 2016, https://www.local10.com/news/2016/06/06/a-look-back-at-muhammad-alis-roots-in-south-florida/. Also see *Muhammad Ali: Made in Miami*, produced by Gaspar González and Alan Tomlinson, 2008. The film discusses Black–White race relations in the context of early- to mid-1960s Miami but does not delve into racial differences among Cuban fighters themselves.

15 Mandy Baca, "Miami Black History: 1940s to 1960s," *New Tropic*, February 11, 2015, https://thenewtropic.com/miami-black-history-1940s-1960s/.

16 Lin, *The Power of Urban Ethnic Exchang*es, 112–13.

17 For limits on the dismantling of White supremacy in Cuba, see Devyn Spence Benson, *Antiracism in Cuba: The Unfinished Revolution* (Chapel Hill: University of North Carolina Press, 2016).

18 For an example of favorable early revolutionary press coverage of Rodríguez, see "Luis Manuel Rodríguez … un boxeador que debió ser pianista [a boxer who should have been a pianist]," *INRA* 1:6 (June 1960): 74–77.

19 Associated Press, "U.S. Plane Seized; Flown to Havana," *New York Times*, July 25, 1961; "33 Passengers Listed Aboard Seized Airliner," *New York Times*, July 25, 1961.

20 Pacheco, *Tales from the 5th Street Gym*, 146.

21 Lloyd Garrison, "Cuba Said to Fail to Lure the U.S. Negro," *New York Times*, August 28, 1961.

22 Cynthia A. Young, *Soul Power: Culture, Radicalism, and the Making of a U.S. Third World Left* (Durham, NC: Duke University Press, 2006), 18–53, quote on p. 30.

23 Michael O. West, "Afterword: Quilting the Black-Eyed Pea," in *To Turn the Whole World Over: Black Women and Internationalism* (Champaign: University of Illinois Press, 2019).

24 Eldridge Cleaver, *Soul on Ice* (New York: Dell, [1968] 1991), 117–19; emphasis in original.

25 Ibid., 117–18.

26 For instance, see W. K. Stratton, *Floyd Patterson: The Fighting Life of Boxing's Invisible Champion* (New York: Houghton Mifflin Harcourt, 2012). The subtitle refers to Stratton's claim that Patterson, as the book jacket reads, was as a boxer "overshadowed by Ali's theatrics and Liston's fearsome reputation" and as an activist by many luminous names of the civil rights era.

27 Cleaver, *Soul on Ice*, 116.

28 "*Playboy* Interview: Muhammad Ali," in *The Muhammad Ali Reader*, ed. Gerald Early (New York: Harper Collins, 1998), 132–59, quote on pp. 138–39. Emphasis in original.

29 Gerald Early, "Introduction: Tales of the Wonderboy," in *The Muhammad Ali Reader*, vii–xiv, quote on p. xi.

30 Sam Pollard, interview with Muhammad Ali, February 16, 1989, http://digital.wustl.edu/e/eii/eiiweb/ali5427.0743.004marc_record_interviewer_process.html.

31 Tex Maule, "He'd Rather Be Red than Rich," *Sports Illustrated*, March 18, 1974.

32 Jonathan Eig, *Ali: A Life* (Boston: Mariner Books, 2018), 472.

33 Matt Schudel, "Teofilo Stevenson, Olympic Boxing Champion and Hero in Castro's Cuba, Dies at 60," *Washington Post*, June 12, 2012. Predictions ran much higher for Stevenson when the bout was first discussed in the 1970s, and George Foreman still thought "Stevenson was better than all of us," meaning himself, Ali, and Joe Frazier. See Michael Woods, "Foreman: Stevenson Was Better than Ali," ESPN.com, June 18, 2012, https://www.espn.com/blog/new-york/boxing/post/_/id/1651/foreman-stevenson-was-better-than-ali.

34 Lawrence Linderman, "Muhammad Ali—A Candid Conversation with the Greatest—and Prettiest—Poet in the World," November 1975, in *The Playboy Interviews: Larger than Life*, ed. Stephen Randall and the editors of *Playboy* Magazine (Milwaukie, OR: M Press, 2006), 323–24. Emphasis in original.

35 "People in Sports," *New York Times*, March 30, 1974.

36 Vincent M. Mallozzi, "No Rest until Kid Gavilan Has Peace," *New York Times*, March 13, 2005.

37 William M. LeoGrande and Peter Kornbluh, *Back Channel to Cuba: The Hidden History of Negotiations between Washington and Havana*, updated edition (Chapel Hill: University of North Carolina Press, 2015), 268–344.

38 60 Minutes Overtime, "1996: 60 Minutes Profiles Muhammad Ali."

39 ESPN Films, 30 for 30 Shorts, *Ali: The Mission*, directed by Amani Martin, 2013.

40 Jorge Alfonso, "La pelea que nunca se celebró," *Bohemia*, 88:3 (February 2, 1996): B26–B29; Talese, "Boxing Fidel."

41 CNN.com, "Ali, Asner Deliver Medical Supplies to Cuba," September 13, 1998, http://www.cnn.com/WORLD/americas/9809/13/cuba.muhammad.ali/.

42 See, for instance, David Plotz, "Muhammad Ali: How the Greatest Became an Islamic Teddy Bear," *Slate*, February 8, 2002.

43 Talese, *Boxing Fidel*. This was a translation of Castro's words to interviewer Ed Bradley.

44 Ryan Teague Beckwith, "Read President Obama's Speech to the Cuban People," *Time*, March 22, 2016, https://time.com/4267933/barack-obama-cuba-speech-transcript-full-text/.

45 Eig, *Ali: A Life*, 530.

46 The Ali Center, "Six Core Principles," https://alicenter.org/about-us/muhammad-ali/.

References

60 Minutes Overtime. "1996: 60 Minutes Profiles Muhammad Ali." June 4, 2014. https://www.cbsnews.com/news/60-minutes-muhammad-ali-ed-bradley/.

Alfonso, Jorge. "La pelea que nunca se celebró." *Bohemia* 88:3 (February 2, 1996): B26–B29.

Ali Center. "Six Core Principles." https://alicenter.org/about-us/muhammad-ali/. 2020.

Associated Press. "33 Passengers Listed Aboard Seized Airliner." *New York Times*, July 25, 1961.

———. "U.S. Plane Seized; Flown to Havana." *New York Times*, July 25, 1961.

Baca, Mandy. "Miami Black History: 1940s to 1960s." *New Tropic*. February 11, 2015. https://thenewtropic.com/miami-black-history-1940s-1960s/.

Beckwith, Ryan Teague. "Read President Obama's Speech to the Cuban People." *Time*. March 22, 2016. https://time.com/4267933/barack-obama-cuba-speech-transcript-full-text/.

Benson, Devyn Spence. *Antiracism in Cuba: The Unfinished Revolution*. Chapel Hill: University of North Carolina Press, 2016.

Cleaver, Eldridge. *Soul on Ice*. New York: Dell, [1968] 1991.

CNN.com. "Ali, Asner Deliver Medical Supplies to Cuba." September 13, 1998. http://www.cnn.com/WORLD/americas/9809/13/cuba.muhammad.ali/.

Dundee, Angelo, and Bert Randolph Sugar. *My View from the Corner: A Life in Boxing*. New York: McGraw-Hill, 2009.

Early, Gerald. "Introduction: Tales of the Wonderboy." In *The Muhammad Ali Reader*, ed. Gerald Early. New York: Harper Collins, 1998: vii–xiv.

Eig, Jonathan. *Ali: A Life*. Boston: Mariner Books, 2018.

ESPN Films. 30 for 30 Shorts. *Ali: The Mission*. Directed by Amani Martin. 2013.

Garrison, Lloyd. "Cuba Said to Fail to Lure the U.S. Negro." *New York Times*. August 28, 1961.

LeoGrande, William M., and Peter Kornbluh. *Back Channel to Cuba: The Hidden History of Negotiations between Washington and Havana*. Updated edition. Chapel Hill: University of North Carolina Press, 2015.

Lin, Jan. *The Power of Urban Ethnic Places: Cultural Heritage and Community Life*. New York: Routledge, 2011.

Linderman, Lawrence. "Muhammad Ali—A Candid Conversation with the Greatest—and Prettiest—Poet in the World." November 1975. In *The Playboy Interviews: Larger than Life*, ed. Stephen Randall and the editors of *Playboy* magazine. Milwaukie, OR: M Press, 2006.

"Luis Manuel Rodríguez … un boxeador que debió ser pianista [a boxer who should have been a pianist]." [No byline.] *INRA* 1 (6, June 1960): 74–77.

Mallozzi, Vincent M. "No Rest until Kid Gavilan Has Peace." *New York Times*. March 13, 2005.

Maule, Tex. "He'd Rather Be Red than Rich." *Sports Illustrated*. March 18, 1974.

McDougall, Tony. *The Fight We Never Saw*. London, Ontario: Lucha Comics, 2020. https://aliversus.com/.

Muhammad Ali: Made in Miami. Produced by Gaspar González and Alan Tomlinson. 2008.

Newfield, Jack. "The Meaning of Muhammad." *Nation*. January 17, 2002.

Organizing Committee of the Games of the XVII Olympiad. *The Games of the XVII Olympiad: The Official Report of the Organizing Committee*. Vol. I. Rome, 1960.

Pacheco, Ferdie. *Tales from the 5th Street Gym: Ali, the Dundees, and Miami's Golden Age of Boxing*. Gainesville: University Press of Florida, 2010.

"People in Sports." *New York Times*. March 30, 1974.

"*Playboy* Interview: Muhammad Ali." In *The Muhammad Ali Reader*, ed. Gerald Early. New York: Harper Collins, 1998, 132–59.

Plotz, David. "Muhammad Ali: How the Greatest Became an Islamic Teddy Bear." *Slate*. February 8, 2002.

Pollard, Sam. Interview with Muhammad Ali. February 16, 1989. http://digital.wustl.edu/e/eii/eiiweb/ali5427.0743.004marc_record_interviewer_process.html.

Pope, Edwin. "Memories of Ali on His Way to Fight Liston." *Miami Herald*, January 19, 2017.

Reuters. "Cuba's President Remembers Muhammad Ali." June 4, 2016. https://in.reuters.com/video/watch/cubas-president-remembers-muhammad-ali-id368785519 (video since disabled).

Rose, Chanelle N. *The Struggle for Black Freedom in Miami: Civil Rights and America's Tourist Paradise, 1896–1968*. Baton Rouge: Louisiana State University Press, 2015.

Schudel, Matt. "Teofilo Stevenson, Olympic Boxing Champion and Hero in Castro's Cuba, Dies at 60." *Washington Post*. June 12, 2012.

Stratton, W. K. *Floyd Patterson: The Fighting Life of Boxing's Invisible Champion*. New York: Houghton Mifflin Harcourt, 2012.

Suarez, Carlos. "A Look Back at Muhammad Ali's Roots in South Florida." Local10.com. June 6, 2016. https://www.local10.com/news/2016/06/06/a-look-back-at-muhammad-alis-roots-in-south-florida/.

Talese, Gay. "Boxing Fidel." *Esquire*. September 1996, 138–47.

The Ring. "Angelo Dundee: The Best I've Trained." RingTV.com. September 23, 2010. https://www.ringtv.com/124373-angelo-dundee-the-best-ive-trained/.

Woods, Michael. "Foreman: Stevenson Was Better than Ali." ESPN.com. June 18, 2012. https://www.espn.com/blog/new-york/boxing/post/_/id/1651/foreman-stevenson-was-better-than-ali.

Young, Cynthia A. *Soul Power: Culture, Radicalism, and the Making of a U.S. Third World Left*. Durham, NC: Duke University Press, 2006.

Chapter Nine

MUHAMMAD ALI: *THE GREATEST* ADVOCATE FOR PEACE AND HUMANITY

Rebecca Hankins

Introduction

"Those who forget the past are doomed to live in Texas" is a quote that comedian and comedy writer Larry Wilmore jokingly stated. This quote sums up how the broader public views Texas. How representative is this statement if we look at Texas historically? That past that Wilmore mentions is buried and intentionally forgotten. It is for good reason that Texas chooses to ignore a history that is less than 20 years old; it was a much more progressive past that our current ultraconservative Texas leaders would like forgotten, erased from the history books and the state's collective memory. This progressive history connects the subject of this essay, Muhammad Ali, considered one of the greatest boxers in American history and a champion advocate for Black people worldwide. This essay will detail Ali's travels during two periods that also coincide with his visits to Texas and how those visits tell us some intimate details about why he is considered one of the greatest athletes and humanitarians. A Texas link to Muhammad Ali has not been explored in an essay, but this surprising connection is representative of the profound history of both the man and the state.

Texas

Twenty states have never elected a female governor, including two of our most liberal states, California and New York. Contrastingly, Texas has had two, Miriam Ferguson (1925–35) and Ann Richards (1991–95). Both women came into office at troubling times for the state. Ferguson came during the time of popularity of the Ku Klux Klan that she actively opposed, and Richards was a feminist icon whose opponent refused to shake hands with her.[1] Texas is also the state where the appointment of a Muslim mayor in a US municipality first occurred, an African American by the name of Charles Bilal. More on this will be addressed later in the essay.

There have been many times when Ali has surprised the world—from his earliest defeat of Sonny Liston, to his conversion to Islam, to his worldwide travels to promote peace, and the iconic lighting of the 1996 Olympic torch during the opening ceremonies in Atlanta, Georgia. These are all episodes where Ali triumphed against all odds. He did what he felt was important not just for his reputation but for all people. Ali's life was full of these surprises both big and small where he used his celebrity status and presence to work toward tolerance and understanding worldwide, to highlight communities, and to support Black peoples wherever they resided.

During my research on Muhammad Ali, I came across two visits he made to Texas that are the focus of this essay. He visited Texas A&M University and the community of Kountze at the invitation of Mayor Charles Bilal. Ali made numerous trips to Texas, including for a fight in San Antonio in 1972 that included a startling story about another fighter having knocked him out. "It had been seven years since Ali had been stripped of his title for refusing to answer his draft notice, and since being reinstated in 1970, his four-year odyssey to win it back had been up and down."[2] Ali saw many triumphs and failures during these times, his boxing privileges having only been reinstated in October 1970, but his legal case continued to wind its way through the courts eventually landing before the Supreme Court. The legal fight under the case name, *Cassius Marsellus Clay, Jr. v. United States*, was argued before the US Supreme Court on April 19, 1971. Finally, in June 1971 the US Supreme Court reversed Ali's 1967 conviction. Ali, facing financial straits due to the case and years of not fighting, looked for any opportunities to make money. Arguably, it was these stressors that were in play during his first fight with Joe Frazier, where he lost. In his second fight with Frazier in 1975 and after the Supreme Court decision, he finally had the opportunity to train without all the baggage of clearing his name and was able to defeat Frazier. He continued to fight, becoming the first champion to win back his title three times. Ali initially retired in 1979 but tried to revive his career after losing to Larry Holmes in 1980, then one more fight before hanging up his gloves in 1981. He was finally done with boxing, but not with what became his enduring legacy, his fight for peace, tolerance, and understanding. He modeled these behaviors in his visits to Texas A&M University in 1978 and to Kountze, Texas, in 1994.

Texas A&M University and the Champ

Texas A&M University was founded in 1866 as a land-grant institution, and it therefore had an obligation to educate all of Texas citizens, including African Americans, women, Latinos, and indigenous individuals. However, that mandate did not prevent the Texas legislature in 1876 from declaring that African Americans (both men and women) and all other women would not have this opportunity. These two were the only groups not permitted to fully enter the school as students until 1963; restrictions on full enrollment for women as undergraduates continued until 1970. This was also when sisters Ellen and Evelyn Smith with Early Douglas became the first Black women to join the track team. Black students were making themselves known, forming the Black Awareness Committee and advocating on behalf of their community.

The idea to bring Ali to campus was the desire of the Memorial Student Center (MSC) Great Issues Committee that reached out to the MSC (now the Woodson) Black Awareness Committee (WBAC). The WBAC has consistently brought in African American speakers, programming, and activities since its founding in 1970. Its signature event is the annual Martin Luther King, Jr. Memorial Breakfast that has brought in such Black luminaries as Angela Davis, Harry Belafonte, Ruby Bridges, and in 2020 Temple

University's Dr. Marc Lamont Hill. It is also worth noting that the Muslim Students Association of Texas A&M and the Muslim community of Bryan/College Station purchased an ad in the Battalion to welcome Ali to the university.

At the time of Ali's visit to Texas A&M University, he had donated $100,000 to relieve the suffering caused by the drought in South Africa, had spoken at the United Nations about world hunger, and formed an organization to raise money to help promote world peace.[3] Muhammad Ali's visit to Texas A&M University, on September 25, 1979, was less than 10 years after the school opened to all African Americans. His talk was titled "Future World Peace," where he was quoted as saying, "There's only one thing that can straighten out the world, and that's the heart."[4] It's an interesting quote with him holding a paper and a balled fist, but it represents who Ali was. He spoke these similar words so eloquently when he lost his license to box, "I did not lose a thing up until this very moment, I haven't lost one thing." "I have gained a lot. Number one, I have gained a peace of mind. I have gained a peace of heart."[5] Ali's visit to A&M was representative of events he would attend throughout his suspension and continued afterward; he was especially interested in going to college campuses where his following was strong and supportive even during his suspension.

When Ali arrived on A&M's campus, he was greeted by throngs of students with over 1,200 in attendance for his talk on friendship, world peace, and tolerance. He spoke about racial and religious turmoil in the world, and one of his many worthy quotes that stood out in his talk was when he spoke of himself: "The real Ali is spiritual. [...] I'm for the rights of everybody who deserves right, and I'm against wrong and those who commit wrong."[6] At the time of his visit, Muslim students did not have a mosque or Islamic Center for prayers; it was built in the 1980s, so it is unclear if Ali made prayers with the group. His visit was a huge success and exemplifies his lifelong goal to bring people together and show our similarities and desires.

International Travels

It was essential to show the dichotomy of Ali's life, working for world peace, but anticipating the need always to be ready for the fight. He understood the importance of representation for a Black man in America, and his travels were representative of this during the year of his visit to A&M. In 1979 Muhammad Ali was only 37 years of age, a young man by anyone's standards, but he had already begun to show signs of the deterioration of his health from the brutality of boxing. Ali was also aware that he was the target of the FBI from his first contact with the Nation of Islam, to his conversion to the religion of Islam, to his travels, where he was followed consistently and his every movement was detailed. (A 142-page dossier was compiled on him by the FBI for just the year 1966!) That did not stop his mission to spread peace and goodwill. A chronology of his travels demonstrates his love of life and the need to support his people all over the world. In February 1979, Ali traveled to Auckland, New Zealand, for a boxing exhibition for a crowd of over ten thousand.[7] While there, he also found time to visit with the local sound archive to promote his album on dental hygiene![8]

Ali continued his travels, visiting Australia in March 1979; he traveled to Melbourne, where the Aboriginal people had long lived as second-class citizens. When Ali visited, he was considered the height of celebrity and Black activism for the community. "Ali was the pinnacle. He was a Black Power luminary, a man who spoke up for oppressed people all over the world, probably the best-known black man on the planet at the time. And he was a boxer. Boxing, says Aunty Alma, was a powerful force in the Aboriginal community, going back to the Sharman tent boxers."[9] Wherever Ali traveled, he made it a particular mission to meet Black people, learn about their conditions, and be an inspiration.

One particularly significant trip that Ali took was to Guyana in April 1979. At the time of his visit, Guyana had been reeling from the horrific Jim Jones's Jonestown massacre that took place in 1978, where over eight hundred people, a large percentage of them African Americans from the United States, were among the dead. That Ali chose this time to offer a positive spotlight on the country is speculative, but his reception was unprecedented. He was swarmed by his fans as soon as he left the plane despite the almost midnight arrival. People followed his car in a procession that was at least a mile long. Former mayor of Georgetown, Guyana, George Hamilton Green, who was responsible for Ali's visit, noted that

> the then government did not anticipate the number of Guyanese who were Ali fans and this was reflected by the huge turnout at the airport during the wee hours of the morning, to welcome their hero. The Timerhi Airport was not the only place that had crowds of Ali's fans, but people from villages along the East Bank Demerara road stayed awake to line the road all the way to the city.[10]

While there, Ali took pains to engage the people while also performing some ceremonial activities, as noted in the newspaper: "Ali, who identified with the oppressed peoples of the world, is seen laying a wreath at Liberation Monument."[11] Green noted: "He was a people's person, humanitarian, teacher, yes, he was very intelligent. He was everything and he ensured he met as much of his fans as possible."[12] Always, when possible, combining his love of the people with his spiritual beliefs, Ali also met with the Muslim leadership of Guyana and dedicated the opening of the Whim Islamic Center.

One final notable trip of Ali's in the year 1979 was his short visit to China in December. This is noteworthy because China had banned boxing since 1956, but as stated by Menelik Mitchell, "hatred of a group is ignored and mitigated when it comes to popularity and celebrity." In 1979 Muhammad Ali's popularity was worldwide and transcended cultures. "Ali met senior vice-premier Deng Xiaoping in the Great Hall of the People. [...] Deng told Ali China was 'worthy of being a friend' and said it would be easy for the people of the United States and China to foster a relationship."[13] We saw Ali's goal to bring world peace and friendship, as he stated at Texas A&M earlier, being realized. Ali agreed to return in six weeks to China to train the Chinese Olympic boxing team. While there in 1979, Ali visited Vietnamese refugee camps noting the same sentiments again on his time at A&M. "I thank the Almighty God, Allah, who has blessed me with such charisma," said Ali, as dozens of Vietnamese children clambered over one another to hug him. His mission, he said, was to spread the word that the refugees were still in need of help, adding: "There's only one big family in this world, and that's the human family."[14]

Kountze, Texas: Charles Bilal

Throughout his travels, Ali sought to spread love and tolerance, but when possible, he never shied away from acknowledging his religious convictions, his Islamic faith as the motivation for his work. He was steadfast in his willingness to assist a Muslim in need if possible, as noted above. As noted previously, Ali was known for helping to raise money for worthy causes, and when called upon by Charles Bilal, the first Muslim mayor in America, he answered that call.

Bilal was appointed mayor of Kountze, Texas, in May 1991. What is also remarkable is that Kountze at the time was a town of a little over two thousand residents, 70 percent of them White.[15] Born and raised in Kountze, Bilal was a well-known businessman, who after winning a seat on the City Council by nine votes was appointed mayor by the "all-white City Council, a white city attorney, a white city treasurer, a white city manager and a white city judge."[16] Mayor Bilal had known Muhammad Ali through their shared faith for two years, and that was the impetus for his visit.

Bilal's main goals as mayor of Kountze were to create jobs and improve his community. He knew that the youth needed to have positive outlets in their lives, or it could lead to problems. According to Bilal, "The nearest (youth) center is at least 40 miles from Kountze, and we need something that can help the children."[17] He contacted Ali to ask him to assist in helping to raise money to build a city youth center. Ali wrote to the mayor in January 1994 offering to do what he could to help the city,[18], and visited the city on March 20 of that same year. Within that short time frame, the mayor, with many other citizens of Kountze, had organized a parade and a banquet, and had created a program. Ali signed autographs and waved to his fans. During his visit, Ali's Parkinson was known, but he was able to take part in activities without much assistance. His fourth wife, Lonnie Ali, the former Yolanda Williams, was there, as always throughout their 30-year marriage, to assist and support him.

Fifteen years younger than Ali, they first met when she was a first-grader in Louisville, their hometown.[19] Not one to enjoy the limelight, Lonnie would say about Ali, "He belongs to the world."[20] The people of Kountze recognized her devotion but wanted to honor her too. The beautiful seven-page program created by the Kountze community not only celebrated Ali but also included Lonnie's name on the front of the page: "Mayor Charles Bilal and the City of Kountze welcome Muhammad and Lonnie Ali."[21] The program had a separate tribute page dedicated to Lonnie Ali and spoke of her life, love, and commitment to her husband. Muhammad Ali's visit on Bilal's invitation left a legacy that continues to this day. The memorable quote in the program that is attributed to Ali states, "My main goal is helping people and preparing for the hereafter."[22]

Conclusion

This essay sought to share insights with and contextualize some of the little-known stories of Muhammad Ali, arguably America's greatest boxer. The year of Ali's visit to Kountze, Texas, South Africa was holding its first multiracial elections after the end of Apartheid, an undertaking that would elect Nelson Mandela as the first Black African president; this after he had spent his youth in a prison, an amazing triumph. Ali had the opportunity to see Mandela as president, playfully sparred with him for the cameras, and shared their mutual respect. In June 2003 they were both in Dublin to attend the Special Olympics World Summer Games and had a chance to speak. Both men understood what it meant to lose their freedom and their livelihood while standing up for their beliefs and principles. Unfortunately, in another part of Africa, during 1994, we saw the start of a civil war in Rwanda, also known as the Rwandan genocide against the Tutsi. The mass slaughter resulted in estimates of over half a million people being killed from April 7 through July 15, the outcome of hate and intolerance that Ali worked hard to address.

Muhammad Ali was known not only because of his prowess or wins in the ring but also for an extraordinary life as a human being. He received innumerable medals and awards, including the Presidential Medal of Freedom in 2005, one of the highest honors for an American citizen. Ali understood that these types of accolades could only take one so far; he always sought to be the "people's champion." Wherever he traveled, he was loved and admired for his convictions, his honesty, and his willingness to fight for others. His strong faith and the need to share it with others, not by proselytizing, but by being an example, was a model for those who say they believe. This memorable statement sums up the life of a man who continues to inspire people who knew him as *The Greatest*, "Thirty years after bursting upon the scene as a gold medal winner at the Rome Olympics, Ali remains a magical figure, known and loved throughout the world. He is deeply religious, generous, kind, and a showman in and out of the ring."[23] There will never be another like him; he is and always will be *The Greatest*.

Notes

1 *Texas Monthly*, "Ann Richards," https://www.texasmonthly.com/category/topics/ann-richards/.
2 Byron Sandford, "The Shot Not Heard Round the World." *Texas Monthly*, December 2004.
3 Todd Hedgepeth, "Ali Booked through 'Friend.'" *Battalion*, September 18, 1979.
4 Speaker Series on "Great Issues," Texas A&M University Yearbook, 53, https://bookreader.library.tamu.edu/book.php?id=yb1980&getbook=Go#page/n53/mode/2up.
5 Krishnadev Calamur, "Muhammad Ali and Vietnam." *Atlantic*, June 4, 2016. https://www.theatlantic.com/news/archive/2016/06/muhammad-ali-vietnam/485717/.
6 Cynthia Thomas, "Ali on Friendship." *Battalion*, September 26, 1979.
7 Sid Sideline, "The Origins of the Ali Trip." *Sun Live*, no date. https://www.sunlive.co.nz/blogs/12686-the-origins-of-ali-trip.html.
8 Jesse Mulligan, "Sound Archives on Ali's Visit to Auckland in 1979." *RNZ*, June 8, 2016. https://www.rnz.co.nz/national/programmes/afternoons/audio/201803704/sound-archives-on-ali%27s-visit-to-auckland-in-1979.
9 Joe Gorman, "'He Came to See Blackfellas!' When Muhammad Ali visited Fitzroy." *Guardian*, June 14, 2015. https://www.theguardian.com/sport/2015/jun/15/when-muhammad-ali-visited-fitzroy.
10 "Muhammad Ali Was Guyana's Champ Too." *Stabroek News*, June 12, 2016.
11 Shareief Khan and Raschid Osman, "Ali Fever Grips Guyana." *Guyana Chronicle*, April 22, 1979.
12 Starbroek News, 2.

13 Martin Choi, "How Muhammad Ali Wooed 'Self-Sufficient' China on 1979 Visit: 'I Just Admire Them so Much.'" *South China Morning Post*, December 21, 1979. https://www.scmp.com/print/magazines/post-magazine/short-reads/article/2178852/how-muhammad-ali-wooed-self-sufficient-china.

14 Ibid., 2.

15 Bruce Taylor Seeman, "Muslim School Gets Help from Texas Town's Mayor/The Nation's First Muslim Mayor Visited Norfolk to Help the School Raise Money." *Virginian-Pilot Newspaper*, February 21, 1993.

16 Ibid., 1.

17 Dave Ryan, "Still the Greatest." *Enterprise News*, March 20, 1994, 3A.

18 Ibid., 1A.

19 Karen Crouse, "Muhammad Ali Was Her First, and Greatest, Love." *New York Times*, June 9, 2016. https://www.nytimes.com/2016/06/10/sports/muhammad-ali-wife-lonnie-ali.html.

20 Ibid., 5.

21 *Don Kelly Research Collection on Gay History and Culture*, Cushing Memorial Library & Archives, Texas A&M University, Album 11—signed program "To Mr. Kelly Thanks Bilal." March 19, 1994.

22 Ibid., 2.

23 Ibid.

Chapter Ten

MUHAMMAD ALI, AKA "THE GREATEST": DEMONSTRATION OF UBUNTU

Derek Wilson

When examining the psychological function of those from a particular culture, one can assume the universal underpinnings reflective of its operations. Conversely, features of mental practices related with the human spirit ought to be thought of as unmistakable and specific to the culture from which one speaks (Nobles, 2015). In like manner, the influence and application of the mind and spirit can be seen as cultural exhibitions of exceptional specific individuals. The psychological underpinnings ought to mirror the social importance of the individuals being inspected. Each part of the human experience must be culturally grounded for precise mental comprehension to be accomplished (Nobles, 2015).

Thus, this work is guided by the conviction that the African episteme provides a more accurate assessment to advance and identify the image and interest of an extraordinary individual in the psyches of millions. Along these lines, this African-centered psychology must reflect at the center an expository, restorative, and reaffirmative process from an African-centered episteme on the impact of such an individual on the minds of those who hold him dearly.

Looking at the unbelievable legend of Muhammad Ali as a contextual investigation model, this discourse will examine the role of connectedness, competency, and consciousness as factors in Ali's demonstration of Ubuntu. In attesting a bona fide hypothetical disposition, a Black psychological perspective will permit us to comprehend the mind of a great African emancipator. This undertaking will demonstrate how African episteme and cosmology lay the framework for a comprehensive, sensible model for universal consumption concerning Muhammad Ali. It will likewise elucidate the mental nature of humanness, *Ubuntu*, as characterized by Ali, who is of African descent, while applying particular beliefs of socially organized ideas to his well-being and mental working (Nobles, 2015).

How do we describe a man who represented the understanding of courage, commitment, character, competence, consciousness, and confidence? Some would see him with delectation, lionization, indomitable spirit, quintessence, aggrandized reputation, refulgence, rectitude, mellifluousness, and ostentatious demeanor.[1]

Muhammad Ali is the "Greatest" of all time. Not only did he exhibit strength, will, and character, but he was also principled in his religion, his family, and his Blackness. He was a man for the people and the world. His infectious personality demonstrated wit, intelligence, charisma, and above all, love for humanity. Muhammad Ali, an idol and icon for centuries to come, was the greatest Black male athlete of my lifetime. I am reminded of the slave versus the master recognition of humanity. Simply put, one who acknowledges the humanity in others and whose humanity is not mutually acknowledged is for the most part seen as a slave. One whose humanity is accepted but not mutual to others is seen as the master (Nobles, 2015). Ali's desire to fight the political structure, to have his humanity recognized at a time when Blacks were not fully free, speaks of his courage and tenacity to deal with the devil eye-to-eye, face-to-face, man-to-man, in essence, to make his humanity known. This discussion will center on how Muhammad Ali demonstrated the greatest Ubuntu ever at the risk of losing it all. How many of us are willing to do just that while at the pinnacle of our success? He was a global icon, an inspiration to all of humanity, but more importantly, he set the image for the Black male to take his rightful place in the world! This work will examine Muhammad Ali through a triadic analysis of a model of Ubuntu, which incorporates (a) examining his demonstration of connectedness; (b) competence from Black personality (confidence and courage); and (c) consciousness (Wilson & Williams, 2013) through an African traditional interpretational analysis (character and commitment) (Nobles, 2015). Relying upon African epistemic reflections (Nobles, 2015), Muhammad Ali through these themes will be identified by his life's legacy. This is best clarified in the meaning of Black psychology by Kambon (1998):

African (Black) Psychology is defined as a system of knowledge (philosophy, definitions, concepts, models, procedures, and practice) concerning the nature of the social universe from the perspective of African cosmology. Black psychology is nothing more or less than the uncovering, articulation, operationalization, and application of the principles of the African reality structure relative to psychological phenomena. (p. 242)

The African philosophy of Ubuntu allows us to understand and define the life of Ali from an African point of view, which is absent in Western psychological discourse. While Ubuntu assists with characterizing the capacity of humaneness, it additionally embraces an arrangement of rules that are logically in contradiction with current Western values (Wilson & Williams, 2013). For example, linking the spirit of the man Muhammad Ali within the context of connectedness, competency, and consciousness (Wilson & Williams, 2013) *reflects his desire to establish unity, righteousness, and equality*—the audacity of a man to be ostentatious in his rebuke of society and his display for flare in and out of the ring. One could imagine that as a young Black male growing up during this era, he was a lionized figure, and his character and charisma were delectations for young brothers like to me to see. He represents Ubuntu, the essence of profound connection with others, "I Am Because We Are." Essentially, Ubuntu represents an essence of togetherness and congruence.

Defining Ubuntu

My colleagues and I (Wilson et al., 2016) in an ongoing conversation of Ubuntu proposed that the essence of being human is our association with others' humanity (Wilson & Williams, 2013). Perceiving one's full possibility and limitless potential to affect the world requires a vibe of unity between being human and the genuine self (Noble, 2012; Nobles, 2015).

In revealing African sensibilities and practices of Ubuntu, we must initially explore native African comprehension schemes and reenter Bantu-Kongo origin beliefs and the essential logic of *Ubuntu* through African tongues. Ubuntu is a Zulu term that defines the substance of being human—*Muntu* = "a human being", *Ntu* = "human." In Zulu linguistics, "Umuntu Ngumuntu Ngabantu," that is, we are individuals because of other individuals (Janz, 2004; Panse, 2006; Brooke, 2008; Wilson & Williams, 2013; Nobles & Mkhize, in publication).

This implies we are individuals in view of others perceiving the requirement for relating with different people because of other people recognizing the need for relating with other humans (Janz, 2004; Panse, 2006; Hanks, 2007; Wilson & Williams, 2013). Embodied within the Ubuntu deep-thinking psychology is the African concept of humaneness. I am because you are. In turn, all behavioral lexes of human performance reflect our understanding of relating to the world, including psychological healthiness and well-being. While scholars (Edwards et al., 2004; Janz, 2004; Panse, 2006; Wilson, 2005, 2012; Wilson & Williams, 2013) have intellectualized the theory of Ubuntu, previous discourse failed to provide accurate contextualization of full spiritual connotation and functioning of Ubuntu.

What is Ubuntu actually? Ubuntu derives from one of the Bantu idioms within Africa. Nobles (in publication), articulates,

> *UbuNtu* from the concept *Ntu* which is assumed to be the unanimous manifestation of ethereal force. *Ntu* inextricable from *Umu* is "Being" itself (Kagame 1989). Theoretically, *Ntu* as a modal fact or idea at which spirit as *being* shoulders tangible form, is reproduced in four kinds of expression in *BaNtu* thinking. In effect there is one essence with four categories of expression. Human beings (*Mu Ntu* or Muntu) reflect spiritual vigor (*Ntu*). Place and Time (*Ha Ntu* or Hantu) are equally expressions of heavenly influence (*Ntu*). All the material objects (*Ki Ntu* , Kintu or i-*ziNto*) like mountains, other animals, rivers, and so on, are celestial expressions (*Ntu*). Joy, beauty, laughter, love, emotions, and so on (*Ku Ntu* or Kuntu) are equally unworldly expressions (*Ntu*). "*UbuNtu*" is, therefore, spirit in which Being and Beings unite. It is the cosmic universal dynamism. (emphasis original)

Ubuntu, given to us through deep philosophical thought, expresses the relational essence of ethereal foundation, which informs our character, morals, mutual support of others, and demand to be treated as human (Brooke, 2008; Wilson & Williams, 2013). Being human is to be spirit, energy, or power. Being spirit is to be one who breathes and transfers within and is conjoined with the sea of waves/radiations of soul (vitality or power) (Nobles, in publication). A person is "spirit" when they assert their humankind by perceiving the humankind of others and on that premise build accommodating relations with them. The examination of Muhammad on all accounts demonstrates a man who was perceptually and spiritually a human being within the framework of Ubuntu. The following sections will explore how "The Greatest" exhibited *Ubuntu* orientation around the themes of connectedness, competency, and consciousness (Wilson, 2012; Wilson et al., 2016).

Quintessence Ubuntu within "The Greatest"

Ali's Consciousness: "Umuntu Ngumuntu Ngabantu"
"When the human spirit is well, whole, and healthy, the Spirit being in a reality of spirit is characterized by confidence, competence, and a sense of full possibility and unlimited potentiality."

(Nobles, 2010)

As indicated by Ubuntu, a comprehensive understanding of well-being and personhood includes putting the most noteworthy value of life on our interpersonal connections between different people (Wilson & Williams, 2013, Fernando, 2010). Ali advises us that well-being is the mutual connection of one's presence to other people. This humanity is controlled by maintaining quality, reliable relationships—"I am because you are."[2] Muhammad Ali was a man of principle. His stance against the government, his activism for social justice and equality, speaks to his spirit within "Umuntu Ngumuntu Ngabantu." Ogundiran (2009) states, "Ubuntu asks us to work towards equity, peace, and harmony as the foundation […] for each and every one of us. […] Ubuntu recognizes the humanity of all, and charges us to rediscover who we are, to rediscover our own human qualities through our interactions with peoples who are different from us" (p. 2).

Ali's demonstration of Ubuntu reflects his spirit and his spiritual quest for standing up for what was right. What is the soul of a man whose his legacy lives on for generations? This subjective evaluation of how Ali the man carried himself recognizes his sense of being to all. His connection to social, cultural, and historic contexts reflects his uniqueness, and, if any of these are abused, his Ubuntu is damaged; the community and his profound essence debilitates. Yet Ali remained indomitable. In Ubuntu, another emotional quality is the satisfying of pure mental operation of fitness and self-governance (Ryan & Deci, 2000). We should investigate and trade our insight, knowledge, and culture to manufacture one community (Ogundiran, 2009; Wilson, in publication). The cultural substance within Ubuntu recommends that the worth of congruous relationships is a significant manifestation of wellness (Wilson, 2012).

This Ubuntu, when perceived, can be shown in Muhammad Ali. For example, when Ali stood against the government in his appeal for being drafted, it was a major statement for a Black man during that time. It was his Ubuntu spirit that recognized how self-consciousness involves an extreme battle amid binary conflicting energies that requires being recognized by others. I remember his major statement, "Why should I go kill others in a different country that has done nothing to me?" Ali recognized that by engaging in affirmative action against his principles, as a man he demonstrated both pro-political and pro-social behavior. It was essential for Ali that if one were able and confident in their capability to fight against the master/slave dynamic, they should have the right to fight to death for humanity. Ali's demonstration of Ubuntu reflects an image that all men should concentrate on. What associations are expected to build up the effect of shared methods of functioning and authentic development of the Black man? For instance, the character improvement of Ali started in a setting of his geographic area—urban educational encounters, White condition denouncing his humanity, which yielded important expressions of connectedness, competency, and consciousness. The next section examines Ali's life in contexts of the consciousness part of the Ubuntu model.

Consciousness

Muhammad Ali was like a sleeping elephant. You can do whatever you want around a sleeping elephant but when it wakes up it tramples everything.
—Malik Bowens, *When We Were Kings* (1996)

The question of consciousness is critical to understand the psychological underpinnings and the spirit of Muhammad Ali. It was Ali's consciousness (ideas, beliefs, etc.) that promulgated open declarations proclaiming his Blackness during his lifetime. This act of declaration reflected deep consciousness. Consciousness as captured by Nobles (2015) is defined as "the process of understanding, examining, and explicating the meaning, nature and functioning of being human for African people by conducting a deep, profound and penetrating search, study and mastery of the process of illuminating the human spirit." Basically, that which exudes from our human awareness endorses important arrangements and equalization for our material and otherworldly hardship. Ali was obstinate in his understanding for the Black man to take his rightful place in the world; he never wavered from the individual being in complementarity to his group. This spirit energy for the African male unreasonably holding fast to an opinion, reason, or course disregarding reason, contentions, or influence makes him mindful of his effect on the humanity of others and conveys with it a definitive articulation for his conduct (Wilson & Williams, 2013).

Ali's experience of consciousness or self-actualized capacity was demonstrated by his changing his name. He was anointed the name Muhammad Ali replacing his European government name, Cassius Clay. This allowed him to attain positive and correct mental status. However, there is trepidation around the decline of this collective consciousness today, initiated and maintained through the negative typecasts of the Black male in our Western culture. While Ali adopted a Muslim religion where Allah is the father, the creator of the human being, through the teachings of the Honorable Elijah Muhammad, everything that the Black man is capable of doing lies within. Consciousness and identity are inextricably connected. The consciousness that Ali exhibited recognized that we are all creators who rule over all the pieces of the human body, mostly the head, the contemplations, and the human condition. As revealed the next morning after the Foreman fight, Ali addressed the many African delegations that came to see him and expressed "that Afro Americans are not as good as you are. Some of us are richer than you are but you have a dignity in your poverty that we don't have. We are spoiled in

America. We have lost what you still have in Africa. You must keep that." Ali's expression went further by his explanation at the time that a shattered consciousness (Nobles, 2015) exists within African Americans. He expressed how Africans in America operated from an unhealthy consciousness. Unhealthy consciousness results in fractured identity, alienation, and distorted malfunctioning. The result is sickness or an unhealthy state being passed on to future generations (Nobles, 2015). He stated, "We have no knowledge of self. Black people have no knowledge of themselves. We have been made just like white people mentally. White people made us just like them that we are now like white people. We have to re-brainwash them." This shattered consciousness represents a fractured identity—a state of damaged spirit. His understanding of re-brainwashing reflects the "restoration of shattered consciousness and shattered identity" (Nobles, 2015, p. 129) as key elements to regaining full healthy consciousness. Consciousness is, however, more than potentiality contained within itself. Hence, as a knowing and knowable spirit, motion, or energy, consciousness is simultaneously "potentiality" and intentional in our humanity (Nobles, 2015). His exhibition of this form of consciousness emanates from a level of brilliance and competency.

Ali's Competency

What brilliance of a man radiant with resplendent quality or state?

—Muhammad Ali

The second general concept demonstrated by Muhammad Ali is that of *competency*, which gives direct access to intellectual processes and worth inside inner functioning. The idea of competency takes into consideration epistemological reflection within, making sense of the reality one lives and revealing their reality through discourse. Muhammad Ali had wit and intelligence beyond measure rarely exhibited by an athlete and boxer. His refulgent character and intellect were evident by his quick wit of expressions in conducting interviews and giving lectures at universities. What other Black boxer would be asked to give a commencement speech at Harvard? And in his speeches he continued to speak on meaningful contextual race-related issues and discussions (Zittoun, 2008), taking into consideration that an actor develops healthy ideas working toward mastering his condition/environment (Khatib & Murray, 1998). Ali suitably used the materials and assets around him. He was captured reciting a brilliant poignant poem representing Ubuntu, "Me, We." This force for an African male defined his world—the most significant reality to define that mirrored the importance of his own human beingness (Nobles, 2012; Nobles, 2015). His fulgent and upright character is recognized by his quality of beinghonest and morally correct.

Ali was not the greatest benefactor of his own humanity; we all were. He revealed for us the future through his secrets; he was a great oracle. He was additionally an extraordinary healer, and the individuals who disregarded his advices experienced the good and bad times delivered by him. Ali spoke to the insight, the knowledge, and the keenness that many enjoyed during his days with us on Earth and after with the many videos capturing who he was and what he still represents. *In this regard, one should recognize that at the human level, conscious competency is always a collective experience and passes from one collective generation to the next.* He exemplifies the astuteness and the chance of impacting our fate. *This conscious competency can never be destroyed.* His aggregated information on the mystery things of the individual and nature, as well as knowledge on the historical backdrop of humanity, makes him brilliant. I believe his soul will manifest into an individual who will choose one's destiny. It speaks to the security, the support, and the encouragement before the vulnerability of life.

Ali's Demonstration of Connectedness

The light in me loves the light in you.
—Brown (2020)

When examining the humanity of Muhammad Ali, the principal purpose of entry is the idea of feeling connected. This concept of connectedness maintains that the most extreme personal satisfaction is predicated on the standards of interrelatedness and reliance (Wilson, 2012; Wilson & Williams, 2013, Wilson et al., 2016). Ali's humanity was made conceivable through the humanity of others (Wilson & Williams, 2013). Connectedness speaks to the link between an individual's need to establish and take part in some resemblance of social bond. Take, for instance, the "Rumble in the Jungle," his fight with George Foreman in Kinshasa, Zaire; it has been well documented that upon his arrival to Zaire, Muhammad Ali saw nothing but beautiful African people. One can imagine how he felt when flying on an all-African plane. He expressed how free he felt flying with all-African pilots and flight crew over the Sierra Desert. His words, "This is beautiful! I am free! I am free!" became famous. I would argue that his "feeling free" was the reconnection to the African spirit born in him. The affect he had was from experiencing the African continent. He expressed his joy to have fought on the continent. The Africans revered Ali for not only his boxing skills but more for his political stance. As it was described, "One of the [Black] children of America was asked to go fight in Vietnam and the response 'me'? You want me to go fight against the Vietcong? They had done nothing to me" (Gast, 1996). Twenty-two million Africans loved and were in support of Muhammad Ali. He was seen as a human extraordinaire at the time to take such a position against the US government. He may have lost millions of dollars, but he gained the esteem of millions of Africans.

He made it a point to walk among the people, and in doing so, the brothers and sisters of Kinshasa came up with the slogan, "Ali, boma ye." Ali's expression of having 100,000 Africans chanting "Ali, boma ye" made his spirit come alive. This group expression of survival was considered of utmost importance. He was perceived as "real person, genuine." It is through his human association that he identifies reciprocal wholesome bonds in his connection with the African brothers and sisters of Kinshasa. This exhibited the shared interests of the provider, Ali, and recipients, the people of Kinshasa, Zaire (Hammack, 2008; Wilson, in publication). Ali was given the ultimate respect when it was stated that "we were all for Muhammad Ali [...] he was defending the good cause for Africans and for the whole world" (Gast, 1996). This communal *connectedness* associates us to our psychological well-being. Winning the championship in Kinshasa affected the social perception that both Africans and African Americans had of each other. . His process for defending the good cause was fighting to uplift young brothers who did not have knowledge about themselves or confidence about their capabilities. His expression of a positive image could serve the purpose of changing the prevalent perception of the African people at home and in the diaspora, which prompts historical, collective, political awareness (Wilson & Williams, 2013). This understanding reflected a spiritual connection he possessed for effectual association of the level of expertise as an African male with correct emotional working.

African Narrative of Ali's life

At its basic understanding, the African episteme of being human (or "of humanity") is the right to be, to exist, to be recognized in the world. The peculiarity of any and all African men, women, or persons frequently offers intra-diverse levels of identity and consciousness (Nobles, 2015). Nonetheless, signs of African culture regenerate to saturate and expose genuine African cultural existence (Wilson & Williams, 2013). Muhammad Ali was no different. Ali was African because Africa is born in him (Higgins, 1994; Nobles, 2015). Ali's purpose was to change the popular consciousness of the African male, which invokes historical, social, and cultural prejudices (Wilson & Williams, 2013; Nobles, 2006). What did his consciousness reveal? Muhammad Ali, I would contend, influenced individuals' feelings and awareness affected by a thought or set of thoughts he presented to society used to award and/or deny worth or confidence of others (Nobles, 1986). He was bold enough to recognize his own greatness when he stated, "I attract people in a way that no other athlete has ever done." He was voted Sports Personality of the World. During the 1960s when Ali demonstrated the greatest upset in boxing history, he stood before the world and announced that he had changed his name from Cassius Clay to Muhammad Ali. Unlike others of his time, America's popular consciousness regarding Black men had not been favorable. For example, Ali was asked a question if he saw himself as being conceited. His response, "I am not conceited; I am confident." The image of the Black male athlete during that time was to not erupt the status quo and to accept what White consciousness wanted of the Black athlete—to be quiet and acquiesce. It was during this time that Whites worked hard to defame, demoralize, and name anything of significance about Black male athletes as crooks, undermining, fierce, unintelligent, uneducated, languid, poor, simply athletic, and musically gifted (Goff et al., 2008). If African American males decided to classify themselves differently, they can do so only in response to Whites' popular consciousness. Since these generalizations were so solid and enmeshed in the mind of White America, Ali knew from the consciousness level of understanding that he must change the image of the Black man. Another great statement provided by Ali was as follows: "For anybody who's doing the right thing they catch a lot of hell. You cannot please God and the devil too." Evidence now demonstrates that Muhammad Ali was right; he needed to demonstrate a sense of consciousness for all Black people so that they can see themselves as worthy of social consideration. This meant that when he stood up for himself, he was standing up for Blacks around the world.

For the Black male athlete, this phenomenon was displayed during the Cleveland Summit in 1967, in which the goal was to advance the position of Blacks in America. Several athletes stood on Ali's side in show of support for his stance against the Vietnam War. He was stripped of his world championship title and charged with draft dodging. What was demonstrated was connectedness by other Black athletes in support of Muhammad Ali by the likes of Jim Brown, Bill Russell, Kareem Abdul-Jabbar (Ferdinand Lewis Alcinder at the time), Carl Stokes, Walter Beach, Bobby Mitchell, Sid Williams, Curtis McClinton, Willie Davis, Jim Shorter, and John Wooten (Bishara, 2016). America's response to these events conveyed an implicit meaning as to the identity, lack of accepted humanity, and devalued Black male during this time in American history (Williams & Wilson, 2015). For Muhammad Ali, this illuminates the impact that by standing up for his personal, community, and religious rights, he had to face the psychosocial forces of dominant culture. Thus, the analysis of Muhammad Ali as a Black man and his demonstration of positive mental health requires a different cultural analysis.

Our most recent analysis of Muhammad Ali reveals that as a Black man his experiences centered around family, representing a strong need to care for his wives and children. Even greater is the fact that he loved his community (Nobles, 2020). This sense of connectedness that he had with the Black community was profound. He could have easily succumbed to the conformity and pressure of the times to not speak. Instead, he exercised his right to free speech. Ali was proud of his Blackness, loved being Black, and demonstrated great love for his family and Black people (Nobles, 2020). The narratives at the time revealed that Ali's cultural appreciations and apperceptions (Nobles, 2015) commonly focused on the stability of family, intense father–daughters interaction, and providing safe community (connectedness). Ali demonstrated Black personality behaviors, and he understood the times around him and used profound inborn convictions (Nobles, 2015) from his religion in adapting to the assaults and attacks of both positive and negative associations with others he came across (competence). The African expressive and explanative talk of Black personality requires the ability to utilize duplicity of private practices, move racially involved pressure, and think about status determined by social, political, and economic factors (Kambon, n.d.) (consciousness). This discourse articulated Ubuntu's underpinnings in the life of Muhammad Ali.

Generally, Ubuntu can be conceptualized as the capacity to live and satisfy the most noteworthy and genuine articulation of ourselves as human beings, being in spirit with others. In other words, "one's spirit and light are made possible through the spirit and light of others." This African axiom recognizes that every person and every life is recognized through their connectedness, competency, and consciousness in their relation with other people with emphasis on understanding (Wilson & Williams, 2013), collaboration, and partnership. From the Akan culture, *obi yiye firi obi* translates as follows: "The human individual is not self-sufficient, he would necessarily require the assistance, goodwill and the relationships of others in order to satisfy his basic needs […] the well-being of man depends upon his fellow man" Gyekye (n.d.). Ubuntu recognizes the humanity in all of us, finding ourselves, settling our own human contrasts within our interactions with each other (Gyeke, 1996; Janz, 2004; Panse, 2006; Brooke, 2008; Hanks, 2007). This spirit of Ubuntu may end up being a substantially more beneficial and enduring applied model while analyzing in contemporary time the life and spirit of Muhammad Ali. Given that, this has the potential to inform a broader, more inclusive understanding of what we ought to become (Wilson & Williams, 2013).

How did Muhammad Ali express his sense of being? He spoke with truth, sincerity, honor, and glory. As Ali stated, "Yes Africa is my home. Damn America and what America thinks. Yeah I live in America but Africa is the home of the Black Man. I was a slave 400 hundred years ago and I am going to back home to fight among my brothers." This articulated "The Greatest's" Ubuntu in him, the bedrock of a man, essence of his spirit, and the caring for his people. At the point when the human soul is completely incorporated as depicted above, being human is then described by our being of connectedness, competency, and consciousness. Ubuntu informs us that the community in which we operate is vital to who we are, where we are, and what we ought to be. I hope I have pleased the spirit of Muhammad Ali by paying homage to the "Greatest Ubuntu" ever! May the eternal light in Ali guide us on our path to truth and glory!

Notes

1 As evident in his interview "Wake up and apologize: Muhammad Ali" with Cathal O'Shannon filmed on July 17, 1972, Dublin, Ireland. https://www.youtube.com/watch?v=J8ZWZzt0bkQ.
2 African philosophy of being.

References

Bishara, M. (2016). "As American sports figures sound off on politics, their European counterparts stay silent." CNN. December 12. https://contenidopatrocinado.cnn.com/2016/12/12/football/where-is-the-european-colin-kaepernick/index.html.
Brooke, R. (2008). "Ubuntu and the individuation process: Toward a multicultural analytical psychology." *Psychological Perspectives*, 51, 36–53. doi:10.1080/00332920802031870.
Brown, M. (2020). *Zen Pig: Book 1, The Art of Gratitude*. San Diego: Puppy Dogs and Ice Cream.
Edwards, S., Makunga, N., Ngcobo, S., and Dhlomo, M. (2004). "Ubuntu: A cultural method of mental health promotion." *International Journal of Mental Health Promotion*, 6(4), 17–22.
Fernando, S. (2010). *Mental Health, Race and Culture*. New York: Palgrave MacMillan.
Gast, L. (1996). *When We Were Kings: Documentary*. http://divxmoviesenglishsubtitles .com /W/When_we_were_ kings.html.
Goff, P. A., Eberhardt, J. L., Williams, M. J., and Jackson, M. C. (2008). "Not yet human: Implicit knowledge, historical dehumanization, and contemporary consequences." *Journal of Personality and Social Psychology*, 94, 292–306. doi:10.1037/0022-3514.94.2.292.
Gyekye, K. (n.d.). "Person and community in African thought." http://home.concepts-ict.nl/~kimmerle/frame Text9.htm.
———. (1996). *African Cultural Values: An introduction*. Philadelphia, PA: Sankofa.
Hammack, P. L. (2008). "Narrative and the cultural psychology of identity." *Personality and Social Psychology Review*, 12, 222–47.
Hanks. T. L. (2007). "The Ubuntu paradigm: Psychology's next force?" *Journal of Humanistic Psychology*, 48, 116. http://jhp.sagepub.com/content/48/1/116.
Higgins, C. (1994). *Feeling the Spirit: Searching the World for the People of Africa*. New York: Bantam Books.
Janz, B. B. (2004). *African Philosophy*. http://pegasus.cc.ucf.edu/~janzb/papers/37AfPhil.pdf.
Kambon, K. K. (n.d.). "Toward the Construction of a Model of African Self-Consciousness Development in Black Children," unpublished manuscript (received July 15, 2014).

————. (1998). "An African-centered paradigm for understanding the mental health of Africans in America." In R. Jones (ed.), *African American Mental Health: Theory, Research and Intervention*, pp.33–50. Hampton, VA: Cobb and Henry.

Khatib, S. M., and Murray, C. B. (1998). "Competency and legitimacy as organizing dimensions of the Black self-concept." In Reginald Jones (ed.), *African American Mental Health: Theory, Research, and Intervention*, 187–208. Hampton, VA: Cobb & Henry.

Nobles, W. W. (1986). *African Psychology: Toward Its Reclamation, Reascension, and Revitalization*. Oakland, CA. Black Family Institute.

————. (2010). "African well-being and the healing of humanity." *Imhotep Journal*, 7.

————. (2012). "Culturecology Model©." In V. D. Woods, N. J. King, S. M. Hanna, and C. Murray (eds.), *"We Ain't Crazy! Just Coping with a Crazy System": Pathways into the Black Population for Eliminating Mental Health Disparities*, pp. 221–24. San Bernadino, CA: African American Health Institute.

————. (2015). *The Island of Memes: Haiti's Unfinished Revolution*. Baltimore: Black Classic Press.

————. (2020). "While sheltering in place: (A guide and workbook) during the time of dread, the corona virus global pandemic." Public document.

Nobles, W. W., and Mkhize, N. (in publication). "The charge and the challenge of illuminating the spirit (skh djr): The question of paradigm, episteme and terminology for therapy and treatment." *Alternation Journal*.

Ogundiran, A. (2009). "Ubuntu: An African Philosophical Reflection on 'One Community, One Humanity.'" Invited address given at the 2009 Unity Day of the City of Newton,' North Carolina, February 8.

Panse, S. (2006). *Ubuntu—African Philosophy*. Buzzle.comhttp://www.buzzle.com/editorials/7-22-2006-103206.asp.

Ryan, R. M., & Deci, E. L. (2000). "Self-determination theory and the facilitation of intrinsic motivation, social development and well-being." *American Psychologist*, 55, 68–78.

Wilson, D. (2005, August). "Multidisciplinary perspectives on issues of health and identity for African Americans." Symposium conducted at the 36th Annual International Convention of the Association of Black Psychologists, South Beach, Florida.

————. (2012). "Competency, connectedness, and consciousness." In V. D. Woods, N. J. King, S. M. Hanna, and C. Murray (eds.), *"We Ain't Crazy! Just Coping with a Crazy System": Pathways into the Black Population for Eliminating Mental Health Disparities*, pp. 159–61. San Bernadino, CA: African American Health Institute..

————. (in publication). "African cultural psychology." *Alternation Journal*.

Wilson, D., Olubadewo, S., & Williams, V. (2016). "Ubuntu: Framework for Black college males positive mental health." In W. Ross (ed.), *Counseling African American Males: Effective Therapeutic Interventions and Approaches*. Greenwich, CT: Information Age.

Wilson, D., & Williams, V. (2013). "Ubuntu: A model of positive mental health for African Americans." *Psychology Journal*,10(2): 80–100. www.psychologicalpublishing.com.

Zittoun, T. (2008). "Speaking in tongues: Commentary on Cubero, de la Mata and Cubero." *Culture & Psychology*, 14, 431–41.

Chapter Eleven

STILL THE PEOPLE'S CHAMP AND RELEVANT IN THE FIGHT FOR SOCIAL JUSTICE: MUHAMMAD ALI'S CONVERSION OF ATHLETIC CAPITAL INTO SOCIOPOLITICAL CAPITAL

Billy Hawkins

Introduction

Activists who are revolutionary never concede, settle, or can be co-opted. They remain committed to the cause, while wearing the mantle of social justice and a passion for the less fortunate to their graves, unfortunately, for some, an early grave. This has been a pattern witnessed with the presence and persistence of Black people in the United States. Regardless of the context, a plantation or Olympic podium, or the methods, the use of violence or nonviolent protest, Blacks have had to and continue to fight for justice to achieve some level of equity and equality in the United States.

Sport and the Black experience in the United States have not been absent of the presence and plight of activists (athletic activism or athletic activist[1]) fighting for racial justice. Although many proclaim and adhere to the belief that sport should be and is apolitical, as a social construction, sport's existence is impossible without being saturated with hegemonic political ideologies of a nation. As a social construction, sport is an ideological state apparatus that is instrumental in promoting capitalist ideals and illusions of democracy, especially in the context of the United States. Concurrently, for those in opposition who are burdened by the prevailing social order, sport has also provided a platform to resist and challenge hegemony in various forms, specifically regarding the Black experience, White hegemony.

Muhammad Ali, without question, is one of this nation's and the world's greatest athletes, and one of the Black community's[2] greatest treasures. He challenged White hegemony within the sport community and in the broader national and global communities. One example we will expound upon in this chapter is when in defiance to enlisting in the US military, he proclaimed to reporters in 1967 in these iconic statements, "I ain't got no quarrel with the Viet Cong. [...] No Viet Cong ever called me Nigger." Never at a loss for words and as a skilled pugilist, Ali crafted his words with precision and authority to land a devastating blow, in this case, a verbal blow against the killing of Brown people across the globe during the Vietnam War to advance White supremacy, specifically, and the broader issue of the global anti-Black and anti-Brown racism and oppression.

Speaking truth to power has been a mantle many Black athletes have had to don to bring attention to social and racial injustices incurred by the Black masses. Whether it was a Jack Johnson, who sought to be a self-identified Black man during the apex of the Jim Crow era; an Ali, who as we shall see in this chapter vocally expressed his disapprobation with the manifestations of White supremacy in the forms of religious and racial oppressions; a Tommie Smith and John Carlos, who raised Black gloved fists on the medal podium during an Olympic medal ceremony; or a Colin Kaepernick, who expressed his discontent with the US version of apartheidism by taking a knee during the playing of the national anthem, there have been many forms of activism expressed in the context of sport and by athletes.[3] Ali has been a role model for converting athletic capital[4] into sociopolitical capital.[5] This chapter will examine his role in carrying the mantle of athletic activism. I intend to discuss how, during critical moments in his career and life, where he converted athletic capital into political capital, provide insight into the controversies incurred by Black athletes, specifically those who use sport as a platform to make a political statement. These insights also inform why some athletes may resist procuring the mantle of athletic activism.

****

Born Cassius Marcellus Clay Jr. in 1942 in a segregated Louisville, Kentucky, he took up boxing as a means of self-defense and self-preservation, yet he excelled and became a highly decorated amateur, Olympian, and later, a professional boxer. Despite his many achievements of winning a gold medal in the 1960 Olympics in Rome, it did not shield him from the covert and overt racist practices inherent in the United States, such as not having access to a downtown restaurant in his hometown. It was the institutionalized racist practices and microaggressions that frustrated Ali to the point of tossing his gold medal into the Ohio River in an act of protest against the hypocrisy of Americanism that was afforded to the White majority but denied to the descendants of enslaved Africans who were kidnapped and bought to the New World to live as colonized property and expendable labor. Furthermore, in his case, as with other athletes who achieve global success, like Joe Louis or Jesse Owens, Ali represented an athletic dominance that fueled this nation's nationalist ideology of superiority. Yet they were constructed as race-neutral pawns who were exploited in this US battle for global White supremacy. Thus, despite being used to advance the political ideology of this nation, they never fully enjoyed the privileges of being American citizens, but were subjected to its racist practices.

In light of his accomplishments on the global sport's stage, Muhammad Ali was the modern-day Jack Johnson, meaning he defied social norms that controlled and oppressed his ability to strive toward self-actualization as a Black man. Remember, Jack Johnson was notorious for not adhering to certain codes of conduct for Black men, generally, and Black professional athletes, specifically. Because of Johnson's lifestyle, certain codes of conduct were imposed on Black athletes like Joe Louis, Jesse Owens, Jackie Robinson, among others, which currently overshadows many Black athletes today. The boxing or sporting enterprise could not define him simply as an athlete or confine him within its narrow frame of reference as it was accustomed to confining his predecessors.

Subsequently, according to A. Bartlett Giamatti, "if for most athletes and spectators sport is work conceived in some special way as play, for Muhammad Ali sport is work conceived as theater."[6] As a seasoned artist/actor, he crafted theatrical presentations in and out of the ring that entertained and inspired millions, as well as challenged traditional conventions for Blacks. In the presentation of his life, we witnessed various acts of converting his athletic capital into sociopolitical capital. Similar to Jack Johnson, he refused to follow the scripts written by others, but choreographed a life of self-actualization. Within the context of this chapter, this lifestyle and process, given the racial tenor during the nadir of his reign as a heavyweight champion, denotes a perfect example of athletic activism. Again, the conversion of athletic capital into sociopolitical capital will be deemed athletic activism.

One act of activism I view in the theatrical presentation of Ali's life was his conversion or transition to the Muslim religious group, more specifically, the Nation of Islam. For a significant portion of the Black community in America, and America for that matter, Christianity was and is the theology of preference and/or persuasion, especially for those who openly expressed their religious conviction. The version of Christianity most Blacks inherited from their parents and grandparents is, for many of us, the only religion we know. For those who strayed from or lurked on the frenzies of the tenets of Christianity we inherited were either heavily criticized or excommunicated from the family. Many in the Black community, specifically, never critically interrogated their religious inheritance or questioned the dissimilarities between the Christianity of America (more specifically, White America) and the Christianity of Christ. Frederick Douglass[7] deconstructed the hypocrisy of the former by informing how it contributed to the institution of slavery and the anti-Black racism that is interwoven in the fabric of this country. Because of the insight about the shortcomings of the Christianity of America this radical slave abolitionist provided, rifts were and are continually created in Black communities along religious lines. Despite this critical deconstruction of America's version of Christianity, during the harsh era of Jim Crow and heated period of the civil rights protests during the 1960s, Christianity reigns as the religion of preference for many in Black communities. Thus, a departure from this theological perspective incurred scrutiny and trepidation.

Regarding the Nation, it was founded by Wallace D. Fard Muhammad in 1930, grew under the leadership of the Honorable Elijah Muhammad, and continues to persevere under the spiritual leadership of Minister Louis Farrakhan. It represents a drastic theological departure from the Black religious norm of Christianity. It was even a departure from the most radical Christian leaders who preached from a liberation theological perspective. Although labeled a hate group, the Nation's popularity grew during the civil rights and Black Power movements because of their philosophy of Black liberation, which included Black Nationalism, racial uplift, self-defense, and self-preservation. They appealed to a segment of Black communities who were sick and tired of waiting on White liberals' legislative processes or the moral development of White racists. This segment of the Black community did not agree with being recipients of the physical racial abuses from police dogs, blasts by firemen fire hoses, or blows from police batons. The Nation straightened the backs of many and strengthened their resolve in not submitting to these types of physical racial abuses for the sake of justice. For certain segments of the Black Christian community, the philosophy of peaceful protest and nonviolent resistance places hope in appealing to the White hegemonic power structure, but these philosophical approaches to address White supremacy, and more specifically White terrorism against Blacks, did not appeal to the philosophy and theology the Nation preached. The Nation sought to confront this racist terrorism with self-defense and in seeking a Black nation-state. This is a brief insight into the context and the reason Ali's conversion to the Nation of Islam (the Nation) encountered criticism, within and beyond Black communities.

****

Thus, when Ali, then Cassius Clay, was 22 years old, he was scheduled to fight Sonny Liston for the heavyweight championship. Controversy surfaced prior to the fight because rumors about Clay's conversion to Islam caused fight promoters to threaten to cancel the fight. The fight, undoubtedly, was not canceled, and Ali went on to win in six rounds due to Liston's refusal to answer the bell at the start of the seventh round. In celebration and customary to his theatrical persona, Ali shouted after the match, "I shook up the world." His victory as the heavyweight champion of the world stunned many in and out of the boxing community. His acts that followed also shook up the world and further set him on a course to converting his athletic capital into sociopolitical capital.

After the Sony Liston fight, Cassius Clay became Cassius X and then Muhammad Ali. He made his conversion to Islam public and his allegiance to the Nation official. His name change from Cassius Clay to Muhammad Ali was a means of disconnecting from his "slave" name, which also denotes a departure from being defined and identified by a system of oppression. It was one controversial step that brought criticism from outside and within Black communities. For example, his conversion to Islam and his name change troubled his father, who considered his son to be brainwashed by this religious organization.[8] Muhammad Ali's alliance with the Nation created additional tension in the sport community and challenged White codes of conduct previously established for professional Black athletes, as well as Whites' expectation of Blacks, in general, especially during this period of racial turbulence. Furthermore, his connection to his previous mentor, Malcolm X, at one time the public face for the Nation and a fierce orator who was adamant and vocal about two of the Nation's provocative beliefs that Blacks were superior and that White people were devils, sparked additional controversy and discontent for Ali. Malcolm X's persona was also controversial for the conservative culture of boxing, specifically, and professional sport, in general, especially with regard to Black upliftment and empowerment. Black professional athletes were supposed to be submissive, appreciative, and most of all loyal to the White power structure that afforded them the opportunity to earn a living as professional athletes. By no means were Black athletes to be outspoken about the social conditions racism spawned or the exploitation they encountered as athletic property. This leads to another key decision that was pro-Black and a means of converting his athletic capital into sociopolitical capital: taking control of his brand as a professional Black male athlete.

Beyond the spiritual development, empowerment, and enlightenment, Ali's alliance with the Nation produced Main Bout Inc. It was a corporate entity that managed ancillary issues (e.g., closed-circuit television rights, etc.) and various aspects of promoting his fights, such as broadcasting rights. Main Bout Inc., the first major multimillion-dollar deal, was Ali's fight against the leading contender, Ernie Terrell. The creation of this corporation was strategically situated with the Nation's Black economic empowerment philosophy. This in and of itself drew considerable criticism from White boxing promoters and sportswriters. According to Michael Ezra, not only were White sportswriters vehemently opposed to the development of Main Bout, but also the controversy (e.g., political, religious, etc.) surrounding Ali and Main Bout created enemies within boxing, such as "rival promoters, closed-circuit-television theater chains, and organized crime."[9] These enemies sought to run Main Bout out of business; thus, "money and politics underpinned opposition to Main Bout."[10] For a Black man, a Black male professional athlete in the profession for boxing during the civil rights era, to have the audacity to take control of his brand was courageous, and it threatened the prevailing system of Black athletic exploitation, which was prevalent in the sport of boxing and other professional sports where there was a premium on Black athletic talent.

Unfortunately, the shelf-life of Main Bout was less than two years, which was no doubt due to various oppositional forces mentioned earlier, as well as the prevailing persistence of White supremacy and its tenacity to control all aspects of Black life. The symbolic empowerment and cultural statement the creation of this company made was co-opted into being a corporation that was fueled by an organization that was anti-American and promoted hate. Often the conversion of athletic capital into political capital is co-opted and misconstrued into something else and something less. Despite the champ's unique abilities, showmanship, and stellar performances in the ring, being able to control his athletic brand was too provocative and a threat to the status quo during this historical period. Also, and again, being the brainchild of the Nation made its existence even more problematic. Despite the token concessions the civil rights era was providing for Blacks, Blacks were still relegated to certain social spaces and given limited political and economic power for development and self-preservation. For example, laws were being passed that allowed Blacks to eat at the lunch counter, but owning the café was out of the question, unless it was in segregated Black communities; Blacks could shop at the S.H. Kress or Woolworth's five-and-dime store, but they could not be managers in these establishments. Therefore, though short lived, Main Bout's demise spoke of the prevalence and persistence of White supremacy's manifestation in various social institutions, in general, and in the institution of professional sports, more specifically. Thus, as a Black professional athlete, you could compete in professional sports, but owning your brand and controlling the mechanisms that enhance your brand identity and exposure was preposterous and unimaginable for the conservative White power structure of professional sports.

Regardless and in spite of its brief shelf-life, Main Bout was a symbolic protest that established precedence for Black athletes and entertainers to control their brands and have more input into their ancillary endorsements. Over 30 years after the formation of Main Bouts, many Black professional athletes are benefiting from the efforts Ali generated in controlling and owning his athletic image, some under the auspices of being "woke" and sociopolitically astute, while others are simply pure capitalist.

****

Back to Ali's conversion: not only was it controversial in and of itself, but the timing of the announcement regarding his conversion to Islam was also controversial—after winning the heavyweight championship. Although it may not have been intentional at the time, this was pivotal and maybe strategic to his life as an activist, which lends to my argument that this activism was a protest for self-actualization. The opportunities for self-actualization have alluded many Black professional athletes, because their lives have been (are) scripted by handlers, managers, and the press, among others. For many prominent Black athletes before Ali, their abilities to stray from the predetermined roles were intensely discouraged. Those who attempted incurred public criticism and condemnation, and ultimately suffered image assassination. For example, as mentioned earlier, Jack Johnson was an outlier and an anomaly because he did not submit to the constructed identity for Black men during his era; thus, he received considerable public criticism and condemnation. Two post-Ali professional Black male athletes who have encountered image assassinations for converting their athletic capital into political capital are National Basketball Association (NBA) players Craig Hodges and Mahmoud Abdul-Rauf (formerly Chris Jackson). The former Chicago Bulls sharpshooter Craig Hodges penned a controversial letter to the then president George H. W. Bush in which he articulated his dissatisfaction with the Bush administration's behavior toward the poor and people of color in his country. His image was assassinated resulting in him being cut from the Bulls and blacklisted from the NBA. Mahmoud Abdul-Rauf was one of the first athletes who used the time during the playing of the national anthem to protest, by either sitting or praying. He was also released from the NBA and never given an opportunity after his image was assassinated. Thus, as a Black male, and more specifically as the heavyweight champion of the world during the 1960s, to avoid public criticism and condemnation, there were certain expectations and prescriptions placed upon Ali, often without his input or consensus.

A life of an activist is a life of making sacrifices and sometimes becoming the sacrifice. Once Ali made his name change and affiliation with the Nation public, his adherence to its ideological and theological practices came to bear for him being drafted into the army and ordered to the army induction center in Houston, Texas, on April 28, 1967. When the name "Cassius Clay" was called out for him to step forward for induction into the US army three times, Ali refused all three times. His refusal to be inducted into the army was another act of activism that was based on his religious beliefs. A week before his induction in 1967, he declared in a statement that he would not travel 10,000 miles "to help murder and burn poor people simply to help continue the domination of white slave masters over the darker people."[11] Thus, as a conscientious objector, Ali solidified his allegiance to his religious beliefs and made a resounding statement against the spread of White supremacy. He further declared the famous words, "I ain't got no quarrel with the Viet Cong. […] No Viet Cong ever called me Nigger." There have been conscientious objectors before and after Ali, but his visibility, popularity, and allegiance to one of the most misunderstood religious organizations during the late 1960s and early 1970s made Ali's stance and statements against the Vietnam War, specifically, and White supremacy, in general, extremely provocative and, in his case, punitive. For example, within the boxing world, Ali stirred considerable controversy that resulted in him being stripped of his titles and basically exiled from boxing for three years. Beyond the boxing world, he was either castigated and labeled "unpatriotic" or celebrated as being courageous for standing up for his religious principles and against a war against poor people, which was also a war that sought to expand the reach of White supremacy over another nation of darker skinned people. Furthermore, he was indicted by a federal grand jury for refusing to be inducted into the draft. He was later sentenced by Judge Joe Ingram of the US District Court for the Southern District of Texas to pay a $100,000 fine and serve five years in jail. He was able to post bail and be released to endure a lengthy appeal process.

His statement and stance about the spread of White supremacy, alone, widen the target on his back and increased his critics' opportunities to assassinate his image and character. During his appeal process, because of the assassination of his image and character of being unpatriotic, many Black civil rights leaders were cautious in publicly supporting him. A small group of Black professional athletes did provide public support. For example, Lew Alcindor, a member of the UCLA basketball team; Sid Williams and Walter Beach of the Cleveland Browns; Curtis McClinton of the Kansas City Chiefs; Bobby Mitchell and Jim Shorter of the Washington Redskins; Willie Davis of the Green Bay Packers; and Gale Sayers of the Chicago Bears.[12]

It wasn't until 1971 that the US Supreme Court issued an 8–0 decision that reversed Ali's conviction. This decision was not reached without much controversy, which space will not permit me to further detail. However, of importance to this chapter, in reference to this decision, is the sacrifice Ali had to make and the sacrifice he became because of his stance against the Vietnam War and his commitment to his faith in Islam, which ultimately cost him three productive years that some classified as the apex of his boxing career.

Subsequent to his battles with the US justice system, Ali went on to stage some of the most iconic fights in boxing history: for example, the "Battle of the Champions," where he met the legendary boxer Joe Frazier for the first time in 1971 in Madison Square Garden; the "Rumble in the Jungle," where he faced George Foreman in Kinshasa, Zaire, in 1974; and the "Thrilla in Manila," hosted in 1975 in Manila, Philippines, which was his third and final fight against Joe Frazier. Besides these and other battles, Ali's greatest contender was Parkinson's syndrome. At the 1996 Olympic Games in Atlanta, Georgia, we witnessed Ali's public fight with this contender as he carried the torch and lit the Olympic cauldron. For 21 years (1960–81) as a professional boxer, the champ bobbed and weaved, jabbed and danced, to win the world heavyweight crown three times. For 32 years, he contended with Parkinson's, but he could not allude its devastating blows to his body and mind.

Conclusion

Converting athletic capital into sociopolitical capital comes at a price. As stated earlier, it requires making a sacrifice and sometimes being the sacrifice. Similar to the sacrifices of Paul Robeson and of other Black athletes in converting his athletic and entertainment capital into political capital to speak out against various global injustices caused by White supremacy, Ali encountered and endured the perils associated with this conversion. One can easily conclude that Colin Kaepernick is having a similar experience, at least to some degree. Kaepernick's conversion of his athletic capital into sociopolitical capital, to date, has cost him years of his career in the National Football League, and possibly his entire career. Unlike Ali and Robeson, his movement has been co-opted and commercialized by the likes of Nike and other sport paraphernalia capitalists who are accustomed to making a profit off a social cause. These corporate messiahs' profiteering patterns are typical in co-opting social movements into something else and something less.

Ali's conversion to Islam, his refusal to be inducted into the army, and the creation of Main Bout are three examples considered in this chapter to be acts of activism and, thus, opportunities where he converted his athletic capital into sociopolitical capital. They inform us of the potential repercussions encountered by Black athletes who choose to use their athletic talents beyond the athletic context for the greater good. Also, it informs us of how sport is not apolitical, but as many scholars have suggested, it is an ideological outpost, a contested terrain, and cultural phenomena that inform, reinforce, and reproduce prevailing ideologies. Despite the use of sport to perpetuate masculine hegemony, racist ideologies, and conservative political beliefs, athletes, social groups, and governments of nations have all sought to use sport and sporting events to make political statements, to advance political ideologies, or to promote social causes. For the Black athlete, they have encountered mixed success in using sport as a counter space and an emancipatory apparatus for social justice. Often, they are not acknowledged or honored until many years after their valiant activist efforts are diluted or forgotten. As with Ali, the pattern of losing the opportunity to compete, thus a loss of wealth, plus the assassination of character occurs for converting athletic capital into sociopolitical capital and, without a doubt, tempers many Black athletes from developing a social justice orientation.

It is interesting to note that similar to martyrs of the movement who have sought to bring attention to racial and social injustices in the United States and globally, some have lost their lives in the process, while others have endured the aforementioned repercussions for their activism. Yet some of these activists have had their once-assassinated images resurrected and now their once-rebellious acts are viewed differently and championed by the masses, whether it is due to selective amnesia, sociopolitical progression, redemption, or the ability of their previous efforts of activism to be co-opted by capitalist elites into something less or something else, which ultimately weakens the power of activism. Regardless, some of these past athletic champions and activists for racial and social justice are worthy of celebrating and remembering—like Ali. As a former Olympic gold medalist, Ali's redemption was witnessed as he carried the torch during the 1996 Olympics and had his gold medal replaced by the International Olympic Committee president,

Juan Antonio Samaranch, during half-time of the US men's basketball game against Yugoslavia.

Despite the ebbs of flows of Muhammad Ali's life, from Louisville, Kentucky, to becoming the world heavyweight champion to being named United Nations' Messenger of Peace, he still remains the peoples' champ and his life is forever relevant in the fight for social justice.

Ali Is Champ

Bronzed by the Gods,
Brown by nature,
Black by culture.
Ali is Champ

Cornered by few.
Celebrated by many.
Crucified by infidels.
Ali is Champ

When Liston didn't answer for the 7th.
He reigned as Champ - the Greatest,
Ali was "A Bad Man," who shook up the world.
Champion of the World

From Cassius to Muhammad Ali to Ali Bomaye,
From Louisville to the Rumble in the Jungle to the Thriller in Manila,
He evolved as a man and prevailed as a boxer.
Stripped of his titles upon his conversion to Islam,
He rebounded and resurfaced to carry the torch at the 1996's Olympic Games.

Finally surrendering to his greatest contender – that fatal pugilist;
The reaper of us all.
Yet, he still remains relevant.
And, he will forever be the people's champ!

Notes

1 Athletic activism is social activism performed in the context of sport and sporting events. Athletic activist are athletes with a social justice orientation and who use their athletic capital to make a sociopolitical statement or ignite a movement.
2 I do not think Black communities are monolithic or homogeneous, but rather heterogeneous due to the intersections of class, education, and other forms of capital.

3 For an in-depth analysis of sport activism, please see: Joseph N. Cooper, Charles Macaulay, and Saturnino H. Rodriguez, "Race and resistance: A typology of African American sport activism," *International Review for the Sociology of Sport* 54, no. 2 (2019): 151–81.

4 Athletic capital is a form of cultural capital in the context of sport. It will be defined as invisible assets an athlete obtains based often on his/her performance, persona, marketability, brand identity and image, and so on. It is a currency that ensures athletic privilege, which potentially leads to social mobility.

5 Sociopolitical capital will be defined as a type of invisible asset or currency that influences social movements and informs policy reform.

6 Angelo Bartlett Giamatti, "Hyperbole's child," in *The Muhammad Ali Reader*, ed. Gerald Early (New York, NY: Harper-Collins, 1998), 166.

7 See Frederick Douglass, *Narrative of the Life of Frederick Douglass: An American Slave* (New York: Collier Books, 1892).

8 Oscar Fraley, "Muslim charge clams up Clay," *Pittsburgh Press*, February 7, 1964. https://news.google.com/newspapers?nid=1144&dat=19640207&id=XF4bAAAAIBAJ&sjid=-04EA AAAIBAJ&pg=5091,2145696.

9 Michael Ezra, *Muhammad Ali: The Making of an Icon* (Philadelphia, PA: Temple University Press, 2009), 193.

10 Ibid.

11 See, for example, John Cottrell, *Man of Destiny: The Story of Muhammad Ali, Formerly Cassius Clay* (London: Frederick Muller, 1967), 335.

12 Arthur R. Ashe Jr., *A Hard Road to Glory: A History of the African-American Athlete Since 1946, Vol. 3* (New York: Amistad, 1993), 85.

Chapter Twelve

INFLUENCING AT THE INTERSECTIONS: BLACK SPORTSWOMEN'S ACTIVISM IN THE ERA OF MUHAMMAD ALI

Akilah R. Carter-Francique

Introduction

During the 1950s and 1960s, a young Cassius Clay rose to prominence exhibiting athletic talent, a boisterous disposition, and a champion spirit. His success yielded an Olympic gold medal in 1960, which included a positive following that embraced his charisma and confidence. Following the Rome Olympics, Clay rose to boxing prominence, a rise that could be described as meteoric due to his ability to secure boxing matches and to win or defend titles against some of the most accomplished boxers of all time like Joe Frazier, Larry Holmes, Leon Spinks, and Sonny Liston. But a shift in Clay's narrative would come after his bout and win against Sonny Liston in 1964. On February 27, 1964, he announced his affiliation with the Nation of Islam (NOI). Days after the affiliation announcement, he would take the name Muhammad Ali, which was chosen by the Honorable Elijah Muhammad, the minister and leader for the NOI.

The NOI was instrumental in nurturing and cultivating Ali interest perspectives. The political terrain and social climate for Blacks in the United States of America during Ali's rise (in the late 1950s and early 1960s) were inclusive of negative racial interactions filled with overt racism and acts of violence in the fight for racial equality. Multiple efforts of groups and leaders were ignited during the struggle to address the race problem (sit-ins; Student Nonviolent Coordinating Committee (SNCC)—Ella Baker, James Forman, Stokely Carmichael; Southern Christian Leadership Conference; National Association for the Advancement of Colored People (NAACP); Freedom Riders; March on Washington—Martin Luther King Jr., Banyard Rustin, A. Philip Randolph). For Ali, the NOI fed that engagement. According to the NOI history:

> The Nation of Islam was founded on the basis of peace and as an answer to a prayer of Abraham to deliver his people who would be found in servitude slavery in the Western Hemisphere in this day and time. […] We have always been taught to respect the laws of the land. We are taught never to carry arms, to make war or to be the aggressor, for this is against the nature of the righteous. We are taught the Principles of Divine Unity and the Universal Brotherhood of Islam. (NOI, 2020)

Hence, Ali's membership with NOI and teachings by the Honorable Elijah Muhammad illuminated a philosophical divide within Black America's approach toward the race problem. In the eyes of White America, it also singed Ali's image and triggered his cultivated following as an Olympic gold medalist, boxing champion, and beloved Black male athlete.

While there was and is an expansive history of Black athletes' interface with the political and legislative landscape (see Jack Johnson, James "Jesse" Owens, Joe Louis, Jackie Robinson, Harlem Globetrotters), Ali's athletic achievement, leadership, prominence, and global consciousness elevated his realm of influence. His global consciousness and influence would collide in 1966, when he refused to serve in the Vietnam War. Ali opposed the notion of war, and his teachings diametrically opposed war as well. He stated:

> "I am a member of the Black Muslims, and we don't go to no wars unless they're declared by Allah himself. I don't have no personal quarrel with those Vietcong." (Fitzpatrick, 1966)[...]
> He later stated, "My conscience won't let me go shoot my brother, or some darker people, or some poor hungry people in the mud for big powerful America. And shoot them for what? They never called me nigger, they never lynched me, they didn't put no dogs on me, they didn't rob me of my nationality, rape and kill my mother and father. [...] Shoot them for what? How can I shoot them poor people? Just take me to jail. (Noble, 2011)

His expressions, and ultimate refusal to serve during the war, resulted in him being identified as a "draft dodger" and banned from boxing for four years. Arguably, Ali's stance and steadfast nature regarding his position toward the war and understanding of other social justice issues grew stronger during his appeal period. In 1971, upon the US Supreme Court overturning his case, he would regain his title as the heavyweight champion of the world.

Ali's lived experience was deemed the prime activist example, and he had the ability to influence leaders (e.g., Malcolm X, Martin Luther King Jr.) and galvanize organizations (e.g., SCLC, SNCC) that had the same goals but divergent ideological beliefs (Ezra, 2016). Ali's sport affiliation allowed him to permeate the walls of politics, religion, and global borders. And, while related yet beyond the scope of this chapter, Ali as a "political entity and global sporting racial project" (Carrington, 2010, p. 2) would take a turn through his socialization, conception of resistance, and expression of Black activism. Consequently, in the world of sport, he became the standard and model of Black athlete activism, deemed the greatest while living then and holding rank still after his death. Hence, the purpose of this chapter is to examine Muhammad Ali the political activist's efforts and his influence of Black sportswomen, and compare and contrast his brand of activism to that of Black sportswomen.

Defining, Operationalizing, and Categorizing Activism

The opportunity to examine the similarities and differences of Ali's lived activism to that of Black sportswomen is an exciting, but daunting endeavor. The concern for this endeavor is based on gender and how gender roles frame identity and the embodiment of action. Thus, while enmeshed in patriarchy, this section will illuminate how activism is defined, operationalized, and categorized.

Defining Activism

Activism in the 1960s was steeped in race, sex, socioeconomic, and political interests. Numerous groups emerged to address these interests and social inequalities by using multiple methods to promote social justice. Consequently, activism has multiple definitions. An activist is defined by Webster's dictionary as "one who advocates or practices activism; a person who supports cases or supports strong actions (such as public protests) in support of or opposition to one side of a controversial issue." During this time period, youth and college students like the aforementioned SNCC or in sport the Olympic Committee for Human Rights (OCHR) and the Olympic Project for Human Rights (OPHR) led the way in activist efforts, which are defined as "activities for the purpose of creating social change, such as protest and community engagement" (Hernandez, 2012, p. 680).

Focusing on Black activists' efforts, Cooper, Macauley, and Rodriguez defined activism as "engagement in intentional actions that disrupt oppressive hegemonic systems by challenging a clearly defined opposition while simultaneously empowering individuals and groups disadvantaged by inequitable arrangements" (Cooper et al., 2019, pp. 154–55). This comprehensive definition also considers and centers oppressive systems (e.g., race, sex, socioeconomic status) as the focal point of activists' actions. Employing this definition is useful as it further inculcates how individual or group efforts connect with a larger social justice agenda through "expressing specific demands for social change and operate in tandem with broader social justice movements" (Cooper et al., 2019, p. 155). Identifying how Black activists' efforts are operationalized is another important aspect to movements and achievement of identified activist goals.

Operationalizing Activism

Focusing on Black athlete activist efforts, it is important to highlight one of the most prolific and impactful movements of the 1960s and still today (Hawkins, 2012). The OPHR occurred in 1968 with the goal to

(a) stage an international protest of the persistent and systematic violation of Black people's human rights in the United States; (b) expose America's historical exploitation of Black athletes as political propaganda tools in both the national and international arenas; (c) establish a standard of political responsibility among Black athletes vis-a-vis the needs and interests of the Black community, and to devise effective and acceptable ways by which athletes could accommodate the demands of such responsibilities; and (d) make the Black community aware of the substantial "hidden" dynamics and consequences of their sports involvement. (Edwards, 1979, p. 2)

Importantly, this movement also included the social justice cause of Muhammad Ali's boxing career with the listed demand for the "Restoration of Muhammad Ali's title and right to box in this country [United States]" (Edwards, 2017, p. 53).

The OPHR picked up the mantle of Ali's activist efforts by using the platform of sport and athleticism, which in turn reaffirmed the importance of the athlete voice, promoted the need for structure in sport activism, and demonstrated that this idealized cultural institution of sport could be a terrain contested outside of the realm of play and entertainment. The OPHR movement formalized and in many ways created a "blueprint" that employed five imperatives to operationalize and guide its activists initiatives that included: (a) a substantial and organically sustained pool of aggrieved plaintiffs seeking redress; (b) a relentless and expanding demand for change, legitimized not only by aggrieved populations but also by collaboration "outside" interests and even, unwittingly, by some detractors; (c) a threatened "establishment interest" that makes the changes demanded more reasonable and appealing to the establishment in terms of cost-reward outcomes than maintaining the status quo; (d) substantively factual arguments and supporting ideological "scaffolding" and "framing" to successfully surmount and overcome two characteristically employed adversarial "ploy"; and (e) a sustaining ideology beyond that professed by adversaries and that legitimizes goals and means that enable vigorous "push back" against tendencies toward definitional hegemony and retrenchment relative to compelled changes (Edwards, 2017). The operationalization of activism is imperative for organizers to recognize the viability of their personal efforts to influence social issues and identify the ways that they can promote social and political change.

Categorizing Activism

Once organization takes place, identifying the multiple ways that social and political change have been and can be achieved is advantageous. Highlighting the scholarly work of Cooper and colleagues (2019), *Race and Resistance: A Typology of African American Activism* shares the ways in which Black athletes made a difference and promoted social change. More specifically, Cooper and colleagues (2019) describe five Black-centered categories within the typology to include symbolic activism, scholarly activism, grassroots activism, sport-based activism, and economic activism.

Each of these categories serves as a reflection and response to hegemonic notions of oppression, and if we examine the life span of Ali, we could identify that he embodied the reflected categories: (a) symbolic activism focuses on social awareness and structural change in the areas of economic, education, politics, and social engagements; (b) scholarly activism focuses on the promotion of critical awareness through the transmission of ideas and theoretical analyses to provoke thought, understanding, and influence policy reform within oppressive systems; (c) grassroots activism focuses on broader social uplift efforts that counter hegemonic notions of engagement that will eventuate a proximal impact; (d) sport-based activism focuses on "actions taken by athletes" to challenge and/ or alter a specific rule or law that maintains oppressive systems/associations/culture; and (e) economic activism focuses on the "actions by individuals and/or groups" business development to promote fiscal empowerment and social uplift in historically marginalized communities (Cooper et al., 2019). As presented, the definition of activism and how it is operationalized and then categorized are valuable aspects of understanding the complexity of activism in general and of Ali's activism specifically.

These multiple and dynamic efforts as well as the longevity and steadfast nature of Ali's activism would impact the world's social issues and influence generations as detailed throughout this book and respective chapters (e.g., views on military service and war, religious expression, support of the Civil Rights movement, support of the human rights movement, alignment and collaboration with thought leaders). Ali's span of influence is, in my opinion, widely understood and constantly compared when activism is performed by Black sportsmen. But with the growth in Black women's sports participation, accomplishments, and leadership roles as coaches, administrators, faculty, managers, directors, and beyond, I believe it is of value to understand how Ali's activism influenced generations of Black sportswomen and gave space for Black sportswomen to express their activist traditions.

Black Feminist Socialization, Resistance, and Activism

Blacks', or African Americans', resistance to systemic racial and class oppression is ever present and not bound by a generation or time span. Black women during the 1950s, 1960s, and 1970s understood this reality; therefore, they realized that for Black women and the greater Black community to include its children, there must be an understanding of the need for group survival. Black women's acknowledgment of Black group survival as well as the need to reject negative stereotypes helps to centralize the resistance efforts, to include activism, by Black women.

The centralization of thought and effort is rooted in the interlocking nature of Black women's oppression based on their race, gender, and social class (as well as ethnicity, politics, religion, sexual orientation, and education) within the American context and beyond. The result of multiple oppressions (King, 1988), or double burden (St. Jean and Feagin, 1998), is experiences of marginalization to include being silenced and being invisible. Focusing on the political activism aspect of this chapter, there is ample literature on efforts, issues, and personas of Black men (e.g., Stokley Carmichael, W. E. B. Du Bois, Medgar Evers, James Farmer, Martin Luther King Jr., Joseph Lowery, Thurgood Marshall, A. Philip Randolph, Malcolm X, Andrew Young) and Black sportsmen (e.g., Henry "Hank" Aaron; Arthur Ashe; Lewis Alcindor, today known as Kareem Abdul-Jabbar; Ralph Boston; Jim Brown; James Meredith; Jackie Robinson; Bill Russell). In addition, there is ample literature on the efforts of White women (e.g., Betty Friedan, Alice Paul, Gloria Steinem, National Organization of Women (NOW)) and White sportswomen (e.g., Roberta "Bobbi" Gibb, Katherine Switzer; Wolfe, 2015). The dearth of acknowledgment to and contributions of Black women, who live at the intersections, often leaves the people and groups of all ages, genders, and educational levels believing only a portion of their efforts or that these women do not exist.

For example, in 2018, I was interviewed about efforts of activism by Black sportswomen. The initial request alluded to a perception that Black sportswomen were not engaged in activism and when engaged they did not sacrifice their livelihood to the same degree as Black sportsmen (e.g., Muhammad Ali; Curt Flood; Chris Jackson, today known as Mahmoud Abdul-Rauf; Colin Kaepernick). My initial reaction was a mix of anger and confusion. Anger due to my own knowledge of the numerous Black sportswomen that have endured and sacrificed participation, professionalization and wealth, family, and mental health and well-being (e.g., Theodora "Tidye" Pickett, Louise Stokes, Lucy Diggs Slowe, Althea Gibson, Luisa Harris). Confusion due to not understanding how the afore-mentioned experiences were not viewed as sacrifice. Thus, my initial comment was, "We as Black women are often invisible, so we don't get that credit" as performing activism (Holland, 2018). That invisibility resides in their intersectionality and is often embodied in a phrase that often reflects society's recognition of Black women: "All the women are white, all the Blacks are men," or more specifically as Hull et al. (1982) write, "All the women are white, all the Blacks are men, but some of us are brave."

Socialization to Resist

The bravery of Black women is instilled at a young age. Black girls are socialized to resist, their awareness and consciousness of marginalization and interlocking oppressions is instilled, and they develop the knowledge of the importance of defining themselves for themselves. First, Collins (2000) expresses in *Black Feminist Thought: Knowledge, Consciousness, and the Politics of Empowerment* that Black girls and women live, work, and play within the matrix of domination. In the quest for empowerment, Black girls and women must nav-igate four domains (e.g., interpersonal, hegemonic, disciplinary, structural) of oppressive interactions that can independently and simultaneously limit their influence and affect their holistic well-being. Therefore, Black mothers and othermothers (i.e., fictive kin) shared and continue to share these truths with their "daughters" through words and actions to help them understand the impact of oppression on their personal engagements and the women, men, and children of the greater Black community.

Consciousness to Resist

Second, socialization of Black girls and women continues through the development of consciousness. Black girls' and women's race, sex, and social class status intersect, interlock, and are forever connected in the aforementioned matrix of domination, or oppressive systems. This lived reality necessitates the need to develop an independent consciousness. The ability to promote Black women's consciousness serves as a space where Black women can experience freedom. Experiencing negative treatment and man-aging racism, sexism, and then classism force attentiveness to an oppositional dichot-omous mindset (Collins, 2016). Thus, doing the work to achieve consciousness is a necessary endeavor toward empowerment. Absence of this knowledge and journey can leave Black girls and women vulnerable to conscious marginalization and an inability to resist individual, group, and institutional injustices.

Black women's resistance is activism. According to Collins (2000), Black women's activism addresses the struggle for (a) group survival and (b) institutional transformation. When addressing the struggle of Black women, or group, consciousness is critical to their activism and cultivating the political struggles in which to engage. Furthermore, consci-entious activism for group struggle promotes an autonomous voice that in turn serves to assist in the formulation of coalitions and collaborations with other groups in hopes to address the second aspect of Black women's activism. The struggle for institutional transformation encompasses Black women's efforts to challenge and change discriminatory policies and actions that promote and justify legislation and governance that marginalize Black women (and other historically marginalized people and groups). These two distinct but connected aspects of Black women's activism can be considered private and, therefore, contribute to the notion that Black girls and women do not sacrifice and/or are not activists. But Black women activist traditions are not governed by dominant society; the tradition is governed by self.

Resist to Self-Define and Self-Valuate

Third, Black women recognize the power of resistance resides in their ability to self-define and self-valuate. In the development of self, Black women embodied the themes of Black feminist thought by recognizing the interlocking oppressions of race, sex, and social class and how that oppression is operationalized. Recognition, plus reflection, yielded understanding and value of Black women's culture. Instilled with this history of importance and experience of negative myths and stereotypes in society and sport (Bruening, 2005; Carter-Francique & Richardson, 2016; Collins, 2000; Richardson & Carter-Francique, 2020), Black women know that they must define themselves and identify their own self-worth. Hence, resistance is further imbued through the practice of self-definition and self-valuation, and equals activism.

Black Sportswomen's Activism

There is a legacy of activism and sport activism that predates Muhammad Ali for both Black men and Black women. Yet I would argue that the three aspects (socialization to resist, consciousness to resist, and resistance to self-define and self-valuate), grounded in Black feminism, also governed Ali's activism. For Black women, sport activism is steeped in the aforementioned notions of group survival and institution transformation (Carter-Francique, 2012; Richardson & Carter-Francique, 2020). As presented, Black women live, work, and participate in institutions that were not created for them to thrive. Thus, like Ali, Black sportswomen used their platform as athletes to bring attention to a range of issues that affect them personally, their children, and the Black community, as well as the larger population beyond the Black community. Arguably, unlike Ali, Black sportswomen's social location reflected an even more limited sphere of influence as their voices, respectability, and networks were also restricted and often muted (Abney, 1999; Bruening, 2000; Bruening et al., 2005; Oglesby, 1981; Smith, 1992, 2000).

While I recognized and learned as a young girl that Black sportswomen's participation as "the first" was an activist endeavor, during my doctoral studies I would garner a greater understanding and appreciation for the way in which representation, group survival, and institutional transformation were employed to aid in identity development (Carter, 2008). This was "activist mothering." Naples (1992) explains activist mothering as a Black woman's "community othermothering" tradition. Activist othermothering is an extension of community othermothering that is rooted in political activism (Naples, 1991,

1992, 1996). In 1992, Nancy Naples explicated the term in "Activist Mothering: Cross-Generational Continuity in the Community Work of Women from Low-Income Urban Neighborhoods." In this article, Naples argues that activist mothering is a more comprehensive articulation of the activities in which Black women, and Latina women, engage. More plainly, Naples states that this term

> provides a new conceptualization of the interacting nature of labor, politics, and mothering—three aspects of social life usually analyzed separately—from the point of view of women whose motherwork has often been ignored or pathologized [...] in sociological analysis. (1992, p. 446)

Naples (1992) suggests that activist mothering reflects the "power of knowledge generated from 'self-defined, subjugated standpoints' to decenter dominant frameworks" (p. 446). Nevertheless, Black women utilized a range of platforms from which to engage in social justice efforts (Barnett, 1993; Collins, 2000; Naples, 1992). Again, this is a practice of social justice engagements utilized by and reflected in the span of Ali's lifetime.

Black Sportswomen Activists: Mothers, Daughters, and Granddaughters

Once again, as members of the Black female collective, Black sportswomen are socialized to resist, care for, and uplift the Black community (Carter-Francique, 2012, 2014; Richardson & Carter-Francique, 2020; Smith, 1992). So, they too have engaged in a range of activism and used their platforms nationally and internationally to promote social change through the aforementioned sport activism typologies (Cooper et al., 2019). And what may become apparent is that the Black sportswomen presented reflect Ali's declaration, in their respective ways, and his embodiment of "I don't have to be what you want me to be, I'm free to be who I want."

For example, and prior to Ali's rise in the 1960s, tennis pioneers Lucy Diggs Slowe (1885–1937), Ora Washington (1899–1971), and Margaret (1915–2004) and Matilda Roumania (1917–2003) Peters, known as "Pete" and "Repeat" (participated in 1930s–1950s and reigned as tennis doubles champions and record holders in the American Tennis Association), also contributed to the sport activist waves[1] of gaining legitimacy, acquiring political access and positional diversity, and demanding dignity and respect through their expressions of symbolic activism and grassroots efforts through their "representational firsts" (Crenshaw, 1991) participation and service. Nannie Helen Burroughs (1879–1961), a pioneering educator and founder of the National Training School for Women and Girls (established in 1909), contributed to sportswomen's grassroots activist efforts through providing a counterspace for Black girls and women in the United States and beyond (Canada, Haiti, Puerto Rico, and African countries) to obtain an education, trade skills, and religious studies *and* participate in physical education and the sport of basketball.

Expressing economic activism, Effa Manley owned, managed, and operated (along with her husband) the Newark Eagles, a Negro Baseball League team from 1935 to

1948. Manley was the only woman to manage an all-male professional baseball team. In 1934 she organized a boycott in response to department stores that refused to hire Black salesclerks. Demonstrating grassroots activism, Manley served as treasurer for the Newark National Association for the Advancement of Colored People (NAACP) as well as raised money for The Booker T. Washington Community Hospital, and through symbolic activism in 1939, she hosted an "Anti-Lynching Day" at Ruppert Stadium in Newark, New Jersey. Based on all of her social justice efforts in and beyond baseball, in 2006 Effa Manley was the first woman inducted into the National Baseball Hall of Fame.

Black Sportswomen of the 1950s and 1960s

Examining the activist mothers in the 1950s and 1960s, a number of women were recruited by the US government, to serve in the international goodwill campaign; however, I argue that "White capitalistic patriarchy" did not recognize the power of Black women's resistance socialization, consciousness, and self-definition and self-valuation. See Table 12.1.

For instance, Davis (2018) in a reflective analysis of Black sportswomen's activism share that "the United States Information Agency (USIA) identified sports as a particularly useful vehicle for Cold War propaganda because sports were supposedly apolitical, and athletes were seen as less likely to be outspoken—particularly Black women." Thus, sport and the notion of Black women's passivity were soon disrupted when Earlene Brown debunked the USIA's message with her candid expressions of racism and explication of racist interactions and treatment experiences of Blacks by Whites in the United States.

Moreover, the nurturing hands of the Black women's collective instilled the constant questioning of purpose and an activist mothering standpoint that permeated the lives of Black sportswomen as expressed by Wilma "Skeeter" Rudolph:

> When I was going through my transition to being famous, I tried to ask God, why was I here? What is my purpose? Surely it wasn't just to win three gold medals. There has to be more to this life than just that. (Rudolph, 1977)

This purpose-filled spirit was reflected in the following generations of Black sportswomen activism, particularly for those sportswomen that lived in the post–Title IX era.

Black Sportswomen Post-Title IX

Title IX of the Education Act of 1972, or Title IX, is a US federal civil rights law that was passed to prohibit discrimination on the basis of sex in federally funded educational programs and/or activities to include sport (Department of Justice, n.d.). During this era, a number of Black sportswomen experienced the unintended consequences (i.e., racism, sexism) of this law (Carter-Francique & Richardson, 2015; see Table 12.2). The intersectional marginalization of race, sex, and social class left Black women vulnerable and exposed to overt acts of racism and sexism as participants and coaches in sport.

Table 12.1 Black Sportswomen Activists of the Civil Rights Movement, 1950s and 1960s: Mothers

Athlete	Sport	Year: Activism
Marcenia Lyle Alberga aka Toni Stone	Baseball	1953, 1954: One of three Black women to play in the all-male Negro Baseball Leagues. Second baseman for Negro Baseball Leagues Indianapolis Clowns in 1953 and Kansas City Monarchs in 1954. 1985: Inducted into the Women's Sports Foundation's International Women's Sports Hall of Fame.
Connie Morgan	Baseball	1954–55: One of three Black women to play in the all-male Negro Baseball League. Second baseman with the Indianapolis Clowns.
Mamie "Peanut" Johnson	Baseball	1953: First female pitcher in the all-male Negro Baseball Leagues' Indianapolis Clowns.
Althea Gibson	Tennis and Golf	1948: First Black female Wimbledon champion. Arguably, Gibson was not interested in being the first to break the color barrier in women's tennis for the sake of social justice; she was interested for the sake of competition and winning. In 1956 she was the first African American to win a Grand Slam title.
Wilma Rudolph	Track and field (Athletics)	1956, 1960: Olympian. First American woman to win three gold medals in a single Olympics—1960 Rome, Italy. Founded the Wilma Rudolph Foundation. 1960: Following Olympic win, "Welcome Wilma Day" was held in Clarksville, Tennessee. At the demand of Rudolph, the festival, parade, and banquet was a racially integrated event. This was the first fully integrated municipal event in the city's history. In 1961, she set the world record in 100 meters. 1963: Served as a global goodwill ambassador for the US State Department. Upon return to the United States and Clarksville, Tennessee, participated in civil rights protests to integrate city restaurants.
Wyomia Tyus	Track and field (Athletics)	1964, 1968: 100 meters Olympic gold medalist in 1964 and 1968. First back-to-back gold medalist in the 100 meters. Fought for racial equality and equal pay and professional opportunities for women athletes.
Erosenna Robinson	Track and field (Athletics)	1952: Worked to integrate a Cleveland, Ohio, skating rink. 1959: High jumper who refused to stand for the national anthem at the Pan-American Games in Chicago, Illinois. Refused to serve as a global ambassador with the US State Department to portray positive race relations. 1960: Participated in a nonviolent protest in her refusal to pay federal taxes, which resulted in a one-year prison sentence inclusive of a hunger strike. Example served to purport the creation of the National War Tax Resistance Coordinating Committee. 1961: Experienced racism and refusal of service when dining at a restaurant. Experience led to integration of restaurants along Route 40 in Maryland.

Table 12.1 *Continued*

Athlete	Sport	Year: Activism
Tennessee Tigerbelles	Track and field (Athletics)	1953–94: Led by two-time Olympic coach (1960, 1964) Ed Temple. This team comprised of greats like Chandra Cheeseborough, Isabelle Daniels, Mae Faggs Starr, Martha Hudson, Madeline Manning Mims, Edith McGuire Duvall, Barbara Jones Slater, Kathy McMillan and Wilma Rudolph, Wyomia Tyus, Willye White, and Lucinda Williams. Under Temple's leadership, the Tigerbelles won a total of 23 Olympic medals (13 gold, 6 silver, 4 bronze). Sport analysts and scholars deemed this team the reason US athletics remained relevant internationally. All women graduated with 4-year degrees, 32 master's degrees, and 8 doctorate degrees.
Earlene Brown	Track and field (Athletics) & Roller Derby	1956, 1960, and 1964: Olympic medalists in the shot put (bronze—1960) and discus (fourth—1956). Only shot putter to compete in three consecutive Olympic games. 1959: Pan-American Games gold medalists in shot put and discus. 1960s: Being vocal about civil rights and women's rights in the 1960s. Recruited by the US Information Agency, along with other Olympic athletes, to spread a message of peace and positive race relations. Brown pushed back this propaganda and spoke honestly of racism on tours.

Note: This is not a complete list of Black sportswomen.

Whether at play or on the sidelines, Black sportswomen posturing in the same fashion as Ali endured a level of retaliation that was often more detrimental to their image than to that of Black men. For example, in 1971 at Creighton State University and in 1973 at Brown University, the Black women cheerleaders, respectively, did not appear and did not stand for the playing of the national anthem prior to the start of a basketball game. The consequences of their symbolic activist actions lead to a three-year disbandment of the team at Creighton and community, media, and legislative outcry in Providence, Rhode Island (Nemitz, 2011; Quick, 2020; The Editors, 1973).

Further, Carter-Francique and Richardson (2015) capture the sport-based activist experiences in the context of Historically Black Colleges and Universities (HBCUs) with access to training facilities, uniform inequalities, and pay equity of Linda Spencer and Sanya Tyler. Tyler voiced her concerns with pay equity as the head women's basketball coach at Howard, sued, and won the first Title IX lawsuit in history (Armour, 1993).

Many of the sportswomen served as the "representational first" in their respective sport participation and coaching appointments, thus still working to gain legitimacy, acquiring political access and positional diversity, demanding dignity and respect, like that of their Black male counterparts. One pioneering woman, Tina Sloan Green, famed lacrosse coach at Temple University, reflected on her activist efforts in 2017:

Table 12.2 Black Sportswomen Post–Title IX: Daughters

Athlete	Sport	Year: Activism
Sheryl Swoopes	Basketball	1995: First female athlete to obtain a shoe contract with Nike for the Nike Air Swoopes. 1996: First player signed to the WNBA with the Houston Comets. 1996, 2000, 2004: A three-time Olympic gold medalist in basketball. 2016: Inducted to the Naismith Memorial Basketball Hall of Fame. 2017: Inducted into the Women's Basketball Hall of Fame.
Sanya Tyler	Basketball	1980: First full-time women's head basketball coach at Howard University (HBCU). The team would go on to win five MEAC season titles, nine MEAC tournament titles, and earn more than 300 wins. 1993: First Title IX win and awarded $1.1 million for sex discrimination suit against Howard University.
Lynette Woodard	Basketball	1984: Olympic gold medalist in basketball. 1985: First female on the all-male Harlem Globetrotters. 1997: Signed to the WNBA's Cleveland Rockers. 2005: Inducted to the Naismith Memorial Hall of Fame.
Nikki Franke	Fencing	1975, 1980: Gold medalist, champion, in foil for the United States Fencing Association (USFA). 1976, 1980: Member of US fencing team. 1979: Inducted into the Brooklyn College Hall of Fame Temple University as being the first and only Black female head coach (46 years and counting). 1992: Cofounder of the Black Women in Sports Foundation (BWSF) that advocates for the underrepresentation of Black women and women of color in sport as athletes, coaches, administrators, and academics.
Wendy Hillard	Gymnastics	1978: First Black US national team member in rhythmic gymnastics. 1979, 1981, 1983: First Black gymnast to represent the United States in international competition, which included three world championship teams. 1995–96: First Black president of Women's Sports Foundation. 1996: Founded the Wendy Hilliard Gymnastics Foundation that provides free and low-cost gymnastics for over fifteen thousand urban youth in New York, New York, and Detroit, Michigan. 2008: Inducted into US Gymnastics Hall of Fame.

Table 12.2 *Continued*

Athlete	Sport	Year: Activism
Tina Sloan Green	Lacrosse	1969–73: First Black to play for the US national field hockey team. 1975–92: First Black head coach in National Collegiate Athletic Association (NCAA) lacrosse. Served as head coach for the women's lacrosse team at Temple University. Team won national championships in 1984 and two additional years. However, Sloan Green did not receive coach of the year and would not for over 10 years, as race played an influential factor. 1992: Cofounder of the Black Women in Sports Foundation that advocates for the underrepresentation of Black women and women of color in sport as athletes, coaches, administrators, and academics. 1997: Inducted into US National Lacrosse Hall of Fame. 2013: Inducted into Philadelphia Sports Hall of Fame.
Jackie Joyner-Kersee	Track and field (Athletics)	1984, 1988, 1992, 1996: Olympic medalists in 1984 (silver in heptathlon), 1988 (gold in heptathlon and long jump), 1992 (gold in long jump), and 1996 (bronze in long jump). 1987, 1991, 1993: Medalist at world championships—1987 (gold in heptathlon, long jump), 1991 (gold in long jump), and 1993 (gold in heptathlon). Served as a board member for US Track & Field (USATF). 1988: Founder of Jackie Joyner Kersee Foundation in East St. Louis, Illinois, which promotes academic and athletic engagement. She is deemed an advocate and philanthropist for children's education, racial equality, and women's rights. 2007: Cofounder of Athletes for Hope, a charitable organization that supports professional athletes' involvement in charities. 2011: Collaborated with Comcast to provide Internet essentials for low socioeconomic families to attain laptops and wifi connections at low cost.
Florence Griffith-Joyner	Track and field (Athletics)	1984: Silver 200 m 1988: Gold 100 m, 200 m, 4 × 100; silver 4 × 400 1989: Co-chaired the President's Council on Physical Fitness.

Continued

Table 12.2 *Continued*

Athlete	Sport	Year: Activism
Zina Garrison	Tennis	1988: Olympic gold medalist in women's doubles and bronze medalist in women's singles. 1990: Runner-up at Wimbledon in women's singles. 1987, 1988, and 1990: Three-time Grand Slam mixed doubles champion (1987 was Australian Open, and 1988 and 1990 were Wimbledon). 1988: Founder of the Zina Garrison Foundation for the Homeless. 1992: Founder of the Zina Garrison All-Court Tennis Program that supports inner-city tennis in Houston, Texas. 1997: A former member of the US President's Council on Physical Fitness and Sports.
Flo Hyman	Volleyball	1984: Olympic silver medalist in volleyball and later lobbied with other female athletes for Title IX legislation. 1987: After Hyman's death from Marfan syndrome in 1986, the National Girls and Women in Sports Day (NGWSD) was created in her honor. It was created and is supported by Girls Incorporated, Girl Scouts of the United States, the National Association for Girls and Women in Sport, the Women's Sports Foundation, and the YWCA of the United States.

Note: This is not a complete list of Black sportswomen.

I was very proud to be the first, but I never wanted to be the "only." That pride is unbelievable. I wanted to represent my family and friends, the university and, most importantly, the African American community. I realized the importance of that—and, if I messed up, then [all African Americans] would be judged by my actions since I am the first. (Richcreek, 2017)

Sloan Green's reflective account of symbolic activism as the "first" Black woman embodies Black feminist thought's community othermother work (Collins, 2000; Naples, 1992). Thus, it is not just about her personal advancement; it is about Black girls, women, and children identifying opportunities, acquiring access, and developing a knowledge base to aid in their maintenance, retention, and promotion to positions of leadership. Therefore, while symbolic activism was imperative, like Ali, Sloan Green recognized the important value of grassroots, sport-based, and economic activism through the cofounding of the Black Women's Sport Foundation (see the BWSF website for mission and detailed efforts).

Black Sportswomen from 2000 to Present

Examining Black sportswomen granddaughters, and as stated earlier, there is a notion that Black women are not engaged in activism or advocacy; thus, they are not subjected to risks or willing to make sacrifices. It is my hope that this chapter has shed light on the historic legacy of Black women's activism in society and sport. That said, contemporary Black sportswomen's activism is receiving greater acknowledgment and media coverage than in the past decades. See Table 12.3. For example, the rise and prominence of sisters Venus and Serena Williams in the white-collar sport of tennis, despite the efforts of Diggs Slowe, Washington, the Peters sisters, Gibson, and Garrison, remains difficult due to their race (and the politics of colorism and skin tone) and socioeconomic status (hometown: Compton, California).

Nevertheless, the Williams sisters have utilized their athletic success as an activist platform to address a range of social issues to include Venus's sport-based and economic activism for the achievement of pay equity at Wimbledon in 2007 (see the film *Venus Vs.* directed by Ava DuVernay). Serena's sport-based and economic activism for maternity leave in tennis rankings and symbolic efforts pushing the medical profession's adoption of diversity training (i.e., cultural competence to aid in maternal health treatment; Toole, 2019) reflects notions that "personal is political" (Collins, 2000). And both sisters shared racist boos and racial epithets at Indian Wells in 2001, which led to a 13- to 14-year boycott. In a 2016 *Players Tribune* article, Venus utilized scholarly activism to explain "Why I'm Going Back to Indian Wells." Her "big sister" narrative expressed her felt racism, consciousness, and responsibility to family and sport with a level of sophistication, elegance, and Black respectability that embodied an understanding of activist mothering (Williams, 2016).

Black sportswomen continue to use their respective platforms to address issues of social injustice. One of the most noteworthy examples of symbolic activism was in 2016 when Black sportswomen in the Women's National Basketball Association (WNBA) demonstrated their alliance with the grassroots activism movement Black Lives Matter (BLM). Founded by Alicia Garza, Patrisse Cullors, and Opal Tometi, all Black women (Black Lives Matter, 2020), this global network was created to "build local power and intervene in violence inflicted on Black communities by the state and vigilantes" (BLM, 2020). Recognizing this mission, the women of the Minnesota Lynx, Black and White, took the lead in protest through wearing black shirts during their pregame warm-up and not answering any questions from the media that were not about police shootings of Black people during the postgame interviews. The sportswomen of the New York Liberty, Indiana Fever, and Phoenix Mercury followed suit in their actions. The result was a $5,000 fine and penalties ($500 individually for wearing a T-shirt) from the WNBA for using team membership and NBA affiliation as a platform for their activism (Cauterucci, 2016). Upon further review, discussion, and public criticism by the players themselves (e.g., Tina Charles's Twitter statement), the fine and corresponding penalties were rescinded by WNBA president Lisa Borders (Eilerson, 2016; Helsel, 2016). (Note: Black male NBA players LeBron James and Derrick Rose staged a similar "I Can't Breathe" protest in 2014 after the shooting death of Eric Garner with no fines or penalties.)

Table 12.3 Black Sportswomen from 2000 to the Present: Granddaughters

Athlete	Sport	Year: Activism
Mo'ne Davis	Baseball	2014: First female and Black female to pitch in the Little League Baseball World Series. This accolade was followed by hate verbiage directed to her on Twitter. 2019: Currently attending Hampton University, a Historically Black College and University, to play basketball and softball, and obtain her undergrad degree.
Aryiana Smith	Basketball	2014: Knox College basketball player who protested Michael Brown's death by police shooting during the national anthem in a game against Fontbonne University in Clayton, Missouri. Her "hands up, don't shoot" gesture and lying on the floor for four minutes thirty seconds was symbolic of the four hours and thirty minutes that Brown laid on the street in Ferguson, Missouri.
Brittney Griner	Basketball	Only NCAA basketball player to block 500 shots and score 2000 points. 2013: WNBA player with the Phoenix Mercury and multiple accolades since her drafting. 2016: Olympic gold medalist in team basketball. 2017: Griner and Layshia Clarendon (Atlanta Dream) penned an op-ed letter against a Texas legislature bill drafted toward make transgender people use restroom facilities based on their birth certificate birth designation.
Dawn Staley	Basketball	1996, 2000, 2004: Olympic gold medalist basketball. 1999: WNBA player with the Charlotte Sting. 2013: Naismith Memorial Basketball Hall of Fame. 2017: Head coach of University of South Carolina women's basketball team. First Black female head coach of NCAA championship team. 2020: Naismith Memorial Basketball Hall of Fame—Coach of the Year.
Maya Moore	Basketball	2011: WNBA first round and first overall draft pick to the Minnesota Lynx. Four-time WNBA champion (2011, 2013, 2015, 2017) and two-time Olympic gold medalist in basketball (2012, 2016). 2020: Took a hiatus from WNBA to engage in and focus on criminal justice reform.

Table 12.3 *Continued*

Athlete	Sport	Year: Activism
Natasha Cloud	Basketball	2019: Member of the Washington Mystics. Performs a range of advocate and service work in her local Washington, DC, community and shares her voice with organizational panels, K–12 school career days, guest lecturer at colleges and universities, lending her voice and growing influence to a variety of organizations and causes. She visited local schools for their career days, shared her story during a Girls on the Run NOVA fundraiser, chatted with journalism students at the University of Maryland, and spoke about the future of coaching at the Aspen Institute.
Toni Smith-Thompson	Basketball	2003: A college basketball player at Manhattanville College who protested both systemic inequality and the Iraq War in 2002. 2011: After college she became an organizer and advocate for nonprofit social work New York Civil Liberties Union.
Women's National Basketball Association (WNBA)	Basketball	2016: Minnesota Lynx women's professional basketball team—Seimone Augustus, Rebekkah Brunson, Maya Moore, and Tanisha Wright—held a press conference while wearing T-shirts that read "Change Starts with Us: Justice & Accountability." Acknowledging the lost lives of Philando Castile and Alton Sterling, who were shot and killed by police—as well "Dallas Police Department," which had just lost five officers to gun violence, and "Black Lives Matter." New York Liberty, Indiana Fever, and Phoenix Mercury followed suit. Players wore Black Lives Matter T-shirts before the game while warming up to honor Philando Castile and Alton Sterling. Due to wearing a non-WNBA-approved uniform, the women on aforementioned teams were fined. The WNBA later rescinded the fine and penalties.
Laila Ali	Boxing	2002–4: IBA Female Super Middleweight title. IWBF Female Super Middleweight title. 2004: IWBF Female Light Heavyweight. 2002–7: WIBA World Super Middleweight title. 2005–7: WBC World Super Middleweight title. 2011–13: President of the Women's Sports Foundation. A champion of fitness, nutrition, and wellness and of gender equity in sport.

Continued

Table 12.3 *Continued*

Athlete	Sport	Year: Activism
Ibtihaj Muhammad	Fencing	2016: Olympic bronze medalist in fencing and the first American woman to wear a hijab in the games. She is a five-time senior world medalist and world champion. With her experiences, she has used her platform to engage in gender equality and diversity discussions globally.
Dominique Dawes	Gymnastics	1992, 1996, 2000: Olympic medalist in artistic gymnastics. First Black woman to win a medal in artistic gymnastics. 1992 bronze team, 1996 gold team, bronze in floor exercise; 2000 bronze team. 2004–6: President of the Women's Sports Foundation. 2010: Appointed cochair for the President's Council on Fitness, Sports, and Nutrition by President Barack Obama.
Briana Scurry	Soccer (Fútbol)	1994–2008: Goalkeeper for US women's soccer team. 1996, 2004: Olympic gold medalist. 1999, 2003: World Cup gold medalist. 2017: First woman goalkeeper and Black woman to be inducted into the National Soccer Hall of Fame. Advocate for LGBTQ rights.
Simone Manuel	Swimming	2016: Olympic medalist and first Black woman to win an individual gold medal, set an Olympic record, and American record in swimming. 2016 gold medals in the 100 m freestyle and 4 × 100 meter medley. Silver medal in the 50 m freestyle and 4 × 100 m freestyle. 2018: Signed an unprecedented TYR sponsorship contract with an inclusion rider that stipulates "meaningful opportunities to traditionally underrepresented groups and that diversity be reflected in creative efforts she [Manuel] pursues with the brand."
Serena Williams	Tennis	Serena and sister, Venus, endured return to Indian Wells 13 years after experiencing racist heckling and accusations of match fixing, where she publicly partnered with Bryan Stevenson and the Equal Justice Initiative to raise funds and vocalize concerns about systemic racism and death penalty. Maternity leave as an athlete and an advocate for Black women's maternal health and cultural competence of physicians and medical staff.

Table 12.3 *Continued*

Athlete	Sport	Year: Activism
Venus Williams	Tennis	Five-time Wimbledon champion (2000, 2001, 2005, 2007, 2008) and four-time Olympian: 2000 gold in singles and doubles, 2008 and 2012 gold in doubles, and 2016 silver in mixed doubles. 2007: Continue Billie Jean King's fight for equal pay at Wimbledon. Won equal pay effort that would eliminate the wage gap between women and men and afford women equal prize money to men.
Gwendolyn "Gwen" Berry	Track and field (Athletics)	2019: Pan-American Games gold medalist in hammer throw. 2019: Stood atop the medal stand with raised fist in protest to President Donald Trump's discriminatory verbal commentary, practices, and policies.

Note: This is not a complete list of Black sportswomen.

Conclusion

Indeed, Muhammad Ali is the Greatest of All Time. His athletic accomplishments are significant, but his activist efforts are everlasting. The dual worlds of athlete and activist in which Ali operated created a space that Black activist sportsmen could pattern themselves and navigate, and that Black activist sportswomen could fulfill a role which was inherent. Ali's presence and felt sacrifice using the sport activist platform uphold notions of activism as a masculine space but utilizing Cooper and colleagues (2019) typologies broaden the scope and provide a welcomed notion that can empower men and women, athletes, and nonathletes to use their platforms to promote social change. Bringing his full self to this platform every time demonstrated how his station in life, exposure to the global power of sport, and religious indoctrination nurtured his socialization to resist, consciousness to resist, and resistance to self-define, self-valuate, and be "free to be who I want."

Note

1 Black sportswomen activists contributed to all waves of athlete activism and service through (a) gaining legitimacy (1900–45), (b) acquiring political access and positional diversity (1946–60), (c) demanding dignity and respect (1960–70), (d) securing and transferring power via economic and technological capital (1970–present), (e) women and gender (1970–present), and (f) LGBTQ+ rights and legitimacy in sports (2019–present) (Carter-Francique, 2012; Carter-Francique & Richardson, 2015; Davis, 1992, 2018; Edwards, 2016; Farmer, 2016; Richardson & Carter-Francique, 2020).

References

Abney, R. (1999). "African American women in sport." *Journal of Physical Education, Recreation & Dance*, 70(4), 35–38.

Armour, T. (1993, July 31). "One woman's rich legal victory bolsters gender equity." *Chicago Tribune*. https://www.chicagotribune.com/news/ct-xpm-1993-07-31-9307310156-story.html.

Barnett, B. M. (1993). "Invisible southern black women leaders in the civil rights movement: The triple constraints of gender, race, and class." *Gender & Society*, 7(2), 162–82.

Black Lives Matter (2020). "About BLM." *Black Lives Matter*. https://blacklivesmatter.com/about/.

Black Women's Sport Foundation (n.d.). Home page. *Black Women's Sport Foundation*. https://www.blackwomeninsport.org/.

Bruening, J. E. (2000). "Phenomenal women: A qualitative study of silencing, stereotypes, socialization, and strategies for change in the sport participation of African American female student-athletes," doctoral dissertation, the Ohio State University.

Bruening, J. E. (2005). "Gender and racial analysis in sport: Are all the women White and all the Blacks men?" *Quest*, 57(3), 330–49.

Bruening, J. E., Armstrong, K. L., & Pastore, D. L. (2005). "Listening to the voices: The experiences of African American female student athletes." *Research Quarterly for Exercise and Sport*, 76(1), 82–100.

Carrington, B. (2010). *Race, Sport, and Politics: The Sporting Black Diaspora*. Thousand Oaks, CA: Sage.

Carter, A. R. (2008). "Negotiating identities: Examining African American female collegiate athlete experiences in predominantly White institutions," doctoral dissertation, University of Georgia.

Carter-Francique, A. R. (2012). "The impact of Dr. Harry Edwards' scholarship and activism." In F. Polite and B. Hawkins (eds.), *Sport, Race, Activism, and Social Change: The Impact of Dr. Harry Edward's Scholarship and Service*, pp. 125–44. San Diego, CA: Cognella.

———. (2014). "The ethic of care: Black female college athlete development." In J. Conyers (ed.), *Race in American sports: Essays*, pp. 35–58. Jefferson, NC: McFarland.

Carter-Francique, A. R., & Richardson, F. M. (2015). "Black female athlete experiences." In B. J. Hawkins, J. Cooper, A. R. Carter-Francique, and J. K. Cavil (eds.), *Black College Athletes: The Sporting Life at Historically Black Colleges and Universities*, pp. 61–83. Lanham, MD: Rowman & Littlefield.

———. (2016). "Controlling media, controlling access: The role of sport media on Black women's sport participation." *Race, Gender & Class*, 23(1/2), 7–33.

Cauterucci, C. (2016, July 25). "The WNBA's Black Lives Matter protest has set a new standard for sports activism." *Slate*. https://slate.com/human-interest/2016/07/the-wnbas-black-lives-matter-protest-has-set-new-standard-for-sports-activism.html.

Collins, P. H. (2000). *Black Feminist Thought: Knowledge, Consciousness, and the Politics of Empowerment*. New York: Routledge.

———. (2016). "Black feminist thought as oppositional knowledge." *Departures in Critical Qualitative Research*, 5(3), 133–44.

Cooper, J. N., Macaulay, C., & Rodriguez, S. H. (2019). "Race and resistance: A typology of African American sport activism." *International Review for the Sociology of Sport*, 54(2), 151–81.

Crenshaw, K. (1991). "Mapping the margins: Intersectionality, identity politics, and violence against women of color." Stanford Law Review, 43(6), 1241–99.

Davis, A. R. (2018, June 7). "Black athletes, anthem protests, and the spectacle of patriotism." *Black Perspectives*. https://www.aaihs.org/black-athletes-anthem-protests-and-the-spectacle-of-patriotism/.

Davis, M. D. (1992). *Black American women in Olympic track and field: A complete illustrated reference*. Jefferson, NC: McFarland.

Department of Justice (n.d.). "Overview of Title IX of the Education Amendments of 1972." Civil Rights Division. https://www.justice.gov/crt/overview-title-ix-education-amendments-1972-20-usc-1681-et-seq.

Edwards, H. (1979). "The Olympic project for human rights: An assessment ten years later." *Black Scholar*, 10(6/7), 2–8.

———. (2016). "The fourth wave: Black athlete protests in the second decade of the 21st century." Keynote address at the North American Society for the Sociology of Sport conference, Tampa Bay, Florida, November 3.

———. (2017). *The Revolt of the Black Athlete*. Champaign-Urbana: University of Illinois Press.

Eilerson, N. (2016, July 23). "WNBA withdraws penalties for players' 'Black Lives Matter' protests." *Washington Post: Sports*. https://www.washingtonpost.com/news/early-lead/wp/2016/07/23/wnba-withdraws-penalties-for-players-black-lives-matter-protests/.

Ezra, M. (2016). "How Muhammad Ali influenced the civil rights movement." *Aljezzera: United States*. https://www.aljazeera.com/indepth/features/2016/06/muhammad-ali-influenced-civil-rights-movement-160605055700822.html.

Farmer, A. (2016, October 14). "Black women athletes, protest, and politics: An interview with Amira Rose Davis." *Black Perspectives*. https://www.aaihs.org/black-women-athletes-protest-and-politics-an-interview-with-amira-rose-davis/.

Fitzpatrick, T. (1966, February 18). "Cassius Appeals; Muslims Not at War". Chicago Daily News, p. 29.

Helsel, P. (2016, July 23). "WNBA rescinds fines issued over 'Black Lives Matter' protest." *NBC News: Sports*. https://www.nbcnews.com/news/sports/wnba-rescinds-fines-issued-over-black-lives-matter-protest-n615536.

Hernandez, E. (2012). "The journey toward developing political consciousness through activism for Mexican American women." *Journal of College Student Development*, 53(5), 680–702.

Holland, J. (2018, March 2). "Serena Williams champions issues on, and off, tennis court." *Philadelphia Sun*. https://www.philasun.com/diaspora/serena-williams-champions-issues-off-tennis-court/.

Hull, G. T., Bell-Scott, P., & Smith, B. (1982). *All the Women Are White, All the Blacks Are Men, but Some of Us Are Brave: Black Women's Studies*. New York, NY: Feminist Press.

King, D. K. (1988). "Multiple jeopardy, multiple consciousness: The context of a Black feminist ideology." *Signs: Journal of Women in Culture and Society*, 14(1), 42–72.

Naples, N. A. (1991). "'Just what needed to be done': The political practice of women community workers in low-income neighborhoods." *Gender & Society*, 5(4), 478–94.

———. (1992). "Activist mothering: Cross-generational continuity in the community work of women from low-income urban neighborhoods." *Gender & Society*, 6(3), 441–63.

———. (1996). "A feminist revisiting of the insider/outsider debate: The 'outsider phenomenon' in rural Iowa." *Qualitative Sociology*, 19(1), 83–106.

Nation of Islam (NOI). (2020). "Brief history on the Nation of Islam." *Nation of Islam*. https://www.noi.org/noi-history/.

Nemitz, T. (2011, July 26). "Great teams: 1973–74. White and blue review." http://whiteandbluereview.com/great-teams-1973-74-part-i/.

Noble, G. (2011, February 20). "Ali: A Living Legend". WABC-TV: Like It Is.

Oglesby, C. A. (1981). "Myths and realities of Black women in sport." In T. S. Green, C. A. Oglesby, A. Alexander, and N. Franke (eds.), *Black Women in Sport*, pp. 1–13. Reston, VA: American Alliance for Health, Physical Education, Recreation, and Dance.

Quick, N. (2020, August 5). "Black athletes have never stuck to sports so why should they start now?" *Revolt*. https://www.revolt.tv/21353533/black-athletes-stick-to-sports-social-justice-history.

Richcreek, K. (2017, June 22). "Tina Sloan Green on Title IX and founding the Black Women in Sport Foundation." *ESPN*. https://www.espn.com/espnw/culture/story/_/id/19687038/tina-sloan-green-title-ix-founding-black-women-sport-foundation.

Richardson, F. M., & Carter-Francique, A. R. (2020). "Black women's sporting experiences beyond the game." In D. Brown (ed.), *Sports in African American life: Essays on History and Culture*, pp. 141–58. Jefferson, NC: McFarland.

Rudolph, W. (1977). *Wilma: The Story of Wilma Rudolph.* London, England: Penguin Publishing Group.

Smith, Y. R. (1992). "Women of color in society and sport." *Quest,* 44(2), 228–50.

Smith, Y. (2000). "Sociohistorical influences on African American elite sportswomen." *Racism in College Athletics: The African American Athlete Experience,* 2, 173–97.

Staurowsky, E. (2012). "Is multiple jeopardy the name of the game for Black women in sport?" In F. G. Polite and B. Hawkins (eds.), *Sport, Race, Activism, and Social Change: The Impact of Dr. Harry Edwards' Scholarship and Service,* pp. 113–24. San Diego, CA: Cognella.

St. Jean, Y. S., & Feagin, J. R. (1998). *Double Burden: Black Women and Everyday Racism.* Armonk, NY: ME Sharpe.

The Editors. (1973, June 24–30). "Under the elms: The cheerleaders and the national anthem." *Brown Alumni Monthly.* http://www.archive.org/stream/brownalumnimonth737brow/brow nalumnimonth737brow _djvu.txt.

Toole, T. (2019, July 18). "Serena Williams invests in project aimed at improving women's maternal health." *The Undefeated.* https://theundefeated.com/features/serena-williams-invests-in-proj ect-aimed-at-improving-womens-maternal-health/.

Williams, V. (2016, March 1). "Why I'm going back to Indian Wells." *Players' Tribune.* https://www. theplayerstribune.com/en-us/articles/venus-williams-indian-wells-tennis.

Wolfe, J. F. (2015, February 16). "10 Surprising sports heroes of the civil rights movement." *Listverse.* https://listverse.com/2015/02/16/10-surprising-sports-heroes-of-the-civil-rights-movement/.

Chapter Thirteen

CARING FOR THE MINDS OF OUR HEROES: A BRIEF OVERVIEW OF COMMON MENTAL HEALTH IMPAIRMENTS, TREATMENT MODALITIES, AND VETERAN ADMINISTRATION RESOURCES

Karen E. Alexander, Ryan Moore, Jeanette Anderson, William Kouba, and Waveney LaGrone

Introduction

War creates scars. The battles that soldiers endure, both on and off the battlefield, can leave lasting impressions on their body, mind, and emotions. Unfortunately, this is often the experience of veterans who served in the US military. When veterans return from service, they often come back changed in some capacity, and in many cases, the change is not for the better. Many civilians lead lives of service off the battlefield yet experience similar wounds. This notion brings to mind another fighter, Muhammad Ali, who, throughout his dynamic life experiences and legendary career, tackled many complex issues that also resulted in lasting scars. Ali, a multifaceted man whom many would call a hero, was primarily known for three major things: championship boxing, civil rights activism, and his fight with Parkinson's disease.

In many ways, Ali, a longtime fighter—both in and out of the ring—and veterans who have served in the military have much in common. Both having lived experiences deeply impacted by the casualties of war and a life dedicated to service and sacrifice. Whether actual military combat, the battle for civil rights, or fighting in a professional boxing ring, many of our heroes overcame fear, faced significant danger, and withstood major adversities that often pose lasting effects on their emotional, mental, and physical outcomes throughout their life span.

For both civilians and veterans, healthcare workers, particularly nurses, play a vital role in treating these conditions. From a nursing practice perspective, it is important to remember our heroes' sacrifice not only in dying but also in living with the scars born of their heroic actions. Moreover, it is also important to recognize that soldiers and veterans comprise a vulnerable population with a wide variety of needs resulting from the complexities associated with a life dedicated to military service. As nurses, it is a responsibility and solemn duty to deliver safe and effective care for veterans based on the prescribed therapies and Veterans Administration resources available. Nurses should understand what methods are currently being used to support the delivery of much-needed care and appraise their outcomes. As the rate of veterans diagnosed with mental health issues increases, nurses will be at the forefront of caring for these patients. As such, it is warranted nurses understand various care options availed or prescribed to support the mental and emotional health of veterans. Further, nursing education curriculum should include objectives that address care delivery based on evidence-based practice for these veterans as a vulnerable population experiencing mental illness.

Muhammad Ali, a hero to many, lived a life filled with great complexities. Ali, whose birth name was Cassius Marcellus Clay Jr., was born on January 17, 1942, in Louisville, Kentucky. By the age of 24, Ali was at the height of his career as a boxer and a world champion. He fought some of history's most well-known fighters and earned the name of "The Greatest of All Time" (GOAT) (Al-Madina Institute, 2016). Shortly after the spectacular upset in sports history, the win against Sonny Listen, then Cassius Clay Jr. announced he accepted the teachings of the Nation of Islam. After that he took the name Muhammad Ali, conferred to him by his spiritual mentor, Elijah Muhammad. Eventually, Ali left the Nation of Islam, an African American religious movement, and stirred toward mainstream Sunni Islam as it is practiced around the world. He came to know himself as a minister of the religion of Islam (Britannica, 2020; Al-Madina Institute, 2016).

During this transition, the US military draft summoned Ali to appear to be sent as a soldier to the Vietnam armed conflict. This would be the beginning of a constant battle, as he faced many complex issues unlike anything Ali had to face in the ring (Aleph, 2016). Markedly, in 1967, he refused to enlist in the US army during the Vietnam War. His decision was grounded in personal and religious reasoning, thus making him a conscientious objector to service in the war (Rummel & Blakely, 1988). This decision resulted in a chain of events, including his arrest and the suspension of his boxing license. In addition to his licensure suspension, Ali was banned from boxing in the United States and stripped of his world heavyweight title by the World Boxing Association (Rummel & Blakely, 1988).

Before the 1971 Supreme Court decision that reversed his conviction, Ali traveled the world for four years to continue boxing abroad. His journey outside of the United States led him to become a three-time winner of the heavyweight boxing title. While traveling across the globe as a professional boxer, he also was in service of the people. For example, Ali hand-delivered food and medical supplies to needy sites such as the Harapan Kita Hospital for Children in Jakarta, Indonesia; the underserved youth of Morocco; and Sister Beltran's orphanage for Liberian refugees on the Ivory Coast.

Ultimately, Ali's titles were returned to him by the US Supreme Court, and Ali was able to continue his career in the United States. However, his return to the States did not impede his efforts to serve others (Rummel & Blakely, 1988). In 1981, for example, Ali talked to a distraught young 21-year-old Vietnam veteran who threatened suicide by jumping from a ninth-floor fire escape in Los Angles. After that, Ali accompanied the man to a Veterans Administration Hospital for further treatment and promised to help him find a job (Slate, 2016).

Ironically, despite his refusal to serve in the army, many parallels arise between Ali and the nation's service men and women. He served both the Nation of Islam and as a dedicated and committed professional boxer. Furthermore, the religious principles he lived by, known as the *six cores* (Muhammad Ali Center, 2020), are congruent with many of the militaries core values such as *selfless service* and *personal courage.*

An example of selfless service can be seen in the willingness of many soldiers to serve their country and fulfill their duty loyally without thought of recognition or personal gain. For soldiers, it means to put the welfare of the nation, the military, and your subordinates before your own (Military Leadership Diversity Commission [MLDC], 2009). This notion selfless service is akin to *dedication* and *giving*, which were counted among Ali's six cores. Dedication is defined as the act of devoting all of one's energy, effort, and abilities to a certain task. Additionally, the core principle of giving, which is characterized as to present oneself voluntarily without expecting something in return (Muhammad Ali Center, 2020), also aligns with the spirit of selfless service.

Moreover, similarities also exist between Ali's core value of *conviction* and the military core value of *personal courage.* The military core of personal courage is, in part, defined as enduring physical duress and at times risking personal safety. This value is also characterized by a willingness to confront fear or adversity, especially if taking those actions are not popular with others (MLDC, 2009). Similarly, Ali held a firm belief that one should show great courage and stand behind personal beliefs—despite pressure to do otherwise. Such convictions are part of what led Ali to use the platform provided by his championship boxing career to fight for the causes he believed in.

In addition to the similarities seen across Ali's religious ideology and the military's core principles, Ali also maintained a significant commonality with veterans. In perhaps one of the greatest ironies of his life, Ali, like many of the men and women who have served in the nation's armed forces, would eventually succumb to mental and physical injuries and the challenges associated with living with head trauma resulting from his long career as a professional boxer. Ali's experiences with traumatic brain injury are akin to the issues faced by a multitude of veterans who battle traumatic brain injuries and its consequences—both experiencing the neurological complexities as a result of a life filled with service in some capacity. Perhaps most importantly, whether boxing icon or veteran, all our heroes living with these types of scars are deserving of care. For both civilians and veterans, healthcare workers, particularly nurses, play a vital role in providing such care.

From a nursing practice perspective, it is important to remember our heroes' sacrifice not only in dying but also in living with the scars born of their heroic actions. Moreover, it is also important to recognize that soldiers and veterans comprise a vulnerable population with a wide variety of needs resulting from the complexities associated with a life dedicated to military service. As nurses, it is a responsibility and solemn duty to deliver safe and effective care for veterans based on the prescribed therapies and Veterans Administration resources available. Nurses should understand what methods are currently being used to support the delivery of much-needed care and appraise their outcomes. As the rate of veterans diagnosed with mental health issues increase, nurses will be at the forefront of caring for these patients

Enduring the Aftermath of a Life of Service: Common Mental Health Diagnoses and Resources for Military Veterans

A veteran is defined as a person who served in the active military, naval, or air service who was discharged or released under conditions other than dishonorable, according to Kemp and Bossarte (2012). There are currently about 22.5 million living US military veterans, including nearly 17 million wartime veterans, according to the US Census Bureau (2010). Serving in the military is an experience that has no complement in civilian life. From the outset, individuals in the armed forces share unique experiences that transform the typical socioeconomic and racial or ethnic boundaries of civilian life. Often for returning veterans, those experiences go unspoken, but the scars of mental health remain.

In the case of military veterans, the negative effects of combat on mental health have been documented for many years (Kulka, 1988; USDVA, 2018). Overall, approximately one-third of all returning soldiers have at least one mental health condition (Tanielian & Jaycox, 2008). Some of these conditions include traumatic brain injury (TBI), post-traumatic stress disorder (PTSD), and substance use disorder (SUD). Physical wounds and battle scars are often recognizable, but nurses might not associate a patient's emotional issues or mental health conditions with military service. Besides, the mechanism of an injury must be considered to ensure a comprehensive assessment and appropriate treatment plan (Belanger, 2005).

As part of a nursing education evidence-based project, this chapter provides a brief overview of veterans' unique healthcare issues, focusing particularly on TBI, PTSD, and major depressive disorder MDD). Evidence-based treatment modalities relate to these identified mental health issues. Also, there is a consequent relationship of TBI and PTSD to SUD, criminal behavior, and/or suicide in the veteran population, and the interrelated resources of the Veterans Administration. Specific treatments (cognitive-behavioral therapy [CBT], medications, animal therapy) are briefly discussed.

Common Diagnoses among Military Veterans

The return home for combat soldiers can be difficult. Military culture and experiences affect a veteran's reintegration into civilian life once the service ends. Physical or psychological injury can further complicate the transition to a stable home life. Besides, there is an ongoing stigma attached to mental illness, which most often leads to individuals with psychological problems concealing their conditions, in part due to a feeling of shame or guilt (Johnson, 2013). Hence, when veterans do seek care, nurses as frontline caregivers need to be attentive to these patients who have served in the military to appropriately understand their needs and assess outcomes. Furthermore, there is a need to understand prescribed treatments as they relate to evidence-based practice and veteran-specific resources through the Veterans Administration.

Traumatic Brain Disorder. A TBI, which is a result of a bump, blow, and/or jolt to an individual's head or a penetrating head injury, disrupts the normal function of the brain (Wortzel & Arciniegas, 2010). In addition, TBI studies have indicated an increased likelihood of violent behavior for those that suffer from this injury and may result in criminal consequences for the individual (Yerramsetti et al., 2017). Individuals who have sustained severe TBI may exhibit organic aggressive syndrome, characterized by unplanned, nonpurposeful violence in response to seemingly trivial stimuli (Wortzel & Arciniegas, 2010).

In the case of Ali, the numerous blows to the head that he endured as a boxer for 35 years led to the diagnosis of Parkinson's disease in the early 1980s. Parkinson's is a degenerative disease in which the body's motor skills become less responsive; it is characterized by slurred speech, difficulty in moving the body and face, stiffness, and tremors. Furthermore, research has correlated Parkinson's syndrome to be caused by TBI (Rettner, 2016).

Posttraumatic Stress Disorder. For centuries, veterans of war have suffered from nightmares, irritability, flashbacks, and other symptoms of PTSD. Historically, PTSD was referred to as "shell shock" during World War I and "combat fatigue" or "combat neurosis" during World War II (Bonwick & Morris, 1996; Nicholson, 2004).

PTSD is an anxiety disorder characterized by the persistent reexperience of a highly traumatic event that involved death or serious injury to self or others to which an individual may respond with intense fear, helplessness, or even horror (Halter, 2015). Most often, the PTSD checklist-military version (PCL-M) self-report instrument is used to assess PTSD symptomatology in war veterans (American Psychiatric Association (APA), 2000).

The trauma of PTSD can change the way the brain interprets stimuli from the environment. Changes to the hippocampus and amygdala are implicated in PTSD, suggesting an effect on fear conditioning, emotional processing, and stress responses (Wortzel & Arciniegas, 2010). The prevalence of PTSD in the returning veteran population is troubling. Besides, the number of veterans with PTSD varies by service era. About 11–20 out of every 100 veterans (or between 11 and 20 percent) who served in Operations Iraqi Freedom (OIF) and Enduring Freedom (OEF) have been diagnosed with PTSD in any given year. Moreover, approximately 12 out of every 100 Gulf War veterans (or 12 percent) have been diagnosed with PTSD per year. Additionally, approximately 15 out of every 100 Vietnam War veterans (or 15 percent) were diagnosed with PTSD by the late 1980s (Kulka, 1988), and the diagnoses continue to rise (USDVA, 2013). Furthermore, it is estimated that about 30 out of every 100 Vietnam War veterans (or 30 percent) have had PTSD in their lifetime (USDVA, 2018). If a person has feelings of disturbing or distressing memories or thoughts that last more than thirty days, then that person may have this disorder (USDVA, 2018). PTSD affects about 7 percent of the general population; however, in the veteran population, it affects three times as many individuals (Haveman-Gould & Newman, 2018).

Substance Abuse. SUDs often comprise illicit drugs, prescribed medications, tobacco, or alcohol (or a combination of these) (APA, 2000). A recent Institute of Medicine (IOM) report found that many veterans from the Vietnam War as well as more recent conflicts necessitate assistance with SUDs (IOM, 2010). Often SUD in veterans is a coping measure derived as a result of the stressors of active military service, combat, frequent loss of peers, and military sexual trauma. Moreover, SUD is associated with PTSD, increased risk of anxiety, and depression (Skidmore & Roy, 2011; IOM, 2010). Taken together, the prevalence of mental illness, in particular PTSD and TBI, and the neuropsychiatric and behavioral consequences of these conditions, confounded by the disinhibiting effects of substance abuse, suggest that veterans present a distinct subset of the criminal justice-involved population with particular mitigating factors and treatment needs (Yerramsetti et al., 2017). Moreover, studies suggest veterans with comorbid PTSD and SUD are more difficult and costlier to treat because of poorer social functioning, higher rates of suicide attempts, poorer quality treatment adherence, and less improvement during treatments than those without comorbid PTSD (Reisman, 2016).

Suicide. Suicide is a concern for veterans. It is estimated that 18 to 22 US veterans commit suicide daily, which accounts for about 20 percent of all completed suicides in the United States (Kemp & Bossarate, 2012). Moreover, veterans are routinely trained in firearms use as part of military training, resulting in firearms being the most frequent means of completed suicide in the general adult population. Suicide by firearm accounts for 41 percent of completed suicides of all military personnel (Hoffmire & Bossarte, 2014; Miller & Hemenway, 2008; US Department of Defense [USDD], 2010). In addition, younger veterans aged 18 to 34 had higher firearm suicide and total suicide rates as compared to their civilian counterparts (Healthy People, 2020; Kaplan et al., 2009).

Risk Areas Addressed by the Veterans Administration for Veterans

Veterans are at serious risk for violent actions due to mental health problems. Moreover, veterans are twice as likely to die by suicide as civilians, and approximately eighteen to twenty-two veterans commit suicide every day (Haveman-Gould & Newman, 2018). Consequently, the mental and emotional scars of their service can make them a danger to themselves, and in some cases to others as well. Despite recent increases in the number of treatment programs aimed at addressing the myriad problems associated with PTSD, high-risk behaviors such as suicide attempts, violence, and substance abuse persist among veterans with PTSD even after treatment. Several studies indicate veterans with PTSD experienced higher rates of interpersonal violence compared to veterans without the disorder (Miles, 2010). Studies have shown that the greater risk of violence in veterans who suffer from PTSD is associated with more severe hyperarousal symptoms, higher alcohol consumption rates, lower socioeconomic status, and participating in near sector violence (Tanielian & Jaycox, 2008; USDVA, 2018). As a result of the chronicity of PTSD and its association with high-risk behaviors, there is a great need for predicting when patients are at a greater risk for relapse and serious harm (Haveman-Gould & Newman, 2018; Hartl et al., 2005).

Veterans Administration Resources and Treatment Modalities

To address these risk factors, the Veterans Administration examined ways to intercede and offer support. In 2012, the National Steering Committee of the Veterans Health

Administration (VHA) Veterans Justice Outreach Program set strategic goals. These included the matching of justice-involved veterans with the medical, mental health/psychiatric, vocational, and social services that would improve health and optimize successful community integration and safety for veterans (Blodgett et al., 2013). A published report by Blodget et al. (2013), on behalf of the VHA, identified treatment needs, assessment tools, and treatment methods to reduce recidivism and barriers to access to treatment. This report prompted additional intervention to be offered by the Veterans Treatment Courts (VTC); the first Veterans Court was established in Harris County, Texas. The first docket was five veterans facing felony charges (Yerramsetti et al., 2017). The primary purpose of VTC is to focus on providing treatment, as opposed to a penalty. In other words, when individuals who are led into the criminal justice system as a result of mental illness, the mental healthcare system exemplifies the realization that treating the illness is more productive than punishing the crime (Yerramsetti et al., 2017).

VTC serve to assist in various ways. They work to ensure treatment for mental illness is applied, which may aid those who avoided treatment due to stigma. The program also includes drug testing, probation appointments, and visits with designated mentors. However, the expectation of requirements for veterans to meet is numerous, and treatment may be longer than a penalty such as a sentence. The requirements, combined with the stigma of mental health treatment, can deter veteran participation. However, the limited available studies have shown positive results in the reduction of re-offense and increased quality of life for the participants (Wortzel & Arciniegas, 2010; Yerramsetti et al., 2017).

Appraisal of Veterans Administration Resources for Veterans. The Veterans Health Administration, a branch of the Veterans Administration, is currently the largest healthcare system in the country, with over 150 hospitals, over 800 community-based outpatient clinics, and more than 130 nursing homes (USDVA, 2012, 2013). As the primary responsible agency for the care of veterans, the Veterans Administration has mobilized efforts to combat the issues of relapse and serious harm. To support this effort, the Veterans Administration mental health budget was increased from less than 3 billion dollars in 2007 to nearly 7 billion dollars in 2014 (USDVA, 2018). Moreover, from 2005 to 2011, the Department of Defense (DoD) and Veterans Administration increased the availability of formulary prescription psychiatric drugs to patients who require them, nearly seven hundred percent faster. This increase is more than thirty times faster than the civilian rate of availability (O'Meara, 2016). Additionally, one in six American service members is on at least one psychiatric drug. Despite this mobilization of funds and availability of pharmaceuticals, symptoms and risk behaviors persist (Hartl et al., 2005).

One method of considering the effectiveness of current VHA services is the comparison of suicide rates for those receiving the services versus those who are not. A study conducted by Katz et al. (2012), which compared suicide rates among veterans, found that VHA services help to lower the rate of suicide for those veterans who utilize them. However, this was only for those veterans who were younger than 30 years old receiving VHA services. In contrast, for veterans older than 30, utilization of VHA services was associated with an increased rate of suicide.

These findings in the literature suggest a current division with the VHA services being offered. Furthermore, findings in their study suggest the decrease in rates of suicide for younger veterans may be linked to the increased diagnosis of mental health disorders in this population and as a result increased distribution of services. In contrast, for older veterans, it is possible they are not diagnosed with as many disorders and therefore did not receive as much care from the VHA. From the findings in this study, there is optimism that the decreased suicide rates of younger veterans who utilized VHA services were significant when compared with those who did not utilize VHA services (Katz et al., 2012). This study also implies that older veterans who receive the same care and attention may also see decreased suicide rates in the future. Furthermore, a paucity of additional research in the literature currently exists to further support why this trend exists.

Cognitive-Behavioral Therapy. The use of psychological intervention is regarded as a first-line approach for PTSD by a range of authoritative sources (Reisman, 2016). Of the wide variety of psychotherapies available, CBT is considered to have the strongest empirical evidence for reducing symptoms of PTSD in veterans and to be more effective than any other nondrug treatment (Reisman, 2016; Wang, 2018). The most frequent types of CBT found in the literature are cognitive processing therapy and prolonged exposure (PE) therapy. These two forms of CBT are recommended as first-line treatments in PTSD practice guidelines jointly issued by the Veterans Administration and the DoD (Reisman, 2016).

Appraisal of Cognitive-Behavioral Therapy. To compare CBT with other treatments, its effectiveness must be considered. CBT has been shown to increase symptom relief when used in conjunction with medications. Additionally, in a randomized, controlled clinical trial, administrators of the Veterans Administration Department set out to measure evidence-based treatments that included the cognitive processing therapy that the Veterans Administration offers to its patients who are diagnosed with PTSD. The Department of Veteran Affairs recommends a trauma-focused cognitive type of treatment that consists of a written trauma account in conjunction with group therapy. The results of the study concluded that patients who completed the requirements of the Veterans Administration's cognitive processing therapy showed a significant reduction in PTSD and depressive symptoms (Lamp et al., 2019).

Antidepressants. Antidepressants are currently the preferred initial class of medications for PTSD, with the strongest empirical evidence supporting the use of selective serotonin reuptake inhibitors (SSRIs). Currently, sertraline and paroxetine are the only drugs approved by the Food and Drug Administration to treat PTSD (Reisman, 2016). Although SSRIs are associated with an overall response rate of approximately 60 percent in patients with PTSD, only 20 to 30 percent of patients achieve complete remission. The once highly controversial eye-movement desensitization and reprocessing (EMDR) has been gaining acceptance and is now recommended as an effective treatment for PTSD in both combat-related and civilian cases in a wide range of practice guidelines (Clevenger et al., 2017). The general theory behind EDMR is that focusing on other stimuli while revisiting the experience helps patients reprocess traumatic information until it is no longer psychologically disruptive (Reisman, 2016).

Second-line therapies for PTSD are less strongly supported in the literature and may have added side effects as opposed to other primary treatment options. These second-line therapies include nefazodone, mirtazapine, tricyclic antidepressants, and mono-amine oxidase inhibitors. Prazosin is effective in randomized clinical trials in decreasing nightmares in PTSD (Wang et al., 2018). These drugs act to block the noradrenergic stimulation of the alpha receptor. Its effectiveness for overall PTSD symptoms other than reducing nightmares has not been currently determined. Besides, the VA and DoD Clinical Practice Guidelines for PTSD caution against any use of benzodiazepines to manage core PTSD symptoms as evidence suggests they are not as effective and may instead be harmful (Reisman, 2016).

Appraisal of Antidepressants. In reviewing the literature, medications remain the most effective treatments currently available (Clevenger et al., 2017; Reisman, 2016). Initial medication treatment of contemporary antidepressant drugs to decrease anxiety and depressive symptoms related to PTSD may include SSRIs such as citalopram (Celexa), fluoxetine (Prozac), or sertraline (Zoloft). Additionally, serotonin-norepinephrine reuptake inhibitors (SNRIs) like desvenlafaxine (Pristiq), duloxetine (Cymbalta), and venlafaxine (Effexor) are also used to treat anxiety and depressive symptoms. Tricyclic antidepressants (TCA) like amitriptyline (Elavil) or mirtazapine (Remeron), which are norepinephrine- and serotonin-specific antidepressants, are typically used to treat anxiety and depressive disorders if contemporary psychotropic drugs are not tolerated or deemed less effective (Halter, 2015).

A cohort study conducted by Wang et al. (2018) reviewed contemporary antidepressant drugs. The study findings suggested that both SSRIs and SNRIs have better safety profiles than TCAs. The study also reported that almost half of the patients prescribed a psychotropic treatment would eventually discontinue the medication due to adverse effects like sexual dysfunction, dry mouth, gastrointestinal upset, bleeding, and seizures.

In a randomized case-control study, conducted by Clevenger et al. (2017), researchers found that SSRIs and SNRIs effectively treat depressive symptoms. However, due to patient medication adherence issues, only about 10 percent patients with MDD receive or maintain a proper drug regimen. The findings of the study suggested a combination of therapies approach to include not only SSRI and SNRI drug treatments but also CBT to increase patient adherence issues and to decrease relapse.

Schnurr and Lunney (2019) conducted a cross-sectional study in which the findings supported current PTSD medication treatments such as duloxetine (Cymbalta) are to some extent effective. Additionally, the results of the study noted that almost 70 percent patients retained anxiety symptoms even after adhering to a psychotropic medication regimen. Furthermore, in patients diagnosed with depressive disorders who used duloxetine to treat the disorder, 60 percent retained depressive symptoms, 50 percent maintained insomnia symptoms, and about 70 percent retained anxiety symptoms. Finally, the results of an analysis that compared PE therapy to CBT indicated that individual symptoms and symptom clusters, on average, improved in patients who participated in both treatments. The overall implications in the study suggested recommendations that CBT is used as a congruent form of treatment for patients as a possible method to improve the effectiveness of mediation therapies (Schnurr & Lunney, 2019).

Although antidepressants have been the central focus of pharmacotherapy research in PTSD, better treatments are necessary. Currently, there is growing interest in novel medication development rather than simply relying on SSRIs. The role of the inhibitory neurotransmitter gamma-aminobutyric acid (GABA) and the excitatory neurotransmitter glutamate in PTSD is beginning to be investigated. Both GABA and glutamate play a role in encoding fear memories and therapeutic research. Targeting these systems may open new avenues of treatment for PTSD (Schnurr, 2019; Wang, 2018). Anticonvulsants or antiepileptic drugs affect the balance between glutamate and GABA by acting indirectly to affect these neurons when their neuronal receptor sites are activated. These could, therefore, offer a useful option in the treatment of PTSD symptoms in first-line pharmacotherapy (Reisman, 2016).

Animal Therapies and Service Dogs. A more recent inclusion in therapy modalities has been service dogs. Psychiatric service dogs are increasingly being sought out by military veterans as a complementary intervention for PTSD. After receiving a service dog, many veterans continue training their service dogs at home. Psychiatric service dogs for PTSD are a specialized type of service dogs specifically trained to perform a variety of tasks designed to mitigate the symptoms of PTSD. In the United States, a service dog must be individually trained to do work or perform tasks for a person with a disability (Bergen-Cico et al., 2018; Lafollette, 2019). For individuals with PTSD, these tasks may include responding to the veteran's anxiety, "watching" the veteran's back in public, and waking them up from nightmares (Lafollette, 2019).

Appraisal of Animal-Assisted Interventions (Dogs). Limited studies regarding animal-assisted interventions (AAIs) exist in the literature. Additionally, research has been impeded by limitations such as small sample size and/or the lack of an adequate control group. While studies have shown that AAIs appear to have a positive effect on mental health, the lack of empirical evidence available is problematic in evaluating effects in repeated studies (Bergen-Cico et al., 2018).

Appreciatively, a recent study conducted by Bergen-Cico et al. (2018) using a longitudinal method compared veteran PTSD sufferers who had received service dogs with those on a control waiting list who had not. Those participants in the control group continued to engage in other treatments. The results were promising, as veterans who received service dogs showed decreased rates of PTSD symptoms, decreased perceived stress, increased self-compassion and self-judgment, and lower rates of isolation. In contrast, the control group showed no significant change in these categories and had slightly worsening symptoms in most of them, particularly isolation (Bergen-Cico et al., 2018).

The most significant improvement for veterans with service dogs was found in the categories of self-compassion and self-judgment. This is postulated to be linked to the nonjudgmental attitude of animals, such as dogs (Bergen-Cico et al., 2018). Fundamentally, dogs love their owners without reservation or bias, and this love allowed the veterans to have more compassion for themselves. The study findings also indicated that while treatment was effective, it was just below the 5-point change in the PCL-M score that is considered to be the threshold for clinically determining whether an individual has responded to PTSD treatment (Bergen-Cico et al., 2018, p. 1172). So, while the intervention was quite effective, it was not as effective as other treatments. Still, this is a significant finding for therapy considerations in future studies.

Discussion

The literature in this area (Lamp et al., 2019; Schnurr et al., 2019; Bergen-Cico et al., 2018; Reisman, 2016) broadly conveys that no one treatment is effective for all veterans and that treatment options are highly individualized. Studies also indicate that numerous variables such as socialeconomic status, availability of resources, and the compliance of individual patients must be considered in the development of a treatment plan. In other words, treatment plans must be tailored to suit the lifestyle and capability of each patient.

Current trends also suggest that no single form of therapy is best and that multiple therapies may be necessary to effectively treat those experiencing mental and physical health disparities described above. For example, though CBT was found to be effective, effectiveness is increased when combined with medication (Johnson et al., 2013; Reisman, 2016; Wang, 2018). Also, of note, the introduction of medication may pose side effects that must be evaluated when this type of treatment is used.

Furthermore, CBT requires a patient to attend meetings that they must schedule, and they need to have the available resources to be able to attend. While medication may be effective, it requires continued adherence, which a veteran with unstable income may not be able to maintain. Additionally, medications have documented side effects that may be unacceptable for certain patients, thus endangering compliance. Care providers should be mindful of the fact that services availed through the Veterans Administration, both voluntary and involuntary, may not be accepted or adhered to by the veteran.

In addition to CBT, animal therapy is reportedly a promising treatment modality. The animals used in animal therapy also require a variety of care and attention, which means a veteran must be able to care for (i.e., feed or walk) animals when necessary and rein-force training at home (Veterans Health, 2019). Though research in this area is fairly new, and the effect does not appear to be as dramatic as with other therapy modalities (i.e., CBT), such approaches show restorative effects when utilized. Overall, the best treatment regimen must be mutable and specific to the veteran being treated.

The trends in literature on the effectiveness of CBT, specific medicine modalities, and animal therapy, as well as supportive measures of the Veterans Administration, support the need for further study. At this time, the most prescribed treatment modality is medi-cation, which often leads to unpleasant and, at times, serious and adverse side effects that may cause a reduction in patient compliance with treatment and can further endanger health. Additionally, medication regimens change as more evidence on side effects or adverse effects and benefits is discovered, such as the use of tricyclic antidepressants and monoamine oxidase inhibitors being less supported by new research. Much of the liter-ature conveys that medication can be beneficial; however, it may not be the best or only treatment consideration for all. Thus, careful evaluation of the current trend of relying on medications to treat the common conditions experienced by veterans is warranted.

The ultimate sacrifice that veterans make for this country merits care options that are beneficent and support positive outcomes. Nurses can help advance treatment in many capacities, including advocating for care practices that decrease the likelihood that veterans will experience additional physical trauma and risk in the effort to treat their mental health disorders. Nurses can also promote innovative care practices such as non-medication-based treatments (i.e., animal therapy).

Conclusion

After departing from the military, veterans often continue to grapple with the costs associated with years of sacrifice and service. As evidenced by the health conditions detailed throughout this chapter, a life dedicated to service can result in complex impairments to one's mental and physical health. Many of our nation's service personnel are challenged with military-related mental health diagnoses that leave lasting impressions, often changing the trajectory of their lived experiences.

Like many of our veteran soldiers, Muhammad Ali had scars. Ali was an American professional boxer and social activist who engaged in various "battles" throughout his lifetime, both in and out of the ring. As a civil rights activist, he also used his platform to advocate for the rights of people, and most famously, he resisted to enlisting with a military force for a country that actively discriminated against Black Americans. Although Ali did not serve in the US military, he served in the Nation of Islam and his dedication to personal freedoms permeated his devotion to fighting a war. Nevertheless, for both Ali and military soldiers, serving can be an ongoing war in which they have faced fear, danger, or adversity that can affect physical, moral, and/or mental outcomes. For Ali, in his ongoing battle, damage was occurring inside, where it was not readily apparent or would have been easily recognized as ongoing scars.

Though Ali was the first fighter to win the world heavyweight championship on three separate occasions and successfully defended that title 19 times (Britannica, 2020), he was also challenged by mental and physical ailments related to his boxing career. After retirement, he continued to work to bring awareness to Parkinson's and other conditions through his various philanthropic endeavors. Ali fought for over thirty-five years and lost his final battle to Parkinson's disease resulting from traumatic brain injury on June 3, 2016, in Scottsdale, Arizona.

Both Ali and military soldiers have been credited with personal courage by standing up for and acting upon the things that they felt are honorable. Be it Muhammad Ali or veteran soldiers, our nation's heroes, many of whom have made great sacrifices for the greater good, deserve access to the healthcare need to sustain the highest quality of life possible. Literature focused on TBI and other mental health impairments tells signals that current treatments may not be as effective as desired. Healthcare providers, such as nurses, should recognize that the rates of mental illness experienced by veterans are ever increasing. Many soldiers face physical, mental, and social issues upon returning from service, which situates them in a vulnerable population.

The needs of veterans with mental illness are serious, often resulting in debilitating or life-threatening outcomes, which quite often require extensive and intensive interventions. More research is needed to enhance understanding of various treatment modalities and their effect on veterans with mental illness. Nurses are particularly well situated to advocate for continued research focused on veterans who experience mental health issues. The field would benefit from qualitative studies—which were scarce in the literature—aimed at furthering understanding of the lived experiences of the veterans who are undergoing these treatments. Increased knowledge of personal perspectives may lead to more effective interventions and influence nursing education of caring practices for veterans who will experience military-related mental illness in the future.

This brief overview serves to inform, raise awareness, and provide some understanding of specific mental illnesses and various treatment modalities in the care for veterans. Additionally, the Veterans Administration resources are congruent with the modalities that are availed. When veterans come back to us, as care providers, nurses must give them the best in care delivery, to support their reintegration back into society. With continued research and a commitment to excellence in nursing care, we can give our heroes the care they deserve.

References

Aleph, F. (June 18, 2016). "A true warrior must know when to raise his fists and when to seek paths to peace." Warrior and Rebels. https://www.faena.com/aleph/articles/muhammad-ali-vs-the-war-in-vietnam/. Ali Center (2020)

Al-Madina Institute (June 5, 2016). "Muhammad Ali: The legacy of the greatest boxer of all time." https://almadinainstitute.org/blog/muhammad-ali-the-legacy-of-the-greatest-boxer-of-all-.

American Psychiatric Association. (2000) *Diagnostic and Statistical Manual of Mental Disorders: DSM-IV-TR.* 4th revised ed.. Washington, DC: American Psychiatric Press.

Belanger, H. G, Steven G. Scott, S., Scholten, J., Curtiss, G., and Vanderploeg, R. D. (2005). "Utility of mechanism-of-injury-based assessment and treatment: Blast injury program case illustration." *Journal of Rehabilitation Research and Development* 42, no. 4: 403–12. https://doi.org/10.1682/JRRD.2004.08.0095.

Bergen-Cico, D., Smith, Y., Wolford, K., Gooley, C., Hannon, K., Woodruff, R., Spicer, M., and Gump, B. (2018). "Dog ownership and training reduces post-traumatic stress symptoms and increases self-compassion among veterans: Results of a longitudinal control study." *Journal of Alternative and Complementary Medicine* 24, no. 12: 1166–75. https://doi.org/10.1089/acm.2018.0179.

Blodgett, J. C., Fuh, I. L., Maisel, N. C., & Midboe, A. M. (2013). *A Structured Evidence Review to Identify Treatment Needs of Justice-Involved Veterans and Associated Psychological Interventions.* Menlo Park, CA: Center for Health Care Evaluation, VA Palo Alto Health Care System.

Bonwick, R., and Morris, P. (1996). "Review: Post-traumatic stress disorder in elderly war veterans." *International Journal of Geriatric Psychiatry* 2: 1071–76.

Britannica. (July 24, 2020). "Muhammad Ali American boxer." *Encyclopaedia Britannica.* https://www.britannica.com/biography/Muhammad-Ali-boxer.

Clevenger, S., Malhotra, D., Dang, J., Vanle, B., & IsHak, W. (2017). "The role of selective serotonin reuptake inhibitors in preventing relapse of major depressive disorder." *Therapeutic Advances in Psychopharmacology*, 8, no. 1: 49–58. https://www.ncbi.nlm.nih.gov/pmc/articles/PMC5761909/.

Fatsis, S., & Levin, S. (2016). *Muhammad Ali Was Not a Saint, and He Was Not a Teddy Bear.* Brooklyn, NY: Graham Holdings Company.

Halter, M. J. (2015). *Varcarolis' Foundations of Psychiatric Mental Health Nursing: A Clinical Approach,* 7th ed. St. Louis, MO: Elsevier.

Hartl, T. L., Rosen, C., Drescher, K., Lee, T. T., & Gusman, F. "Predicting high-risk behaviors in veterans with posttraumatic stress disorder." *Journal of Nervous and Mental Disease* 193, no. 7:. 51–58.

Haveman-Gould, B., & Newman, C. (2018). "Post-traumatic stress disorder in veterans: Treatments and risk factors for nonadherence." *JAAPA: Journal of the American Academy of Physician Assistants* 31, no. 11: 21–24. doi:10.1097/01.JAA.0000546474.26324.05.

Hoffmire, C. A, & Bossarte, R. M. (2014). "A reconsideration of the correlation between veteran status and firearm suicide in the general population." *Injury Prevention* 20, no. 5: 317–21. https://doi.org/10.1136/injuryprev-2013-041029.

Institute of Medicine (IOM), (2010). *Returning Home from Iraq and Afghanistan: Preliminary Assessment of Readjustment Needs of Veterans, Service Members, and Their Families.* Washington, DC: National Academies Press.

Johnson, B. S., Boudiab L. D., Freundl, M., Anthony M., Gmerek, G. B., & Carter J. (2013). "Enhancing veteran-centered care: A guide for nurses in non-VA settings." *American Journal of Nursing* 113, no. 7: 24–39. doi: 10.1097/01.NAJ.0000431913.50226.83.

Katz, I. R., McCarthy, J. F., Ignacio, R. V., & Kemp, J. (2012). "Suicide among veterans in 16 states, 2005 to 2008: Comparisons between utilizers and nonutilizers of Veterans Health Administration (VHA) services based on data from the National Death Index, the National Violent Death Reporting System, and VHA." *American Journal of Public Health* 102, no. S1: S105–10.

Kulka, R. S. (1988). *Contractual Report of Findings from the National Vietnam Veteran Readjustment Study.* Washington, DC: Veterans Administration.

Lafollette, M. R., Rodriguez, K. E., Ogata, N., & O'Haire, M. E. (2019). "Military veterans and their PTSD service dogs: Associations between training methods, PTSD severity, dog behavior, and the human-animal bond." *Frontiers in Veterinary Science* 6, no. 23. https://doi.org/10.3389/fvets.2019.00023.

Lamp, K. E., Avallone, K. M., Maieritsch, K. P., Buchholz, K. R., & Rauch, S. A. (2019). "Individual and group cognitive processing therapy: Effectiveness across two veterans affairs posttraumatic stress disorder treatment clinics." *Psychological Trauma: Theory, Research, Practice, and Policy* 11, no. 2: 197–206. http://dx.doi.org/10.1037/tra0000370.

Kaplan, M. S, McFarland, B. H, & Huguet, N. (2009). "Firearm suicide among veterans in the general population: Findings from the national violent death reporting system." *Journal of Trauma* 67, no. 3: 503–7.

Kemp, J., & Bossarte, R. (2012). *Suicide Data Report, 2012.* Washington, DC: US Department of Veterans Affairs, Mental Health Services, Suicide Prevention Program. www.va.gov/ opa/ docs/Suicide-Data-Report-2012-final.pdf.

Miles, D. (2010). "VA strives to prevent veteran suicides." *American Forces Press Service* (April). https://www.nationalguard.mil/News/State-Partnership-Program/Article/577195/va-stri ves-to-prevent-vet-suicides/.

Military Leadership Diversity Commission (MLDC). (2009). "Department of Defense core values." Issue Paper 6. https://diversity.defense.gov/Portals/51/Documents/Resources/Com mission/docs/Issue%20Papers/Paper%2006%20-%20DOD%20Core%20Values.pdf.

Miller, M., & Hemenway, D. (2008). "Guns and suicide in the United States." *New England Journal of Medicine* 359, no. 10: 989–91.

Muhammad Ali Center. (2020). "Be great: Do great things." Louisville, KY. https://alicenter.org/about-us/muhammad-ali/.

Nicholson, M. (2004). "Caring for war veterans—victims or heroes? Undiagnosed and untreated symptoms of post-traumatic stress disorder affect many World War 11 veterans at Auckland's Ranfurly Veteran Centre. Nurses and caregivers need education to care for veterans appropriately." *Kai Tiaki: Nursing New Zealand*, 10, no. 4 (May): 18–20.

O'Meara, K. P. (2016). "Federal legislation proposes investigating connection between psychiatric drugs and veteran suicides." Published by Citizens Commission on Human Rights International (CCHR). The Mental Health Watchdog. April 7, 2016. Los Angeles, CA. https://www.cchr int.org/2016/04/08/legislation-will-investigate-psych-drugs-and-veteran-suicides/.

Reisman, M. (2016). "PTSD treatment for veterans: What's working, what's new, and what's next." *P&T* 41, no. 10: 623–34.

Rettner R. (June 6, 2016). "Live science. Muhammad Ali's death: Can head injuries cause Parkinson's?" https://www.livescience.com/54986-muhammad-ali-head-injury-parkinsons.html.

Rummel, J., & Blakely, G. (1988). *Muhammad Ali*. Chelsea House Imprint.

Schnurr, P. P., & Lunney, C. A. (2019). "Residual symptoms following prolonged exposure and present-centered therapy for PTSD in female veterans & soldiers." *Depression & Anxiety (1091– 4269)* 36, no. 2: 162–69. doi:10.1002/da.2287.

Skidmore, W. C., & Roy, M. (2011). "Practical considerations for addressing substance use disorders in veterans and service members." Social Work in Health Care, 50, no. 1: 85–107. DOI: 10.1080/00981389.2010.522913.

Tanielian, T. L., & Jaycox, L. (2008). *Invisible Wounds of War: Psychological and Cognitive Injuries, Their Consequences, and Services to Assist Recovery*. Santa Monica, CA: RAND.

US Census Bureau, Statistical Abstract of the United States. (2012). Table 520. Veterans by Selected Period of Service and State: 2010, p. 340. Washington, DC: US Census Bureau..

———. Table 521. Veterans Living by Period of Service, Age, and Sex: 2010, p. 340. Washington, DC: US Census Bureau.

US Department of Defense Task Force on the Prevention of Suicide by Members of the Armed Forces. (2010). *The Challenge and the Promise: Strengthening the Force, Preventing Suicide and Saving Lives* [final report]. Washington, DC: US Department of Defense.

US Department of Veterans Affairs, National Center for Veterans Analysis and Statistics. (2013). *Department of Veterans Affairs Statistics at a Glance.*

US Department of Veterans Affairs, National Center for PTSD. (2018). *How Common Is PTSD in Veterans?*

US Department of Veterans Affairs. (2013). *National Vietnam Veterans Longitudinal Study (NVVLS)*, pp. 2–18.

Veterans Health—Mental Health. (January 16, 2019). "Dog ownership and training reduces post-traumatic stress symptoms and increases self-compassion among veterans: Results of a longitudinal control study". Defense & Aerospace Week, Studies in the area of mental health reported from Syracuse University. http://search.proquest.com/docview/2165842487/.

Wang, S. M., Han, C., Bahk, W. M., Lee, S. J., Patkar, A. A., Masand, P. S., & Pae, C. U. (2018). "Addressing the side effects of contemporary antidepressant drugs: A comprehensive review." *Chonnam Medical Journal* 54, no. 2: 101–12.

Wortzel, H. S., & Arciniegas, D. B. (2010). "Combat veterans and the death penalty: A forensic neuropsychiatric perspective." *Journal of the American Academy of Psychiatry and the Law* 38, no. 3: 407. doi:10.7249/mg720ccf.

Yerramsetti, A. P., Simons, D. D., Coonan, L., & Stolar, A. (2017). "Veteran treatment courts: A promising solution." *Behavioral Sciences & the Law* 35, nos. 5–6: 512–22. doi:10.1002/bsl.2308.

Chapter Fourteen

THE COMPLEMENTARY DUO OF SPORTS AND ACTIVISM: CRITICAL REFLECTIONS ON MUHAMMAD ALI AS A FORMIDABLE ATHLETE AND ACTIVIST

Howard Bartee Jr.

Only a man who knows what it is like to be defeated can reach down to the bottom of his soul and come up with the extra ounce of power it takes to win when the match is even.

—*Muhammad Ali*

African Americans in sports have prompted much debate about the role of activism, particularly given the platform that athletes assume publicly and the potential for making a difference in the broader society. The extraordinary life of Muhammad Ali reflects an American hero as one whose contributions as a formidable athlete and activist gave voice to the voiceless in the ongoing pursuit of social justice. As a renowned boxer, Muhammad Ali garnered worldwide attention, which he used as his unique platform to highlight injustices and inequalities affecting African Americans. From fighting abroad as an athlete to fighting domestically as a social activist, Muhammad Ali showed first-hand sports as a mechanism through which individual and collective causes could be voiced for the local community and broader country and the world in which he lived (Ali & Durham, 1975; Collins, 2001; Korn, 2016). The expansive reach of Muhammad Ali as an athlete-turned-activist in a complementary duo provides the basis of his public persona to be considered as the "Greatest of All Time" (GOAT) and, in his own words, remain the one who could "come up with the extra ounce of power it takes to win when the match is even."

Research has shown how athletics is a unique platform used to engage youth in meaningful ways (Lugetti et al., 2017). This research has shown that sports is a cultural asset for youth, particularly from socially vulnerable backgrounds, where they can feel safe and protected as well as be able to dream about possibilities beyond the ring. As an athlete, Muhammad Ali understood how his individual talent of boxing could be used to show the power of athleticism. Muhammad Ali, a native of Louisville, Kentucky, whose former name was Cassius Clay and one who often faced difficulties as a growing youth, was an Olympic gold medalist as well as a boxing heavyweight champion of the world. Research has also shown how activism is used by athletes to advance causes of social justice purposefully (Bredemeier & Shields, 2019). The research indicates the following:

> Character education in sport contexts can promote social justice. […] The character of the team provides a nexus within which to develop individual character, which is elaborated in terms of four types of character: moral, civic, intellectual, and performance character. To promote commitment to social justice, character educators can focus on three elements of moral character: moral reasoning, the circle of moral regard, and moral identity. (p. 202)

An integrative approach of promoting character as part of sports is critical toward achieving establishing foundations for participants. With that said, as an activist, Muhammad Ali believed in this viewpoint as his religion assumed importance within his life and informed his activism. He demonstrated how exercising freedom of speech, collectively, could be used to either challenge or uphold American democracy. He protested the Vietnam War, participated in the civil rights movement, and was involved in related human rights efforts. How Muhammad Ali lived inside and outside the boxing ring shows how athletes and nonathletes alike can pursue matters of social justice using the platform they have.

Thus, this chapter uses narrative inquiry to explore, qualitatively, perspectives on athletics and activism through highlighted aspects of the life of Muhammad Ali. Huber (2010) states: "Narrative inquiry […] is the study of experience understood narratively. It is a way of thinking about, and studying, experience. Narrative inquirers think narratively about experience throughout inquiry" (p. 436). Narrative inquiry allows for me, as a writer, to reflect upon the complementary experiences of athletics and activism encountered by Muhammad Ali. Connelly and Clandinin (1990) identify narrative inquiry as involving the collection of information for the purpose of research through storytelling. Narrative inquiry then allows me, the writer, to create a narrative of the experience. To that end, the abbreviated narrative explores Muhammad Ali as a human and social being and how those experiences offer insight into his formidable, complementary roles as athlete and activist. Such experiences propel Muhammad Ali as "athlete among athletes" and "activist among activists" and the implications therein for athletes and nonathletes today.

Muhammad Ali as Athlete among Athletes as a Human Being

Part of understanding the complementary duos of athletics and activities through the experiences of Muhammad Ali as an athlete among athletes and is the recognition of who he was as a human being. First, it was the knowledge of self that Muhammad Ali possessed. From growing up in Louisville, Kentucky, to the heights of pro boxing, Muhammad Ali always sought to be, as he once said, "a bad man." His reflections on not being a bad man was not in a negative sense, but a "bad man" in the context of being a great fighter. He would be a great fighter who all his opponents feared, knowing that he was the better fighter in the ring on a given day. Much of the exemplification of Muhammad Ali being an athlete among athletes is a result of his knowledge of self.

Muhammad Ali (2012) stated the following: "When I was a young man, the motto 'I am the greatest' brought publicity to me and inspired young people who saw me as their hero. My boxing was just the beginning of my life" (p. 2). Understanding who he was allowed him to be able to relate to others in a broader sense and not just through sports.

Second, it was the ability of Muhammad Ali to relate to others. He knew others thought of him as hero, and through boxing, he could maintain his heroism as the icon many might have needed. Muhammad Ali (2012) also expressed the following:

> In my current career, I am trying to help all young persons find their own greatness. Very often great and beautiful things are difficult to discover. Gold is buried under layers of rock. Pearls are hidden in shells lying in the debris at the bottom of the ocean. We have to work to find them. Our challenge is to search for greatness in the most unlikely places, even in youth who frustrate or frighten adults. (p. 2)

The quote shows how Muhammad Ali had a respect for others and what they could become. He considered it as a mission, in many ways, to help others come to know and explore their own greatness. The mere recognition of "their own greatness" as individuals serves as the foundation for uncovering the uniqueness within. There was also a sense that Muhammad Ali considered every human being as being able to accomplish greatness when investments are made within them regardless of their stage of life (i.e., "youth who frustrate or frighten adults").

The work of Gaston-Gayles et al. (2012) suggests that athletes have a sense of self and/or others beyond their affiliation with the institution (i.e., colleges, universities, schools, programs) as well as the sports they might be connected to:

> Although it would be ideal if athletic participation on its own accord enhanced civic values and behaviors, it is reassuring to know that institutions committed to fostering these values and behaviors across the entire student body—and those that provide student athletes with opportunities to participate in cocurricular activities within and beyond the athletic program—may encourage all students to develop congruence between their civic values and behaviors. (p. 551)

Such perspective shows the importance of athletes knowing who they are prior to engaging in sports. They are to believe in themselves beyond anything else that might exist and/or in which they participate, which then influences interactions with others. This belief in self exists as a part of and/or separate from institutions, programs, and/or individuals.

Third, it was how Muhammad Ali accepted his own abilities of flash and flair combined with intelligence and loyalty that defined him. Each of these qualities played a role in how he approached the sport of boxing and his ability to channel these qualities in a way that shaped and prepared him accordingly. Particularly, from his childhood days as Cassius Clay to his name change to Muhammad Ali, it was the flair of Muhammad Ali that could excite masses of boxing fans, both domestically and internationally. Flair is a skill of instinctive ability to appreciate or make good use of something. The manner in which Muhammad Ali conducted himself is evidenced in how he would participate in jump rope exercises and the types of quotes that he would make, "Float like a butterfly, sting like a bee. The hands can't hit what the eyes can't see." Moreover, the intelligence of Muhammad Ali cannot be denied as part of his recognition of who he was as a human being. Muhammad Ali embraced his intellectual talents and his ability to use his athletic prowess to cross barriers in race, sports, and religion and advocate for the interests therein. From this level of confidence with his unique flair, "Muhammad Ali forced America to confront itself" (Gems et al., 2017). Muhammad Ali would continue to use his flair to generate support and buy-in toward causes for social justice.

The work of Orosz and Mezo (2015) addressed how high levels of self-efficacy and the belief in who one is influences one's athleticism. The study particularly looked at an integrative model of sports talent focusing on the role of how psychological factors in football get developed. Findings from the study suggest that the development of psychological factors (e.g., concentration, lack of anxiety, self-confidence, coping skills, and social skills) in an integrated approach can enhance personal efficiency in developing football giftedness. Orosz and Mezo (2015) stated the following:

> The more psychical capacity someone can mobilize to develop themselves, the better results they will be able to achieve in the future. The development of psychological factors can be supported by programs with long-term and well-developed concepts and strategies. Introducing such programs at football clubs would facilitate the development of talent. The fruits of success can be harvested later; therefore, it is necessary to emphasize the development's long-term concept. The more a factor affects the deeper layers of personality, the slower the change may occur. (p. 74)

The perspectives show the importance of having intra- and interpersonal skills. In this case, they allowed the football players to have better success in the long term. The perspectives also indicate the need to be intentional to further develop those skills. Through participation in formal programming efforts, those skills can be more strongly developed into reaching their fullest potential. The participation of Muhammad Ali in amateur boxing programs, as a young boy, in Louisville, Kentucky, helped to solidify his athletic capacity.

Thus, reflecting upon Muhammad Ali as a human being and how we might better understand his capacity to engage successfully with the complementary duos of sports and activism highlights him as having the knowledge of self, respect for others, and recognition and acceptance of his own abilities. His *knowledge of self* is evidenced by the understanding of what it meant to be the greatest. Muhammad Ali understood the importance of his responsibility to be the best he could be, and that would serve to encourage individuals to be the best they could be. His *respect for others* provided the means for him to help them discover their own purpose. Muhammad Ali saw this type of respect as an opportunity for investing in the hopes and dreams of others. His *recognition and acceptance of his abilities* resulted in an appreciation of his own intellect and talents for being able to cross cultural, racial, and geographical lines. As a human being, the genius of Muhammad Ali transcended boundaries, which contributed to his rise as an athlete among athletes as well as a model for how sports and activism can coexist.

Muhammad Ali as Activist among Activists as a Social Being

Understanding the complementary duos of athletics and activities through the experiences of Muhammad Ali as an activist among activists is the recognition of who he was as a social being. Muhammad Ali, the activist, helped to bring attention to those people that felt unfairly treated in the 50 states, and he did so with intentionality. It was the commitment of Muhammad Ali to social justice and sports and how they could be used simultaneously as a platform to make a difference. Muhammad Ali won a number of fights including amateur championships (i.e., Kentucky Golden Glove, National Golden Glove, Amateur Athletic Union). With regard to heavyweight championships, one particular fight emerges where Muhammad Ali fought Joe Frazier and lost in a 15-round decision. In a rematch, in 1974, Ali would win and then face George Foreman for the heavyweight championship (Ali & Durham, 1975; Collins, 2001; Korn, 2016). Known for his "rope-a-dope" style of boxing, he would beat George Foreman for the heavyweight championship. This was one of his biggest fights ever occurring in 1975 called "Thrilla in Manila," and it was a fight against Joe Frazier again. In the end, Muhammad Ali would win with a 14th-round technical knockout. Having won this fight, he would finish his career in the late 1970s. The collective impact of these heavyweight championships continued to propel Muhammad Ali on the international scene.

Notwithstanding, while fighting within the boxing ring, the treatment of so many concerned Muhammad Ali, and therefore, his platform strategically brought attention to their plight of economic disparity, social relevance, and educational inequities, and other areas of concern. One of the more challenging times of Muhammad Ali and his commitment to social justice was when he evaded the military draft in 1967. Ali's refusal to join the army and fight in Vietnam was based upon obtaining a conscientious objector status based upon his religious belief. While taking this stance was within his constitutional rights, it brought a great deal of attention and ability for him to continue fighting in the ring. Once his request was denied by the US government, he also received a five-year prison sentence and a $100,000 fine. Additionally, as he awaited an appeal to the US Supreme Court, state boxing associations banned him from the sport. He was also stripped of his title and unable to pursue his livelihood, thus making him more celebrated as the antiwar movement continued to grow (Gems et al., 2017). The transcendence of Muhammad Ali was his ability to endure losses and gains as an athlete and activist for the sake of social justice.

Muhammad Ali also had the ability to control the public narrative through media outlets about issues affecting the African American community and their implications for America. While he remained loyal to his craft of boxing and to his family as well as his religious beliefs, he was indeed an athlete who showed loyalty not only to his background but also to the greater society. Muhammad Ali was often criticized for this type of stance although he would later experience transcendence from "a black rebel into a conservative American, who favored steady progress for his people within American society" (Wiggins, 2010). Muhammad Ali, too, had a way with words, to say the least, and, oftentimes, pundits would flock to him seeking some statement because of the language he used. An example of this language is found in the statements released to Krishnadev Calamur in the *Atlantic* (2016). Muhammad Ali stated:

"My conscience won't let me go shoot my brother, or some darker people, or some poor hungry people in the mud for big powerful America," he said at the time. "And shoot them for what? They never called me nigger, they never lynched me, they didn't put no dogs on me, they didn't rob me of my nationality, rape and kill my mother and father. […] Shoot them for what? How can I shoot them poor people? Just take me to jail."

The quote shows the intentionality and thoughtfulness with which Muhammad Ali operated. He pointed out issues both inside and outside the African American community. Consciousness is needed for everyone, and Muhammad Ali did not consider any one group to have any more ownership of it. According to Korn (2016), Muhammad Ali also stated:

Ask yourself—was it worth all this, what you did to get in here? You think you'll never get caught. But why are we in here if we never get caught? Way before you there were bad cats, Al Capone and Dillinger, and for some reason they never won either. Life is too short to spend in a place like this. […] You wake up in the morning and you're in jail. Nothing to do but wait for sleep and then sleep comes and you wake up the next morning and you're still in jail. You can't get in your car and drive anyplace you want. Can't eat the food you like. Can't get out, run around, take a jog in the park or be with your loved ones, a wife or girlfriend. Don't spend your life in no jail. What could you get that could be worth all this? Ten million dollars—and I know you didn't get no ten million dollars—Ten million dollars ain't worth two years in jail.

Muhammad Ali did not mince words related to messages uniquely targeted for the African American community. He sought to hold his own community responsible for actions as well as the broader country. Communication through the media about issues unique to African American community and beyond became a part of his platform as an activist among activists.

Individuals, too, across the world marveled at the talents he displayed as a boxer. Because of this popularity, people would look to him for insight and voice about issues beyond the boxing rink. Gorsevski and Butterworth (2011) talked about his ability to connect with people and express their ideas meaningfully. They state the following:

While Muhammad Ali has been the subject of countless articles and books written by sports historians and journalists, rhetorical scholars have largely ignored him. This oversight is surprising given both the tradition of social movement scholarship within rhetorical studies and Ali's influential eloquence as a world-renowned celebrity espousing nonviolence. Ali's rhetorical performances played a pivotal role in radicalizing the civil rights movement as it (d)evolved into twin forces: Black Power and anti-Vietnam war movements. Ali's rhetoric conjoins messages of Martin Luther King, Jr. and Malcolm X, enabling critics to re-envision civil rights texts. Ali's enduring rhetoric provides a model for analyzing texts and social movements invoking the paradox of the violence in nonviolent civil disobedience. (p. 50)

Such perspectives highlight the ability of Muhammad Ali to use persuasive communication to impact change. Furthermore, after having had an illustrious career, Muhammad Ali would join a government envoy to Africa and travel to Iraq to help free 15 American hostages and participate in other acts of activism. According to Gems et al. (2017), as an athlete, rebel, and social protagonist, Muhammad Ali remained a symbol of a defiant generation and of the revolution he helped to spur in American society. After succumbing to Parkinson's disease, he would continue being a public servant. A more memorable event would be in 1996 when, having come full circle from protesting the Vietnam War during the 1960s, he would light the Olympic torch to open the Atlanta Games held in Atlanta, Georgia.

Thus, reflecting upon the social being of Muhammad Ali and how we might better understand his capacity to engage successfully with the complementary duos of sports and activism highlights him as using sports as a conduit for activism and using the media to communicate messages unique to the African American community and beyond. His *prowess as a sports figure* gave him a platform to advocate for issues unique to social justice. Both domestic and global audiences would flock to Muhammad Ali because of his sporting ability within the ring. His *use of the media and language* offered the outlet for communicating important issues. Muhammad Ali knew the power of words and was able to draw upon this talent in a way that media pundits would seek him out to determine what he had to say about issues. As a social being, Muhammad Ali understood how to utilize his talents to become an activist among activists as well as a model for how sports and activism can coexist.

Implications for Athletes and Nonathletes from the Critical Reflections of Muhammad Ali as a Human and Social Being

What we have learned as athletes and nonathletes alike is that Muhammad Ali, as a human being, understood the importance of having self-knowledge, respect for others, and an appreciation of abilities (Ali & Durham, 1975; Collins, 2001; Korn, 2016). High self-efficacy and lack of self-centeredness establishes a foundation to be able to engage one's individual purpose. On a human level, across the world, we have dealt with COVID-19 pandemic, and the lack of sports in our society has created a world of social distancing and Zoom technology where we have watched *The Last Dance* docuseries about Michael Jordan and virtual sports training in sports including boxing. In fact, the championship of the National Basketball Association (NBA) was even played in a bubble where the Los Angeles Lakers ascended as champions. The new norm that we are experiencing is much like the words of Muhammad Ali when he stated: "Champions are made from something they have deep inside them—a desire, a dream, a vision." With that said, the life of Muhammad Ali has taught us the importance of being able to adapt and connect on a human level for it is within that space we are able to connect meaningfully.

What we have learned as athletes and nonathletes alike is Muhammad Ali, as a social being, understood the need to be able to communicate effectively and how to use the platform that he had been given (Ali & Durham, 1975; Collins, 2001; Korn, 2016). From the many interviews that Muhammad Ali engaged in with the late Howard Cosell, who as a reporter for the American Broadcasting Company (ABC) would often engage in playful conversations with Ali, to the lives of children he touched while training and running with them before fights, the widespread impact of Muhammad Ali is observed today in the expanded role of how athletes are engaging the public as social beings.

LeBron James, as part of the NBA, is engaging socially with his "more than just an athlete" approach. Colin Kaepernick, a former National Football League (NFL) quarterback, has engaged to protest police brutality by taking a knee. Like Muhammad Ali, athletes of today are engaging the public purposefully and intentionally for the cause of social justice.

What we have learned as athletes and nonathletes alike is that Muhammad Ali, as both a human and social being, learned to embrace criticism as a natural part of the pursuit of social justice (Ali & Durham, 1975; Collins, 2001; Korn, 2016). Muhammad Ali enacted his religious values through his protest of the Vietnam War as well as through his name change from Cassius Clay to Muhammad Ali when he became a member of the Nation of Islam. Yet, he was criticized. The intellect and integrity of Muhammad Ali was tested when he entered into activism as a professional boxer, particularly given that athletes were to be athletes only. Such criticism, in many ways, mirrors what Los Angeles Lakers' LeBron James faced when he was told to "shut up and dribble." While, in both instances, Muhammad Ali was criticized, he would later regain his respect as his actions transcended race, sports, and religion (Ali & Durham, 1975; Collins, 2001; Korn, 2016). Engaging both as a human and social being, the life of Muhammad teaches the importance of exemplifying courage while under fire in the pursuit of social justice.

Conclusion

As a young man growing up during the 1970s, to this day, I recall watching the boxing matches of Muhammad Ali on television with my parents including my mother and my late father, along with my sister, my uncle, my aunts, and my cousins. I often wondered about who gave him the greatness he demonstrated in the boxing ring. I had also become aware of how the greatness of Muhammad Ali thrilled fans, both domestically and globally. The flair and appeal of Muhammad Ali became evident through his declaration of himself as "the greatest," which takes a unique sense of self-confidence, self-esteem, and self-endurance. Thus, through the narrative exploration of this chapter, what Muhammad Ali offered as a human and social being is understood within the context he served. Such reflections apply to both athletes and nonathletes alike given the transformational and transcendental impact of Muhammad Ali. And now, in 2021, while we do not know what the future holds for the sport of boxing, we do know the legacy of Muhammad Ali forever lives on.

References

Ali, Muhammad. (2012). "Discovering Greatness." *Reclaiming Children and Youth*, 21, 5–6.
Ali, Muhammad, & Durham, R. (1975). *The Greatest: My Own Story*. New York: Random House.
Bredemeier, B., & Shields, D. L. (2019). "Social Justice, Character Education, and Sport: A Position Statement." *Quest*, 71 202–14.
Calamur, K. (2016). "Muhammad Ali and Vietnam." https://www.theatlantic.com/news/arch ive/2016/06/muhammad-ali-vietnam/485717/.
Connelly, F. M., & Clandinin, D. J. (1990). "Stories of Experience and Narrative Inquiry." *Educational Researcher*, 19(5), 2–14.

Collins, M. (eds.). (2001). *Muhammad Ali through the Eyes of the World.* London: Sanctuary Publishing.

Gaston-Gayles, J., Bryant, A., & Davis, H. (2012). "Civic Responsibility and the Student Athlete: Validating a New Conceptual Model." *Journal of Higher Education*, 83, 535–57.

Gems, G., Borish, L., & Pfister, G. (2017). *Sports in American History: From Colonization to Globalization.* Champaign, IL: Human Kinetics.

Gorsevski, E. W., & Butterworth, M. L. (2011). "Muhammad Ali's Fighting Words: The Paradox of Violence in Nonviolent Rhetoric." *Quarterly Journal of Speech*, 97, 50–73.

Korn, H. (2016). "Muhammad Ali Retrospective." http://www.henryjameskorn.com/2016/06/14/excerpt-from-muhammad-ali-retrospective/.

Luguetti, C., Oliver, K., Kirk, D., & Dantas, L. (2017). "Exploring an Activist Approach of Working with Boys from Socially Vulnerable Backgrounds in a Sport Context." *Sport, Education, and Society*, 22, 493–510.

Orosz, R., & Mezo, F. (2015). "Psychological Factors in the Development of Football-Talent from the Perspective of an Integrative Sport-Talent Model." *Journal for the Education of Gifted Young Scientists*, 3(1), 58–76. doi:http://dx.doi.org/10.17478/JEGYS.2015112018.

Wiggins, D. (2010). *Sport in America: From Colonial Leisure to Celebrity Figures and Globalization.* Champaign, IL: Human Kinetics.

Chapter Fifteen

NOSTRA AETATE, INSHALLAH: MUHAMMAD ALI IN COMMUNITY DIALOGUE WITH CATHOLIC COMMUNICATORS

Autumn Raynor

Introduction

In the American worship of sport, Muhammad Ali's iconolatry is undeniable. Many athletes are deified in their respective sports, but what sets Ali apart is his Abrahamic reach throughout disparate sports fandoms and communities of people who are largely uninterested in his athleticism. The material culture of the United States has reflected Ali's status as champion emeritus for five decades. His corporal image and bombastic quotes provide some of the most recognizable pop culture ephemera but are also relevant to contextualizing the political identity expectations of the historical Black public figure. Ali was frequently placed on worldwide "most famous" and "most influential" lists. Eurocentric news organizations that devoted column inches and broadcast segments to Ali often published his direct quotations and allowed his team control of the accompanying images.[1] In the times when the thoughts and interpretations of journalists and handlers dominated a Black athlete's narrative, Ali managed his public face and communicated facets of his identity and agenda on his own terms.

Through mediated communication channels of pictorials, interviews, and film, Ali proved himself a change agent in the realms of professional sports, activism, cultural pride, and religious expression. The latter carried with it an especially distinct context as Ali negotiated his spirituality, political beliefs, and public face in international media. As his career hit celebrity echelons, Methodist-raised Cassius Clay Jr. remerged in the papers as student of Islam Cassius X and was soon reintroduced as Nation of Islam brother Muhammad Ali.[2] Throughout history, when a Black man public figure outwardly participates in radical Black political identity, White-aligned media often paints him as a heel: disrespectful, ungrateful, problematic, un-American.[3] After years have passed, White-aligned media may manipulate the social memory of its audience by depicting White opposition to Black political agency as the long bygone, misguided ignorance of a small group of disenfranchised White reactors.[4] In this ritual of ahistorical whitewashing, the Black political man is now bold, progressive, and righteous, but his original actions maintain status as violations to Whiteness and its racialized social hierarchy. Muhammad

Ali experienced some of the ritualized agency invalidation, but he also had some support from White audiences during his most controversial moments.

White media coverage and Black media coverage suggest that each of their respective targeted publics varied in their attitudes about Ali's name change, spiritual conversion, and draft refusal. In short, he was not fully villainized in White media and not heralded as a hero by all Black narrators. Black and White receivers of information about Ali both supported and rejected his movement through the Black radical tradition. In this view, the Black political man is neither turned from heel to hero by one group nor maintained as constant hero by the other, as he never occupied either space exclusively. As a case study, a defining characteristic of Ali's religio-political liminality is found in the quantity and quality of his language and image-based public self-definition. The Black political man spoke for himself as he challenged inequality. Ali rooted his arguments in themes of human universality, universal respect of spirituality irrespective of denomination, cultural diversity, and interfaith tolerance. Publics understood him, and many people believed that he had strongly held beliefs. He chose words that reflected a universal spiritual identity.

In its most simplistic form, Ali's social memory is encircled by a universal story on which denominations of fans, historians, and casual observers agree; a world-class protestant athlete converted to Islam and lived his life as a spiritually inclusive man of great conviction. After death, the American social memory of Ali holds him as one of the most famous and celebrated American Muslims. When the champion's religiosity and spirituality are inspected for less salient, but enduring, contextures, an interesting picture comes into focus. In addition to being a celebrated Muslim American, Muhammad Ali experienced lifelong relationships with people and institutions associated with the Catholic Church. This chapter uses Afrikan worldview framework and speech creolization theories in an effort to place Muhammad Ali's universally appointed communication skillset in conversation with his biographical necessity to create universal speech pathways and his tangential exposure to the Catholic faith. Later, the piece will explore a brief photo retrospective of Ali evoking ecumenical image aesthetics.

Worldview Creolization: Universal Languages

An exemplar of Africana oratorical tradition, Ali was an entertaining and impactful wordsmith. Ali outwardly discussed his Blackness, his pride in Black people, and his awareness of its structural politics. Ali's biographers count his childhood experiences as a preamble to his willingness to publicly discuss the human requirements of his Blackness in ways that were normatively suppressed in Eurocentric publications.[5] Emerging as a boxing powerhouse at the age of 22, Ali had already experienced the discrimination, segregation, and racism rampant in Louisville, Kentucky. In those times, Afrocentric media could engage the peculiar circumstances surrounding a Black athlete's fame and cultural politics without subjecting the athlete to White contempt. The White gaze was an ever-present threat to the income opportunities and safety of Black athletes. Athletes were often invited to sacrifice their bodies while being discouraged from speaking their truths.[6] Although the White ownership class continues to penalize Black athletes who promote the realities of Blackness, Ali's use of corrective ontology in spaces of White control was a dangerous, groundbreaking, step toward the future.

As a man born in segregated Kentucky, in 1942, the descendant of enslaved Africans, Ali would likely be versed in the speech acts and interpersonal communication codes necessary to mitigate the ire of White oppressors.[7] Instead of cowing to the irrational speech codes of his opposition, he deliberately made space for conversations located in direct contrast to the raceless, apolitical, Negro aggressor personality White media readily promoted. While the motions and outcomes would be unprecedented for a man of his time, position, and celebrity, this identity negotiation is a typical outgrowth of Africana duality. Du Bois's double consciousness explains that the survival of the Afrikan in America requires hyperawareness of the mechanisms of Whiteness while simultaneously immersed in one's own diasporic Africana worldview.[8] Survivalist "twoness" of African American people involves complete mastery of the contexts and behaviors of the oppressive hegemonic class, most often facilitated thorough the complete integration of a contrasting worldview.

Whereas Azibo, Carruthers, and Dixon correctly define Blackness, or the Afrikan worldview, as containing elements of universality among all diasporic Africana people, the Eurocentric worldview investment in separation and distinction is weaponized against Afrikan people.[9] This is not to say Africana people are monolithic and White people are not, but this truth rather indicates the ability of illegitimate power to invoke the opposite. Despite unparalleled geographic and cultural diversity, Whiteness regards Africana people as one-dimensional members of a singular origin and disposition while requiring Africana people to communicate with actual one-dimensional members of a singular origin and disposition as individuated sovereigns. In truth, Blackness is a suite of physiological and cultural indicators and Whiteness is the possession of only one artifact: supremacist social capital.[10] In this effort, Whiteness calls on a structural oneness to steal power while demanding that Africana people become fluent in social information particularized by artificial ecologies.

A reality-based illustration gestures toward Du Bois's double consciousness. Muhammad Ali and his family interacted with White women and men, young and old: agricultural workers, religious figures, shopkeepers, police officers, educators, financial professionals, and many other situational White typologies. The family interacted with Africana members of these categories, as well. Each group in Black communities and White communities would carry with it its own social mores and vernacular expectations. However, penalties of miscues within intercultural interactions would likely outweigh those of intracultural miscommunications. Those damages would be incurred by Africana people regardless of accuracy. While Whiteness would be the absolute basis of the "violation," additional severity would be applied for interactions colored by Eurocentric power dynamics. For example, Black teenagers may banter and joke with each other without strict gender limitations. However, a Black teen boy using sarcasm with a White teenaged girl could be incriminated for offending her Whiteness, her girlhood, and even her father's social status.

An analysis of Ali's historical preparedness for speech-based power negotiations mirrors that of diasporic responses to colonization and illegitimate disempowerment: Africana people in colonized spaces must have multifaceted consciousnesses situated in highly individualized, yet shifting, contexts. When devising a communication strategy, Whiteness isn't the only personal membership the Africana communicator must consider. In contrast,

Whiteness mandates that Blackness is the only factor that supersedes all other personal characteristics. Malcolm X summarizes the point thusly: "A white bum speaks to a Black doctor and a Black janitor the same way—as if they are beneath him."[11] Indeed, intra-supremacist power and class variation exists, but ownership of Whiteness is the sole qualifier affording White-identified people universal entitlement to engage the sociopathy of racialized ontological violence. There exists no natural rationale for members of an entire culture to be ruled over by another in perpetuity. The premise itself is absurd, and subsequently, Africana people survive in the knowledge that the creators of these constructs are not rational actors. This concept is simplified in an African American vernacular English expression: one cannot argue with crazy; one can only try to manage it.

When viewed linguistically, as a survivalist grammar of perception and reaction, complex negotiations of identity and communication indicate a blending, a formation approaching a construct more closely related to a creole than a traditional code-switch.[12] The African American survivor *interprets* in Whiteness, *selects* reaction strategies rooted in Blackness, and *responds* in a lingua franca. The lingua franca carries the reactionary expectations of White and Black receivers, and thus must be universally encoded for audiences with diverse worldviews. African American grammarians are burdened with outsized consequences of miscommunication.[13] Therefore, although the vocabulary necessary to respond to Whiteness is located in the creole, intense interpersonal communication customization is employed as a form of risk management. Speech communication scholarship illustrates a direct pathway from a communicator's worldview schema to encoding and decoding competencies.[14] Increased knowledge of communicator archetypes provides access to increased amounts of potential outcomes advantageous to one's best self-interest. A person equipped to quickly process social information for all involved communicators will likely have increased confidence and better response outcomes than a person with limited social knowledge. We find demonstrations of this phenomena during Muhammad Ali's media coverage.

Ali was hyperaware of the impact of his words and imagery. He leveraged his close relationship with sports broadcaster Howard Cosell into positive coverage about his religion, name change, draft refusal, and boxing license reinstatement.[15] He invited several journalists and photographers to his training camps, including longtime friend and collaborator Howard Bingham. Cosell was White and Jewish, Bingham was a Black Christian, and Ali was now Muslim. Ali prioritized parts of his communication repertoire for different audiences. The record suggests he used his heritage experience with duality, and its survivalist grammar, to employ messaging strategies for maximum impact. Ali's family and community modeled discourse strategies and taught him to survive with his words. Blackness is not a mandatory precursor to the development of intercultural speech competency, but learning to customize effective intercultural communication strategies is certainly an education vital to Black survival.[16]

The Nation and the Faithful

Muhammad Ali's intercultural communication prowess traversed numerous contexts and publics. He spoke to people from multitudinous backgrounds on and off camera, captivating people in each country he visited. Photos and articles depict Ali hugging babies, conversing with world leaders and disenfranchised Africana laborers.[17] Ali was a skilled pugilist; he was quick, decisive, a forceful puncher, and an agile defender. He began advertising his dominance and verbally berating impending opponents via media, sometimes months before stepping into the ring. His rhymes and upbraids were products of the Afrocentric toasting tradition; he played the dozens with opponents that did not realize they were invited to a verbal battle until they were called out in the media.

Ali was celebrated and criticized for his verbosity. Eurocentric annoyance with Ali's word games turned to outrage when Ali rebuked the oppression of his people.[18] Uniquely, the boxer enjoyed a strong White and non-White fan base all over the world. Competing values of double consciousness and Eurocentric expectations were tested during Ali's transition out of his previous surname, and he faced additional scrutiny when he refused to be drafted for the Vietnam War in 1968. In each incident, Ali articulated his motivations confidently and succinctly as he focused on each audience. Muhammad Ali declared himself a conscientious objector and refused to enter the draft. The US government charged and convicted him, the boxing administration stripped his titles, and he lost his livelihood in the prime of his career. He spoke plainly about his religious beliefs, and his reluctance to kill communities that had not harmed him. He spoke about refusing to kill on behalf of Eurocentric Americans who had harmed him and his people.[19]

While banned from boxing, Ali began to take paid speaking engagements to support his wife and daughter. The interpersonal communication prowess that balanced indignation and spiritual universality in print and interviews did not initially translate to Ali's public-speaking comfortability. He stood before liberal college audiences and stoically repeated Nation of Islam talking points. Ali would eventually come into his confidence and deliver more of his own character during speeches.[20] He still covered the ideas of the Honorable Elijah Muhammad, but he did so with the energy and generic spirituality creoles he'd previously devoted to his interpersonal conversations. On May 19, 1968, Muhammad Ali presented a speech at the University of Notre Dame. Ali was invited as the school's first speaker in its newly created 'Student Union Academic Commission's' speaker series.[21] The speech was titled "The Solution to the Black and White Problem as Taught by Elijah Muhammad."

Ali's universal message of racial and spiritual respect, however couched in Nation of Islam rationale, allowed the divorced, Muslim, athlete with the race relations platform to be embraced by a receptive audience at America's flagship Catholic university. Forty-four years prior to Ali's speech, from May 17 to 19, 1924, the students of Notre Dame physically clashed with the Klu Klux Klan (KKK) when it arrived in their city. The violent racism of the KKK was well known, and the students of Notre Dame acknowledged the KKK as an anti-Catholic terrorist organization.[22] While it is unknown if Ali knew Notre Dame students once battled the Klan, the archive reveals that current and historical themes of devotion, persecution, and religiosity had made granular allies of Catholics and Muslims.

Islam and Catholicism shared connections beyond their respective Abrahamic origins. Muhammad Ali's draft refusal was familiar and understandable to many Catholics who knew of, or utilized, the conscientious objector refusal during the Vietnam War.[23] The social programming supported by Catholic-facing media presented Muhammad Ali as having a reputation for speaking about truth, justice, and accountability. Islamic media postured Muhammad Ali as a persecuted figure, maligned for his spiritual conviction. Catholicism promotes great respect for people who stand in their faith against unjust opposition.[24] Muslims and Catholics could converge around each religion's dogmatic rigidity, scheduled rituals, and respect for holy days. Islam and Catholicism were visibly *actionable* religions: leaders and participants could be identified by their dress, their pushback against secular norms, their almsgiving, their worship spaces, and their rituals. In short, Islam and Catholicism are mutually intelligible: lexical differences are present, but a lingua franca unites them into the universality of strong tie spiritual devotion.[25] Muhammad Ali's ability to create universal dialogue with Catholic people began during his adolescence. He maintained connections to Catholic people and institutions throughout his lifetime (Figure 15.1).

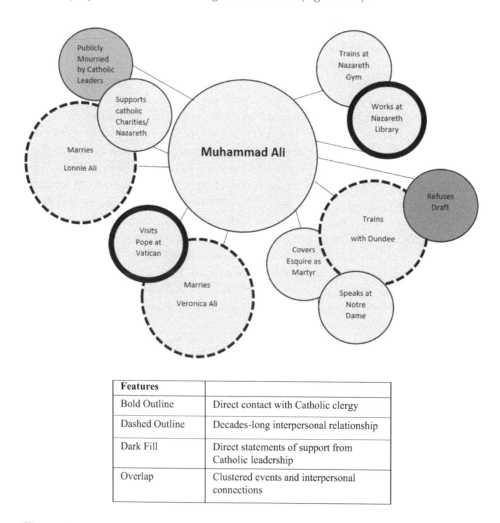

Features	
Bold Outline	Direct contact with Catholic clergy
Dashed Outline	Decades-long interpersonal relationship
Dark Fill	Direct statements of support from Catholic leadership
Overlap	Clustered events and interpersonal connections

Figure 15.1 Culturagram representing Muhammad Ali's interconnected Catholic social network.

Karol and Cassius

Muhammad Ali began his career as a self-designed student athlete. As a teenager, he worked at the library reception area of Nazareth College and would conduct his first boxing workouts at its gym. The college's resident nuns, Sisters of Charity of Nazareth, provided a space that was racially integrated, a rarity in Louisville at the time. Nazareth College is now Spalding University and remains a Catholic institution.[26] Ali maintained a decades-long connection with the school and its member. He continued to pay respect years later as he brought flowers to funerals of the sisters who were there during his adolescence. Ali's start at the Catholic college would have undoubtedly exposed him to the broad rules and practices of Catholicism. Later in life he would be lauded for his interfaith approach to spirituality. The young Methodist boy began his career manning the card catalog at a Catholic college. Ali's trainer and confidant of 20 years, Angelo Dundee, helped him achieve his athletic goals. In a 1989 interview, Dundee said of Ali, "I hope I was as good of a Catholic as Ali was Muslim."[27] Ali's faith grew into that of a devout Muslim that would exchange autographs with His Holiness the Pope.[28] When Ali was received by Pope John Paul II in 1982, he was accompanied to the Vatican by his third wife, Veronica Porche Ali. Mrs. Porche Ali was raised Catholic, as was Ali's fourth wife, and partner until his death, Lonnie Williams Ali.[29]

John Paull II and Muhammad Ali shared a few similarities in their journeys. Both men were fervent students and practitioners of their faiths. Both experienced a faith transition that required a name and identity conversation. During their lives, both men were devoted to justice and charity. Muhammad Ali and his wife Lonnie quietly donated to various schools and charities, including Catholic resource centers. The Muhammad Ali Parkinson Center is a medical facility within the Christus St. Joseph Hospital Group.[30] Both Ali and John Paull II aged to be ambassadors for continued faith and dignity within affliction as they attended public events while exhibiting the tremors of Parkinson's disease. Their lives were celebrated while they lived to enjoy the laurels, and their legacies were honored upon their deaths. Muhammad Ali lived to see John Paul II canonized, changing his moniker again to Saint John Paul II. Ali's interaction with sainthood, an illustration of a martyr's reality, preceded John Paul's by 46 years.

Aesthetics of a Catholic Ali

In the prime of his career, Ali was one of the most photographed, and subsequently recognizable, men in the world. Photographers were able to capture the urgency and beauty of the Black political man in ways that elevated documentation to art. Narratives surrounding Ali's photos are conveyed magnanimously through film. Ali's photo archive contains thousands of culturally important images. Contemporary social memory correctly ruminates on the intersecting Islamic, political, and athletic aesthetics. The photos described below offer a new characterization that reflect overtly catholic aesthetics. Whether staged or serendipitous, a receiver with a passing knowledge of catholic iconography will recognize familiar postures and narratives. This section recounts select photographs that place Ali within the Catholic visual imagination (Figures 15.2–15.6).

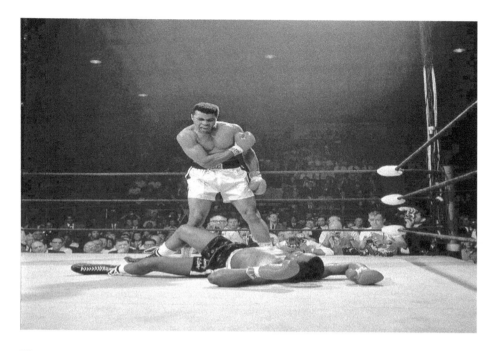

Figure 15.2: "Get up sucker!" (Ali–Liston II, St. Dominic's Arena, May 25, 1965).
Source: Photograph by Neil Leifer.
Sports photographer Neil Leifer was a friend and frequent shooter of Muhammad Ali. This shot would go on to be considered one of the best sports photos of all time. In the lead-up to the fight, Ali roasted Liston in the media. Although Ali was taller and heavier than his opponent, he called Liston "a big old bear."[31] He promised to down him. When the controversial knockout happened early in the fight, this image presents Ali as David to Liston's Goliath.

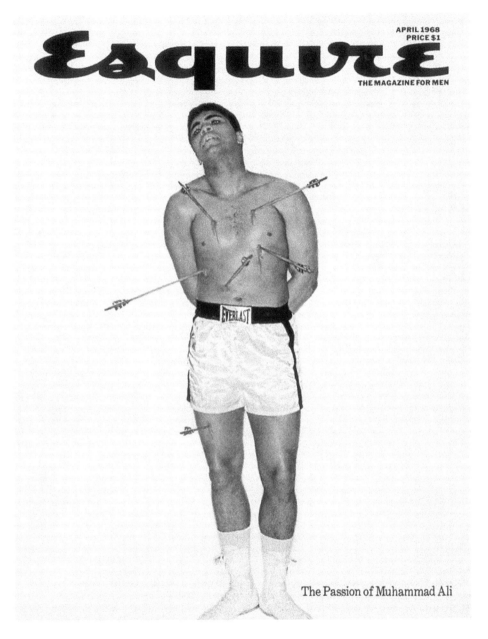

The Passion of Muhammad Ali

Figure 15.3: "The passion of Muhammad Ali" (April 1968).
Source: Esquire magazine, photograph by Carl Fischer.
Esquire Art Director George Lois showed Ali a postcard drawing of Saint Sebastian and asked if he would pose as the Catholic martyr for the cover.[32] Ali agreed, and photographer Carl Fischer immortalized the champion during his exile from boxing. The connection was overt: like Jesus, Ali was being persecuted for his certainty in his identity and faith.

Figure 15.4: "Ali enters the city" (Kinshasa, Zaire, October 1974).
Source: Photograph by Howard Bingham.
Howard Bingham shot hundreds of pictures of Ali during their trip to Kinshasa during the Rumble in the Jungle event. Residents were excited to see the star, forming crowds during his official appearances and unannounced training activities. The presence of the massive crowd, the uniformed guard, and Ali's travel through the crowd return us to Jesus's passion narrative in the 1968 *Esquire* photo. Ali is photographed triumphantly riding into a space to lovingly greet his people although he knows he will be hurt.

Figure 15.5: "I am" (Kinshasa, Zaire, October 1974).
Source: Photograph by Howard Bingham.
Howard Bingham previously captured Ali entering the city with frenzied onlookers. He was dressed in Western clothing and appeared a bit hot and disheveled. The motion is evident in the photo. This Bingham shot, taken just days later, is a contrast stunning in its stillness. The crowd is calm. Ali is standing on his own feet, staring directly into the camera. He has traded his collared shirt for a dashiki. In the days between the two photos, the crowd shifted from around him to behind him. He was fighting for them. He entered the fight as the underdog. George Foreman abused Ali for several rounds, and then Ali rose up and claimed the victory. The win was a metaphor for his exile from boxing and return.

Figure 15.6: "Apostle" (November 2017).
Source: GQ magazine, photograph by Martin Schoeller.
A little over a year after Ali's death, athlete-activist Colin Kaepernick was photographed for *GQ* magazine. Kaepernick's choice to protest the racism and inequality lodged against his people resulted in his sport rejecting him and preventing him from making a living through football. Kaepernick knew what was at risk; Ali's exile experience was a warning strong enough to travel generationally. The *GQ* creative team noted that Kaepernick was Ali's spiritual successor in activism and asked him if he would pose for an "Ali" shot. The young activist brought his own dashiki.

Conclusion

Muhammad Ali's social memorialization will always be associated with his unwavering faith, conviction, rejection of inequality, and commitment to win. Ali's public image is a study in the Afrocentric logic of both/and.[33] He was a fighter and a lover; a champion who lost; a boastful sportsman who silently helped people who needed it. In sum, Muhammad Ali was a lot of things to a lot of people. Biographers surmise he relied so much on the power of speech because he was dyslexic.[34] Africana studies and communication scholars can see the technique and immediacy of his words as indicators of his advanced knowledge of the tools his background afforded him. Muslims, Catholics, and other religious members can identify with his devotion to his faith. Perhaps through the methods Ali used to form communication connections by way of multiple consciousnesses, scholars can study more branches in pursuit of mutually intelligible interactions among seemingly disparate speech communities.

This piece's foray into a less-canonical aspect of Ali's biography does not presume to suggest his connections with Catholicism were pivotal to his life's work and experiences. Islam, his spiritual center, provides the most compelling window to Ali's approach to communication coding and interfaith fluency. Just as a peripheral event may influence a day, or a life, in ways that one may not be aware, the presence of the universal church, and its people, may or may not have greatly impacted Ali's interfaith speech repertoire. However, had he wanted to exercise his interfaith rhetoric with longtime interpersonal communication partners, Catholic people, spaces, and iconography were regular fixtures in his life. Intimate and significant parts of Ali's social network and public experiences are associated with Catholicism, although if he was not a member of that faith. Muhammad Ali transcended denominations, using his universal spiritual communication to fight for his people and all people with kind spirits.

Notes

1　Norman Miler, *The Fight* (Boston, MA: Little, and Brown, 1975).
2　Kevin Mitchell, "From the Vietnam War to Islam: The Key Chapters in Ali's Life." *Guardian*, June 2016.
3　Howard Bryant, *The Heritage: Black Athletes, a Divided America, and the Politics of Patriotism* (Boston, MA: Beacon Press, 2018).
4　S. Towsend, M. Phillips, & G. Osmond, "Remembering the Rejection of Muhammad Ali: Identity, Civil Rights and Social Memory." *Sports in History*, 38 (2018): 267–88.
5　Thomas Hauser, *Muhammad Ali: His Life and Times* (New York: Simon & Schuster, 1991).
6　Jonathan Eig, *Ali: A Life* (Boston, MA: Houghton Mifflin Harcourt, 2017).
7　Thomas Hauser, "The Importance of Muhammad Ali," *ESPN Magazine* online, June 2016.
8　W. E. B. Du Bois, *The Souls of Black Folk* (New York, NY : Gramercy, 1994).
9　Karanja Carroll, "Africana Studies and Research Methodology: Revisiting the Centrality of the Afrikan Worldview." *Journal of Pan-African Studies* 2 (2008): 4–27.
10　Cheryl Harris, "Whiteness as Property." *Harvard Law Review*, 106, no. 8 (June 1993): 1707–91.
11　Malcom X and Alex Haley, *The Autobiography of Malcolm X* (New York: Grove, 1965).
12　Charles DeBose, "Codeswitching: Black English and Standard English in the African American linguistic repertoire." *Multilingual Matters*, 13 (1992): 157–67; John McWhorter, "Pidgins and Creoles as Models of Language Change: The State of the Art." *Annual Review of Applied Linguistics*, 23 (2003): 202–12.
13　Minkah Makalani, "Black Lives Matter and the Limits of Formal Black Politics." *South Atlantic Quarterly*, 116 (2017): 529–52.
14　Kai Alter, Erhard Rank, Sonja Kotz, Ulrike Toepel, Mirelle Besson, Annett Schirmer, and Angela Friederici ., "Affective Encoding in the Speech Signal and in Event-Related Brain Potentials." *Speech Communication*, 40 (2003): 61–70.
15　David Kindred, *Sound of Fury: Two Powerful Lives, One Fateful Friendship* (New York: Free Press, 2006).
16　Charles DeBose, "Codeswitching."
17　William Strathmore, *Muhammad Ali: His Life in Pictures* (Bath, England: Parragon, 2016).
18　Eig, *Ali: A Life*.
19　Les Carpenter & Laughland Oliver, "Shunned by White America, How Muhammad Ali Found His Voice on Campus Tour." *Guardian*, June 2016.

20 Bill Siegal, *The Trials of Muhammad Ali*. Documentary, 2013.

21 Staff, The Observer (May 1968) Muhammad Here Sunday Vol 2 No 74

22 Staff Reporter (February 2011) 78 Years ago: Notre dame battles the KKK. Irish Echo

23 Father Raymond De Souza, "The Contradictions of Muhammad Ali." Catholic Education Resource Center, Washington, DC, June 2016.

24 US Catholic Church, *Catechism of the Catholic Church* (New York: Double Day, 2003).

25 Paul Helm, *Philosophy of Religion* (New York: Britannica, 2010).

26 Jessica Able, "Muhammad Ali Got His Start Working at a Louisville Catholic College." The Catholic Register Online, 2016.

27 Louis Massiah, "Blackside Inc Interview with Angelo Dundee." Washington University Libraries, 1989.

28 Mark Zimmerman, "Lives and Deaths of John Paul II, Muhammad Ali Intertwined." Crux online, 2016.

29 Patricia Sheridan, "Breakfast with Lonnie Ali." *Pittsburgh Post Gazette*, December 3, 2007.

30 Dignity Health Directory online, April 7, 2020.

31 David Remnick, *King of the World: Muhammad Ali and the Rise of the American Hero* (New York: Random House, 1998).

32 Jill Hudson, The Undefeated Online, May 31, 2017.

33 Carroll, "Africana Studies and Research Methodology."

34 Theresa Maher, "Muhammad Ali: Dyslexic Role Model Fought in the Ring and for Social Justice." RespectAbility Online, February 2018.

Chapter Sixteen

ALI: STANDING FOR SOMETHING

Brandon Allen

Initiating an engagement about the late heavyweight champion Muhammad Ali is a perplexing endeavor. Consequently, on April 28, 1967, tensions ran high in downtown Houston. The Vietnam War was underway, and many did not approve. Likewise, a large crowd protested and waited outside the US Customs office, hoping to see how one man's belligerent response might affect the nation's overall mood. A little before 8 a.m., the antagonist arrived. People began to chant, "Hep! Hep! Don't take that step!"[1] as the heavyweight boxing champion, Muhammad Ali, made his way through the crowd. Ali moved through the crowd with grace and poise. He was not in Houston for a heavyweight fight. Furthermore, he was about to experience the battle of his life: a three-and-a-half-year struggle with the US government, over his refusal to take part in the war with Vietnam.

Ali entered the courthouse carrying the consciousness of Black people on his broad shoulders. As a proud minister of the Nation of Islam (NOI), he was a public voice of freedom for the Black community and, as such, a conscientious objector of the Vietnam War. As Ali climbed the stairs to the courthouse, he understood why activist H. Rap Brown and students from Texas Southern and other Historically Black Colleges were spiritually and physically with him along this journey. The weight of his situation was not lost on him. He fully understood the complexities of his actions and how they would affect African American self-perception. An elderly woman stopped Ali before he entered and said, "Stand up, brother! We're with you! Stand up! Fight for us! Don't let us down!"[2] There was a sense of human possibility in the environment. Protestors believed that Ali carried the power to articulate their position and thus shift the American war politic. Coincidently, protesters' presence was saying *our general has arrived, and we will not fight!* The fact that Ali was standing up meant that others could too. A collective dissent was forming, giving Black people confidence that their protest would not be in vain. Most knew Ali as the heavyweight champion of the world, but that day, he emerged as the cultural hero of righteousness they had been praying for.

In truth, Ali's decision to refuse the draft defined a culture. Despite facing five years in prison and a $10,000 fine, Muhammad Ali's defiance shaped African Americans' 1960s cultural memory. His resistance provoked metaphysical violence upon Black people and caused many to consider Black folks' cowardice un-American. Phrased another way, Ali's refusal unleashed terror ontologically upon Black bodies in that Whites read his behavior as anti-American sentiment. This chapter aims to examine how Muhammad Ali's political stance against the Vietnam War influenced Africana cultural memory and thus invited rhetorical and metaphysical violence upon the Black community.

Conscientious Objector

Due to the high rate of casualties during the Vietnam War, the United States lowered its draft status drafting more young men into the military. Consequently, this new military draft status included Ali, thus making him at once eligible to be drafted into the military. Ali's earlier score disqualified him from selection; nevertheless, Ali decided to stand on his religious principles as a conscientious objector, refusing to enter the military with the lower requirements. A conscientious objector is any person who refuses to serve in the armed forces or bear arms on moral or religious grounds. Considering this military change, in his draft status, Ali filed a draft exemption as a conscientious objector with the government; Ali stated that "to bear arms or kill is against my religion. And I conscientiously object to any combat military service that involves the participation in any war in which the lives of human beings are being taken."[3] Ali proclaimed his fundamental objections were religious and socially justifiable.

Moreover, Ali doubled down on his stance, telling reporters, "No Viet Cong ever called me Nigger."[4] His quote provoked the government and others because his declaration of freedom challenged the construct of White supremacy. Before his induction ceremony in Houston, Ali established why he philosophically objected to the war when he stated,

> If I thought going to war would bring freedom and equality to twenty-two million, my people, they wouldn't have to draft me. I'd join tomorrow. But I either have to obey the laws of the land or the laws of Allah. I have nothing to lose by standing up and following my beliefs. We've been in jail for four hundred years.[5]

To put it more simply, Ali refused to change his moral principles to appease the government. Regardless of the consequences of an anti-black world, Ali was willing to stand his ground.

Freedom Is Not Free

In his book *Ontological Terror*, Calvin Warren explains how an anti-Black world defines Black Being as nothingness. According to Warren, "The Negro is black because the Negro must assume the function of nothing in a metaphysical world. The world needs this labor."[6] Ali may not have understood the extent to which an anti-Black America would respond to his political stance. His body was not his own; its only purpose was entertainment and labor, not a political protest. During the Maafa, America intentionally created systems to perpetuate Black Being as nothing or having no value, ensuring that the Negro body remains a laborer. America's forefathers described in the Declaration of Independence as inalienable rights life, liberty, and the pursuit of happiness.

Furthermore, the authors of the US Constitution created the three-fifths compromise that "allowed a state to count three-fifths of each Black person in determining political representation in the House (African American Registry, 2017; Sneddon, 2016; Rigueur, 2016). It was an early American effort to avoid the intersectionality of race, class, nationality, and wealth for political control."[7] Consequently, African Americans have never been considered full human beings, and when they challenge this ontological terror, violence erupts.

The day Muhammad Ali refused to be drafted into the Vietnam War, metaphysical violence at once erupted because he chose to stand up for what he believed in challenging White supremacy. Furthermore, Warren explains the response of the US government and every boxing commission in the country was because Ali challenged the ontological boundaries of freedom. According to Warren, "Black freedom is a form of violence for the human, violence that must be met with extreme force."[8] Furthermore, throughout America's history, whenever African Americans fought for their human rights, they were confronted with extreme force. It did not matter whether it was on the street or in the courtroom.

Consequently, Blacks who saw their Being as "Free" faced a violent backlash from White citizens. For instance, when Black citizens wanted to end segregated schools and attain civil and voting rights, White citizens would come together as angry mobs and physically terrorize, suggesting Blackness is void of being in an anti-Black world. Consequently, today, police officers murder unarmed Black men and women, while rarely facing justice is a reality for Black people. Additionally, Ali, considering himself a conscientious objector, was enough of an ontological offense for the government to convict him of draft evasion, sentence him to five years in prison, fine him $10,000, and take away his passport. They made it impossible for him to fight anywhere globally and make a living to support his family.

Moreover, the boxing commissions in different states revoked Ali's license to fight. To put it another way, Ali was the victim of metaphysical violence that White supremacy used when Black people threatened to disrupt the power structure. On the contrary, Ali continued to voice his idea of Black freedom juxtaposing his view of liberation to Whites' Black subjugation view. To put it bluntly, White Americans tried to destroy Ali for his stance against the Vietnam War, being a Muslim and a conscientious objector, protesting and voicing their hate for Ali's political stance. There is no question that antipatriotic criticism for Ali would be the most significant criticism he would receive in his life. A case in point, television personality David Susskind told Ali during an interview,

> I find nothing amusing or interesting or tolerable about this man. He's a disgrace to his country, his race, and what he laughingly describes as his profession. He is a convicted felon in the United States. He has been found guilty. He is out on bail. He will inevitably go to prison, as well as he should. He is a simplistic fool and a pawn.[9]

Despite the criticism from the public, the media, and the government, Ali stood on his principles of refusing to fight for a country fighting an unjust war.

Furthermore, the degradation of Ali continued with Maine governor John Reed. Reed declared his hate for Ali despite trying to schedule a fight for him in his state. Reed stated that "Ali should be held in utter contempt by every patriotic American. Maine sons and daughters are fighting in Vietnam. I don't think Maine people want our state to be used to further the ambitions and gains of an individual of Ali's character."[10] Ali's stance and lack of contrition infuriated the White power structure; the consequence was they closed off all possibilities of him earning money. Asked about giving Ali a boxing license, former California governor Ronald Reagan said, "Forget it. That draft dodger will never fight in my state."[11]

Wherever Ali encountered racist White people, they would remind him of his place in the American caste system. He was a slave, and he does not get to dictate the terms of his freedom. A case in point, on the day of his induction, as he left, an older White woman approached Ali, chastising him for his draft decision. She yelled at him,

> You goin' straight to jail. You ain't no champ no more. You ain't never going to be champ no more. You get down on your knees and beg forgiveness from God! My son's in Vietnam, and you no better'n he is. He is there fightin', and you here safe. I hope you rot in jail. I hope they throw away the key.

This woman's response suggests that Ali was America's villain.

In Houston, Ali had decided to forgo the draft, making him a villain in an anti-Black world, and White Americans took every chance they could to remind him of his social status. Ali was not their champion. He was White America's entertainment. Furthermore, Ali was not supposed to think or make political statements, especially when he made millions of dollars. Ali was villainized because he challenged the White supremacist construct and disrupted the metaphysical holocaust.

Moreover, Ali refused to back down from his principles, no matter the cost. Despite the hate he received from White America, Black America would stand with Ali. In other words, Ali's decision not to enter the draft made him Black America's champion, and most would rally around him.

Fight the Power

Ali's position as a conscientious objector was problematic for the US government. They wanted Ali's body for their personal use to boost the soldiers' morale in combat and increase support among American citizens who viewed the war as controversial. Consequently, Ali could not turn back if he wanted to; there were too many people worldwide watching him and rooting for him, idolizing him. There is no question, Ali had to stand and fight for those who had no voice, and the black and brown people all over the world would agree. According to Uruguayan writer and journalist Eduardo Galeano's poem "Memory of Fire: Century of the Wind,"

> They told him that a good boxer confines his fighting to the ring. He says the real ring is something else, where a triumphant black fight for defeated blacks, for those who eat leftovers in the kitchen.

They advised discretion. From then on, he yells.
They tapped his phone. From then on, he yells on the phone, too.
They put a uniform on him to send him to Vietnam. He pulls it off and yells that he isn't going because he has nothing against the Vietnamese, who have not harmed him or any other black American.
They took away his world title. They stopped him from boxing. They sentenced him to jail and a fine. He yells his thanks for these compliments to his human dignity.[12]

Increasingly important was how Ali's political stance influenced Africana cultural memory, inspiring and stimulating Black consciousness. For instance, during a speech challenging the war, Dr. Martin Luther King stated, "No matter what you think of Mr. Muhammad Ali's religion, you certainly have to admire his courage."[13] Conversely, Dr. King supported Ali despite their religious differences. King's speech encouraged attendees to file as a conscientious objector to prevent them from going to war. Additionally, activist H. Rap Brown chanted with the crowd in support of Ali outside Houston's courthouse. National Football League (NFL) running back Jim Brown organized a group of Black athletes that included basketball players Bill Russell and Kareem Abdul Jabbar supporting Ali's decision to refuse the draft. Russell stated,

I didn't go to Cleveland to persuade Muhammad to join or not join the Army. We were just there to help, and I was struck by how confident he was, how totally assured he was that what he was doing was right. [...] Philosophically, Ali was a free man. Besides being the greatest boxer ever, he was free. And he was free at a time when historically it was very difficult to be free no matter who you were or what you were. Ali was one of the first truly free people in America.[14]

Figure 16.1 is a sequential flow of examining issues of power, economy, and culture. Concerning Muhammad Ali, he centered his experiences working with the NOI from a cultural analysis, which allowed him to adapt and adjust an Afrocentric perspective. Ali's stance would become a beacon of hope for African Americans. A hope that they could be free in a country that historically oppressed Black Americans. Kareem

Figure 16.1 A sequential flow of examining issues of power, economy, and culture.

Abdul-Jabbar, like Russell, was amazed that a Black man stood up for his principles and represented Black freedom. According to Abdul-Jabbar,

> I was a hundred percent behind Muhammad's protesting what I thought was an unjust war. [...] Ali didn't need our help because, as far as the black community was concerned, he already had everybody's heart. He gave so many people courage to test the system. A lot of us didn't think he could do it, but he did and succeeded every time.[15]

To put it another way, Ali had profoundly affected Black people and changed their perspective of what it meant to be free. He was creating a new gaze for Blacks shifting them away from a hegemonic White paradigm. Inspired Black athletes took a stand for justice and freedom. For instance, during the 1968 Olympics, African American sprinters John Carlos and Tommie Smith took the medal stand during the US national Anthem's playing. They gave the Black Power salute supporting Ali, human rights, and social justice.

In the film *The Trials of Muhammad Ali,* John Carlos said, "The number one statement in my mind was to have Muhammad Ali vindicated from all the nonsense and the negativity they tried to put around him and give him the right to be the champion."[16] Ali's stance continued to affect African Americans in all areas profoundly. Author and professor Gerald Early recalled how he felt as a young boy in 1967 in his essay "Tales of the Wonderboy":

> When he refused, I felt something greater than pride: I felt as though my honor as a black boy had been defended, my honor as a human being. He was the grand knight, after all, the dragon-slayer. And I felt myself, little inner-city boy, that I was, his apprentice to the grand imagination, the grand daring. The day that Ali refused the draft, I cried in my room. I cried for him and for myself, for my future and his, for all our black possibilities.[17]

Ali was willing to give up his career as a boxer and the heavyweight champion of the world, and people all over the world were ready to resist and stand with him.

The 1960s was an epoch of political unrest between Black and White Americans. Respecting the accomplishments of those in the civil rights era, young Black activists began to fight for freedom more aggressively. The shouts of "We Shall Overcome" were replaced with "Black Power." Ali's political stance was an event that helped to usher in this new era of self-determination and Black pride. The 1960s saw the Student Nonviolent Coordinating Committee's Stokely Carmichael as a Black Power movement leader. Huey P. Newton and Bobby Seale founded the Black Panther Party for Self-Defense. The Black Panthers instituted programs that addressed social injustice. Other activists and artists such as Amiri Baraka, Jacob Carruthers, Angela Davis, Nikki Giovanni, H. Rap Brown, Assata Shakur, Dick Gregory, Sonja Sanchez, and many more were seen and unseen activists. All were attacking the power structure of White supremacy. Like Muhammad Ali, all of them saw their beingness outside of the White gaze and wanted to be free of it. They were all constructing a new radical aesthetic that announced to an anti-Black world that their Black beingness was free. Free to be Black, free to be a woman, free to be a man, free to be gay or straight, free to be loved, free to be creative, free to be an artist, free to imagine a life without White restriction. They were free to *be.*

Ali's draft defiance stance against an anti-Black world was a declaration of independence. He believed freedom was more important than money, and he would sacrifice his prime boxing years and millions of dollars to make his point. White America would not control his being no matter what they took from him economically. He was unapologetically free, and White supremacy hated him for it. They tried to destroy him, but he still prevailed.

Conclusion

In this chapter, I argue that in 1967 Muhammad Ali refused to be drafted in the US military and directly and indirectly impacted Africana cultural memory. Furthermore, I discussed his declaration of independence provoked metaphysical violence from an anti-Black world, not willing to see his being or any Black Being as having value or being free. Despite being stripped of his titles, facing five years in prison, and his character attacked by the media and American citizens, Ali remained steadfast in his peace and freedom principles. He was the people's champ, and he did not need validation from White supremacy.

I used Calvin Warren's *Ontological Terror* and the Afro-pessimism theoretical framework he uses in his book, examining why anti-Black America attempted to enact metaphysical violence on Ali. Further research is needed on Afro-pessimism to understand why Black Being is a threat to White supremacy? How has this dynamic affected the contemporary professional athlete? Colin Kaepernick is an example of the White power structure destroying a person's career because Kaepernick dared to challenge the White supremacist construct. Like Ali, White America punished Kaepernick for kneeling during the national anthem and refusing to show contrition to the White power structure. Additionally, further research should study why African American NFL players did not stand in solidarity with Kaepernick and boycott the league? Were they willing to give up their morals for a paycheck?

Moreover, researchers must take it further and produce reasonable solutions to Black ontology as nothingness. How do we shift the White supremacist paradigm? Additionally, how have these events affected Africana cultural memory? Afro-pessimism is a research topic that addresses the dynamic between Blackness and Whiteness. Using Afro-pessimism as a frame of reference can help to shift the White supremacist paradigm. Researchers should continue to examine using Black aesthetics to usurp the European gaze, creating an Africana gaze that allows Black beingness to see itself as free without validation from Whiteness.

Conversely, this cannot be the only way. More solutions must be found to continue moving the Africana discipline forward and understanding how White supremacy uses 400-year-old tactics to dominate Black bodies. Scholars and students should do more research, asking questions such as: How does the White gaze blind the Black eye? Does becoming wealthy aid in this blindness to White supremacy because affluent Blacks see themselves from skewed views? There are plenty of problems to address within a White power structure using a Eurocentric frame of reference. Conversely, additional research is needed to find solutions to the Black problem. We must continue to base our analysis on an Afrocentric theoretical frame of reference.

Notes

1 Muhammad Ali and Richard Durham, *Muhammad Ali the Greatest My Own Story* (Los Angeles: Gray Malkin Media, 1975), 167.
2 Ibid.
3 Ibid.
4 Gerald L. Early, *The Muhammad Ali Reader* (Manhattan: Ecco, 2013), 194.
5 David Remnick, *King of the World* (New York: Vintage Books, 1998), 291.
6 Calvin L. Warren, *Ontological Terror: Blackness, Nihilism, and Emancipation* (Durham: Duke University Press, 2018), 6.
7 African American Registry, "The Three-Fifths Compromise," 2017, https://aaregistry.org/story/the-three-fifths-compromise/, accessed April 17, 2020.
8 Warren, *Ontological* Terror, 53.
9 *The Trials of Muhammad Ali*, directed by Bill Siegel, 2013. New York: Independent Lens.
10 Rob Sneddon, *The Phantom Punch: The Story behind Boxing's Most Controversial Bout* (Lanham: Down East Books, 2016), 216.
11 Leah Wright Rigueur, "When Muhammad Ali Endorsed Ronald Reagan," *Washington Post*, June 10, 2016, https://www.washingtonpost.com/posteverything/wp/2016/06/10/when-muhammad-ali-endorsed-ronald-reagan/, accessed November 6, 2020.
12 Eduardo Galeano, "Memory of Fire: Century of the Wind," walterlippmann.com, https://walterlippmann.com/eduardo-galeano-on-muhammad-ali-1967/, accessed April 16, 2020.
13 Dr. Martin Luther King Jr., quoted in *The Trials of Muhammad Ali*, Netflix.
14 Thomas Hauser, *Muhammad Ali: His Life and Times* (New York: Open Road Media, 2012), 173–74.
15 Ibid., 173.
16 John Carlos, quoted in *The Trials of Muhammad Ali*, Amazon Prime.
17 Remnick, *King of the* World, 293.

Bibliography

African American Registry. "The Three-Fifths Compromise." *African American Registry.* July 17, 2017. https://aaregistry.org/story/the-three-fifths-compromise/ (accessed April 17, 2020).
Ali, Muhammad, and Durham, Richard. *Muhammad Ali the Greatest My Own Story.* Los Angeles: Gray Malkin Media, 1975.
Ali, Rahaman. *My Brother, Muhammad Ali: The Definitive Biography.* London: John Blake, 2019.
Early, Gerald L. *The Muhammad Ali Reader.* Manhattan: Ecco, 2013.
Galeano, Eduardo. "Memory of Fire:Century of the Wind." *Walterlippman.com.* 1967. https://walterlippmann.com/eduardo-galeano-on-muhammad-ali-1967/ (accessed April 16, 2020).
Hauser, Thomas. *Muhammad Ali: His Life and Times.* New York: Open Road Media, 2012.
Remnick, David. *King of the World.* New York: Vintage Books, 1998.
Rigueur, Leah Wright. "When Muhammad Ali Endorsed Ronald Reagan." *Washington Post*, June 10, 2016.
The Trials of Muhammad Ali. Directed by Bill Siegel. 2013.
Sneddon, Rob. *The Phantom Punch: The Story Behind Boxing's Most Controversial Bout.* Lanham: Down East Books, 2016.
Warren, Calvin L. *Ontological Terror: Blackness, Nihilism, and Emancipation.* Durham: Duke University Press, 2018.

Chapter Seventeen

MUHAMMAD ALI AND HEALTH AND WELLNESS

Angela Branch-Vital, Andrea Mcdonald,
Park Esewiata Atatah, Catherine Kisavi-Atatah, and
James L. Conyers Jr.

Life History (Child-Rearing That Led to Boxing)

Muhammad Ali was born in Louisville, Kentucky, on January 17, 1942. His birth name was Cassius Marcellus Clay. He grew up in the low socioeconomic community of Louisville, in a household with his sister, four brothers, and both parents. Muhammad's family was from African slave descent. His parents supported their family by working as a painter (father) and home cleaner (mother). Ali attended the Central High School in Louisville. During school, he was diagnosed with dyslexia, a disorder that affects areas of the brain that process language. This can cause problems in identifying speech sounds and learning. Therefore, Ali faced difficulties in reading and writing.

The champ grew up in a community where racial segregation was very high. According to the dictionary, segregation is the enforced separation or isolation of a race, class, or ethnic group. This practice prevents social intercourse in educational facilities and institutions. During Ali's upbringing, he encountered various racial segregations and the murder of Emmett Till. For example, children of color in their community were not allowed to participate in some community activities. Through these experiences, Muhammad became frustrated and got involved in the vandalization of railroad yards.

Ali started his boxing career at a very early age. He was first introduced to boxing by a police officer (Joe Martin) through his personal vendetta. At age 12, Muhammad owned a bicycle, which he kept at his front doorway. One morning he woke up to find that a thief had stolen his bike. His parents called the police, and upon the arrival of the police, Muhammad was so indignant that he wanted to seek revenge. However, the police officer Joe Martin invited Muhammad to the community center to learn boxing lessons. Equally, he also tried to discourage Muhammad from thinking about attacking the thief by telling him the only way we could hurt a thief is through learning boxing. At first, Muhammad ignored the invitation from Joe Martin. After more investigations, he decided to start his first boxing lessons with another trainer, Fred Stoner, who actually provided him with real experience as a boxer.

Table 17.1 Ali Boxing Matches, 1961 to 1963

Fight dates	Boxer's name	Results
January 17, 1961	Tony Esperti	Ali won 3rd round TKO
February 7, 1961	Jim Robinson	Ali won 1st round TKO
February 21, 1961	Donnie Fleeman	Ali won 7th round TKO
April 19, 1961	LaMar Clark	Ali won 2nd round knockout
July 22, 1961	Alonzo Johnson	Ali won 10th round Uanimous decision
November 29, 1961	Willi Besmanoff	Ali won 7th round TKO
March 23, 1962	George Logan	Ali won 4th round TKO
November 15, 1962	Archie Moore	Ali won 4th round TKO
March 13, 1963	Doug Jones	Ali won 10th round Uanimous Decision
June 18, 1963	Henry Cooper	Ali won 5th round TKO

Subsequently, Muhammad started his training and boxing career at 12 years of age. Between 1955 and 1960, Ali fought 100 amateur boot and 2 national championships. He also won two national Amateur Athletic Union boxing titles, a gold medal in the light-heavyweight bracket in 1960, in Rome. After he returned, Ali became a professional boxer with an unprecedented combination of both his speed, strength, stamina, and personal magnetism. From 1961 to 1963 Ali's boxing record consisted of 19 wins by knockout. Table 17.1 provides a charting and listing of these bouts.

Religious/Spiritual Beliefs and Nutrition

Muhammad Ali was raised in a Baptist household and later changed his spiritual beliefs and practices to Al-Islam in 1961. The Nation of Islam (NOI) was founded by Wallace D. Fard Muhammad on July 4, 1930, in Detroit, Michigan, with the leadership being transitioned to the Honorable Elijah Muhammad in 1933 and the organization's geographic move to Chicago, Illinois. Their primary aim is to improve the spiritual, mental, social, and economic conditions of African Americans in the United States. According to the literature, Muhammad decided to switch from Christianity because his personal beliefs were not aligned with the practices of the Bible and he transformed to the sacred text of the Holy Quran. Contextually, he interpreted the disperse of Baptist scriptures and believed Christianity emphasized the subordination of Blacks in enslavement, which is presented from a Eurocentric hegemonic perspective.

Muhammad's affiliation with the NOI began in 1959, in Chicago, during the Golden Gloves tournament fight. He attended the first national NOI meeting in 1961. This was where Muhammad met Malcolm X, his spiritual and political mentor. Malcolm X was a Muslim minister and a Black political and human rights activist. Growing up as a teenager, Muhammad Ali was furious about racism among African Americans. He believed that joining the NOI would allow him to speak out about integration. Therefore, he began to attend lectures and rallies of Malcolm X and Elijah Muhammad, a chief religious disciple.

In 1964, the professional boxer and goal medal champion converted his name from Cassius Marcellus Clay to Muhammad Ali, which meant "beloved of Allah." Just before his fight against Sonny Liston in 1964, he announced his name changed.

The Honorable Elijah Muhammad first published his classic text, *How to Eat to Live*, in the year 1967. Reflective of his agrarian background, Muhammad became conscious of the preexisting illnesses that affected African Americans in the deep South. Much of this is aligned to poor diet, lack of exercise, and continuity of systemic racism imposed through a Jim Crow system of segregation. Once Muhammad Ali accepted membership into the NOI, he adopted the diet, moto development, and knowledge of self, to engage in and dismiss the labels assigned to African Americans to the level of subordinate group status.

Unlike many of the boxing professionals of his era, Ali had a diet of organic supplements, rather than performance enhancers, which allowed his body to prepare and heal naturally. Ironically, in the contemporary space of sport, diet and training are correlated to the continued careers of professional athletes in football, baseball, basketball, and boxing, to name a few sports. Although we have been able to cite Ali as a stalwart in this contribution to sport, beyond athletic activity, it is the wisdom and knowledge of the Honorable Elijah Muhammad that provided the base and context to coordinate diet and exercise, with mental and physiological stamina. Figure 17.1 illustrates a basic cycle of the intersection and relationship of these areas of diet and exercise, which affected and impacted Muhammad Ali.

Consequently, the text *How to Eat to Live* is a standing testimony of the trajectory and worldview of African Americans to describe and evaluate the concept of diet from a cultural perspective. Muhammad assigned the Black community to eating one meal per day. A selective appetite of fruits, vegetables, breads, and protein. He writes the following:

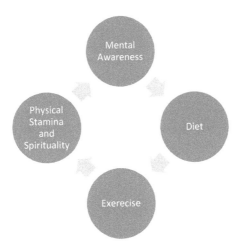

Figure 17.1 Intersectional relationship of diet and exercise.

The Muslims who try to live according to the teachings of the Holy Qur'an will not eat the wrong food when they know what that food is.

Of course, those who are becoming converts to Islam in America, my followers, are being tried. The Christians, white and black, try to force or deceive my followers into eating foods they know we the Muslims do not approve.

In prison, they almost starve my followers trying to force them to eat the filthy, poisonous swine flesh. This I know, because when I was in prison they did the same to me.

Thanks to the coming of Allah in the Person of Master Fard Muhammad, if we obey what He has given to us in the way of proper foods and the proper time to partake of these foods, we will never be sick or have to pay hundreds, thousands and millions of dollars for doctor bills and hospitalization. (Muhammad, 1967)

Ali followed this dietary rubric, along with the spiritual awareness of the NOI, which has cited him as one of the most well-known athletes internationally and the greatest boxer of various weight classes of all time.

Muhammad Ali's Training Routine and Diet Plan

To become a champion, Ali knew he had to train like one. As soon as he was introduced to boxing as a teenager, Ali knew he wanted to become the greatest boxer ever and for that he was willing to do the work and become the best. Ali's personal trainer, Angelo Dundee, told that Ali would run to the gym, and when he finished there, he would run all the way back home as well. The distance from his house to the gym was seven miles. Ali stated in several interviews that he woke up at 5.30 a.m. and did some light stretching followed by a six-mile run, which he would usually do in 40 minutes. Ali was known for his hand and foot speed. He was also a surprisingly powerful puncher. He was a hard worker in training camp and used diet and exercise to get in top condition.

Nutrition and Diet

Muhammad Ali's diet was wholesome and nutritious food. He would eat food like chicken, rice, steak, vegetables, potatoes, and fruits. A normal breakfast for him consisted of eggs, wholesome toast, and orange juice. A normal lunch and dinner consisted of either chicken steak with potatoes or vegetables. He would often snack on fruits throughout the day as well as kept himself hydrated by drinking tons of water and juice. It was often reported that Ali never smoke or consumed alcohol. He believed in taking care of his body and mind, and felt that smoking and alcohol consumption were more damaging than good.

Physical Conditioning

Ali was a dedicated runner when he was in training camp. He was interested in building stamina because in the era that Ali fought professionally—1960 through 1981—heavyweight title fights often went for 15 rounds. The only way to last in those fights was to do the running needed to build endurance. Ali would wake up early at 5:30 a.m. and go for his run. He would normally run six miles per day, six days a week.

When it came to training, Ali adapted an old-school style of boxing training. He didn't really lift weights and relied on calisthenic training like push-ups, sit-ups, and pull-ups. At times he would do the old-school Rocky IV–style training, like chop wood, hit sledgehammers on tires, and run while wearing heavy boots. His speed for a heavyweight was blistering fast, and he would be able to evade oncoming punches with ease. Ali was known for his footwork as well as coining the "Ali shuffle," something that helped him confuse his opposition.

He never had a set routine, and in different phases of his boxing career, he had different routines, but Ali worked as hard in the gym as any fighter of his era. A typical Ali workout included 15 minutes of warm-up exercises to work up a good perspiration prior to serious training. Ali would start off with 5 three-minute rounds of shadow boxing. He would take a 30-second break between rounds. Ali then moved to the heavy bag for 6 more three-minute rounds. He used the heavy bag to work on his punch combinations and endurance. Ali would then do 15 minutes of floor exercises. He would vary his routine, but he did bicycle crunches, sit-ups with a medicine ball, and leg raises as his primary exercises. Ali would then put his bag gloves back on and hit the speed bag for nine minutes. He would close out his boxing drills by skipping rope for 20 minutes. Ali would always move while skipping and refused to stay in the same place.

Through the early part of his career, Ali would spar hard. But once he became champion by beating Sonny Liston in 1964, he was not a fan of sparring to get ready. For one, he did not like to beat up his sparring partners and he was more interested in sharpening his defensive skills. Consequently, he took a lot of punches while sparring. Longtime trainer Angelo Dundee often grew exasperated when Ali would take punches while sparring. "Ali never won a decision in the gym," Dundee told the *New York Daily News* in 1996. "He took shellackings in the gym only because that was the way he wanted to train."

Muhammad Ali's Refusal to War

The Vietnam War was a long, costly, and divisive conflict that pitted the communist government of North Vietnam against South Vietnam and its principal ally, the United States. The conflict was intensified by the ongoing Cold War between the United States and the Soviet Union. It is believed that the Vietnam War goes down in history as one of the worst wars ever in the world. The war also pays close attention to the development of a massive anti-war movement and counterculture that divided the country into "hawks" and "doves."

On April 28, 1967, Ali faced his last chance to join the army. He reported to the US Armed Forces Examining and Entrance Station in Houston, Texas. After a morning of physical exams and filling out forms, Ali was ushered into a ceremony room. Each draftee was to step forward when his name was called. This symbolic step indicated each young man's official induction. But when Ali's name was called, he did not move. The officer repeated his name. When Ali remained motionless, the officer asked for a written explanation of why Ali refused military service. His refusal to enter the draft raised many issues. First, he felt he should be exempt from military service as an active minister of the NOI. As an African American, he felt he could not kill other people of color. He also noted that his induction seemed unfair, because no Blacks were on the Louisville, Kentucky, draft board.

Ali refused to be inducted into the armed forces, saying, "I ain't got no quarrel with those Vietcong." "Why should they ask me to put on a uniform," he said, "and go 10,000 miles from home and drop bombs and bullets on brown people in Vietnam while so-called Negro people in Louisville are treated like dogs and denied simple human rights? [...] I have nothing to lose by standing up for my beliefs. We've been in jail for four hundred years." Muhammad Ali's defiance could be due to his religious beliefs as a Muslim and/or the state of the country as it relates to African Americans for that time period. The Vietnam War happened during a time that African Americans were not treated equally and some stated that African Americans were treated as inhuman and as second-class citizens.

Ali's refusal to fight in the Vietnam War was believed to be well received with the African American community. It was viewed that he was standing for justice and humanity. To these African Americans and other civil rights activists, Ali became a high-profile leader in their movement. But he still had to deal with the federal government. Immediately, a lawyer from the Louisville Sponsoring Group visited Ali. He pointed out that more than a million dollars were at stake. Contracts for commercials and public appearances were in danger. His refusal to not join the US army to fight in the Vietnam War came with a cost. However, his religion would not allow him to be in the military in any form.

On June 20, 1967, Ali was convicted of draft evasion, sentenced to five years in prison, fined $10,000, and banned from boxing for three years. He stayed out of prison as his case was appealed. But he found that he no longer had a career as a professional athlete. The trouble started when the New York State Athletic Commission stripped Ali of his boxing license as he refused to step forward at his draft induction. Other states followed suit. They would not grant him approval to fight for pay. Meanwhile, the judge had taken away Ali's passport, which was a common practice when someone was convicted of a felony. But not being able to travel stopped Ali from seeking work as a boxer outside the United States. He had earned several hefty paychecks competing in Canada, Germany, and England in 1966. Ali lost more than his boxing license when he refused to step forward. The World Boxing Association also stripped Ali of his championship title. Without boxing, Ali found another job: public speaking. He was paid to give lectures at college campuses. Young people disillusioned with the war welcomed the high-profile voice.

Ali returned to the ring on October 26, 1970, knocking out Jerry Quarry in Atlanta in the third round. On March 8, 1971, he fought Joe Frazier in the "Fight of the Century" and lost after 15 rounds, the first loss of his professional boxing career. On June 28 of that same year, the US Supreme Court overturned his conviction for evading the draft.

Muhammad Ali and Parkinson's

In 1984, at the age of 42, Muhammad Ali was diagnosed with Parkinson's. His diagnosis came approximately three years after his retirement. Researchers have found repeated blows to the head can increase an individual's rate of developing Parkinson's. It is not known when Ali developed Parkinson's. Whether it was three decades of being hit on the head or whether it was his genes that led to the condition, the answer is still unknown and may never be known.

Since the 1920s, doctors have known about the correlation between a career in boxing and a series of symptoms that include slurred speech and tremors. The connection was compelling enough for them to dub the syndrome dementia pugilistica. It's now known as chronic traumatic encephalopathy (CTE), and scientists today have a deeper understanding of how trauma to the brain might contribute to Parkinson's as well as to other brain diseases like Alzheimer's. (CTE is still hard to diagnose; for now, it can only be done posthumously.) At present, several experts in the neurodegenerative-diseases world or others believe the reason Ali wound up with Parkinson's was brain trauma over the course of his career.

Muhammad Ali's Contribution to Society

Muhammad Ali passed away from Parkinson's-related complications in 2016 at the age of 74, but his mission lives on. Ali left the ring for the final time, with a 56-5 record. He is the only fighter to be a heavyweight champion three times.

Ali is often remembered as the greatest boxer of all times. In addition, he is known as a philanthropist and a humanitarian. Ali established the multicultural Muhammad Ali Center. The center develops programs that cultivate six principles: confidence, conviction, dedication, giving, respect, and spirituality. In addition, the center holds his legacy and inspires others to be great.

References

African Exponent (2019). https://www.africanexponent.com/post/9032-muhammad-ali-refused-to-fight-for-the-us-in-the-vietnam-war,

Ali, Muhammad, with Hana Yasmeen Ali (2004). *The Soul of a Butterfly: Reflections on Life's Journey.* New York: Simon and Schuster.

Anonymous. "New Evidence Links Traumatic Brain Injury with Parkinson's." July 13, 2016. https://www.parkinson.org/blog/science-news/science-article/traumatic-brain-injury-parkinsons.

Erenberg, L. A. (2012). *The Rumble in the Jungle: Muhammad Ali and George Foreman on the Global State.* Chicago: University of Chicago Press.

———. (2012). "'Rumble in the Jungle': Muhammad Ali vs. George Foreman in the Age of Global Spectacle." *Journal of Sport History,* 39(1), 81–97. www.jstor.org/stable/10.5406/jsporthistory.39.1.81.

Ezra, M. (2009). *Muhammad Ali: The Making of an Icon,* Philadelphia: Temple University Press.

From the Archive (April 29, 1967). "Muhammad Ali Refuses to Fight in Vietnam War," *Guardian* (US ed.). https://www.theguardian.com/theguardian/2013/apr/29/Muhammad-ali-refuses-to-fight-in-vietnam-war-1967.

Hauser, Thomas (1991). *Muhammad Ali: His Life and Times.* New York: Simons and Schuster.

——— (2005)., *The Lost Legacy of Muhammad Ali.* Toronto, Ont.: SportClassic Books.

History.com (2019). https://www.history.com/this-day-in-history/muhammad-ali-refuses-army-induction, https://www.history.com/topics/vietnam-war/vietnam-war-history.

John Micklos Jr. (2010) *Muhammad Ali: I am the Greatest.* Berkley Heights, NJ: Enslow.

Marks, H. S. (2018). *Muhammad Ali.* Ipswich, MA: Salem Press Biographical Encyclopedia.

Mazrui, A. (1977). "Boxer Muhammad Ali and Soldier Idi Amin as International Political Symbols: The Bioeconomics of Sport and War." *Comparative Studies in Society and History,* 19(2), 189–215. www.jstor.org/stable/178176,https://boxrec.com/media/index.php/Main_Page.

Muhammad, Elijah (1967). *How to Eat to Live.* Chicago, IL: Nation of Islam.

Owens, Tom (2011). *Muhammad Ali: Boxing Champ & Role Model (Legendary Athletes).* Minneapolis, MN: Adbo.

Parkinson's New Today (2019). "The Complicated Link between Muhammad Ali's Death and Boxing." https://parkinsonsnewstoday.com/2019/10/23/muhammad-ali-legacy-advocacy-boxing/.

Stefan Fatsis (June 2016). "No Viet Cong Ever Call Me Nigger: The Story behind the Famous Quote That Muhammad Ali Probably Never Said," *Slate.* http;//www.slate.com/articles/sports/sports_nut/2016/06/did_muhammad_ali_ever_say_no_viet_cong_ever_called_me_nigger.html.

Thomas, J. (2009). "Ali, Muhammad: (b. 1942) Boxer." In N. Bercow & T. Ownby (eds.), *The New Encyclopedia of Southern Culture: Volume 13: Gender,* pp. 291–93. Chapel Hill: University of North Carolina Press.

TIME Health (2016). "The Complicated Link between Muhammad Ali's Death and Boxing." https://time.com/4358063/muhammad-ali-dead-parkinsons-boxing/.

CONCLUSION

Christel N. Temple

We finalized this volume from fall 2020 to fall 2021 during the COVID-19 pandemic, a period when families were doing everything they could to keep themselves amused and entertained while sheltering in place at home. My family celebrated Martin Luther King Jr. (MLK) Day on January 18, 2021, and now that youtube.com is available as a television app, I searched for King documentaries or videos on MLK Day to show my fourth grader a *living* and *laughing* Dr. King. King was on a nighttime talk show telling a joke.

When we finished viewing King, I turned to channels that documented Muhammad Ali. In the zombifying world of video games, especially during the pandemic, that tied our children to their homes and indoor activities, I reveled in the chance to introduce my son to the visual, not the storybook, version of Muhammad Ali. In the storybook that we own, *Muhammad Ali: Champion of the World* (2007) by Jonah Winter and François Roca, even though the designated age group is 4- to 8-year-olds, there is a sentence that says, "Jack Johnson was hated and booed all over America just for the color of his skin" and a reference to "the white slave master who had owned his African ancestors." Our pre-school and first- through third-grade children would learn about "racism" in this book and how "African Americans were supposed to know their place and keep their mouths shut." Our babies would learn about killing, the Vietnam War, and how the judge told Ali, "It's jail time for you." In my house, we are saving this Muhammad Ali children's storybook for later when he is until he is older and has a better grasp on society's racism. Then, he can also enjoy the liberating and proud parts of the book that celebrate Ali's triumphs.

When I found Ali footage on youtube.com, Ali was smiling and bouncing around, chanting his famous lyrics of bravado. There was also a video of Ali's workout regimen. He was up at dawn, and he ran many miles on an empty country road. His skin was glistening in healthy sweat. He was talking about being healthy and fit and having endurance. I watched my son glance up to see Ali on the screen. He lost interest in his iPad for a moment. He was drawn in by the sensational persona of Ali. The COVID-19 pandemic has challenged the world's physical fitness by keeping us indoors more and away from organized sports, the roller skating rink, and playgrounds. Fewer children have been playing outside. Parents have been glued to online Zoom meetings. I purchased a rowing machine and moved the mini trampoline into our family room and in front of the television as a step to inspire greater physical activity.

Later that night at bedtime, my son announced that, like Ali, he, too, wanted to run at the track, to run for hours at a time, like Muhammad Ali did every morning. So, in just 20 minutes of experiencing the *living, laughing* Ali, the proud talk, the boxing superiority, the craft of strategic sportsmanship, the motivational speech about saving his strength for the final stretch of a boxing match, *Ali's heroic athleticism positively influenced my son*. It is a contemporary privilege to have images of Ali at our fingertips from the comfort of our homes. On MLK Day, we enjoyed seeing the earnestness of Ali's facial expressions, his prowess and skill, and the sheer beauty of his masculinity and physicality. Of course, there is more to Ali than charisma and aesthetics.

This collection on Ali's role in Africana cultural memory reflects the maturity of meditating on a hyperheroic African American figure to reach the heights of critical engagement and valuation. We get exposed to and have the opportunity to evaluate our heroes cyclically. We have age-appropriate encounters like I describe above through fun video footage, then through young adult encounters with books, and finally in our more sophisticated adult knowledge base that guides children into their emerging social awareness. Like Paul Carter Harrison, Danny Glover, and Bill Duke, who shared their sense of community heroics and compiled the youth and family book of heroes, *Black Light*, we are charged to find new ways to ensure that cultural memory and mythological structure are routine parts of the African American processes of gaining confidence, building self-esteem, and utilizing our culture's many options for heroic modeling.

As these essays reflect, there is an aspect of sacred remembrance in the reason for and the methods of honoring cultural heroes whose achievements and feats are source material for our cultural memory. Some of Ali's contemporaries, each heroic in his own right, died in the midst of their activism. They were assassinated and became martyrs, while Ali lived to die of natural causes through Parkinson's disease (even though it is a consequence of the concussions that come with the sport of boxing). Different types of passing warrant different types of memorialization. This volume reminds us that even though society may be less familiar with the critical process of itemizing a legend's cultural value in terms of the newer academic tools for assessing memory, myth, heroics, mythology, resisting, and surviving, there are many critical possibilities for stabilizing cultural reflection through commemoration and meditation.

Ali is a force to be reckoned with and an icon to be recalled because of his role in a tradition of African Americans strategically using sport for an activist platform while they also excel in contests of physicality and bravery. Ali (re)claimed his masculine physicality for more than an auction block or for exploited labor in a capitalist system that has valued his potential as a low-paid physical laborer more than it valued his mind. Ali's identity as a Black man striving and winning principled and physical battles is an entry also in the narrative of African people's spirituality and personhood. It is the critical process of evaluating Ali through the Africana Studies paradigms, lenses, and epistemological frameworks that has prompted this collection's visions of him that are meaningful and functional for people of African descent, in particular in our own community contexts and worldviews. We learn that Ali's iconic status, when observed and deciphered from a Black psychology lens, offers cultural perspectives far beyond static superlatives related to an alleged colorblind Americanism. For once, in engaging with a version of intellectual biography on Ali, Black readers do not have to cringe when, repeatedly, they hear about his meaning to America rather than his meaning to African America. Additionally, contributors have given us a sense of Ali's acclaim beyond the shores of the United States, and this internationalism is not limited to his prize fights in Kinshasa in Zaire or Manila in the Philippines.

Every contribution in this collection has had something important and functional to offer in the collective effort of Africana Studies and its allied practitioners to use our cultural memory of history and heroes to increase the life chances and life experiences of Black people, as we have combed through Ali's archive to mine original cultural meaning.

CONTRIBUTORS

Karen E. Alexander is a native New Yorker and registered nurse for over 35 years. Dr. Alexander has worked in many facets of nursing. Additionally, she retired from the US Air Force having served 22 years, both as a noncommissioned and commissioned officer with several deployments. She is currently an assistant professor and the founding director of nursing at the University of Houston Clear Lake—Pearland, Texas. Her research focus is vulnerable populations (fathers of preterm infants, veterans, and adolescent food insecurity) and nursing education. She dedicates time to serve her professional and personal community through various organizations, as a role model, and mentor.

Brandon Allen is a graduate student at Clark Atlanta University. The central focus of his thesis research examines how Muhammad Ali's and Colin Kaepernick's cultural resistance shaped Africana cultural memory using a theoretical framework exploring how Black athletes' cultural resistance historically shaped Black consciousness. He also studies liberation from an Afrocentric perspective, redefining the identity of Africans in America, as well as their role in the world.

Jeanette Anderson was raised in Texas and has a diversified career, choosing a nursing degree as a registered nurse in her fourth decade of life, graduating in 2007. Later, she completed her BSN at the University of Houston-Clear Lake in 2019. Currently, she enjoys a rewarding career as an adolescent psychiatric nurse at the Menninger Clinic in Houston, Texas. In her role, she helps young adults navigate the difficult years of adolescence through mindfulness teaching and compassion. Prior to her nursing career, she worked for NASA as a neutral buoyancy diver for 5 years. Additionally, she participates in Ironman competitions.

Molefi Kete Asante is a professor and chair at the Department of Africology, Temple University. He is the founder of the *Journal of Black Studies*, the theory of Afrocentricity, and the first PhD program in African American Studies at a major university. Also the author of 95 books, Dr. Asante is an international thought leader.

Park Esewiata Atatah earned his PhDs from Walden University in 2013 in public policy administration and specializes in criminal justice and health services. He earned his master's degree from Texas Southern University (TSU) in master's of public administration, majoring in public policy, and a bachelor's degree from TSU in BBA, majoring in Management. He is currently an assistant professor at Prairie View A&M University (PVAMU) College of Education, Department of Health and Kinesiology. He worked with Texas Department of Criminal Justice-Institutional Division for almost twenty-three years and retired as a unit supervisor in 2017. His research interests are in healthcare issues, criminal justice, special-needs clients, minorities' issues, disproportionality, under-served issues, and globalization issues.

Howard Bartee Jr. is an assistant professor of health and kinesiology—sport manage-ment at Prairie View A&M University. Dr. Bartee, an avid sports historian and in higher education for over twenty years, has authored the book *The Next Level: Six Perspectives on the College Choice Process of Student Athletes* and enjoys being a husband, father, son, and brother. Dr. Bartee holds an EdD in sports management (US Sports Academy), an MS in admin-istration and information resource management (Central Michigan University), a BA in political science and accounting (Tougaloo College), and a data analytics and visualiza-tion certification (Rice University).

Angela Branch-Vital holds a doctorate in behavioral science/health promotion with a concentration in epidemiology and biostatistics from the University of Texas School of Public Health. Dr. Branch-Vital has secured nine grants and served as the principal investigator on five of the nine grants and the coprincipal investigator on the remaining four. She has secured funding from top-tier funding sources such as the National Institute of Health, the US Department of Food and Agriculture/National Institute of Food and Agriculture, and the National Center on Minority Health and Health Disparities. Dr. Branch-Vital's areas of research interest include social inequalities, health disparities and social change, developing interventions within the communities, evaluation and redesign of health services, and multilevel models in public health.

Akilah R. Carter-Francique is the executive director at the Institute for the Study of Sport, Society and Social Change and an associate professor at the Department of African American Studies at San Jose State University. Her research encompasses the intersection of sport, society, and social justice inclusive of issues of diversity, social movements, and the dynamics of social change and development. Carter-Francique served as the 2018–19 president of the North American Society for the Sociology of Sport (NASSS) and is the coeditor of *Athletic Experience at Historically Black Colleges and Universities: Past, Present, and Persistence* and *Critical Race Theory: Black Athletic Experiences in the United States.*

James L. Conyers Jr. holds a PhD in African American studies from Temple University and was the director of the African American Studies Program, director of the Center for African American Culture, and university professor of African American Studies at the University of Houston. He authored and edited over forty books, served on various editorial boards, and served as the editor of two book series. He was an accomplished author, philanthropist, scholar, mentor, and activist.

Rebecca Hankins is the Wendler Endowed Professor and certified archivist/librarian at Texas A&M University. She is affiliated faculty in the Interdisciplinary Critical Studies Program that includes Africana Studies, Women's and Gender Studies, and Religious Studies. She develops and implements collection development policies for Africana studies, women's and gender studies, race and ethnic studies, and area studies, and provides counseling for the integration of these materials into the curriculum, incorporating information and archival literacy components. She is also responsible for creating library guides and other tools for instruction. She provides comprehensive reference and instructional services in person and virtually.

Billy Hawkins is a professor at the University of Houston in the Department of Health and Human Performance. He is the author of several peer-reviewed articles and books, and he serves on several journal and book editorial boards. His teaching and research contributions are in the areas of sociology of sport and cultural studies, sport management, and sport for development. He received his PhD from the University of Iowa in Health and Sport Studies, an MS degree in exercise and sport science from the University of Wisconsin at La Crosse, and a BS degree in business administration from Webber International University.

Ruby Holden-Pitre is a freelance writer who specializes in Africana literature and Black women studies.

Bayyinah S. Jeffries is an associate professor in the Department of African American Studies at Ohio University. She is the author of "Race Relations in Higher Education: The Case of the OSU 34" (*Journal of Ohio Valley History*), "Black Religion and Black Power: The Nation of Islam's Internationalism" (*Genealogy*, special issue: Global Black Movements), *A Nation Can Rise No Higher than Its Women: Black Muslim Women in the Movement for Black Self-Determination* (2014, " 'Raising Her Voice:' Writings by, for and about Women in *Muhammad Speaks* Newspaper, 1961–1975" (*African American Consciousness: Past & Present*), and other works. Dr. Jeffries's research focuses on African American social movements; Black nationalism; African American women's history; issues of identity and resistance in relation to the intersections of race, gender, religion, and nationalism; expressions of self-determination; and comparative Black history.

Catherine Kisavi-Atatah has worked in the medical field for the past 20 years. She earned her PhD in health services and specialized in health policy. She has two primary research areas. She focuses on educational studies about how to educate underserved minorities, nationally and globally, about some previously and currently emerging and reemerging tropical diseases generally. The secondary focus of her research is on globalization. This research comprehensively deals with the identifications of tropically neglected diseases such as insect-borne diseases like malaria and reemerging previously eliminated diseases such as waterborne diseases like dysentery in underserved countries in Africa and globally.

William Kouba is a native Houstonian and registered nurse for the past three years. Mr. Kouba possesses a passion for helping others. He is a recent graduate from the University of Houston-Clear Lake RN-BSN program. He strives to always devote the highest respect to our military veterans. He currently works for the Department of Veterans Affairs. In this role he identifies and credentials healthcare providers to perform specific exams for military veterans so that they may receive their pensions. He has a special interest in veterans and applauds the sacrifices they made to ensure we all have the freedoms we enjoy today.

Waveney LaGrone was born in Jamaica, West Indies, and migrated to the United States in the mid-1990s. Ms. LaGrone started her nursing career as a nursing assistant in Texas. Later, she pursued a certificate in vocational nursing, associate degree in nursing, and a BSN from the University of Houston-Clear Lake in 2019. As a registered nurse her practice areas include geriatrics and individuals with mental health issues and mental retardation. Currently, she is working at the Auberge in Kingwood, Texas, a memory care and Alzheimer's assisted living facility as the health services director. This assisted living facility has a strong veteran community.

Andrea McDonald is an assistant professor of health and current curriculum chair in the Department of Health and Kinesiology at Prairie View A&M University. She earned a doctorate in health education from Texas A&M University, College Station, and an MS degree in human sciences concentration in dietetics and nutrition from Prairie View A&M University. Her research focuses on underserved minority youth and behavioral risk factors within the United States and Caribbean. McDonald has taught more than ten thousand students and served as an advisor for Eta Sigma Gamma. She is a fellow for Texas Public Health Association and a member of the American Academy of Health Behavior.

Ryan Moore is a native Houstonian, growing up from coast to coast in California, Long Island, New York, and Dallas. He started his nursing career as a licensed vocational nurse. Mr. Moore later earned his associate degree in nursing, becoming a registered nurse. He is a recent graduate from the University of Houston-Clear Lake RN-BSN program. As a registered nurse for four years, he is currently employed at the Caplan Surgery Center in Houston, Texas, as a perioperative nurse. He is a dedicated nurse who serves the community in excellence in care delivery. This care is inclusive of a large Texas veteran population.

Suzuko Morikawa is an associate professor of history at Chicago State University. She is a native of Japan and became the first Japanese to receive a PhD from the African American Studies Program at Temple University, the first PhD program in African American Studies in the United States. Her areas of specialization are US racial and ethnic history, cultural-historical studies on African Africans in a global context, and African American sport history. Her works have been published in *The Journal of Black Studies, Emerging Voices: The Experiences of Underrepresented Asian Americans*, and *The 1980s: A Critical and Transitional Decade*.

Wade W. Nobles is a Skh Shetist, Professor Emeritus of Africana studies and Black psychology at San Francisco State University, a cofounder (and past president) of the Association of Black Psychologists, and the founder and executive director of the Institute for the Advanced Study of Black Family, Life and Culture, Inc (retired). He is the author of over one hundred articles, chapters, research reports, and books, including *African Psychology: Toward Its Reclamation, Reascension and Revitalization, Seeking the Sakhu: Foundational Writings in African Psychology*, and *The Island of Memes: Haiti's Unfinished Revolution*. Dr. Nobles is the chairperson of the ABPsi Pan-African Black Psychology Global Initiative.

Abul S. Pitre is a professor and department chair of Africana studies at San Francisco State University He holds a BS in social studies education, an MA in social science from Southern University Baton Rouge, and a PhD in education and human resource studies from Colorado State University. He has authored and coedited 25 books, with his most recent being *The Gloria Ladson-Billings Reader, A Critical Black Pedagogy Reader: The Brothers Speak, Research Studies on Educating for Diversity and Social Justice,* and *Perspectives on Diversity, Equity, and Social Justice in Educational Leadership.* In addition, he has written several journal articles, book chapters, and book reviews. He is also the series editor for the following book series, *Critical Black Pedagogy* (Rowman and Littlefield); *The Africana Experience and Critical Leadership Studies* (Lexington Books); and *Elijah Muhammad Studies* (Hamilton Books).

Autumn Raynor is a professor of speech communication at Houston Community College and an adjunct lecturer of African American studies at the University of Houston. Her most recent article publications include "Black Spaces" (2019) and "Anti-Black Ontological Violence in Undergraduate Textbooks" (2020).

Anju Reejhsinghani is an assistant vice provost for strategic diversity, equity and inclusion administration at the University of Wisconsin-Madison. She is a former tenured associate professor of history and international studies at the University of Wisconsin-Stevens Point and also previously served as an executive director at the Institute for Regional and International Studies at University of Wisconsin-Madison. She works on race, gender, and transnational sport in the Americas and is completing a monograph on Cuban boxing.

Christel N. Temple is a professor of Africana studies at the University of Pittsburgh. She works at the intersections of history and literature, with a focus on cultural theory, comparative Black literature, and cultural mythology. She is the author of *Literary Pan-Africanism: History, Contexts, and Criticism, Literary Spaces: Introduction to Comparative Black Literature,* and *Transcendence and the Africana Literary Enterprise.* Her most recent book, *Black Cultural Mythology,* helps to establish a theoretical and methodological framework for the subfield of Africana cultural memory studies.

Natalie Williamson is a graduate from the Educational Leadership Doctoral Program at Prairie View A&M University. Her research interests are in diversity, equity, and social justice leadership.

Derek Wilson is an associate professor of psychology at Prairie View A&M University. Dr. Wilson is the director of the Ubuntu Positive Mental Health Research Lab at PVA&MU. He teaches courses on sociocultural psychology, human diversity, clinical psychology, and research methodological approaches with African-centered framework perspective. Additionally, he has published research articles on the positive mental health model for those of African descent, African-centered therapeutic approaches, cultural competency, and mental health disparities. Dr. Wilson is currently the chair of the Certification of African-Centered Black Psychology for the Association of Black Psychologists.

INDEX

Bold number indicates figure and table.